The 1984 Presidential
Election in the South

The 1984 Presidential Election in the South

Patterns of Southern Party Politics

Edited by

**Robert P. Steed,
Laurence W. Moreland,
and Tod A. Baker**

PRAEGER SPECIAL STUDIES • PRAEGER SCIENTIFIC

New York • Philadelphia • Eastbourne, UK
Toronto • Hong Kong • Tokyo • Sydney

ROBERT MANNING
STROZIER

Library of Congress Cataloging in Publication Data

Main entry under title:

APR 17 1986
The 1984 presidential election in the South.

Bibliography: p.
Includes index.
Tallahassee, Florida
   1. Presidents—United States—Election—1984—
Addresses, essays, lectures.   2. Southern States—
Politics and government—1951–   —Addresses,
essays, lectures.   3. Political parties—Southern
States—History—20th century—Addresses, essays,
lectures.   I. Steed, Robert P.   II. Moreland,
Laurence W.   III. Baker, Tod A.
E879.A15   1985   324.973'0927   85–12246
ISBN 0–03–000538–8

Published in 1986 by Praeger Publishers
CBS Educational and Professional Publishing, a Division of CBS Inc.
521 Fifth Avenue, New York, NY 10175 USA

© 1986 by Praeger Publishers

6789   052   987654321

Printed in the United States of America on acid-free paper

INTERNATIONAL OFFICES

Orders from outside the United States should be sent to the appropriate address listed below. Orders
from areas not listed below should be placed through CBS International Publishing, 383 Madison Ave.,
New York, NY 10175 USA

Australia, New Zealand
Holt Saunders, Pty, Ltd., 9 Waltham St., Artarmon, N.S.W. 2064, Sydney, Australia

Canada
Holt, Rinehart & Winston of Canada, 55 Horner Ave., Toronto, Ontario, Canada M8Z 4X6

Europe, the Middle East, & Africa
Holt Saunders, Ltd., 1 St. Anne's Road, Eastbourne, East Sussex, England BN21 3UN

Japan
Holt Saunders, Ltd., Ichibancho Central Building, 22-1 Ichibancho, 3rd Floor, Chiyodaku, Tokyo,
Japan

Hong Kong, Southeast Asia
Hold-Saunders Asia, Ltd., 10 Fl, Intercontinental Plaza, 94 Granville Road, Tsim Sha Tsui East, Kow-
loon, Hong Kong

**Manuscript submissions should be sent to the Editorial Director, Praeger Publishers, 521 Fifth
Avenue, New York, NY 10175 USA**

Contents

Acknowledgments

The idea for this book dates back to March 1983. In the early stages of planning the Fourth Citadel Symposium on Southern Politics to be held approximately a year later, we thought that it might be appropriate and interesting to begin work on a manuscript containing state-by-state analyses of the 1984 presidential elections in the South. We were successful in interesting a number of our colleagues in participating in the project, and by October 1983 arrangements for each of the proposed chapters had been completed. A number of these contributors participated in two panels on recent developments in state politics at the Fourth Citadel Symposium on Southern Politics held at The Citadel in March 1984. In a variety of ways, then, this book is related to the series of Citadel southern politics symposia and related publications, which have focused our attention on southern politics over the past eight years.

To assure a central unifying thread in the analyses, we provided the following general guidelines for each of the state chapters: (1) a short section discussing the major political developments in the state in recent years (especially since roughly 1972), (2) a brief section on the pre-nomination campaign in the state, (3) a section examining the general election campaign(s) in the state, (4) a more extensive description and analysis of the election results, and (5) a concluding section designed to suggest ways in which the 1984 election fits into the state's recent political history (with some room for speculation about its meaning for the state's political future). However, we also wanted to allow a great deal of room for variations in style, approach, and coverage in recognition of the rich diversity that has long characterized southern politics and southern politics research. Additionally, while the central focus of the book is the 1984 presidential election, we invited our contributors to include some discussion of other contests as a part of the broader context of their state's electoral politics. Since the number and nature of these other elections varied dramatically from one state to another, it was even more important to allow maximum flexibility in treatment and coverage from chapter to chapter. The result, we believe, is a book that has a basic unity underlying a range of interesting styles and treatments.

Our debts in this work are numerous. Major General James A. Grimsley, Jr., President of The Citadel, has been a firm and constant supporter of the Symposium and all its publishing byproducts; and Brigadier General George Meenaghan, Vice President for Academic Affairs and Dean of the College at The Citadel, has encouraged and supported our work at every point. The present project is no exception. We are indebted to both for their continuing efforts to assist us specifically and to help create and maintain an atmosphere conducive to professional scholarship at The Citadel. Professor Milton L. Boykin, Head of the Department of Political Science at The Citadel, has also provided significant encouragement and administrative support as this manuscript has been developed. A large number of our colleagues at other institutions have contributed to this work through their participation in our symposia on southern politics and through their willingness to engage in intellectual exchange with us and with others who share an interest in the politics of the region. Finally, we are deeply appreciative of The Citadel Development Foundation's financial support, without which this project could not have been completed.

Robert P. Steed
Laurence W. Moreland
Tod A. Baker

April 1985
Charleston, South Carolina

Part I

Introduction

1

Southern Politics: A Prelude to Presidential Politics in 1984

William C. Havard

In view of the sheer bulk and variety of literature produced by political scientists, historians, sociologists, journalists, and general social
commentators on southern politics over the forty years since the end
of World War II, one might well have expected that at least one book,
and perhaps a handful of essays in periodicals, would have appeared
during this time on the general theme of the South and the presidency. Presidential electoral politics has, of course, been the subject
of much analysis and comment, but the political relations between
the region and the presidential institution in all of its functions and
the processes by which those functions—both symbolic and practical—have been carried out in a time of great change seem to have
been scanted, so far as systematic analysis is concerned. The apparent
absence of even scholarly interest in studying the relations between
the enigmatic South and the nation's chief executive (by 1945 not
only the chief of state and symbolic personification of national unity,
but also the focal point of central authority in both domestic and
foreign affairs) is a hiatus that cannot easily be either explained or
filled.

Perhaps the explanation is a simple one: The South's political relation to the presidency may be perceived as a subject lacking the
regional distinctiveness that was characteristic for so long of so many
other features of the South's overall political culture—the exclusion
of blacks from all but token participation in politics, the one-party

system, an inverted emphasis on political activity in which participation was most intense at the grass roots and tended to diminish
rapidly as the electoral units became larger, the offices at stake more
powerful, and public issues of greater and more lasting consequence.
But politics is too much a part of the woof and warp of our social
and cultural fabric to permit us to be satisfied by easy answers. Symbolic factors seem to prevail over much of the specific historical circumstances of accommodation and conflict by means of which the
South and the nation have converged and diverged in their political
practices and in their regional interrelations.

In this respect, one of the major symbols has been produced by
the effective denial of access to the presidential office by southerners
during the century following the end of Reconstruction. Taken literally, the long-standing presumption has been that a national political party with a southerner at the head of the ticket could not win
the election; but the pragmatic situation was more complex because
the sectional party alignments were such that even before the Civil
War the Democratic Party faced strategic difficulties in the Northeast,
and increasingly in the Middle West, as a result of the need to ac-
commodate the South, which was a major geographic component in
the forging of winning coalitions in national elections. In fact, the
last southerner elected President on the Democratic ticket prior to
the Civil War was James K. Polk in 1844 and the last southerner
elected to that office in the antebellum period was Zachary Taylor
in 1848, but he was the nominee of the Whig Party in that year. The
sectional split in the national Democratic Party in 1860—Stephen
Douglas of Illinois was the nominee of the Democrats in a convention
session in Baltimore, and John C. Breckinridge of Kentucky, Vice
President during President Buchanan's administration (1857–61),
was the nominee of a protest convention of southern states following
the breakup of the convention in Charleston, South Carolina—assured Lincoln's triumph in the 1860 election. Beyond that, it paved
the way for both the displacement of the Whig Party by the Republicans as the "other" major party in the American two-party system
and a regional realignment of party electoral tendencies that enabled
the Republican Party to become the national majority party for some
seventy years thereafter.[1] This realignment was based on a shift of
the usual political affinity of the Midwest with the South during the
pre–Civil War years to a joining of electoral forces of the midwestern
states with the Northeast, an alignment that was sustained in its early
years by the symbols of sacrifice and victory of those states that had
been engaged in the common cause of preservation of the Union
and the abolition of slavery through force of arms. In election after

election, the "waving of the bloody shirt" was part of the campaigns that held this new regional coalition together and enabled the Republican Party to maintain its position as the national "majority party" until 1932.

During Reconstruction (circa 1865–77) the South was an occupied territory, with the white males who had participated in the "rebellion" disfranchised, and the Reconstruction leadership opportunistically ambivalent on both the issue of the South's place in the nation and on the question of which institution—the Congress or the President—was primarily responsible for the reconstruction of the South. As the Congress became more radical and seized the initiative on Reconstruction from the President, readmission of the southern states to the Union was made conditional on the fulfillment of stringent requirements in terms of loyalty oaths, the ratification of the Fourteenth Amendment, and the adoption of new state constitutions in strict conformity with the laws enacted by a growing radical Republican congressional majority. Southern politics was thus largely in the hands of various combinations of newly enfranchised blacks, carpetbaggers, (northerners who moved south to seek economic and political advantage in the chaotically unsettled conditions of the region), and scalawags (white southerners who became Republicans). These actions turned Reconstruction away from the expressed intentions of Lincoln to bind up the nation's wounds, assist the newly freed former slaves to assume their places as citizens entitled to full civil rights, and get on with the job of restoring the region's devastated economy.

Ironically, the President during the early period of Reconstruction (1865–69) was a southerner, Andrew Johnson of Tennessee, an opponent of secession (a War Democrat) who had been elected Vice President as Lincoln's running mate in 1864 on the euphemistically denominated National Union Party ticket. Following his accession, Johnson moved firmly and swiftly to try to reunite the country by providing for a general amnesty covering all but the major officials and higher grades of military officers of the Confederacy, making provision for setting up civil governments, and arranging for restoration of congressional representation from the seceding states. In doing so he ran afoul of the congressional radicals, and one of the greatest conflicts between executive and congressional authority in American history ensued. Early in 1868 the House of Representatives brought impeachment charges against the President, the first and only time this action has been taken against a President. Even though the trial in the Senate on the impeachment charges failed by one vote to convict Johnson, his reputation and the constitutional grounds of executive power had been so severely damaged that he could no longer resist what he regarded as usurpation of presidential authority by the Congress.

Although Johnson barely avoided removal from office and was a badly battered and ineffective chief executive thereafter, his arguments against radical reconstruction were well borne out by subsequent experience. He had contended on numerous occasions that failure to reunite the sections by permitting the South to renew its allegiance and come back into the Union immediately and as fully a part of the constitutionally ordained governing arrangements as possible would not only lead to accumulating resentment and further conflict of a sectional nature, but would make for increasing tensions in relations between the races. Once scorned as a traitor in the South, where his frontier populist views on the social and economic conditions of the "ordinary" people and his opposition to the political leadership of the large planter class led him to continue to support the Union, he now had to face the recriminations of the radicals of the North for being so soft on the unreconstructed states of his region that he might be considered a sort of double agent whose loyalties to the nation were suspect to say the least.

That the congressional leaders of the Republican Party and their agents (both official and from the ranks of volunteer opportunists seeking government favors) were more interested in the short-term political and economic gains to be had from Reconstruction than in the welfare of the black "freemen" was demonstrated in the manner in which Reconstruction ended. In the 1876 presidential election, the Republicans nominated Rutherford B. Hayes, after the scandal of "Mulligan letters" derailed the favorite, James G. Blaine, and the Democrats nominated the popular governor of New York, Samuel J. Tilden. By this time enough of the disfranchised southerners had been restored to citizenship, and the Democratic Party had been remobilized to the point at which it was competitive enough to enable it to carry the southern states in a presidential election. Tilden also carried New York, New Jersey, Connecticut, and Indiana, with the election turning largely on issues of corruption, not just in the carpetbag governments of the South, but within the Grant administration and in other Republican-dominated states as well. When the count was made Tilden led Hayes by 250,000 votes in a total popular vote of 8.3 million, and in electoral votes by 203 to 166. The Republicans challenged the election returns in three southern states— Florida, South Carolina, and Louisiana—on the grounds that black voters had been prevented from going to the polls, and in Oregon on the contention that the Democratic governor had illegally thrown out one Republican elector and certified a Democrat in his place.

From all of those states, two sets of returns were reported. Party leaders in Congress got together and arranged for passage of a special act setting up a bipartisan commission to resolve the deadlock. The commission consisted of five members of the House of Representatives, five from the Senate, and five from the Supreme Court. Seven of the members were Republicans, seven were Democrats, and Justice David Davis of the Supreme Court was considered an independent. However, Davis was elected to the Senate in the interim and was replaced by Justice Bradley, a Republican who had first written an opinion favoring Tilden, but under Republican pressure he shifted his vote to Hayes. The vote of the commission was 8 to 7 (strictly according to party lines) in support of Hayes, thus giving him all of the contested electoral votes and a 185 to 184 margin in the electoral college.

The continued controversy over this outcome forced a further "compromise" before congressional certification of the election was possible. In exchange for support of the commission's decision by southern Democrats, the Republicans promised to withdraw federal troops from the South, to appoint at least one southerner to the Cabinet, and to appropriate funds needed for southern internal improvements. In March 1877 Hayes duly took office.

The outcome of the 1876 election effectively wrote an end to Reconstruction, but it left nearly all of the issues that its proponents and administrators were supposed to address in abeyance. The black populations of the southern states found themselves legally free; but with their economic and social condition largely unchanged, and thus they were returned to a status of dependence on their former masters or the land-holder successors to those masters. The promises symbolized by the phrase "forty acres and a mule" were left unfulfilled, and several specific provisions of the "Civil War Amendments" (XIII, XIV, and XV) and of the Civil Rights Acts of 1866 and 1875 proved to be vulnerable in the absence of an externally imposed authority to implement them in practice. With most of its capital resources either destroyed or sequestered and with little in the way of financial aid forthcoming from Washington, the South lapsed into a static agricultural economy.

From a conquered and occupied province, the South's relation to the nation moved at the end of Reconstruction to a position that has been designated as neocolonial dependency in which the old balance of interests shifted to northern dominance, both economically and politically. With the Republican Party established as the national majority party, the federal government could get on with the enactment of policies that favored the advancing American industrial revolution even as the country moved toward completing the continental territorial expansion that had been slowed by the drawn out disputes over the North-South balance of power and wealth involved in the controversy over admission of territories as free or slave states. In matters of international trade, transportation, taxation, and finance, public policy promoted the interests of industry over agriculture, with the result that the South remained a producer of primary goods— agricultural products and raw materials to fuel the furnaces and provide the natural products for the mills and factories of the growing industrial cities of the Northeast and Midwest. The region was also a supplier of cheap labor for the absentee-owned or -controlled extractive industries.

In brief, the South was substantially alienated from mainstream American for some seventy years following Reconstruction, partly by its own choice, but certainly as much or more by the imbalance of political and economic power in favor of the North that was a direct result of the outcome of the Civil War and Reconstruction, followed by the consolidation of the Republican Party's position as the new national majority party and the inauguration of economic policies that signalled the advent of large-scale corporate financial and industrial capitalism.

The internal political struggles in the South for the next generation turned largely on the restoration of self-determination of the southern states or, in other terms, the "redemption" of the South from the remaining vestiges of externally imposed rule, which involved a complex interplay of ideas and actions, as real or perceived political crises invariably do. Overall, this meant concentration on the replacement of two major negative symbols of southern defeat and humiliation by two positive symbols of southern cultural identity and political solidarity. On the one hand, this symbolic transformation (perceived by white southerners as a Manichaean transition from evil to good) involved the elimination of the Republican Party as an effective instrument of political power in the South; and on the other hand, it required strengthening the determination (as historian Ulrich B. Phillips put it in the 1920s) to see that the South remained a white man's country. The 1877 compromise traded the future possibilities of a competitive party system in the South for a national "sustaining" victory that would prove useful in buying time in office for the consolidation of a Republican majority coalition in the rest of the country. Even before 1877 the southern states had already begun to restore the Democratic Party to its former dominant competitive position in state and local politics, as well as in congressional elections, as the old leaders, now further enobled in the popular mind as heroes of the lost cause (including many former Whigs who had been converted into conservative Democrats) were restored to citizenship and restitution of political rights. The fragile southern Republican coalition of carpetbaggers, newly freed blacks, and scalawags could not stand up to the Democratic challenge for very long, as the charges of corruption leveled at the reconstructionists were contrasted with the growing legend of an idyllic and unsullied antebellum South, whose guarantee of survival could be insured only by political solidarity under the embracive symbol of the Democratic Party.

As indicated above, it took approximately a generation (or roughly into the turn of the century) to accomplish the purposes of purging the Republican influence on southern politics, and simultaneously making the North-South political estrangement semipermanent. It took a bit longer (roughly through the first decade of the twentieth century) to exclude blacks from effective participation in southern politics and thus provide long-range assurance of white supremacy in the social, economic and political life of the South. The estrangement of the races in the South could be said to complement the estrangement of the South from the nation, inasmuch as the failure to maintain more than a token political presence in the South after 1877 tacitly left the region to its own devices in race relations, and thus contributed to the widening gap between North and South in the cultural underpinnings of their respective social structures, economic systems, and political practices.

Many historical retrospectives on the South have treated post-Reconstruction politics in the region as undifferentiated and unchanging in its principal characteristics over a period of 50 to 75 years, both internally and in national affairs. The cultural bonds, at least among the whites of all classes, were perceived as strong and as derived from a shared sense of history that made the region distinctive and easily distinguished from other areas of the United States. This unity was reflected politically in a one-party system in which real competition was minimal and popular participation was maintained at consistently low levels. These conditions were attributable mainly to deliberate exclusion from access to the ballot and to participation through the mediating institutions, most notably the primary of the Democratic Party, as was the case with blacks generally, and with some whites, especially those in the lower socioeconomic classes.[2] In this view, issues played little or no part in election contests, except for the general issue of race, which often stayed below the threshold of popular consciousness except when brought out for diversionary purposes as serious (or sometimes even minor) rifts among white voters threatened to disrupt the established rule of the bourbon planters in the black belt and their allies drawn from what the late Professor Jasper Shannon called the "county seat elite."[3] In this environment nominations by the Democratic Party became the key to access to public office and here the process of party selection became the closest thing to democratic politics that the South attained in its old-style political arrangements.

The primary system of nominations was instituted throughout the South in the early part of this century as part of the aforementioned effort to establish the Democratic Party's hegemony so completely that any serious attempt at a Republican challenge would be fore-doomed at the outset. The Democratic Party was a private, not a public, institution in the South, and as such, it was exclusively white in its composition and largely upper-class in its leadership. The party was loosely organized; and the competition for nomination in the primaries (usually a dual-election system because of rules requiring the winner to obtain a clear majority for nomination, thus necessitating a second or run-off primary election if no candidate received a majority in the first primary) turned on the nature of factional alignments among Democrats in each of the states of the South. The factional struggles (sometimes bifactional, but more often multifactional, geographically personalized, localized, and constantly changing) were an attenuated substitute for broad-based party alignments. The commonplace descriptive phrase for the general effect of these arrangements was that in the South a victory in the primary was "tantamount to election."

How was this system related to the national political process through which the election of members of Congress and the President took place and formed the basis for the organization and functioning of the national government? Since the congressional elections were also administered by the states, the process was the same as that used for election of state officials, at least after the Seventeenth Amendment was adopted in 1912 requiring the popular election of U.S. Senators. The national convention method of nomination of presidential candidates made the primary moot until quite recently, and delegates were largely a combination of professionals and Democratic citizens-at-large named by party committees and subject to the "unit rule," whereby the vote of the entire delegation from a given state was delivered to the candidate who received a majority of votes in the delegation caucuses preceding the roll call vote from the floor. In any case, the outcome of the general election in the region was assured inasmuch as the South would duly deliver each state's electoral vote to the Democratic candidate, with the Republican strength having been reduced to a few mountain strongholds in East Tennessee,

western North Carolina and Southwest Virginia (from which a scattering of congressional districts returned Republicans to the Congress), a scattering of "blacks and tans" who kept the party heritage
of Reconstruction alive and enjoyed the benefits of local control of
national patronage under Republican administrations, and a similar
scattering of "presidential Republicans" who were registered or declared Democrats but regularly voted Republican in presidential elections. The South was nearly as solidly supportive of the national
Democratic Party regionally as the individual southern states were in
relation to state and local Democrats.

The South's participation in national governmental affairs was active despite the apparent social, economic, and political isolation of
the region, a seemingly unalterable commitment to the national minority party, and tacit exclusion of southerners from access to the
presidency (even when Virginia-born Woodrow Wilson was nominated and elected in 1912 and 1916, his political career had been
confined to New Jersey and his southern origins were overlooked or
excused on those grounds). Democratic politicians from the South
had certain bargaining advantages vis a vis northern Democrats, and
in some instances these extended to Republican Party members as
well. In the first place, the South constituted the single, broad geographic base of continuing support for the national Democratic Party,
which meant that it was essential to the very survival of the national
minority party during the long period of Republican dominance.
While southerners were no more eligible for nomination as candidates for the presidency by the Democrats than by the Republicans,
they did have a major role in the nominating process, including a
veto on potential candidates by reason of the rule requiring a two-
thirds vote of the Democratic convention delegates for nomination.
Although that rule was rescinded for the 1936 convention and thereafter, the South had more than one-third of the delegates before that
time and could thus block the nomination of candidates who where
objectionable to the southern leadership. In the Congress, the southern delegations constituted a majority of the Democratic representation, so their united strength played a major role in decisions there.
Furthermore, southerners tended to be long-termers once they were
elected, so their experience, coupled with the practice of longevity
in determining committee positions, gave them both the positions of
power and the parliamentary skills to use them effectively.[4] In addition, southerners had a somewhat freer mandate so far as their
stands on issues were concerned than was the case with many Senators
and Representatives from other areas. As long as they did not violate
the southern mores on racial matters, their places in Congress were

usually safe and they could be a determinative force in many areas of policy. Contrary to conventional wisdom, this power was not consistently conservative or reactionary; and when a Democrat occupied the presidential office or constituted a majority in Congress, southerners played major leadership roles in both the legislative body and the administration.[5] Conditions resulting from the 1877 compromise largely prevailed through World War II.

At this point the question might well be asked, "Why has all of this seemingly arcane historical background been introduced as the prelude to a book that is about a single national presidential election in the eleven states that collectively constitute 'the South,' or at least that part of the southeastern region of the United States that more than a century ago attempted to constitute a separate nation called 'The Confederate States of America'?" The answer is not a simple one, but it surely has to start with the conception that one cannot begin to understand a single political event, however important it may be in its own right, without recalling (even if only sketchily) the ways in which that event emerged from the historical experience of the society in which it took place. Thus it is that we are able to observe in our concentration on the presidential election of 1984 in the southern states much of the same interplay of social forces and many of the same issues, albeit in residual ways, that were present in earlier eras of American and southern history, going back at least to the time when the South was in the uncertain position of being neither fully in nor out of the Union, after having failed to separate from it completely. We must ask questions about the underlying social structure in the region (especially the relations between the races), about the way in which the politics of the region and of the nation function, how the parts differ from each other and from the whole, about the ideological ranges among the various groupings of the populace, and how these differences and similarities affect the outcomes of elections and affect the way the governments are organized, including the policies they produce over time.

Both the effort to explain specific political phenomena and to generalize these explanations cumulatively to the point of developing theoretical conclusions (which is the ostensible purpose of political science) inevitably involve careful consideration of the temporal dimension through which social and political continuity and change are reflected. To this point we have discussed briefly and generally the conditions under which the South and the nation-at-large attempted to resolve the crises of civil war, physical conquest of the southern states by the North, and Reconstruction of the South, and to stabilize the internal politics of the South and its relations to national politics. It has been indicated that the reconciliation, although uneasy in many ways, did produce a characteristic "old politics" in the South that persisted (largely as a consequence of a combination of national indifference to the South and white political solidarity in the region) for a period upwards of half a century (assuming the "system" had been fully installed and was operating effectively soon after the beginning of the twentieth century).

Throughout the foregoing account, it has been implied that since World War II southern politics has undergone such a sea change that the "old politics" as usual no longer obtains. As a further setting for the analysis of the 1984 presidential election in the South, we may turn now to a brief discussion of the major factors in, and magnitude of, that change, without attempting to provide any definitive answers to the omnipresent questions about the extent to which southern politics has moved definitively into the mainstream of American politics or has moved out of a state of uncertain transition of forty years' duration into a new politics whose discernible patterns display sufficient regularities to suggest a prospective long-term stability.

The conventions of analysis in discussions of this sort appear to forbid starting from any place other than V. O. Key, Jr.,'s point of departure in *Southern Politics*, published in 1949, one year after the 1948 Democratic National Convention was temporarily disrupted by a walk-out of the Mississippi delegation and half the Alabama delegation following the adoption of a civil rights plank in the party platform, a move that signaled the beginning of a growing disaffection of the South with the national Democratic Party.[6] The simplicity of Key's statement of the "predispositions" that underlie ("color" is his term) the book and his brief list of major structural impediments to a socially effective, democratic politics in the South is often overlooked because of the rich analytical material that, paradoxically, were both contributory to, and derivative from, these conceptions. Key's "predispositions" (basic working assumptions), as stated in the Preface to *Southern Politics* were (1) ". . . a belief in the democratic process as it is professed in the United States"; (2) ". . . a belief that southerners possess as great a capacity for self-government as do citizens elsewhere in the country"; and (3) ". . . the conviction that the best government results where there is free and vigorous competition at the ballot box in contests in which genuine issues are defined and candidates take a stand." Key identified the following as the main structural bars to a democratic politics in which there might be a genuine

sharing of power among all the citizens of the South: disfranchisement, one-party politics, racial segregation, and malapportioned legislative bodies.

In the case of the restraints on democracy in the South, all of those
listed above have now been formally removed or weakened so substantially that individual efforts to retain them can usually be overcome without the long delay and excessive costs required to deny
their general application. The civil rights movement eventually ended
de jure segregation and much of de facto segregation, as well as the
disfranchisement laws and extralegal practices that prevented the
most fundamental act of political participation—resort to the ballot;
one-party politics has given way to a shifting pattern of competitiveness that approaches a two-party system, or perhaps even a multiparty
one; and strict application of the U.S. Supreme Court's ruling in
Baker v. *Carr* to the legislative bodies in the United States, from the
national House of Representatives down to the elective councils and
commissions of local units of government, has made them reflect the
principle of "one man, one vote" as closely as is numerically possible
in a given constituency.

As in all human activities, some loopholes remain in these structures; and even when the loopholes are effectively closed, the results
in practice may still differ from those predicted (or even more from
the results desired by many proponents of the corrective measures),
so the effort to apply the principles that undergird the demands for
change in ways that suit the interests of some individuals and groups
continues to be a normal part of politics. But the competition is no
longer restricted by means that may be considered unwarranted in
a society that professes to operate as a full-fledged democracy.

The extent to which Key's "predispositions" have been realized in
fact is more problematic inasmuch their implementation implies the
development of a comprehensive understanding of a complex and
continuously changing political system, constructed of many parts in
dynamic relation to one another, and then measured in effectiveness
by the standards of an abstractly drawn ideal type.

Such an analysis requires the examination of a wide variety of
variables and their interactions, not only among themselves but also
in relation to other systems. Thus the chapters of this book on the
individual states of the South and the concluding chapter, which
provides an overview of the region as a whole, analyze the way in
which the political system of each state and of the region functioned
in relation to the presidential election of 1984. From the massive and
still accumulating literature on southern politics since World War II,

we are conscious of the comprehensiveness of change in every aspect of the social and political structures in southern life over the past forty years.[7] Demographic change has led to the development of an urban middle class and a skilled working class, that in combination is larger than any other social grouping, produced partly by a net increase in migration south on the part of people from outside the South, as well as by the continuing movement within the region from the farm to the city. Urbanization and industrialization have increased at a rate that now approaches the national average in many southern states rather than in the rim South alone and has made the southern black population an even more urban one than the white population, while largely wiping out the difference between the North and the South in agriculture as compared with other primary occupations and closing the North-South gap in per capita income (although far from completely).

Political change proceeded as rapidly as the changes in demographic characteristics, at first as a result of national activity, especially in the areas of civil rights (the unfinished business of Reconstruction) and equality of representation (redressing, in particular, the imbalance of power between the urban and rural South). The initial changes eventually led to internal action that opened new possibilities for genuine competition, abandoned race as the overriding issue of southern politics, reorganized the mediating institutions, including the political parties, and revamped both the organization of the governing institutions and the processes by which public policy is made and executed in the effort to make them more effective and more accountable. A corollary result was to enlarge issue orientation of southern politics so as to improve and expand government services to all areas of the population and to reduce to some extent the distinction between public and private activities. The relation of the states to the central government has also been vastly altered in the direction of centralization of authority to the point of abandonment of dual federalism, while continuing to increase state and local governmental activity under the impetus provided by federal initiations of programs, but with a corresponding increase in federal surveilance and control.

All of these and related changes are addressed as variables in the analysis of the 1984 presidential election that follows. Although that election was so one-sided not only in the South, but nationally as well, that the simplest conclusion is to suggest that the results verify earlier speculation that the South has so reversed its old politics that it has now become solidly Republican, at least in presidential politics. But again that would be too easy because there are other indicators that raise questions about the directions of change and the possibilities of stabilization of both the national and regional systems in the future. And those are the questions to which the authors search for answers in their analysis, as they seek to understand what continuities and alterations in the general trend lines are evident in the 1984 presidential election.

NOTES

1. In my view the best overall treatment of the historical pattern of national party alignments remains Samuel Lubell's *The Future of American Politics*, rev. ed. (Garden City, NY: Doubleday Anchor Books, 1956). See also Dewey Grantham, "Conceptualizing the History of Modern Southern Politics," *The History Teacher* 17(1): 9–31, 1983.

2. For a thorough analysis of the way in which disfranchisement of blacks (and others) was accomplished to the end of building a one-party system and assuring that the South would remain "white man's country," see J. Morgan Kousser, *The Shaping of Southern Politics: Suffrage Restriction and the Establishment of the One-Party South, 1880–1910* (New Haven and London: Yale University Press, 1974).

3. Jasper Berry Shannon, *Towards a New Politics in the South* (Knoxville: University of Tennessee Press, 1949), Chap. 3, 38ff.

4. A cleverly amusing, though seriously intended, study of the effectiveness of southern politicians is David Leon Chandler's *The Natural Superiority of Southern Politicians; A Revisionist History* (Garden City, NY: Doubleday, 1977).

5. For an excellent statement about the South's positive response to the New Deal, both popular and among members of Congress, see Everette Carll Ladd, Jr., with Charles D. Hadley, *Transformation of the American Party System*, 2d ed. (New York: Norton, 1978), Chap. 3. The centrality of the race issue has obscured the streak of liberality that runs through the southern attitude on economic issues and has affected the issue stands on issues of many more Democratic members of Congress from the South than is generally recognized.

6. V. O. Key, Jr., *Southern Politics in State and Nation* (New York: Knopf, 1949). A new edition (mainly facsimile) was published by the University of Tennessee Press in 1984. With due acknowledgment of the irreplaceability of Key's book, a stimulating challenge to students of politics to "transcend" Key's analysis has been made by Numan V. Bartley in his "Beyond Southern Politics: Some Suggestions for Research," *Perspectives on the American South*, Vol. 2 (London: Gordon and Breach, c. 1984), 35–47.

7. In chronological sequence the major general works since Key include William C. Havard, ed., *The Changing Politics of the South* (Baton Rouge: Louisiana State University Press, 1972); Numan V. Bartley and Hugh D. Graham, *Southern Politics and the Second Reconstruction* (Baltimore and London: The Johns Hopkins University Press, 1975); and Jack Bass and Walter DeVries, *The Transformation of Southern Politics: Social Change and Political Consequences Since 1945* (New York: Basic Books, 1976). Note the way in which the titles of these books emphasize the theme being discussed here. A

more recent extension of the analysis of electoral politics in the South beyond the early and mid-1970s is Alexander P. Lamis, *The Two-Party South* (New York and Oxford: Oxford University Press, 1984). Again the title is worth noting by contrast with that of Alexander Heard's *A Two-Party South?* published in 1952.

Part II

The Deep South

2

Louisiana

*Charles D. Hadley**

Were V. O. Key, Jr.,[1] to visit Louisiana today he would find the state still on the "seamy side of democracy" and its legislature, government, and politics dominated by a powerful charismatic governor, Edwin W. Edwards, in the place of Huey and Earl Long. Over the last decade and a half, political scandals have continued to surface from the use of "lightweight" concrete in its interstate highway system, lucrative insurance commissions for political supporters without regard to expertise, a near-bankrupt tax shelter for state employees (DCCL [Deferred Compensation Corporation of Louisiana]), mail fraud, vote buying, prison pardons, public work for personal gain, and so on. Many powerful Louisiana politicians "vacationed" or are "vacationing" compliments of the federal government in its prison system: former Attorney General Jack P. F. Gremillion, Commissioner of Administration Charles Roemer, Agriculture Commissioner Gil Dozier, Assistant Agriculture Commissioner Frances Picora (in a different administration), Senate President Michael O'Keefe, U.S. Representative Richard Tonry, District Judge Roy Price, and others.

Reminiscent of the colorful gubernatorial campaigns of the past,

*I wish to acknowledge the thoughtful comments of my colleagues Elizabeth E. Allen and Harold W. Stanley on an earlier version of this manuscript, the cooperation of Louisiana Democratic and Republican Party Executive Directors Deborah A. Moore and Greg Beuerman, and the assistance of Chalermpalanuapap Termsak and Brenda J. Butler who helped compile the regional gubernatorial and presidential voting data.

the whirlwind campaign stump of 1983 touched all 64 parishes in some 80 stops in nine days and ended a week before the election. In that stump Edwin Edwards assumed the role of savior. He told the hundreds who greeted him at each stop: "You that are elderly and have seen your funds cut, you that are crippled, blind, poor, disabled, you that have suffered these long three and a half years [under incumbent Republican David C. Treen], take heart. Take heart, for . . . the great healer shall returneth and shall make ye well." Edwards considered himself "a poor man's friend, a little man's God." The quick-witted former governor was never at a loss for words. Treen, responding to a debate question, said, "I'd rather be inept than dishonest" whereupon Edwards shot back, "I'd rather be inept than dishonest, too. But since I'm neither, I have a hard time commenting on the question." The audience laughed. The 1983 gubernatorial campaign, which cost the two major candidates $19 million, excluding in-kind contributions, would have made the Longs proud.[2]

As well, the politicians and electorate adapted to the civil rights and voting rights revolutions and to modern campaign technology as had the rest of the South and nation.[3] By the 1970s, however, the bifactional characteristic of Louisiana politics—Longs v. anti-Longs or reformers—described by Key and others had disappeared, as had the practice of "ticketing."[4] By the 1970s two cohesive Democratic political factions no longer contested Louisiana state elections, if indeed, they ever had.[5]

Moreover, in time for the 1975 gubernatorial election and through the persistent efforts of Governor Edwards, Louisiana, with the permission of the U.S. Department of Justice, put into place the open elections system. Under that electoral arrangement, party symbols that identified separate state (Rooster) and national (Donkey) Democratic parties were removed from the ballot, which was then restructured from party column to office block. All candidates for an office now face each other in a primary election. If no candidate receives a majority of the votes cast, the top two vote-getters, regardless of political party affiliation, if any, face each other in a runoff general election. The traditional general election was eliminated. In effect, this electoral system has institutionalized multifactionalism.

With the implementation of the Voting Rights Act of 1965 the southern system of elections was destroyed;[6] the nationalization of Louisiana and southern politics was complete.[7] The literacy tests and poll taxes used to disfranchise blacks and poor whites were banned and federal registrars were sent to Louisiana to list voters on the rolls, as fewer than 50 percent of its eligible black population was registered to vote in 1964. While Louisiana's 1960 black voter registration (31.1

percent) was slightly higher than the regional average (29.1 percent), it was significantly higher than that of Mississippi, Alabama, and South Carolina and, according to analysis, directly related to its predominant southern Louisiana Catholicism.[8]

From Table 2–1, black voter registration steadily increased in the aftermath of *Smith* v. *Allwright* (1944), which banned the white pri-

TABLE 2–1   Louisiana Voter Registration by Race, 1948–84

	Black			
	*n**	*% Increase*	*% VAP*	*% Total*
1948	28	—	na	3.0
1952	108	73.8	na	10.2
1956	152	29.1	na	14.4
1960	160	13.5	31.1	13.9
1964	165	1.5	na	13.7
1966	239	31.2	na	18.7
1968	281	15.0	na	19.5
1972	377	25.5	61.6	21.9
1976	398	5.2	63.0	22.9
1980	465	14.4	60.7	23.1
1984	561	20.6	na	24.8
	White			
1948	896	—	na	97.0
1952	945	5.1	na	89.8
1956	906	−4.4	na	85.6
1960	993	8.8	76.9	86.1
1964	1,037	4.3	na	86.3
1966	1,042	0.5	na	81.3
1968	1,160	10.2	na	80.5
1972	1,342	13.6	77.1	78.1
1976	1,342	0.0	78.4	77.1
1980	1,550	13.5	74.8	76.9
1984	1,701	9.7	na	75.2

*thousands

Source: "Statement of Registered Voters [October close of registration]," Report of Secretary of State (Baton Rouge: State of Louisiana, 1948–84). The figures reported by the Secretary of State are slightly higher than those from the Commissioner of Elections. The latter does not report voters listed by Federal Registrars in the years following the Voting Rights Act of 1965. Beginning 1980 the numbers are in agreement. The Voting Age Population (VAP) percentages are from: U.S. Bureau of the Census, Statistical Abstract of the United States (Washington: 1984, 1978, and 1974), respectively, 261, 519, and 439.

mary, and again with the implementation of the Voting Rights Act of 1965. Blacks incrementally became a larger segment of the electorate, from 3 percent in 1948 to 14 percent in the 1956–64 period to 25 percent in 1984. Furthermore, it appears that black voter registration reached its peak in 1976 (63 percent of the voting age population) and low point in 1980 (60.7 percent). White voter registration expanded as well, though the white proportion of the electorate steadily declined between 1948 (97.0 percent) and 1984 (75.0 percent). It remained about 14 percentage points higher than that for blacks. The greatest gain came in the 1968–72 and 1980–84 periods.

Electoral success for black candidates came with the significant voter registration gains and with the formation of black political organizations. In addition to those with acronyms like BOLD, COUP, SOUL, ROOTS, BULL, and BLOW, there are those with conventional names: Orleans Parish Progressive Voters League (OPPVL), Black Alliance for Progress, Black Citizens for Better Government, Black Committee for Progressive Change, Black Concern, Black Concerned Souls, Black Old Regulars, Black Women's Caucus, and others.[9] In 1968 Louisiana had 53 black elected officials, only one of whom sat in the state legislature. The increases in black elected officials have been significant and rapid: 124.5 percent, 1968–72 (to 119); 100.8 percent, 1972–76 (to 250); 31.1 percent, 1976–80 (to 363); and 17.1 percent, 1980–84 (to 438). These increases are concentrated in city/parish and educational establishment positions and number more than eight times the 1968 figure. Though modest in number, 12 blacks sit in both houses of the state legislature and form a legislative "black caucus."[10]

The nationalization process continues into the 1980s and affects party politics as well. While Democratic Party voter registration remains overwhelming today (80.6 percent), it has steadily eroded since 1956 (98.7 percent) as shown in Table 2–2. Republican Party voter registration gains are steady but small (1 percent), in 1956; 2.9 percent, 1972; 7.4 percent, 1980; 11.3 percent, 1984). Similar growth has occurred in the category "Other," in which 99.4 percent were independent or unaffiliated in 1984. The Republican Party has made significant electoral gains at the city/parish level (similar to those of blacks), gains attributed to the open elections system. The number of Republican elected officials went from fewer than 50 in 1975 to 118 in 1981, 270 in 1983, and 345 in 1984. In 1983 among their number was the Governor and two of the eight Representatives (down from three).[11] But at the same time, the open elections system appears to have worked against the party at the state level. State legislative candidacies immediately were cut to one-fifth their former number

TABLE 2–2   Louisiana Voter Registration by Political Party,
1948–84 (in percentages)

	Total	Democratic	Republican	Other
1948	924,705	98.9	0.3	0.8
1952	1,056,720	99.0	0.5	0.5
1956	1,057,687	98.7	0.9	0.4
1960	1,152,151	98.6	0.9	0.5
1964	1,201,785	98.1	1.5	0.4
1968	1,451,836	97.4	2.0	0.6
1972	1,780,288	95.3	2.9	1.6
1976	1,865,548	93.5	3.7	2.8
1980	2,015,402	86.6	7.4	6.0
1984	2,262,101	80.6	11.3	8.1*

*99.4% are independent or unaffiliated.
Source: See Table 1.

in Senate elections (1972, 17 [44 percent]; 1975, 3 [8 percent]) and
to nearly one-fourth in House elections (1972, 39 [37 percent]; 1975,
11 [11 percent]). By 1983 Republican candidates for Senate and House
elections had increased to 7 (18 percent) and 16 (25 percent), respectively; the party now holds one Senate seat (through initial special
election) and 11 House seats (five of whom switched parties).[12]
    In the 1970s the Louisiana Republican Party moved from the weak
federal patronage variety to a strong viable party organization. By
1984 it had outgrown its headquarters near the Capitol; hence, the
executive director, the organization director, and the computer department (with a staff of four) moved to new offices while the finance
director, with three support staff, remained at the old headquarters
owned by the party. In 1984, moreover, its annual budget reached
$1.8 million (of which $500,000 was for the presidential campaign
in Louisiana), up from $371,000 a year earlier. These figures put
the Louisiana Republican Party among the best staffed and most
highly financed in the country. By contrast, the Louisiana Democratic
Party operated with an executive director, a special projects director,
a computer technician, and an office manager and with a $250,000
operating budget, both staff and funding respectable by national
standards.[13] Further evidence of the nationalization process is evidenced in voter turnout. In the late 1940s voter turnout in gubernatorial elections far exceeded that in presidential elections as shown
in Figure 2–1.[14] By 1968 greater numbers of Louisiana voters were
participating in presidential rather than gubernatorial elections (+7.4
percent), a phenomenon that has continued through the present with

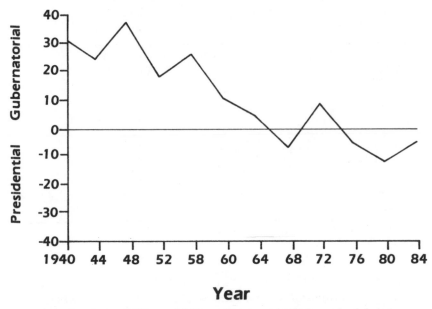

FIGURE 2–1   Differential Voter Turnout in Gubernatorial and
Presidential Elections, 1940–84 (percentage difference).

the exception of the hotly contested 1972 Edwards/J. Bennett Johnson gubernatorial runoff election, which brought out 10.5 percent
more voters than the Nixon/McGovern presidential contest.

The presidential/gubernatorial vote data shown in Tables 2–3 and
2–4 complete the examination of contemporary Louisiana politics.
Several points are evident: Republican support is strongest in Louisiana's cities/urban parishes (excluding New Orleans)—Shreveport,
Lake Charles, Baton Rouge, Jefferson, Lafayette, Monroe, and Alexandria—and the northern Protestant, more conservative area of
the state.[15] Given the strong support for Dixiecrat presidential candidate Strom Thurmund in 1948 (who had the official Democratic
designation on the ballot) and for American Independent presidential candidate George Wallace in 1968, Louisiana has been categorized
among the reactionary or protest Deep South states.[16] With overwhelming support from North Louisiana, Barry Goldwater won the
state in 1964 as did Dwight Eisenhower in 1956, Richard Nixon in
1972, and Ronald Reagan in 1980 and 1984.

The apparent inconsistency between party voter registration (80.6
percent Democratic) and statewide Republican Party success in both
gubernatorial (1979) and presidential elections can be explained by
political philosophy and perceptions of two distinct Democratic Par-

TABLE 2–3   Presidential Vote, North/South Louisiana and Florida Parishes, Urban/Rural, 1940–84 (percentage Democratic)

		Region of State				
	State	North	South	Florida[1]	Urban[2]	Rural
1940	85.9	90.4	83.9	88.2	85.7	86.1
1944	80.6	74.0	83.0	82.8	70.8	77.9
1948	32.3	32.0	32.6	37.5	36.3	28.7
	(49.4)[3]	(55.6)	(45.8)	(46.6)	(41.9)	(57.6)
1952	52.9	50.8	52.5	57.6	50.8	55.8
1956	42.6	40.4	41.0	46.5	40.4	45.7
1960	50.4	39.3	71.8	60.6	59.7	68.9
1964	43.2	22.2	53.1	41.0	43.2	43.2
1968	28.2	23.7	31.3	25.0	30.5	25.9
	(48.3)[4]	(52.8)	(44.6)	(54.1)	(40.8)	(56.1)
1972	28.4	25.9	32.7	33.8	30.9	29.5
1976	51.7	48.2	55.1	53.9	49.9	56.2
1980	45.7	44.0	49.1	46.1	45.5	48.9
1984	38.6	33.8	41.6	35.9	39.4	37.8

[1]The Florida Parishes are those across Lake Ponchatrain and adjacent to the Florida panhandle.
[2]The urban parishes include: Caddo (Shreveport), Calcasieu (Lake Charles), East Baton Rouge (Baton Rouge), Jefferson, Lafayette (Lafayette), Orleans (New Orleans), Ouachita (Monroe), and Rapides (Alexandria).
[3]Dixiecratic vote in parentheses ( ).
[4]American Independent vote in parentheses ( ).

TABLE 2–4 Gubernatorial Vote, North/South Louisiana and Florida Parishes, Urban/Rural, Years with Republican Opposition, 1960–83 (percentage Democratic)

		Region of State				
	State	North	South	Florida*	Urban*	Rural
1960	80.5	93.1	78.1	81.8	77.4	87.9
1964	60.7	53.5	62.9	63.0	51.2	71.5
1972	57.2	42.0	65.5	48.1	52.7	61.6
1979	49.7	49.1	48.5	54.3	44.7	54.0
1983	62.3	60.6	64.6	62.0	57.4	68.2

*See Table 2–3 for explanations.

ties—one state, the other national.[17] Louisiana voters perpetuate a strong state Democratic Party by tradition as evidenced by the state legislative elections and at the same time support the generally more conservative Republican candidates for Congress and the presidency.

1984 PRESIDENTIAL PRIMARY
ELECTION/CAUCUS MANEUVER

After its experience with two political party-operated national convention delegate selection systems in which few registered voters participated (1972 caucuses with less than 1 percent and 1976 primary elections with 3–4 percent), in 1979 Louisiana adopted a state-run presidential primary to be held the first Saturday in April, beginning 1980. The apportionment of delegates to be selected at party caucuses held the third Saturday in April was based on the primary election result. The objective was to increase voter participation. As required by Section 5 of the Voting Rights Act of 1965, the new primary law/caucus system was submitted to and approved by the U.S. Department of Justice (Justice). The anticipated increased voter participation materialized in 1980 when Democratic turnout reached 20 percent.

On the other hand, the state legislature, concerned with potential budget deficits during its regular 1983 session, considered suspending the 1984 primary as an economy move but later chose not to do so. However, several months later (December) in a lame duck special legislative session called to correct the congressional district reapportionment thrown out in federal court, the primary was suspended for 1984 due to revenue shortfalls and presidential politics.[18] Supporters of the Rev. Jesse Jackson—including black legislators, Louisiana Association of Business and Industry (LABI; the major business lobby), and the League of Women Voters—lobbied to keep the primary; on the other side was the AFL–CIO and, for fiscal reasons, the Commissioner of Elections. Argued in highminded fiscal terms, the political argument centered on a delegate selection system perceived to favor Walter Mondale rather than Jesse Jackson.[19]

The state stressed that the primary law suspension was "strictly an economic measure" and provided documentation on that point when it was submitted to the federal Department of Justice for implementation clearance. "Minority" objection to the suspension also was noted at that time.[20] Two days later (7 January), on the motion of a black state legislator, the Democratic State Central Committee (DSCC) nearly unanimously adopted a resolution supporting retention of the presidential primary and forwarding a copy to Justice. A month later,

New Orleans Mayor Ernest N. Morial (Jesse Jackson's Louisiana campaign chairman), Orleans Parish Civil Sheriff Paul Valteau, state Representatives Richard Turnley, Joseph Delpit, and Johnny Jackson, and the Louisiana Black Caucus, among others, filed a "Comment" with Justice objecting to the suspension. The objection was based on (1) discriminatory intention as evidenced by election law discrimination as recent as the 1983 state legislative and congressional district reapportionments, as well as the politics that surrounded the primary law suspension; (2) the return to a delegate selection procedure (1972) that produced very low turnouts that would adversely affect minority voters; and (3) the potential for voting abuses under the party's caucus delegate selection plan.[21]

Subsequently, Justice requested additional information from the state with respect to the suspension of the primary. The requested information included (1) alternatives taken by the state to deal with its financial situation; (2) increased costs to the major political parties as a result of alternative delegate selection plans; (3) support from blacks for the primary law suspension; and (4) state measures to insure that the alternative delegate selection would be "open to all registrants of the respective parties without discrimination on the basis of race or color."[22] On these points the state cited (1) the retroactive increased state income tax passed in the same special session of the legislature; (2) minimal additional costs to the political parties (which planned all along to hold caucuses following the presidential primary); (3) the regular session unanimous vote by black legislators to suspend the primary; and (4) the inability of the state to become involved with the delegate selection process because it was a political party process outside the state election code.[23]

While the legality of the presidential primary suspension remained under consideration by Justice, the Louisiana Secretary of State proceeded to prepare for the primary by qualifying presidential candidates and by preparing the ballot on the assumption that the primary would be held. Eventually the last possible date for printing absentee ballots arrived without any decision from Justice. On 14 March, then, on the opinion of the Louisiana Attorney General and because of the lack of necessary funds, the Secretary of State cancelled preparation for a 7 April primary.[24]

The following day Civil Sheriff Valteau, Mayor Morial, and others who had complained to Justice about the primary law suspension went to the Federal District Court to force the state to hold the presidential primary because, as required by Section 5 of the Voting Rights Act of 1965, the state had no received clearance from Justice and had not sought approval from the Federal District Court for the District of Columbia. Ironically, on 16 March when Federal District Judge Adrian Duplantier issued a temporary restraining order requiring the primary to be held 5 May, Justice refused to clear the suspension:

> [We] cannot help but note the timing of the proposed change, coming in the midst of a political campaign and on the heels of the announcement of the Reverend Jesse Jackson to enter the presidential race. The suspension, if approved, will undeniably reduce the opportunities for blacks to participate meaningfully in the delegate selection process. Not only is use of a large number of polling places eliminated, but voting hours are shortened as well. Where, as here, the state has made no effort to develop a comprehensive alternative process that assures minorities full and equal participation in the franchise, it cannot be said that a temporary suspension of general elections laws is free of discriminatory effect.

Several days later a three-judge federal district court enjoined the state to hold its presidential primary on 5 May.[25] The state applied to U.S. Supreme Court Justice Byron R. White to stay the district court injunction; White refused.

The Democratic Primary and Causes

The Rev. Jesse Jackson made a campaign blitz through most of Louisiana's major cities (Shreveport, Monroe, Lake Charles, Baton Rouge, and New Orleans) during the week before the 5 May primary. While the large enthusiastic crowds of supporters who greeted him at each campaign stop helped Jackson win the election with 43.6 percent of the total votes cast, equally important was the sophisticated $700,000 computer operation that had been developed by his state campaign coordinator Sherman Copelin for Governor Edwards' 1983 election campaign. Copelin's New Orleans-based computer system has in its memory all metropolitan area black voters cross-referenced by ward, precinct, and special interests, the latter developed from physicians' patients lists, church membership rosters, fraternities, and the like. The system—capable of telephoning 125,000 voters per week with personal messages tailored to the campaign at hand (in this case, Jesse Jackson and Muhammad Ali), calling back busy telephone numbers, and purging from its memory disconnected telephone numbers—was used in the Jackson campaign on a limited basis due to insufficient funds. It was effective where used. For example, in a precinct where voter turnout appeared to lag, the computer was pressed into operation at midday; the result was 375 votes for Jackson to Mondale's nine and Hart's five.[26]

The combination of campaign coordinator Copelin's computer operation and several hundred of Mayor Morial's City Hall "volunteers" who worked the streets for his political organization LIFE (and the efforts of other black political organizations such as the Rev. Wilhelmina Cole's People of the Black Community) resulted in an overwhelming Jackson vote (70.7 percent) in the Second Congressional District, where he won all of the convention delegates as shown in Table 2–5. He did extremely well in U.S. Representative Gillis Long's Eighth Congressional District (Alexandria; 46.8 percent and three delegates), as well as the Sixth (Baton Rouge; 43.3 percent and two delegates) and the Fifth Congressional Districts (Monroe; 42.0 percent and two delegates). U.S. Senator Gary Hart, the favorite with delegates at the late March state convention, captured 25 percent of the vote to garner 13 delegates (33 percent) to former Vice President Walter Mondale's 22 percent and ten delegates (26 percent).

The unusually large black voter turnout was the key to Jackson's only statewide victory, which inadvertently may have been helped by Governor Edwards, who called the primary "silly" and "meaningless" when he advocated its boycott on election eve. Jackson received 90.2 percent of the black vote in contrast to Mondale's 6.2 percent and Hart's 1.3 percent. On the one hand, 97.7 percent of Jackson's vote came from the black community.[27] On the other hand, the Democratic turnout (18 percent) was not too different from that in 1980 (20 percent).

By contrast, very few Democrats turned out at the 19 May caucuses (.2 percent), where the actual people to attend the national convention were selected. The greatest number of Jackson supporters turned out in New Orleans (588), while a delegate was selected elsewhere with but nine votes. A number of delegate positions went unchallenged. The sparse caucus turnout was consistent with 1972, when that was the sole mechanism to select most of the Democratic National Convention delegation.

Next, the Democratic State Central Committee met 9 June to select the remainder of the delegation. The total delegation reflected the primary support for Jackson (43.9 percent; 25), Hart (33.3 percent; 19), and Mondale (22.8 percent; 13).[28] The complete delegation was rounded out with 12 uncommitted party and elected officials, six selected at the DSCC meeting and six "super delegates." Governor Edwards (uncommitted) beat Mayor Morial (Jackson) to head the delegation; Morial, who was entitled to attend the convention given his status as Democratic National Committeeman-at-Large, received few votes. Sherman Copelin (Jackson) was elected Vice Chair and Melissa Cloud (Hart) was elected Secretary. The 63 elected delegates reflected national Democratic Party desires with 43 percent blacks and 46 percent women. By background there were 33 percent of the delegates who had never attended a national convention (though 57 percent were party activists), 17 percent state legislators, 25 percent Democratic Parish (county) Executive Committee members, 17 percent union members, and 43 percent in business/professional occupations.[29]

The Republicans

Among Louisiana Republicans there was no contest; hence, voter turnout was very low (8.4 percent). President Ronald Reagan ran in the 5 May primary without opposition and received 90 percent (14,964) of the votes cast to win all the delegates (four per congressional district), the remaining 10 percent (1,723) being cast "uncommitted." As with the Democrats, the people to attend the national convention were selected in caucuses held 19 May. These 32 delegates, an equal number of alternates, and party leaders met 30 June to select the remaining 9 delegates to complete the 41-member delegation and an equal number of alternates.

In direct contrast with their Democratic counterparts, delegates to the Republican National Convention were nearly all whites (97.6 percent) who had business/professional occupations (73.2 percent), including 20 businessmen and ten lawyers. The remaining delegates included ten (24.4 percent) homemaker-civic-political activists and one student. Of the women delegates (37 percent, a number held very responsible national party/convention positions: Betty Heitman, Co-chair of the Republican National Committee; Marilyn Thayer, Co-chair of the Louisiana Reagan-Bush campaign and Chair of the Platform Committee's Human Resources and Opportunity Subcommittee; and Ginny Martinez of the Committee on Arrangements. In addition to its unified commitment to the Reagan-Bush reelection effort, the delegation shared an "unbending" conservative political philosophy.[30]

THE ELECTION CAMPAIGN

The traditional Labor Day start of the general election campaign brought Vice President George Bush to Louisiana for a special world's

TABLE 2–5 Primary/caucus Vote and Apportionment of Democratic National Convention Delegates

	Hart			Jackson			Mondale			Uncommitted			Other		
	Vote	%	Del	Vote	%	Del	Vote	%	Del	Vote	%	Del	Vote	%	Del
A. Congressional District:															
1st	9,871	36.5	3	4,728	17.5	0	8,298	30.6	2	2,350	8.7	0	1,829	6.8	0
2nd	6,158	11.4	0	38,010	70.7	4	7,193	13.4	0	1,157	2.2	0	1,267	2.4	0
3rd	10,596	30.7	2	11,878	34.4	2	8,465	24.5	1	2,154	6.2	0	1,432	4.1	0
4th	10,727	27.2	2	13,716	34.7	2	9,543	24.2	1	3,660	9.3	0	1,850	4.7	0
5th	11,138	25.6	2	18,284	42.0	2	9,043	20.8	1	3,486	8.0	0	1,597	3.7	0
6th	7,248	24.0	1	13,100	43.3	2	7,531	24.9	2	1,411	4.7	0	970	3.2	0
7th	8,783	31.8	2	7,765	28.1	1	8,149	29.5	2	2,118	7.7	0	804	2.9	0
8th	15,072	24.1	1	29,226	46.8	3	12,940	20.7	1	3,073	4.9	0	2,190	3.5	0
Vote Totals	79,593	25.0		136,707	42.9		71,162	22.3		19,409	6.1		11,939	3.7	
Delegate Totals		33.3	13		41.0	16		25.6	10		0.0	0		0.0	0

B. Caucus Vote

Totals	1,456	1,139	1,517

C. DSCC Selection

	1,456		1,139		1,517		Total
Delegates	30.7	4	46.2	6	23.1	3	
Party/elected Officials	40.0	2	40.0	2	20.0	1	6[1]

D. Uncommitted

	1,456		1,139		1,517		Total
Party/elected Officials							6[2]
Total Delegation	33.3	19	42.1	24	24.6	14	12

[1] Governor Edwin W. Edwards, DSCC Vice Chair James Brady, DSCC Treasurer Charlotte Sumlin Cantwell, Robert d'Hemecourt, Cathy Long (Mrs. Gillis W. Long), and Sidney Flynn.

[2] DSCC Chair Jesse Bankston, DSCC Vice Chair Kathy Vick, U.S. Representatives Gillis W. Long, Lindy Boggs, John Breaux, and Jerry Huckaby.

Source: State of Louisiana, Secretary of State, Elections Division, 5 May Primary Election Report, 11 May 1984.

fair celebration; he was introduced by New Orleans Saints Head Coach Bum Phillips, who endorsed the Reagan-Bush ticket: "I don't know how much good I can do, but I want you to know I'm on your side." Bush then spoke to several thousand spectators outside the United States pavilion.[31] In many respects, however, the Louisiana Republican reelection effort had already begun on the floor of the Democratic National Convention when delegation chair and declared Mondale delegate Governor Edwin W. Edwards, anxious to deliver a delegation supporting Mondale, persuaded two elected Hart delegates to vote for Mondale on the first ballot. The switch precipitated a shouting match between Hart delegate State Representative Quentin Dastugue (D-Metairie) and Governor Edwards' brother Marion before reporters and the national television networks. An angry Dastugue noted that "Edwin Edwards talked them into it" and threatened, "We may switch to Jesse Jackson just to let him carry the state" [as he had in the primary]. Not denying his role, Edwards made light of the situation: "A rumor got around the floor that we had some delegates switching, so we talked two of them into doing it so as not to disappoint anybody."[32]

The following day Dastugue alluded to the possibility of switching political parties: "It's becoming increasingly obvious that the Democrats don't want me in their party. They can cater to gays and everybody else, but there's no place in it that fiscal conservatives can get a hearing."[33] A month later, Dastugue, now (R-Metairie), basked in the limelight of the Republican National Convention as a special guest. Moreover, near the end of the convention via telephone from Dallas, the Louisiana GOP welcomed to its ranks fellow conservative state Representative Garey Forster who became chair of the New Orleans Reagan-Bush campaign. By the end of the reelection campaign, three additional state representatives switched to the GOP: Emile "Peppi" Bruneau, Jr. (New Orleans), Archie R. Crosby Morehouse, East and West Carroll), and Charles "Chuck" Cusimano, II (Jefferson). Shortly after the President's impressive reelection, two more Democratic state legislators converted: Senator Kenneth "Ken" Osterberger (Baton Rouge) who headed the East Baton Rouge Parish "Democrats for Reagan" and Representative Vincent "V. J." Bella (St. Martin, St. Mary).[34]

These party conversions, among others, were not accidental. Rather, they were the direct result of an "Elected Officials Conversion Program" developed by Republican state legislators and the state GOP staff, a program requested by other Republican state parties and featured in the January 1985 issue of the Republican National Committee's *First Monday*.[35] Governor Edwards characteristically expressed no surprise at the conversions: "Those that have changed came here [Baton Rouge] as registered, elected Democrats, though with Republican, conservative philosophy. They have reflected that with all of their votes here." He went on to speculate: "It's not going to change their vote in the Legislature. . . ."[36]

Another aspect of the Louisiana GOP reelection campaign that began before Labor Day was a concerted effort to significantly increase Republican voter registration. For example, New Orleans Republican City Councilman Bryan Wagner sent out three mailings that included voter registration change applications and postage-paid return envelopes; 50,000 were mailed just prior to the Republican National Convention. In his "Dear Friend" letter, the Councilman indicated:[37]

> I am writing to you in the hopes that you might want to do something personally to help President Ronald Reagan get reelected. One of the major components that elected officials look at when they make an endorsement is the registration of the candidate's party. A surge in Republican registration would be a great help to President Reagan. It might help convince some Democrat elected officials to endorse the President's reelection.

To the letter he added the following "P.S.":

> I realize that this letter may be received by some people who are Walter Mondale Democrats. Even though you don't agree with me, I hope you applaud my efforts to get people who think Republican to register Republican. Then you can have the Democratic Party all to yourselves.

Though 1984 Republican voter registration increased by 59,442 (30.2 percent) between 1 January and 12 October, the bulk of the increase (54,910; 27.9 percent) came between 1 July and 12 October as a direct result of the GOP effort by Wagner and others around the state. Moreover, 51 percent of the 1984 Louisiana voter registration increase through 12 October (117,769) was Republican followed by Democratic (30 percent) and unaffiliated (19 percent).[38]

While Governor Edwards very early distanced himself from the Louisiana Mondale-Ferraro effort[39] and Mayor Morial focused his sole attention and that of his City Hall "volunteers" on the passage of a metropolitan earnings tax (considered a test vote for a future third-term charter change attempt), the Louisiana Republican Party opened Reagan-Bush headquarters with a fulltime paid staffer in each of its 14 PAC districts around the state and expanded its state headquarters paid staff to 25.[40] Louisiana Black Republican Council chair Eulis Moore took a three-week tour to Louisiana's ten major cities in search of black support for Reagan-Bush, the Louisiana Republican Hispanic Assembly held a major fundraiser featuring U.S. Treasurer Katherine Ortega, and conservative Democratic state Representative John J. Hainkel, Jr. (New Orleans)—House Speaker under Governor David C. Treen—assumed statewide responsibility to organize "Democrats for Reagan."[41] By the end of the campaign, enthusiastic Republican volunteers had identified 290,000 favorable Reagan voters by telephone and another 25,000 through door-to-door canvases.[42]

On the other hand, with the exception of visits by Vice President George Bush's wife Barbara (29 October) and former Vice President Walter Mondale's wife Joan (30–31 October) and some other relatives, the presidential reelection campaign never came through Louisiana after Labor Day, though not for the lack of effort. State Representative Mary Landrieu (D-New Orleans) noted: "We've tired many times to get them [Mondale and Ferraro] here. I guess Louisiana just isn't that high a priority." Rather, the symbolic gesture toward the Deep South was made by both Walter Mondale and Geraldine Ferraro as well as by President Reagan (on behalf of Republican U.S. Senator Thad Cochran) in neighboring Mississippi.[43]

CONCLUSION

In 1984 President Ronald Reagan significantly increased his margin of victory over 1980 in every Louisiana parish except Orleans (New Orleans) by capturing 60.8 percent of the total votes cast. The President's electoral victory rivaled popular Governor Edwin W. Edwards' impressive and unprecedented election to a third term a year earlier when he routed incumbent Republican David C. Treen by garnering 62.3 percent of the total vote in an election campaign in which he spent $12 million. About three-quarters of the state's registered voters turned out for both elections.

Referring back to Table 2–3 and excluding the protest third-party victories of 1948 (Dixiecrat) and 1968 (American Independent), note that only President Richard M. Nixon in 1972 fared better than President Reagan, when Nixon ran against another unpopular Democratic liberal, U.S. Senator George McGovern. The 1984 presidential election has a pattern similar to those beginning with 1960: Republican support continues to be much greater in North rather than South Louisiana and slightly greater in rural rather than urban Louisiana. The urban/rural vote distribution reverses the usual pattern but is consistent with the 1964 and 1972 Republican landslides.

Democrat Walter F. Mondale's Louisiana support was similar to that he received in the rest of the country, as shown in Figure 2–2. In spite of the fact that Mayor Morial and his organization were preoccupied with the metropolitan earnings tax referendum on the same ballot and neglected the Mondale-Ferraro presidential campaign, the Democratic share of the vote increased from 56.9 percent to 57.7 percent (1980–84) in Orleans Parish.[44] Aside from East Carroll and Madison Parishes (upper-right corner of the state) that, like New Orleans, have majority black voter registrations, the Democratic

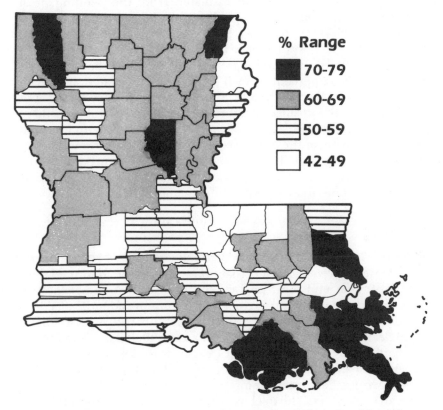

FIGURE 2–2   Distribution of the 1984 Republican Presidential Vote by Parish

Note: Outlined is Congressman Gillis W. Long's Eighth Congressional District; the figure was adapted from one developed by the Louisiana Republican Party.

ticket fared best in Congressman Gillis W. Long's Eighth Congressional District. After New Orleans, it "is the closest thing in the state to a constituency that supports national Democratic policies"; it has a 1980 black population of 36 percent.[45] Seven of the ten parishes won by Mondale-Ferraro were in Long's district. With the exception of Allen (23 percent), they have black voter registrations in the 38–48 percent range. Moreover, while the President did not receive a majority of the vote in East Feliciana Parish (49.5 percent), he did beat Mondale (49.0 percent).

Despite the fact that the congressional and nearly all state/local election contests were settled in the open elections system 29 September primary and were thus insulated from the pending presidential election, nine of 15 Republican candidates rode into office on President Reagan's coattails. Most important for the Republican Party was the election of Bryan Bush as District Attorney for East Baton Rouge Parish (Baton Rouge) with 53 percent of the vote (versus the President's 62 percent), which included an estimated 25 percent of the ballots cast by black voters. Since District Attorney Bush serves the State Capitol and since Louisiana's Attorney General lacks direct authority to prosecute cases involving government corruption (written permission from the appropriate local district attorney is constitutionally required), he has the power to prosecute in Baton Rouge all state government corruption cases. An aggressive Bush potentially could move Louisiana away from the "seamy side of democracy."[46]

The Future

While the Louisiana Democratic Party struggles to keep its liberal/black-conservative/white voter coalition together for continued domination of state and local politics, the Louisiana Republican Party continues to use all means possible, including presidential elections, to build aggressively toward the future. With the support of the Republican National Committee (RNC), the 290,000 pro-Reagan voters identified by several thousand Reagan-Bush telephone bank volunteers are being profiled for computer utilization and added to the 25,000 pro-Reagan voters computerized after identification by Republican canvassers. The data bank will be expanded continually and existing profiles updated with each successive election.

In early 1985 the Louisiana Republican Party will open three regional party headquarters—Lafayette, New Orleans, and Shreveport—with a parttime paid staffer and volunteers in an effort to continue the voter registration momentum developed in the presidential election and to establish precinct programs. It will continue to provide assistance to its candidates in the form of voter lists, telephone bank sheets, direct mail, contributor data, staff advice, "RNC field staff direction, and, in some cases, direct contributions from [the] RNC and the Republican Trust."[47]

Besides the continuing effort to expand its grassroots base, the Louisiana Republican Party, taking advantage of the apparent electoral protection provided incumbents by the open elections system, will continue to court and attempt to convert elected conservative Democrats to its party. One might expect a special effort directed at conservatives in the state legislature where, by the end of 1984, it held 17 of 107 House (12 from conversions) and two of 39 Senate seats (one from conversion).

More than competitive in presidential elections, Louisiana Republicans are quickly moving the state down the road to competitive two-party politics at all government levels.

NOTES

1. V. O. Key, Jr., *Southern Politics* (New York: Knopf, 1949), 156–82.

2. See John Maginnis, *The Last Hayride* (Baton Rouge: Gris Gris Press, 1984). Cf. A. F. Liebling, *The Earl of Louisiana* (Baton Rouge: Louisiana State University Press, 1970); T. Harry Williams, *Huey Long* (New York: Knopf, 1970).

3. Jack Bass and Walter DeVries, *The Transformation of Southern Politics* (New York: Basic Books, 1976), Chaps. 1–3, 8; Numan V. Bartley and Hugh D. Graham, *Southern Politics and the Second Reconstruction* (Baltimore: The Johns Hopkins University Press, 1975); Everett Carll Ladd, Jr., and Charles D. Hadley, *Transformation of the American Party System*, 2d ed. (New York: Norton, 1978), Chap. 3; and James L. Sundquist, *Dynamics of the Party System*, rev. ed., (Washington, DC: The Brookings Institution, 1983), Chaps. 12, 16.

4. V. O. Key, Jr., *Southern Politics*, Chap. 8; Allan P. Sindler, *Huey Long's Louisiana* (Baltimore: The Johns Hopkins University Press, 1956); Perry H. Howard, *Political Tendencies in Louisiana*, rev. and exp. ed., (Baton Rouge: Louisiana State University Press, 1971) and "Louisiana: Resistance and Change," in *The Changing Politics of the South*, ed. William C. Havard (Baton Rouge: Louisiana State University Press, 1972), 525–87. Cf. Alexander P. Lamis, *The Two-Party South* (New York: Oxford University Press, 1984), 107–19.

5. John Wildgen, "Voting Behavior in Gubernatorial Elections," in *Louisiana Politics: Festival in a Labyrinth*, ed. James Bolner (Baton Rouge: Louisiana State University Press, 1982), 319–44; Earl Black, "A Theory of Southern Factionalism," *The Journal of Politics* 45 (August 1983): 594–614.

6. V. O. Key, Jr., *Southern Politics*, Chap. 25–30; Jarrold G. Rusk and John J. Stucker, "The Effect of the Southern System of Election Laws on Voting Participation: A Reply to V. O. Key, Jr.," in *The History of American Electoral Behavior*, eds. Joel H. Silbey, Allan G. Bogue, and William H. Flanigan (Princeton: Princeton University Press, 1978), 198–250.

7. E. E. Schattschneider, *The Semisovereign People* (New York: Holt, Rinehart & Winston, 1960), 78–96.

8. John H. Fenton and Kenneth N. Vines, "Negro Registration in Louisiana," *American Political Science Review* 60 (September 1957): 704–13. On Catholic/Protestant areas of the state, see Wesley Jackson, "Survey 'confirms' north and south Louisiana boundaries," New Orleans *Times-Picayune/States Item*, 16 April 1983, Sec. 3, 10; and John K. Wildgen, *A Political Atlas of Louisiana Gubernatorial Elections*, Research Study No. 30, Division of Business and Economic Research, University of New Orleans, New Orleans 70148. See also Bernard Cosman, "Religion and Race in Louisiana Presidential Politics, 1960," *Southwestern Social Science Quarterly* 43 (December 1962): 235–41.

9. Registered with the Division of Ethics Administration, Campaign Finance Disclosure Office, State of Louisiana, as political committees in 1983.

10. Joint Center for Political Studies, *Black Elected Officials: A National Roster* (New York: UNIPUB, 1984 and indicated years).

11. Greg Beuerman, Executive Director, Louisiana Republican Party, 19 June 1984.

12. See Patrick F. O'Connor, "The Legislature," in *Louisiana Politics,* ed. James Bolner, 47–49.

13. James L. Gibson, Cornelius P. Cotter, and John F. Bibby, "Assessing Party Organizational Strength," *American Journal of Political Science* 27 (May 1983): 199–201; Greg Beuerman, Executive Director, Louisiana Republican Party, 19 June 1984; and Deborah Schaeffer-Moore, Executive Director, Democratic State Central Committee of Louisiana, 19 June 1984.

14. The gubernatorial and presidential general elections, though in the same year through 1972, were held during *different* months. Beginning 1976 the gubernatorial runoff general election is held during October of the year that *precedes* the regularly scheduled November presidential election.

15. Donald S. Strong, *Urban Republicanism in the South* (University, AL: University of Alabama Press, 1960).

16. William C. Havard, "From Past to Future: An Overview of Southern Politics," in *The Changing Politics of the South,* ed. William C. Havard, 719–29.

17. Charles D. Hadley, "Dual Partisan Identification in the South," *The Journal of Politics* 47 (February 1985): 254–68; and see my "The Continuing Transformation of Southern Politics," in *Political Ideas and Institutions,* eds. Edward V. Heck and Allan T. Leonhard (Dubuque, IA: Kendall/Hunt, 1983), 100–101.

18. Republicans and some conservative Democrats voted with black legislators against the suspension. William P. Quigley, Esq., "Comment" submitted to the U.S. Department of Justice in opposition to the primary law suspension, 14.

19. Bill McMahon, "Panel votes to cancel presidential primary," Baton Rouge *Morning Advocate,* 13 December 1983, 10–A.

20. Correspondence to William Bradford Reynolds, Assistant Attorney General, Civil Rights Division, U.S. Department of Justice, from Kenneth C. DeJean, Chief Counsel, Department of Justice, State of Louisiana, Baton Rouge, 5 and 19 January, 8 February 1984.

21. Quigley, "Comment."

22. Correspondence from William Bradford Reynolds to Kenneth C. DeJean, 24 February 1984.

23. Correspondence from Kenneth C. DeJean to William Bradford Reynolds, 1 March 1984.

24. Charles M. Hargroder, "Brown defies U.S., calls of state primary," New Orleans *Times-Picayune/States-Item*, 15 March 1984, 1.

25. *Valteau, ET AL* v. *Edwards, ET AL*, No. 84–1293 (E.D. LA., 16 March 1984; 21 March 1984; Communication from William Bradford Reynolds to Kenneth C. DeJean, 16 March 1984.

26. Dudley Clendinen, "Computer-Aided Black Network Won Louisiana for Jackson," *The New York Times*, 7 May 1984, B–9.

27. Dr. Brian Sherman, "Black Turnout Tripled White Turnout in Louisiana Primary," VEP [Voter Education Project] Press Release, 24 May 1984.

28. The 39 delegates were apportioned to congressional districts with a formula based on population and the average Democratic presidential vote in the 1976 and 1980 elections; the Second District received 4 and the others 5. The proportional award threshold was determined by dividing the number of delegates into 100; it was 25 percent for the Second District and 20 percent for the others. Delegates were awarded to candidates reaching the threshold for each district by dropping the votes for candidates not reaching the required threshold and recalculating the vote percentages.

29. David Snyder, "La. delegation puts differences behind it," New Orleans *Times-Picayune*, 24 June 1984, Sec. 1, 29.

30. David Snyder, "Delegation reflects changes in state GOP," New Orleans *Times-Picayune*, 19 August 1984, A–1, A–12.

31. Quoted in Bridget O'Brian and Gayle Ashton, "Bush speaks at fair," New Orleans *Times-Picayune/States-Item*, 4 September 1984, A–1, A–4.

32. Quoted in Jack Wardlaw, "State delegates prefer to fight and to switch," New Orleans *Times-Picayune/States-Item*, 19 July 1984, A–10. The delegation voted 26 for Mondale, 24 for Jackson, and 19 for Hart.

33. Quoted in Jack Wardlaw and Allan Katz, "One La. delegate seething over convention rift," New Orleans *Time-Picayune/States-Item*, 20 July 1984, A–8.

34. Greg Beuerman, Executive Director, Louisiana Republican Party, telephone interview, 11 December 1984.

35. "Preliminary Year End Report," Louisiana Republican Party, 8 December 1984, 2–3.

36. "Edwards not surprised by deserting Demos," New Orleans *Times-Picayune/States-Item*, 12 September 1984, A–20.

37. Letter from Bryan Wagner, Councilman District "A," The Council, City of New Orleans, 15 August 1984. On the GOP conversion and registration effort, see also David Snyder, "State GOP looks beyond Reagan '84," New Orleans *Times-Picayune*, 26 August 1984, A–1, A–4.

38. State of Louisiana, "Report of Registered Voters," Commissioner of Elections, Quarters ending 31 March, 30 June, and 30 September 1984; and "1984 Voter Registration Summary," appended to "Preliminary Year End Report."

39. Jack Wardlaw, "Edwards limits Mondale support," New Orleans *Times-Picayune/States-Item*, 22 August 1984, A–13; James H. Gillis, "Gov. Edwards keeps his distance," New Orleans *Times-Picayune/States-Item*, 24 August 1984, A–15.

40. Beuerman, ibid.

41. "GOP woos Hispanic, black vote," New Orleans *Times-Picayune/States-Item,* 20 September 1984, B–4; "Demos for Reagan organize," New Orleans *Times-Picayune/States-Item,* 23 October 1984, B–4; and Kim Chatelain, "Leading Demos join the herd of Jefferson's GOP elephants," New Orleans *Times-Picayune/States-Item,* 27 October 1984, A–20.

42. Beuerman, ibid.

43. Jack Wardlaw, "Campaign trail doesn't go through state," New Orleans *Times-Picayune/States-Item,* 24 October 1984, A–1, A–4.

44. A group of women including many associated with the National Organization for Women (NOW) raised the funds, opened, and staffed the New Orleans Mondale-Ferraro headquarters.

45. Michael Barone and Grant Ujifusa, *The Almanac of American Politics, 1984* (Washington, DC: National Journal, 1983), 494–95.

46. Jack Wardlaw, "Baton Rouge's new DA vows to get tough," New Orleans *Times-Picayune/States-Item,* 8 November 1984, A–17, A–21.

47. Beuerman, ibid; "Preliminary Year End Report," ibid.

3

Mississippi

Alexander P. Lamis

MISSISSIPPI POLITICAL HISTORY, 1960–83[1]

As it has for over a century, the race issue has dominated recent Mississippi politics. The premier political development in Mississippi during the last two decades, in addition to the dramatic increase in black voting strength, has been the state's entry into the era of two-party competition. In this regard, the outstanding feature was the difficulty black and white Democrats had in bringing about the bi-racial coalition that became so important for the southern Democratic Party in the post–civil rights era. The situation can only be understood within the context of the state's heavy preoccupation with race.

The successes of Republican presidential candidates in Mississippi are easily linked to the national Democratic Party's advocacy of civil rights for blacks. As early as 1960 an unpledged slate of presidential electors, supported by Governor Ross Barnett and other Democratic segregationists, carried the state with 39 percent of the vote[2] to continue the protest that began in the 1948 Dixiecrat revolt, when Mississippi Governor Fielding Wright was Strom Thurmond's vice-presidential running mate. In 1964 Mississippians gave Barry Goldwater, the Republican standard-bearer, 87.1 percent[3] of their votes, chiefly on the basis of his stance against the 1964 Civil Rights Act. Any doubts about the partisan meaning of the heavy Republican vote in 1964 were dispelled four years later when the Republican Richard

Nixon mustered only 13.5 percent. George Wallace in 1968 carried the Magnolia State with 63.5 percent; Hubert Humphrey received 23 percent. Without Wallace on the ballot in 1972, President Nixon swept Mississippi, holding George McGovern to his lowest percentage in the South, 19.6 percent. These wild fluctuations in presidential voting are illustrated in Figure 3–1.

Into this polarized racial atmosphere, the nascent state Republicans sought to carve out a place for themselves. In the 1964 Goldwater "landslide," Prentiss Walker became Mississippi's first GOP congressman in the twentieth century. Two years later Walker tested the capacity of the state's newly found Goldwater Republicanism by challenging Senator James O. Eastland. Neal R. Peirce described Walker's effort:

> A chicken farmer by profession, Walker had first won notice as chairman of the 1960 unpledged slate of electors in Mississippi. Walker demonstrated his limited political acumen by trying to suggest that Eastland had merely been pretending for 25 years

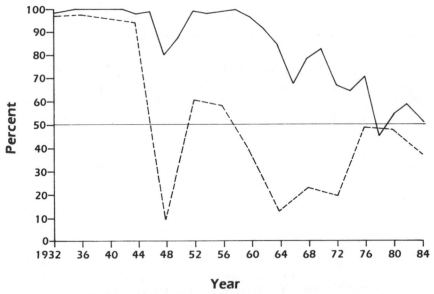

—— David's index of Democratic party strength for Mississippi (composite of the vote for governor, U.S. senator, and U.S. representative)

---- Democratic presidential vote in Mississippi

FIGURE 3–1   Democratic Party Stength in Mississippi, 1932–84

that he was a real conservative. (I have always been amused by the image conjured up by Walker's charge that Eastland, unbeknown to the good people of Mississippi, "hobnobs and prances" with the Kennedy political clan in Washington.) The argument that Walker was the truer Mississippian simply didn't wash; as state AFL-CIO chief Claude Ramsey pointed out, Walker was trying to "outsegregate" Eastland, and "this, of course, was impossible. You just don't outsegregate Jim Eastland."[4]

The Democratic Party strength trend line,[5] displayed in Figure 3–1, demonstrates the failure of the GOP to find a distinct place for itself in the chaotic political environment existing in Mississippi in the late 1960s. One result of the Republicans' difficulties, the figure reveals, was an upsurge of Democratic strength into the early 1970s following the initial decline through 1966. This weakness and disarray among the Republicans was exemplified by the party's failure to run a candidate for Governor in 1971, after it had unsuccessfully contested the 1963 and 1967 gubernatorial elections.

Despite the lack of GOP representation in the 1971 gubernatorial campaign, this election is important for what it discloses about black-white Democratic relations. In most of the other southern states by the end of the 1960s, there was considerable movement toward accommodation and cooperation among white and black Democratic leaders in statewide elections. But in Mississippi, where the resistance to nationally enforced efforts on behalf of blacks was extreme, the white Democratic establishment was unable to breach the gap[6] in any meaningful way untill 1975, and what occurred in the 1978 election suggested that the mid-1970s' compromise contained an easy tendency to become unraveled.

The separation of the loyalist Democrats—the coalition of blacks and white liberals recognized by the national party—from the state's white Democratic establishment contributed to the independent candidacy for Governor in 1971 of Charles Evers, the black civil rights leader, who vigorously espoused the cause of the state's long-oppressed minority. Evers received 22.1 percent of the votes cast, most of them from blacks.[7] William Waller, a former segregationist who won the Democratic primary running as a self-proclaimed populist, was overwhelmingly elected.

From 1972 to 1975 the accommodation and the easing of the race issue that had been apparent in most of the rest of the South since about 1970 took place in Mississippi. Although Governor Waller brought blacks into state government for the first time, it remained for the 1975 campaign and victory of another self-styled populist, Cliff Finch, the Democratic gubernatorial primary winner, to bring the warring white-black factions of the Democratic Party together. A *New York Times* preelection report states:

> Mr Finch has the support of almost all of the state's leading Democrats from Senator James O. Eastland, who is backing him heartily, to Aaron Henry, the black chairman of the liberal loyalist faction, who endorsed him with obvious reluctance. Mr. Finch was once known as a segregationist. . . .
>
> Observers attributed Mr. Finch's black support to his workingman theme, which apparently elicited blue-collar sympathy across racial lines.[8]

Gil Carmichael, a moderate Republican who had unsuccessfully sought to unseat Senator Eastland in 1972, presented himself as a reform Republican in the mold of Arkansas's Winthrop Rockefeller. Carmichael's moderation considerably upset Mississippi Republican leaders, who preferred a more conservative approach. In a 1982 interview, Carmichael elaborated on his differences with the dominant GOP leadership in the state: "Probably the role I play is moderate. That's one of the reasons I'm so aggravating—I'm so dogmatic in my moderate role. I keep talking about bringing the blacks into the Republican party and making it a viable, broad-based party." He said his conception of the party's future runs counter to that of Dixiecrat-turned-Republican leaders who prefer a "lily-white Republican party." Carmichael elaborated:

> Wirt [Yerger, a state GOP leader] had a dream of pulling out the white Dixiecrats [from the Democratic party] and . . . forming the new Republican party. . . . Then a fellow like Carmichael comes along and he goes to Jackson State [a predominantly black university in the state's capital] and as a Republican starts talking to the black people, wanting them in the Republican party. "Come on, join the Republican party. . . ."
>
> I didn't want [there] to be a white Republican party and a black Democratic party. I didn't want that at all. To me that is just destruction. . . . We've gone nowhere if the Republican party in 1990 is the reverse of what [existed in the one-party era, all whites in one party and blacks isolated]. The reason we wanted to be the governor was to break the chain that has kept Mississippi on the bottom since the Civil War.[9]

Newspaper accounts of the 1975 general election campaign stressed the absence of race as an issue.[10] Finch won with 52.2 percent, after having assembled the same black-white coalition that had been winning for Democrats elsewhere in the South since the start of the post– civil rights era. Carmichael, who received 45.1 percent of the vote, said that, despite his effort, his Republican label scared the "black and the poor vote," adding, "What other reason would the redneck and the black person come together, if the [Republican] candidate didn't scare them."[11]

The inauguration of Governor Finch, who in early 1976 was credited with performing a minor political miracle by bringing together the black leadership and the white regulars, set the stage for an organizational unification of the Democratic Party in Mississippi. Both white and black Democratic factions agreed to call precinct meetings at the same time for the selection of delegates to the 1976 national convention, and this led to a unified delegation and the reentry of the regulars into the national party. At the 1976 convention, co-chairmen for the unified party were chosen: Aaron Henry, the loyalist black leader, became one co-chairman; Tom Riddell, a white representative of the regulars, the other. The unified party leadership worked enthusiastically for the election of fellow southerner Jimmy Carter. And in 1976 the Democratic Party's presidential nominee carried Mississippi for the first time since 1956; Carter received 49.6 percent of the votes cast to Gerald Ford's 47.7 percent.

The fragile nature of the black-white Democratic unity forged in 1975 and 1976 was demonstrated at the voter level in the 1978 U.S. Senate election to fill the seat held by Eastland, who had decided to retire. Charles Evers ran as an independent and won 22.9 percent, with most of his votes coming from blacks.[12] Deprived of the black support that had carried the state for Finch in 1975 and Carter in 1976, the Democratic nominee, Maurice Dantin, received only 31.8 percent of the votes cast and was defeated by three-term U.S. Representative Thad Cochran, the Republican nominee, who received 45 percent. Cochran acknowledged the obvious: The black-white Democratic split was the cause of his good fortune. A month before the election, he told a Washington *Post* reporter: "It's a fluke, a most unusual set of circumstances that happen to benefit me. If I had to write a script, I couldn't have done a better job."[13]

Conservative and moderate white Democrats were obviously upset over the Evers-inspired defections. U.S. Representative G. V. (Sonny) Montgomery, one of the most conservative of the southern Democrats in Congress,[14] took issue in an interview with an Evers campaign remark: "[Evers's] statement that the Democrats have not done anything for the blacks is totally wrong. Under the Democratic Congress, the blacks have certainly gained, especially in Mississippi."[15] Montgomery did not point out that he had opposed most of this legislation. And herein lies a tension that has not been lost on Mississippi Republican leaders.

U.S. Representative Trent Lott, the Gulf Coast Republican elected to the House with Cochran in 1972, described the plight of Mississippi Democrats as he saw it (or perhaps as he hoped it would be):

> They're in a bind with the national Democratic party. If they subscribe to the national Democrat party's principles, platform, they are clearly going to alienate the overwhelming majority of the white people in Mississippi. If they don't do it, they are going to offend the black folk in Mississippi. . . .
>
> So if they go with the typical national Democrat base, they wind up with blacks and labor and your more liberal, social-oriented Democrats, white people. Put those groups together and they are a minority in Mississippi. . . .
>
> So, they [statewide Democratic candidates] have got to have some of these old redneck George Wallace white voters. If they have these other groups, they alienate that group.[16]

Generally throughout the South, statewide Democratic candidates have been able to hold together this biracial coalition that Lott viewed as in danger of falling apart in Mississippi. And it must be remembered that in Mississippi the coalition failed in 1978 only because of a fluke resulting from the effort of a charismatic black leader. Other black leaders have not given up on the Democratic Party, nor have white Democrats from Montgomery's conservative side of the spectrum moved to the more liberal side.

In 1979 the Democratic black-white alliance held together long enough to elect a Governor. William Winter, the 1979 Democratic gubernatorial primary winner, assembled this formidable, if volatile, coalition to soundly defeat Republican Gil Carmichael's second attempt for the state's highest office, 60.9 percent to 39.1 percent. Winter, a former lieutenant governor, had been identified as a moderate on civil rights in the 1960s, and this identity was credited with causing his defeat in the 1967 gubernatorial runoff primary by John Bell Williams, the outspoken Democratic segregationist who was elected Governor that year.

During the early 1980s the uneasy biracial Democratic statewide coalition remained in place.[17] Although President Carter narrowly lost the state to Ronald Reagan in 1980, the coalition experienced no serious disruptions unrelated to the national forces prevalent in that election.[18]

When Senator John C. Stennis, the veteran Democrat, ran for a sixth term in 1982 at the age of 81, he drew a well-financed challenge from a 35-year-old Republican, Haley Barbour. On the issues, both men shared the same conservative philosophy. Thus, the Barbour strategy became a one-note attempt to convince Mississippians that they needed, to quote the GOP nominee's slogan, a "Senator for the '80s," and by less-than-oblique implication not a "Senator in his 80s." Stennis won with 63.9 percent to Barbour's 36.1 percent. It was one of the relatively unnoticed ironies of the 1982 elections that Stennis, who in his 30-year Senate career had vigorously opposed civil rights for blacks, received overwhelming black support in this election, support that partly accounted for his wide victory margin.[19]

While black voters were doing Senator Stennis an undeserved favor, white Democratic voters in the Mississippi Delta did not reciprocate for a black Democratic congressional nominee. State Representative Robert G. Clark, the only black to serve in the Mississippi legislature during the first half of the 1970s, defeated several white candidates in the primary to win the Democratic nomination for the court-created Second Congressional District. The creation of the district, which had a 53.7 percent majority of black residents but had less than a black majority among registered voters, resulted from a prolonged legal battle to undo two decades of racial gerrymandering by the Mississippi legislature in the drawing of the state's congressional district lines.[20] After Clark won the nomination, the state's major Democratic officeholders, led by Governor Winter, warmly endorsed him and aided in his campaign. Clark, an amiable politician who had backed Republican Carmichael in 1975, centered his campaign on economic issues, attacking Reaganomics. A *New York Times* reporter wrote that Clark talks cheerfully about "mending fences and really doing something in Mississippi that has never been done before, trying to build a coalition that works two ways rather than just one."[21]

The Republican nominee was Webb Franklin, a former state judge and a Democrat who switched parties to make the 1982 race. Franklin campaigned as an economic conservative, branding Clark as too liberal for Mississippi. While the surface campaign sounded like a standard Democratic vs. Republican affair, the real issue was plain to everyone. A clever *New York Times* headline writer captured it: "Mississippi Race, Whatever They Say, Is About Race."[22] Subtle and not-so-subtle efforts by the Franklin campaign to appeal to racial prejudice appeared throughout the campaign. These included a Franklin television commercial featuring Franklin standing in front of an ornate Confederate monument making an appeal for Mississippians not to forget their sacred heritage as well as the rather unusual approach of putting his opponent's picture in fliers and newspaper supplements, a tactic described by one leading campaign adviser as an effort to remind voters that Mr. Clark was black.[23]

In an extremely close election, Franklin defeated Clark, 50.3 percent to 48.4 percent. What had happened was quite simple: Few white Democrats voted for the black Democratic nominee. Clark's fellow Democrat, Stennis, for example, carried the Second District with 61.3 percent of the votes cast. Robert Walker, Mississippi NAACP field secretary, summed up the situation concisely: "I wouldn't be so foolish to say [Clark] didn't get white votes, because he did. He didn't get enough. . . ."[24]

The Democratic gubernatorial nominee in 1983, Attorney General Bill Allain of Natchez, managed to hold substantial black support despite the presence of a black independent in the race. During the fall campaign, Charles Evers made his third independent bid for statewide office, contending that blacks and other minorities "want our fair share" and asserting that the "state is run by 11 percent of its people . . . mostly stuffy, redneck, old white men."[25] This time most of Mississippi's black leaders shunned Evers. Their 1983 decision to support Allain appeared to represent a triumph of practicality over emotion. David Jordan, a black politician from Greenwood, explained: "We're not going to give Ronald Reagan a base in Mississippi in the governor's office. The trick . . . will not work on us this time. Our eyes are open. We went for that trick in '78 and a Republican senator came in the back door. The game is over and school is out."[26] In the November balloting, Evers's support was miniscule compared to his two previous showings; he received only 3.9 percent and was an insignificant factor in the gubernatorial outcome.

Despite Evers's poor finish, the 1983 governor's race proved to be an explosive—if seamy—affair for singular reasons without parallel in recent statewide partisan conflict. Allain's main opponent was Republican Leon Bramlett, a wealthy Clarksdale planter and champion of the most conservative elements in the state GOP hierarchy. What had appeared through early October to be a humdrum affair was transformed by the end of the month into one of the most spectacular and emotional Governor's campaigns in recent memory. With two weeks left before Election Day, several of Bramlett's major financial supporters, through their attorney, charged that Allain "frequently has engaged in homosexual acts with male prostitutes."[27] The allegations were accompanied by sworn statements from three black transvestites, two of whom described having sexual relations with Allain.[28]

These bizarre allegations stunned nearly everyone in Mississippi who was following the campaign. Allain immediately called the charges "damnable, vicious, malicious lies"[29] and the next day threatened to file a libel suit.

Based on the election returns, the indeterminacy of the homosexual allegations probably had a neutralizing effect. Allain won with 55.2 percent of the votes cast to Bramlett's 38.9 percent. When it had become apparent that Evers had failed to materialize as a significant force in the election and before the GOP bombshell, it was safe to expect the black-white Democratic coalition to deliver Allain about a 55 to 60 percent victory. The allegations probably cost Allain several percentage points, causing him to finish in the low range of the coalition's strength. Thus, despite the sensational events of this election, Allain won the governorship essentially because he was able to hold together Mississippi's potent biracial Democratic coalition, an alliance whose well-being was severely tested in the 1984 election.

THE 1984 PRESIDENTIAL NOMINATION CAMPAIGN IN MISSISSIPPI

Mississippi received considerable attention from the national candidates during the 1984 Democratic presidential nomination campaign. Although Walter Mondale eventually won the bulk of the state's 43 delegates at the San Francisco convention, his path to that victory was far from easy.

Mississippi's four-stage delegate selection process started with 2,000 precinct caucuses on Saturday, 17 March. Conventions in the state's 82 counties met two weeks later on 31 March to select delegates to conventions in the state's five congressional districts held on 14 April; five national convention delegates were chosen at each of these latter gatherings. The final 18 delegates were chosen at the state convention on 4–5 May.

Six presidential candidates qualified to receive delegates in the Mississippi process, but by the time of the precinct caucuses, only Mondale, the Rev. Jesse Jackson, and Senator Gary Hart were still in the race. Senator John Glenn, who ended his candidacy on the eve of the state's caucuses after his weak showing a few days earlier on Super Tuesday, had given considerable attention to Mississippi and had a functioning statewide organization in place at the time of the candidacy's collapse. Glenn's state leaders urged their supporters to go to the caucuses uncommitted to any candidate.[30]

The Mondale campaign had strong backing from education groups, organized labor, and the white party establishment. In the words of a Memphis *Commercial Appeal* reporter, Mondale's was "the most extensive organization in the state, using telephone banks and mass mailings."[31]

Jackson's organization strength was among the state's black activists and was shored up by the candidate's strong appeal to black voters, which was demonstrated by the size and enthusiasm of the crowds Jackson attracted during his personal appearances in the state. Some black leaders, however, such as Aaron Henry, president of the Mississippi NAACP, and several black legislators, supported Mondale. In fact, Mondale's state coordinator asserted: "Jackson is the opposition. We're competing healthily in the black community with Jackson."[32]

Hart virtually ignored Mississippi until his New Hampshire primary victory energized his campaign. In early March a Hart volunteer organizer from Texas surveyed the prospects in the state for a last-minute effort but decided that they did not have enough money to make a major effort.[33]

Under the caucus system the initial showing of strength at the precinct level should be roughly reflected at the end of the process. But several factors worked to add a measure of uncertainty for the remaining stages. First among them was the threshold requirement. In keeping with the national party rules, a 20 percent minimum was required at the congressional district and state levels for a candidate to get any delegates; the threshold was 10 percent for the first two levels. Another element of uncertainty arises from the necessity of a candidate's delegates to show up at succeeding conventions to keep their candidate's strength from being reduced; if some tire of spending Saturday in a long, noisy, and often chaotic meeting, a candidate could lose ground. And finally, the uncommitted category, especially large in Mississippi in 1984, offered growth potential for all candidates.

The precinct caucuses gave a narrow lead to the uncommitted category, followed closely by Mondale and Jackson, with Hart a distant fourth. The percentages were: uncommitted 31.6; Mondale 30.4; Jackson 26.9; and Hart 11.1.[34] Two weeks later at the country conventions, Mondale and Jackson improved their positions, the former overtaking uncommitted for the lead. The figures were: Mondale 31.3; uncommitted 30.7; Jackson 28.7; and Hart 9.3.[35]

In the period leading up to the congressional district conventions, the 20 percent threshold loomed as a major obstacle for the Hart campaign. Based on the county results, the Coloradan did not have 20 percent in any of the five districts.[36] Hart's newly installed campaign director, Wilson Golden, a Jackson lawyer, concluded the obvious: The key to success would be "how successful we can be in electing Hart-leaning [people] as uncommitted delegates."[37]

At the congressional district conventions, at which 25 national delegates were chosen, Mondale won 10, uncommitted 8, and Jackson

7. Failing the threshold, Hart received no delegates. The Hart strategy of winning delegates among the uncommitted also appeared to have failed; only one of the eight uncommitted delegates had initially backed Hart.[38]

The state convention in Jackson completed the selection process. Of the eleven delegates chosen there who could be pledged, four were for Mondale, four uncommitted, and three for Jackson. National rules mandated that the other seven delegates had to be officially unpledged and made up of party leaders and officeholders.[39]

In the weeks leading up to the Democratic National Convention, Lieutenant Governor Brad Dye, the delegation chairman and one of the officially unpledged delegates, joined the Mondale team and lobbied hard to bring aboard other uncommitted delegates. When the roll call was taken in San Francisco on 18 July, Mondale received 26 votes from the Mississippi delegation as part of his first-ballot nomination victory; Jackson won 13 delegate votes from the Magnolia State; and Hart received 4.[40]

THE 1984 GENERAL ELECTION
CAMPAIGN IN MISSISSIPPI

Full comprehension of the partisan developments that occurred in Mississippi during the 1984 general election campaign requires treatment of three races in addition to the presidential contest: the reelection efforts of Senator Thad Cochran and U.S.·Representatives Webb Franklin and Wayne Dowdy.[41]

William Winter, the former Democratic Governor, after months of vacillation, announced in early February that he would seek to unseat the Republican Cochran, and Winter received the Democratic nomination in the June primary over token opposition. In the Fourth District, the Republican Party actively recruited several possible candidates to oppose the Democrat Dowdy, including at least one Democratic state legislator. The search ended near the spring filing deadline when David Armstrong, a 32-year-old Natchez lawyer, expressed interest in making the race. Declaring, "We can beat him," Armstrong said, "It needs to be brought out that Mr. Dowdy is not representative of the people of this district. His voting record is very antibusiness."[42] In the fall campaign, Armstrong delivered on his pledge to mount an aggressive campaign, one that sought repeatedly to benefit from President Reagan's popularity.

Of the three challengers, only the Democrat Robert Clark in the Second District had to work for this party's nomination. Clark let it be known early that he would seek a rematch with the Republican Franklin, who only narrowly defeated him in 1982. Two blacks and a white challenged Clark in the June primary, but the veteran state legislator defeated the field with 62.3 percent of the vote.

The preprimary conventional wisdom held that Clark would be forced into a runoff, probably with Robert Gray, the mayor of the town of Shelby, who argued that Clark was not militant enough in the promotion of black interests.[43] But Gray, who was more closely identified with Jesse Jackson than Clark, received only 9.4 percent of the vote. The other black in the race, Evan Doss, Claiborne County tax assessor, won only 6.6 percent. The runner-up in the race, with 21.7 percent, was Richard Barrett, a Jackson attorney and an unabashed white supremacist. Barrett urged repeal of the Civil Rights Act and the Voting Rights Act and argued that "integration has ruined education in Mississippi."[44]

The Cochran-Winter, Franklin-Clark, and Dowdy-Armstrong races formed the partisan backdrop before which the Reagan-Mondale campaign in Mississippi was fought out. Or, one might argue that, when it became readily apparent in the fall that Reagan would carry the state, the presidential election became the backdrop for the others, as the interest of Mississippians centered increasingly on the importance of 1984 for the state's partisan future. At any rate, all four contests cast considerable light on current Magnolia State politics.

Walter Mondale and Geraldine Ferraro cannot be faulted for ignoring Mississippi in the fall campaign. On 1 August Mondale and Ferraro began their post convention campaign with a visit to Jackson and a nearby farm. Although the issues of the campaign were discussed, the visit is remembered for the "great blueberry muffin test" that Ferraro underwent at the playful hands of Jim Buck Ross, Mississippi's veteran commissioner of agriculture and a self-proclaimed defender of southern manhood. The widely reported exchange took place while Ross was explaining Mississippi's catfish industry to the candidates. When told that the state was developing catfish, crayfish, grapes, and blueberries as new crops, Miss Ferraro remarked that she, too, grew blueberries. Mr Ross then brought laughter from the audience, including Mr. Mondale and Miss Ferraro, by asking if she could cook a blueberry muffin. " 'I sure can,' Miss Ferraro finally responded. 'Can you?' The comment drew longer laughter. Grinning, Mr. Ross said, 'Down here in Mississippi the men don't cook.' "[45] The *New York Times* report of the encounter concentrated on the Ferraro-Ross exchange and relegated Mondale's substantive comments of the day to the end of the article.[46]

Mondale returned to the state once more in mid-September, holding a question-and-answer session in Tupelo, in northeast Mississippi. He attacked President Reagan for failing to offer a deficit-reduction plan and said that during the 1980 campaign he had accurately predicted that Reagan, if elected, would seek to cut Medicaid and Social Security. He warned, moreover, that if Reagan were reelected, he would advocate sharp cuts in Medicare.[47]

At the Tupelo appearance, Mondale received several hostile questions dealing with religion and abortion. He defended the Democratic platform against its description as antireligious, noted that he did not like to see religion being raised in the presidential race, and argued that it would be wrong for government to interfere in the "very difficult personal decision" of abortion.[48]

Mondale visited Tupelo at the invitation of the city's mayor, Jimmie Caldwell, one of the Minnesotan's strongest Mississippi supporters. Caldwell attracted national attention at a meeting of mayors in St. Paul when he defended the Democratic ticket's appeal in the South. "Walter Mondale's and Geraldine Ferraro's cares, concerns, philosophies and family values are just as Southern as catfish, corn bread and cotton," Mayor Caldwell asserted at a news conference, and the colorful sentence was televised throughout the country.[49]

Caldwell, however, was the exception among the state's white Democratic officeholders, most of whom were virtually invisible during the fall presidential campaign. Governor Allain, whose erratic behavior since his election amid the homosexual charges had left the state with its weakest chief executive in decades, snubbed Mondale during the candidate's August visit. During the Tupelo stop, Allain engaged in a publicity charade, tying his support for Mondale to whether the candidate would pledge to give the state a veto over the placing of a nuclear waste site in Mississippi.[50] Mondale eventually gave the pledge, which appeared to produce no noticeable change in Allain's nonexistent role in the campaign. C. B. (Buddie) Newman, Democratic speaker of the Mississippi House, announced at the end of July that he planned "to sit this one out."[51]

When two Democratic officeholders, state Representative Ed Buelow of Vicksburg and Sheriff J. B. Torrence of Rankin County, held a series of GOP-sponsored news conferences in late July to endorse President Reagan's reelection, Steve Patterson, the Democratic state chairman, announced that a provision of the party's constitution would be enforced to bar such dissidents from running for reelection as Democrats.[52] Following Patterson's cue, a week later the Democratic executive committee in Warren County voted to prohibit Buelow's renomination as a Democrat. Issuing an invitation to Buelow and other Democrats like him, Ebbie Spivey, the chairwoman of the Mississippi GOP, said:

> The leadership of that party has gone so far to the left that a majority of Mississippians cannot support their liberal ideas. Mr. Patterson knows full well that Mississippians feel closer to Ronald Reagan than Walter Mondale and I am not surprised to see him using desperation tactics like threatening elected officials. But how can any Democrat, whether elected official or committed citizen, be threatened for doing what is right?[53]

Patterson's threat was partly motivated by potential defections from another direction—some black Democrats were threatening in August to run an independent candidate in the Senate race, a development that is discussed below.[54]

President Reagan visited Mississippi in early October, drawing a huge crowd to a Gulfport rally. He praised the South and stressed his concern with winning the region, criticized Mondale for preaching economic gloom and doom, and attacked the Democrats for wanting to give the American people a massive tax increase.[55]

Vice President George Bush also campaigned in the Magnolia State several times. In Jackson in March, he told Mississippians that the withdrawal of Senator Glenn from the Democratic nomination campaign signals an unfortunate turn to the left, adding:

> It has become all too clear that there is absolutely no room in that national Democratic party race for the values represented by candidates who stand for a strong defense and who stand for these strong, basic family values.[56]

Reagan's strength in Mississippi prompted Bill Minor, the dean of the state's political writers, to compose a column on the subject, stating "Mississippi's love affair with Ronald Reagan is something to behold." Minor continued:

> Reagan's Hollywood style conservatism, his simple answers to complex domestic and world problems, and his repertoire of anecdotes about the virtues of bedrock American values have made him the object of affection of thousands of erstwhile white Mississippi Democrats since he came on the national political scene in 1964. . . .
>
> Mississippi GOP leaders don't want to talk about it, but there is a great deal of underlying racism involved in Reagan's popularity in Mississippi. Reagan is a polarizing figure whether he wants to be or not, in a race-conscious state such as ours.
>
> How else could it be that he is projected an easy winner in Mississippi with three out of four white votes, while showing

virtually no votes in the black community that represents 30 percent of the total vote?[57]

I will return to this theme in the next section.

In the other 1984 statewide race, William Winter carries an initial
handicap resulting from the adverse publicity he received when he
accepted the chancellorship of the University of Mississippi in late
1983 and then changed his mind and rejected the post a few days
later, presumably to run for the Senate.[58] On the stump Cochran
made points with the episode by comparing Winter's longevity as Ole
Miss chancellor with the briefness of Bert Lance's service as chairman
of the Mondale campaign.[59]

Throughout the campaign, Winter argued that Mississippi, one of
the country's poorest states, had been unfairly hurt by the Republican
administration's budget cuts. A *Clarion-Ledger* report described the
appeal:

> Winter said Mississippi's efforts to better itself economically had
> been "stymied" by a "false economy" at the federal level, resulting
> in "disproportionate" cuts in federal aid.
> "I'm not content to see the people of Mississippi enjoy less than
> parity," Winter said, adding that the South needs a "more artic-
> ulate spokesman."[60]

Winter, who was 61 years old, also stressed his 36 years of experience
in state government, contending that he had "worked my way up"
as a state representative, state treasurer, lieutenant governor, and
governor, while Cochran's "first public office [was] an office on the
Potomac."[61] To Cochran's charge that he is a liberal, Winter responded late in the campaign: "If being a liberal means that one is
concerned about seeing that everybody has an equal opportunity,
then I confess being a liberal. They said that back in the 1960's when
I said I thought the constitution ought to apply to everybody in this
country."[62]

Cochran, who was 46 years old, emphasized his Washington experience and his Senate seniority, frequently pointing out that he
chairs the Agriculture Appropriations Subcommittee and is a member of the Defense Appropriations Subcommittee. He said these posts
enable him to "assure Mississippi gets its fair share."[63] The incumbent
charged that "it's not Mississippians who are supporting" Winter, but
rather liberal Democrats in Washington who "dreamed up this campaign."[64] "I don't think we want somebody in Washington just representing the interests of the national Democratic party."[65]

When in a joint appearance Winter criticized Cochran's support
for the 1981 Reagan tax cut, saying, "You cannot cut taxes to the

extent that they were cut and increase appropriations as much as they have been increased, for defense for example, and expect us to have a solvent country," Cochran responded, as reported in the *Clarion-Ledger:*

> "If William Winter had been in the Senate and voted on the other side of that issue, he would have been in a very small minority. And I would say exercising a judgment that wasn't widely shared anywhere in the country."
>
> Cochran said Winter wanted to continue the "economic mess" created by the Carter administration. . . .
>
> "I would say trying to provide workers and consumers in America with more of a share of what they were working to earn was eminently fair and correct. I know that adding one more person to the Democratic side of the aisle in the Senate is not going to help the spending problem there," Cochran said.[66]

As these excerpts from the rhetorical battle indicate, both men embraced the basic positions of their national candidates, although naturally both at various points sought to sidestep national positions or images they viewed as unhelpful to their campaigns. An examination in the next section of the results of this election indicates how closely related the Senate and presidential races became on Election Day.

A final episode from the Senate campaign—an aborted threat of a black independent candidacy—needs brief mention. In early August a group of forty black leaders met and endorsed the idea of running Johnnie Walls, a black Greenville attorney, as an independent in the senatorial race. Walls complained that Mississippi blacks were "tired of being taken for granted [by the white Democratic establishment]. Our real needs have not been met." Referring to the failure of more blacks to win elective office, Walls said, "We don't receive the same support we give whites. . . . They only want us when they need us. That is getting old."[67] The group eventually listed seventeen demands of the state Democratic party.[68] The ones involving increased party support for Robert Clark were eventually met, and through the reconciliation efforts of Chairman Patterson and the last-minute intervention of Jesse Jackson, in early September Walls decided against making the race.[69]

On the surface the Clark-Franklin rematch was fought out once again over economic issues. While Franklin had the incumbency edge, Clark was the beneficiary of a January 1984 court-ordered redistricting that increased the district's black population to 58.3 percent and the black voting-age majority to 52.8 percent.[70] Vagn Hansen, a Delta State University political scientist, characterized the role of race in the 1984 campaign this way: "I really think that race this time is simply implicit in the campaign, that everyone who can be expected to vote knows the racial identification of the candidates. It [that is, racially explicit campaigning] may be less necessary than it was before."[71] The *Clarion-Ledger* recorded the following comments when the two men appeared together at an NAACP meeting in Raymond:

"When Webb Franklin runs my picture and his and says 'I'm one of you,' I believe he's saying, 'I'm one of those who sold my [Clark's] great-grandmother' in slavery," Clark said.

Franklin prefaced his remarks in Raymond by saying he was "sick and tired" of Clark "whining that I have not been responsive to black issues and interests."[72]

A full month before Election Day, the main concern in the Second District had become turnout. "Conceding that Delta voters already have made up their minds," a *Commercial Appeal* reporter wrote in early October, "both candidates in the highly polarized Second Congressional District are focusing their attention on turning out the vote."[73]

In the Fourth District, Armstrong, the GOP challenger, tied his campaign to President Reagan and charged that Representative Dowdy was in league with the "free-spending liberals" in Washington. Vice President Bush, in Natchez to boost Armstrong's candidacy, declared: "A vote for David Armstrong is a vote for President Reagan's programs. . . . Don't tie one hand behind the President's back. Give us David Armstrong."[74]

Dowdy, a personable 41-year-old politician first elected in 1981, stressed his constituency service. As for the charge of being liberal, Dowdy responded: "Some people in Washington would snicker if they heard someone with my voting record called a liberal. I'm a progressive southerner."[75] When the returns were in, of the four Democrats running in Mississippi in 1984, Dowdy was the only one who held together the state's potentially potent black-white Democratic coalition.

ANALYSIS OF THE ELECTION RESULTS

The 6 November balloting produced a convincing Republican triumph. President Reagan soundly defeated Walter Mondale in Mississippi, 61.9 percent to 37.4 percent. Senator Cochran won reelection easily with 60.9 percent to former Governor Winter's 39.1 percent. Representative Franklin again narrowly defeated Robert Clark, 50.6 percent to 48.9 percent. Representative Dowdy became the only Democrat in Mississippi to win a contested election in 1984, holding off a strong showing by David Armstrong, 55.3 percent to 44.7 percent.[76] Each election is examined in turn below, starting with the presidential race.

In 1980 President Carter only narrowly lost Mississippi to Ronald Reagan, 48.1 percent to 49.4 percent. The Georgia native's coalition consisted of overwhelming black support—over 90 percent—plus approximately a third of the white vote.[77] In the 1984 election, black support for the Democratic presidential nominee remained strong. Circumstantial evidence of this black support is provided in Figure 3–2. Here the 15 Mississippi counties with the highest proportion of blacks in the population are compared with Mondale's highest 15 countries, revealing a close relationship. Survey data corroborate the point. A Mississippi State University poll, conducted by Stephen D. Shaffer in April 1984, put Mondale's black support at 85 percent (see Table 3–1). Classified precinct results from Jackson, shown in Table 3–2, suggest the figure was probably higher.

Thus, the major fall-off in Democratic support occurred among white Mississippians. Table 3–1 puts Mondale's white support at 20 percent. The Jackson precinct returns in Table 3–2 show Mondale's white strength even weaker in the state capital. There were variations in degree of support for the Democratic standard-bearer among the state's whites based on differences in income, age, and sex, as is demonstrated in Table 3–3. The less-prosperous whites were more likely to vote for Mondale than were those 60 years of age or older. And the gender gap made a pronounced appearance in 1984. Yet, despite these differences among whites, the overall message from these tables is clear: Few whites voted for Mondale. Why?

Major national factors, which have grown in influence over southern and Mississippi politics since the demise of one-party isolation,

TABLE 3–1   Race and Voter Preference in the Mississippi 1984 Presidential Election

	Whites	Blacks	Total
Mondale	20%	85%	38%
Reagan	80	15	62
Total	100%	100%	100%
N	284	112	396[1]

[1]Only likely voters are considered. Undecideds are omitted.

Source: Mississippi State University Poll, conducted 15–29 April 1984 by Stephen D. Shaffer. Professor Shaffer kindly and promptly responded to the author's request for the cross-tabulations used in this table and Tables 3–3 and 3–4.

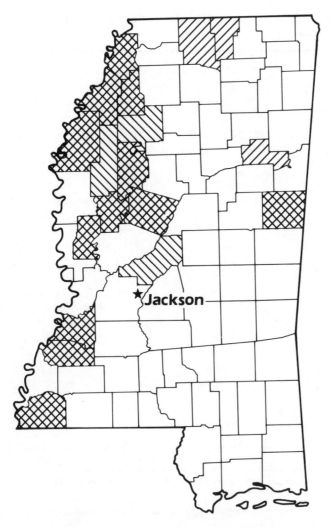

Fifteen counties with highest proportion of blacks in the 1980 census

Fifteen counties giving Democrat Mondale his strongest support

High proportion Black counties giving Mondale strong support

FIGURE 3–2   Race and Democratic Presidential Voting in Mississippi in 1984

TABLE 3–2   Classified Precinct Results by Race and Income
in Jackson, Mississippi

| | Whites | | |
	Low Income[1]	Moderate to High Income[2]	Blacks
1980			
Carter	21.1%	15.3%	96.0%
Reagan	75.6	81.7	2.1
Others	3.3	3.0	2.0
Total	100.0%	100.0%	100.0%
	(N = 9,949)	(N = 11,803)	(N = 8,224)
1984			
Mondale	14.7%	9.6%	94.7%
Reagan	84.8	90.1	2.7
Others	0.5	0.3	2.6
Total	100.0%	100.0%	100.0%
	(N = 9,863)	(N = 13,269)	(N = 9,254)
Winter	15.8%	11.1%	94.3%
Cochran	84.2	88.9	5.7
Total	100.0%	100.0%	100.0%
	(N = 9,771)	(N = 13,146)	(N = 9,010)
Dowdy	29.7%	26.4%	96.2%
Armstrong	70.3	73.6	3.7
Total	100.0%	100.0%	100.0%
	(N = 9,538)	(N = 12,867)	(N = 8,605)

[1]Various precincts from 1980 census tracts with median household incomes ranging from $13,200 to $18,500.

[2]Various precincts from 1980 census tracts with median household incomes ranging from $23,800 to $36,100.

Source: Ted Rhinehart, a University of Mississippi undergraduate, provided this information. He accomplished the laborious task of classifying Jackson's precincts during the fall of 1984 as part of a senior honors independent study project under the author's supervision.

favored the Republican ticket in the 1984 election: an apparently strong economy with low inflation and the personal popularity of President Reagan. But there was something else that motivated some white Mississippians: a subtle appeal to racial prejudice by the Reagan administration. The Republicans deny this, of course, and rely instead

TABLE 3–3   Income, Age, Sex, and Voter Preference of
White Mississippians[1] in the 1984 Presidential Election

	Income		
	Under $10,000	*$10,000 to $20,000*	*Over $20,000*
Mondale	41%	24%	8%
Reagan	59	76	92
Total	100%	100%	100%
N	41	82	125
	Age		
	18–39	*40–59*	*60–98*
Mondale	18%	15%	29%
Reagan	82	85	71
Total	100%	100%	100%
N	140	79	65
	Sex		
	Male	*Female*	
Mondale	16%	24%	
Reagan	84	76	
Total	100%	100%	
N	155	129	

[1]Only likely voters are considered. Undecideds are omitted.

Source: See documentation in Table 3–1.

on imprecise claims that these voters are conservatives. Conservative
on what issues? Race?

As with all subtleties, the GOP's 1984 racial appeal requires a little
effort to pin down. The point was driven home to me during an
interview in 1981 with a political official in the White House who was
expounding on the "new southern strategy" of Ronald Reagan. When
asked if Reagan was appealing to the racist side of the Wallace voter
by attempting to slash domestic programs such as food stamps and
legal services for the poor, the official responded:

> You start out in 1954 by saying "Nigger, nigger, nigger." By 1968
> you can't say "nigger"—that hurts you. Backfires. So you say stuff
> like forced busing, states' rights, and all these things you're talking
> about are totally economic things and a byproduct of them is
> [that] blacks get hurt worse than whites. And subconsciously maybe

that is part of it. I'm not saying that. But I'm saying that if it is getting that abstract, and that coded, that we are doing away with the racial problem one way or another. You follow me—because obviously sitting around saying, 'We want to cut this,' is much more abstract than even the busing thing *and* a hell of a lot more abstract than "Nigger, nigger."[78]

Obviously, how much one is doing away with the race issue in this context is debatable.

The above quotation illustrates the Republican pleasure at the confluence and logical compatibility in the 1980s of economic-class conservatism with the lingering racial protest. The GOP, as the party philosophically opposed to an activist federal government in New Deal-style economic matters (a policy that favored the well-to-do North and South), gained adherents also from those who objected to federal intervention in the racial affairs of the states. In addition, the anti-black image of the administration was bolstered by the Reagan position in support of tax-exempt status for private schools that engage in discrimination, as well as Reagan's appointment of U.S. Civil Rights Commission members who were unrepresentative of the mainstream of the nation's black leadership.

The racial polarization that occurred in the presidential election spilled over to the Senate race. The Mondale-Winter county percentages bore striking resemblance. Of Winter's 15 strongest counties, 14 were Mondale's; the slight difference came only because Winter had a percentage point less support than Mondale in Leflore County and a percentage point more in Tallahatchie County. Thus, Winter's strongest counties were also those with the highest proportion of blacks. Table 3–2 indicates that Winter did only about a percentage point better than Mondale among whites in Jackson. It was this pronounced weakness among whites shown by Winter, a three-decade veteran of Mississippi Democratic coalition politics, that surprised state observers. What had happened was obvious: The dynamics of the presidential race filtered over to the Senate contest to the disadvantage of Winter, who became tied to Mondale in the voters' view. Or, as one white Mississippi farmer, a traditional Democrat, phrased it: "William just got too close to the niggers."[79]

The racial divisions in the Second District persisted in 1984, the election returns showed. Leslie McLemore, a Jackson State University political scientist, put it well: "In broad strokes blacks voted for Mondale, Winter and Clark, and whites voted for Reagan, Cochran and Franklin." McLemore added: "It [Clark's defeat] was a judicious combination of the coattails of Reagan and a very well-organized campaign by Webb Franklin. [Clark] simply did not have the resources that Webb Franklin did."[80]

Precise figures on turnout were not available. However, Karen Hinton, Clark's press secretary and one of his leading strategists, made this assessment after analyzing the returns: "We thought we had a good black turnout. There are some [counties] we would have liked to have won bigger, like Sunflower and Bolivar. But is just didn't happen. We were superseded by a larger white turnout that I think was tied directly to Reagan."[81]

Clark's second defeat fueled continued bitterness among black Democrats. Johnnie Walls, the black who had threatened an independent Senate campaign, commented after the election: "We're going to have to realize that race is a factor in Mississippi and face it head on. White people have to look themselves in the mirror and ask why it's all right for them to represent them and us, but it's not all right for us to represent us and them."[82]

While Mondale, Winter, and Clark came up woefully short of white supporters, Representative Dowdy managed in 1984 to assemble the classic post–civil rights era black-white Democratic coalition. Table 3–2 shows that Dowdy won an average of 28 percent of the support of Jackson's whites. In the rural, small-town counties south of the capital, the former mayor of McComb, which is located in Pike County, did at least as well among whites. For example, in Covington County, which is 34.5 percent black, Dowdy won 60.5 percent of the vote; in Lawrence County, 30.9 percent black, Dowdy received 59 percent.[83]

The next, and concluding, section treats the significance of the 1984 election results for Mississippi's political future.

CONCLUSION

Where does this election leave the partisan situation in Mississippi? No one can deny that the Democratic coalition came under intense strain in the 1984 election. In fact, on the eve of the election, Bill Minor, the veteran political columnist, warned:

> Tuesday could be doomsday for the Democratic Party as we have known it in Mississippi, culminating a party realignment that has been threatening since 1964. . . .
>
> The state could be on the verge of shifting overnight from what was long a one-party Democratic state to a one-party Republican state. The tragedy of it, however, is that the dominant Republican Party would become the "white man's party," and the

Democratic Party the "black and tans," a complete reversal of roles from 100 years ago.[84]

Examination of more 1984 survey data, this time using the partisan identification measure rather than candidate choice, aids the effort to chart the current partisan landscape in Mississippi. The first panel of Table 3–4 illustrates that the Democratic label attracted 45 percent of the state's citizens. Even among whites, Democratic identifiers were more numerous than those claiming allegiance to the GOP. Independents, however, captured the largest share. The other panels of Table 3–4 demonstrate the existence of pronounced income and generational differences among white partisan identifiers. In essence, there existed in Mississippi in 1984 a potentially strong black-white Democratic coalition that showed a tendency among its white group

TABLE 3–4   Race, Income, Age, and Party Identification in Mississippi in 1984

| | Race—All Mississippians | | |
	Whites	Blacks	Total
Democrats	34%	67%	45%
Republicans	23	7	18
Independents	43	26	37
Total	100%	100%	100%
N	397	184	581

| | Income—White Mississippians | | |
	Under $10,000	$10,000 to $20,000	Over $20,000
Democrats	49%	40%	23%
Republicans	22	22	26
Independents	29	38	51
Total	100%	100%	100%
N	72	118	159

| | Age—White Mississippians | | |
	18–39	40–59	60–98
Democrats	28%	32%	51%
Republicans	28	17	18
Independents	44	51	31
Total	100%	100%	100%
N	191	115	91

Source: See documentation in Table 1.

to be stronger in the lower-income categories and among older voters. This situation does not differ remarkably from that found in most Southern states by the early 1980s.[85]

When one penetrates deeper, however, Mississippi becomes quite valuable in a comparative vein because the lack of subtlety in the state's public life highlights sensitive political elements that are often submerged in other states. This view of Mississippi's extreme status is by no means novel. V. O. Key, Jr., wrote in 1949:

> Northerners, provincials that they are, regard the South as one large Mississippi. Southerners, with their eye for distinction, place Mississippi in a class by itself. . . . Yet Mississippi only manifests in accentuated form the darker political strains that run throughout the South.[86]

And perhaps my conclusion concerning the future of Mississippi politics applies, in a less extreme way, to other states of the South.

Into the mid-1980s the Magnolia State continued to fulfill the marvelous analytical role that Key had discerned. Given the fact that Mississippi had the highest proportion of blacks in the nation, 35.2 percent in the 1980 census, and recognizing that Mondale received only 37.4 percent of the vote in Mississippi, it is likely that Mississippi had the lowest proportion of white Democratic support of the fifty states in the 1984 presidential election. This outcome has been explained above as at least partly a manifestation of the subtle appeal to racial prejudice by the Reagan administration. While the appeal may have been subtle, the response of white Mississippians was not.

Does this 1984 performance mean that the state's Democratic Party is soon to be made up only of blacks? Since my preference is to give the upper hand in such matters to political elites, I believe the matter rests with how well the current and next generation of the state's leaders—whites and blacks—are able to handle the bitter legacy of racial antagonism they have inherited.

Although race clearly divides in Mississippi, there are other important cleavages, chief among them economic-class divisions. Among "those who have less," Mississippi, the state with the lowest per capita income in the nation, can count a substantial number of whites along with a majority of its long-disadvantaged black population. If future white and black Democratic leaders in the Magnolia State are able to form and hold together a biracial coalition that seriously concentrates on the economic needs of "those who have less," the Mississippi Democratic Party could yet lead the way to a southern future based on equity and justice. If they fail to find common political ground across racial lines, Mississippi is likely—as it did in 1984—to once again exemplify "the darker political strains that run throughout the South."

NOTES

1. This section draws from Chap. 4, "Mississippi: It's All Black and White," in Alexander P. Lamis, *The Two-Party South* (New York: Oxford University Press, 1984), 44–62.

Research assistance in the preparation of the present chapter was graciously provided by Traci Cook, a University of Mississippi political science major.

2. In 1960 the Kennedy-Johnson Democratic ticket was second with 36.3 percent; the Republicans, led by Richard Nixon, finished third with 24.7 percent. The victorious unpledged slate cast Mississippi's electoral votes for Senator Harry F. Byrd of Virginia.

3. Strom Thurmond and the Dixiecrats had carried Mississippi in 1948 with nearly the exact figure—87.2 percent!

4. Neal R. Peirce, *The Deep South States of America* (New York: Norton, 1974), 196. At least one prominent Mississippi Republican, W. D. (Billy) Mounger, held to Walker's reasoning nearly a decade later. "Eastland is a national Democrat," Mounger told reporters in 1975. "I think he has been playing house with Ted Kennedy and George McGovern behind the scenes in Washington." Jackson *Clarion-Ledger*, 16 May 1975.

5. The trend line plots Paul T. David's Composite B Index, which David presented in his *Party Strength in the United States, 1872–1970* (Charlottesville, VA: University Press of Virginia, 1972). For the 1972, 1974, and 1976 elections, David updated his book in *Journal of Politics* notes; I calculated the index for the more recent elections.

6. White resistance was so vehement in Mississippi throughout the 1960s that there occurred a complete organizational rupture between the state and local white Democratic officeholders, who led the fight for segregation, and a coalition of blacks and white liberals loyal to the national party. The regulars were denied seating at the 1968 Democratic National Convention in Chicago for their failure to remove racial discrimination from party affairs as mandated by the national convention in 1964. Instead the national party recognized the loyalist black-white coalition as the official Democratic party in Mississippi. Charles Evers, brother of Medgar Evers, the murdered civil rights leader, became the state's Democratic National Committeeman. "The Birth of the Mississippi 'Loyalist Democrats' (1965–1968)," *Journal of Mississippi History* 4 (February 1982): 27–45.

7. Ever's county-level vote correlates at .95 with McGovern's and at .94 with the county-level percentage of blacks.

8. *New York Times*, 20 October 1975.

9. Interview with Carmichael, conducted by the author, 31 March 1982, in Oxford, Mississippi.

10. *Clarion-Ledger*. 8 November 1975; *New York Times*, 20 October 1975.

11. Interview with Carmichael.

12. Ever's vote correlates with the county-level percentage of blacks at .86.

13. Washington *Post*, 10 October 1978.

14. Montgomery's rating by the conservative Americans for Constitutional Action in 1972 was 100 percent; his rating by the liberal Americans for Democratic Action that year was zero. Michael Barone, Grant Ujifusa, and Dougles Matthews, *The Almanac of American Politics 1976* (New York: Dutton, 195), 461.

15. Interview with Montgomery, conducted by the author on 26 January 1979 in Washington.

16. Interview with Lott, conducted by the author on 23 January 1979 in Washington.

17. Over the objections of blacks, Governor Winter ended the dual party chairmanship arrangement during the spring of 1980, when he installed his choice, Danny Cupit, as state chairman. The *Clarion-Ledger* wrote that Cupit, who is white, "has walked the fine line of diplomacy between blacks and whites and moderates and conservatives in the party." State Representative Fred Banks, a black politician, said that blacks would not be comfortable with a single party chairman. "Even though I recognize it's time to have one head ... there is not enough trust there yet," Banks asserted. *Clarion-Ledger*, 23 March 1980.

18. Carter's two presidential races in Mississippi correlate at .82.

19. A Mississippi State University survey conducted 7–18 September 1982 found that 80 percent of the state's blacks favored Stennis with 20 percent for Barbour. These results were reported in the *Clarion-Ledger*, which sponsored the poll, on 27 September 1982. There is no reason to suspect that this ratio changed during the remaining weeks of the campaign.

20. For an excellent account of this court struggle, see Art Harris's 1 June 1982 Washington *Post* article on the subject.

21. *New York Times*, 14 October 1982.

22. Ibid.

23. Ibid.

24. Memphis *Commercial Appeal*, 5 November 1982.

25. Jackson *Daily News*, 12 September 1983.

26. *Commercial Appeal*, 21 October 1983.

27. *Clarion-Ledger*, 26 October 1983.

28. Ibid., 6 November 1983.

29. Ibid., 26 October 1983.

30. Ibid., 17 March 1984.

31. *Commercial Appeal*, 11 March 1984.

32. Ibid.

33. *Clarion-Ledger*, 11 March 1984.

34. Ibid., 22 March 1984.

35. Ibid., 14 April 1984.

36. Jackson's forces fell short of the threshold, based on the county results, only in the First Congressional District in the northern part of the state, but managed to make it to 20 percent at the 14 April convention.

37. *Clarion-Ledger*, 8 April 1984.

38. Ibid., 15 April 1984.

39. Ibid., 6 May 1984. The state convention also witnessed a leadership struggle among Mississippi's black Democrats. Aaron Henry, long-time civil rights leader and Democratic National Committeeman, was defeated two-to-one for the committeeman's post by a much younger and a less openly conciliatory black leader, Bennie

Thompson, a Hinds Country Supervisor and a Jesse Jackson supporter. The contest, which was the talk of the convention, symbolically marked the passage of leadership to a new generation of the state's blacks.

40. *Clarion-Ledger,* 19 July 1984.

41. The state's other three U.S. Representatives were either unopposed or faced token opposition. Mississippi elects its legislature, Governor, and other state officials in the odd year before a presidential election.

42. *Clarion-Ledger,* 5 April 1984.

43. Ibid., 1 June 1984.

44. Bolivar (Miss.) *Commercial,* 10 May 1984. Barrett summed up his campaign this way: "I am a ball of cotton in this race and my opponents are three lumps of coal. And come Christmas, I hope the people will not find a lump of coal in their stocking." The primary percentages were reported in *Congressional Quarterly Weekly Report,* 9 June 1984.

45. *New York Times,* 2 August 1984.

46. Ibid.

47. *Commercial Appeal,* 14 September 1984.

48. Ibid.

49. Ibid., 13 September 1984.

50. *Clarion-Ledger,* 12 September 1984.

51. Ibid., 27 July 1984.

52. Ibid.

53. Ibid., 11 August 1984. Buelow and Torrence switched to the GOP within a few weeks.

54. Later in the campaign Patterson adopted a more low-key approach when local Democrats appeared at Reagan rallies. For an account of one such incident in Lowndes County, see "Party chiefs downplay Dems at Reagan rally," *Clarion-Ledger,* 27 September 1984.

55. *Mississippi Press,* 2 October 1984.

56. *Clarion-Ledger,* 17 March 1984.

57. Ibid., 7 October 1984.

58. The affair was fully examined eight months later in a *Clarion-Ledger* article on 26 August 1984, the day after the inauguration of a new Ole Miss chancellor.

59. *Clarion-Ledger,* 26 August 1984.

60. Ibid., 4 April 1984.

61. Ibid.

62. Tupelo *Daily Journal,* 31 October 1984.

63. *Clarion-Ledger,* 26 August 1984.

64. Ibid.

65. Ibid., 15 April 1984.

66. Ibid., 17 June 1984.

67. During the fall campaign, Senator Stennis provided an example of what Walls was talking about. When Stennis needed black support in 1982 to win reelection, he

endorsed Robert Clark's candidacy; in 1984 he declined to state a preference, saying he did not live in the Second District. See Wayne Weidie's column, "John Stennis can endorse two Democrats, but not Robert Clark," in the *Clarion-Ledger,* 28 October 1984.

68. *Clarion-Ledger,* 22 August 1984.

69. When asked about the Walls candidacy, Jackson said this during a mid-September visit to the state: "If he had run, three things would have happened. He would have lost, Winter would have lost, and Cochran would have won without contest. . . . Regular Democrats cannot win without black Democrats. Black Democrats cannot progress without regular Democrats. We can do together what we cannot do separately." *Clarion-Ledger,* 16 September 1984.

70. *Commercial Appeal,* 7 January 1984.

71. *Clarion-Ledger,* 21 October 1984.

72. Ibid.

73. *Commercial Appeal,* 7 October 1984.

74. *Clarion-Ledger,* 31 October 1984.

75. Ibid.

76. The election results reported in this section are percentages calculated from the certified vote totals provided by the Mississippi secretary of state, 28 November 1984.

77. A Mississippi survey for 1980 was not available, but this estimate is based on a national survey that showed 35 percent of white southerners and 93 percent of southern blacks voted for Carter and on an Alabama survey that showed 38 percent of that state's whites and 96 percent of the blacks backed Carter. Lamis, *The Two-Party South,* 214 (Table 15–2).

78. Interview conducted in Washington by the author and a newspaper reporter, 8 July 1981. The official requested anonymity for these remarks.

79. Related to the author by Bill Minor, who overheard the comment during the fall campaign.

80. *Clarion-Ledger,* 8 November 1984.

81. Ibid.

82. Ibid., 11 November 1984.

83. As a result of his 1984 triumph, Dowdy is considered an up-and-coming Democratic star; he has made it known that he wants to succeed Senator Stennis.

84. *Clarion-Ledger,* 4 November 1984. Minor's column carried the headline "State Democrats in real danger of becoming permanent minority."

85. For a discussion of the regional trends, see Chap. 15, "Southern Politics in the 1980s," in Lamis, *The Two-Party South,* 210–32.

86. V. O. Key, Jr., *Southern Politics in State and Nation* (New York: Knopf, 1949), 229.

4

Alabama

William H. Stewart

ALABAMA'S RECENT POLITICAL HISTORY

Political developments in Alabama since the early 1970s may most usefully be examined in the broader context of four important trends that will also aid in interpreting the results of the 1984 presidential election. By relating the outcome of the November balloting to the trends identified at the outset of this chapter, we may also be better able to understand the course Alabama is taking politically in the late twentieth century.

Certainly among the most important trends is the increased black involvement in Alabama politics. The impact of the Voting Rights Act (VRA) has been felt in all political institutions, even more in the 1970s and 1980s than in the mid-1960s when the VRA was originally passed and the names of thousands of blacks were put on voter rolls for the first time.

Blacks have become the most identifiable and easily the most loyal of the groups that presently compose the Alabama Democratic Party. In 1972 two elector slates pledged to McGovern, the regular Democratic slate and a slate put up by the black-dominated National Democratic Party of Alabama, were on the November ballot. Subsequently, however, black support for national nominees has been merged with that provided by the regular party organization. Blacks no longer feel the need to work through separatist political parties. When they promised to support Jimmy Carter, blacks were told that they would be given more influential roles in Democratic Party affairs. This promise was kept by both the national and state party elites. In the 1976 general election, Carter got more than 140,000 of the approximately 150,000 votes cast by blacks. Blacks provided about one-fifth of Carter's total vote. The incumbent President was estimated to have received 94 percent of black ballots in the 1980 presidential election, even as he was being deserted by many other voting groups, both in Alabama and in the nation at large.

A second development in Alabama politics, which rivals the increased involvement of blacks, is the abandonment of George Wallace's presidential hopes. In balloting in May 1972, Wallace had won all places for delegates to the Democratic National Convention in Miami. Then, a few days later, he was shot by Arthur Bremer in Laurel, Maryland. Unable to pursue his own race further, Wallace nevertheless declined to endorse the ultimate convention nominee, George McGovern. Wallace's hostility to the national ticket in 1964 had helped Barry Goldwater romp in Alabama. His disdain for McGovern now probably contributed to the massiveness of Richard Nixon's win. Wallace attempted another race for President in 1976 but with little success in the primaries. When he quit in June, it was clear that he had made his last presidential run. With Wallace's exit from presidential politics, the ongoing efforts to reunite the Alabama Democratic Party with the national Democratic Party, a development that warrants separate consideration, were made significantly easier. Indeed, Wallace has been indispensable in state elections in keeping rural and blue-collar urban whites in the Democratic fold with massive numbers of new black voters.

In 1976 Wallace campaigned actively for a national Democratic ticket for the first time in 16 years (before he became Governor for the first time). In 1982 Wallace was elected again as Governor after four years out of office, winning over Republican Mayor Emory Folmar of Montgomery with the aid of a rural-labor-black coalition. Generally, from 75 percent to 80 percent of the vote in predominantly black counties went to Wallace in his successful bid for a fourth term.

A third trend, closely related to the influx of blacks into the formerly all-white Alabama Democratic Party and the cessation by Wallace of schismatic presidential runs, is this increasingly close identification of the Alabama Democratic Party with the national party (particularly since the mid-1970s). At least in terms of national politics, but also increasingly in the context of state politics, the Democratic Party (an integral part of the national organization) is a genuine party—and it is liberal (by Alabama standards). In short, party means something to officials and apparently also to ordinary voters.

Despite the fact that it has had to reorient itself dramatically in a very short time, the Alabama Democratic Party is actually freer of intraparty strife than it has been in decades. This could be because the most dissident, anti-Washington elements have gotten out (voluntarily or, in some instances, involuntarily) or been silenced.

But what of the Republican Party? The moderate growth of an increasingly ideological Republican Party is the fourth important trend that may be observed in Alabama politics since the early 1970s.

The Alabama Republican Party has experienced no general election in the years of the 1970s and 1980s like that in 1964 in the Goldwater sweep when the party elected five U.S. Representatives, plus many of the local offices where they had bothered to put up candidates. There continued to be two Democratic U.S. Senators and four Democrats and three Republicans in the House of Representatives throughout the 1970s. No change in the partisan lineup of Alabama's congressional delegation occurred until Jeremiah Denton was elected to the Senate. Denton defeated Jim Folsom, Jr., with the aid of Ronald Reagan's coattails in 1980 to become the first Republican Senator from Alabama in 101 years. Now four of Alabama's nine-member congressional delegation were Republican. In 1982, however, this number declined to three when the Birmingham House seat switched from Republican to Democrat. As late as the mid-1970s, Republicans held only one seat (out of 140) in the Alabama Legislature. By the early 1980s, this number had risen to eight.

The Republican Party has become even more ideologically oriented since the early 1970s. The Democratic Party, in contrast, has dropped its old (racist) mindset and accepted much of the program of the pragmatically liberal national Democratic Party as its own. Republican primary voting has come to be dominated strongly by rightist ideologues rather than party organization-minded realists. The Alabama Republican appeal, therefore, frequently is to a rather narrow spectrum of voters. Diversity of belief is not welcomed and, hence, independents and nominal Democrats may not be strongly tempted to vote Republican in other than presidential races, where candidates will make appeals that are attractive to a broader cross-section of urban and suburban white, middle-class voters. But there are large groups who may be persuaded to vote Republican. Republicans frequently are identified by their Democratic adversaries as the country club set. However, this may not be as true as it used to be. An increasing number might be more accurately pointed to as the conservative, Baptist, evangelical set. The Moral Majority was very active in the presidential and congressional campaigns of six states in 1980. Alabama was one of these. Baptist Jimmy Carter had not sought to implement the kind of legislative program desired by other conservative Christians who are increasingly finding political refuge in Republican voting, and many of these religiously oriented voters deserted Carter in favor of Reagan.

The combined result of these four trends, in some respects overlapping but in others quite disparate, is to move Alabama closer to national norms, especially as concerns its voting behavior in presidential elections. If a presidential candidate is popular nationally, he will also probably be reasonably popular in Alabama. Because it still has a majority of relatively conservative white voters, however, Alabama is not likely in the foreseeable future to be solidly in the Democratic camp. True, the moderate, Baptist, southerner Jimmy Carter found substantial support among right-of-center white Alabama voters, particularly in 1976, but his candidacy was probably atypical of the kind Alabama voters can usually expect to find on their Democratic presidential ballots.

Presidential politics is a critical part of the overall pattern of state politics, and the student of southern politics may learn important lessons by studying Alabama. It is to an intensive examination of Alabama and the 1984 presidential election that we now turn.

THE ALABAMA PRESIDENTIAL PRIMARY

Throughout the nation, five primaries and six caucuses were held on 13 March, Super Tuesday. The Alabama presidential primary was regarded as more significant than other southern primaries that day for two main reasons. First, Florida was not as "southern" as Alabama. Secondly, Georgia was viewed as morally bound to support Mondale, Jimmy Carter's Vice President. The primary was also important because it would determine if John Glenn, at one time seen as the strongest Democratic challenger to President Reagan, would even be able to remain in the presidential race. After disappointing performances in the Iowa caucuses and the New Hampshire primary, it was forecast that, "For Glenn, Alabama is . . . the whole ball of wax."[1] Also, in 1980 structural changes were made in the primary. The date was changed from May to March and presidential aspirants' rather than delegate candidates' names were emphasized on the primary ballot. George Wallace was, of course, no longer on the presidential ballot, and he made no endorsement during the primary campaign.

Thirty-five delegates were selected by Democratic voters on Super

Tuesday out of the 62 the state party was allocated. Five were chosen from each of the seven congressional districts. The remaining delegates (27) were selected by the State Democratic Executive Committee to ensure proportionality for presidential candidates, provide adequate representation for minorities and women, and give due recognition to Democratic officeholders and party officials. In the Republican primary, seven delegates were selected at large, three from each congressional district (a total of 28 delegates). Ten additional delegates were chosen by the state party organization, according to party rules, to ensure compatibility with primary voting. In 1984 all delegate candidates were pledged to President Reagan.

Each of the major Democratic candidates campaigned in Alabama, although Hart started later than the rest. The first time he had visited the state was in August 1983. He was now on a roll, however. Two weeks earlier he had won the supposedly crucial New Hampshire primary, one week before delegate contests in Maine, Vermont, and Wyoming. He made a few brief stops in Alabama after his early wins. In contrast, Mondale made ten visits to Alabama during the fall and winter months of 1983–84, including four trips in the two weeks prior to Super Tuesday. Jackson and Glenn also campaigned extensively in Alabama. Alabama traditionally has not been the site of much presidential campaigning. About 25 percent of Alabama's registered voters participated in the primary voting. Eighty-eight percent of these voters cast ballots in the Democratic primary, only 12 percent in the uncontested Republican primary.

The Alabama primary may have done more to give Walter Mondale the Democratic presidential nomination than any other. Syndicated columnists Jack W. Germond and Jules Witcover, writing from Alabama a few days before Super Tuesday, asserted that, "If there is one thing that is clear in the final days of the campaign . . . it is that Fritz Mondale must prevent further inroads into his black support by Jackson if he is to avoid another defeat by the onrushing Gary Hart."[2] This he was, in fact, able to do. It is estimated that Jackson got 53 percent, Mondale 42 percent of the black ballots cast in the Alabama presidential primary. (Estimates vary substantially, depending on which exit polling and other data one consults.) Within Birmingham, due to the endorsement of Mayor Richard Arrington and the political muscle of Arrington's Citizens Coalition, Mondale got about 59 percent of black votes cast compared with Jackson's 37 percent. Mondale had the endorsement of the Alabama Democratic Conference (ADC), the black wing of the Alabama Democratic Party organization. Some components of the ADC supported Jackson and carried their south and west Alabama territories for him, however.

One study found that 40.6 percent of the participants in the Alabama Democratic presidential primary were black.[3] Blacks were estimated to compose about 25 percent of Alabama's registered voters.

Probably the single most important component of Mondale's winning electoral coalition was organized labor. AFL–CIO support was touted nationally as having the winning margin for Mondale in the Alabama primary. Union households represented approximately one-third of the Democratic primary turnout and Mondale won the votes of 44 percent of the voters from these households. He also had the support of the teachers lobby, the Alabama Education Association. Other public employees apparently voted for Mondale in substantial numbers as well.

Of these primary voters identifying themselves as Democrats, a full 40 percent voted for Mondale. Taking his group of voters alone, 78 percent had voted for Carter in 1980. In contrast, 67 percent of Glenn's voters had supported Reagan. Only 39 percent of Glenn's voters even identified themselves as Democrats. The majority were either Republican or Independent. Mondale got more votes from the youngest voters (those 18–24) than Hart (28–23 percent). Alabama was the only state thus far in which this was the case. The largest group of Mondale voters, however, was in the 60 or over age group (30 percent of the Mondale supporters).

Mondale had a superb grassroots organization, far superior to that of any other candidate. Further, he had the money needed for TV spot advertising, which stressed his rural background as the son of a Methodist minister. Of those primary voters who based their decision on the experience of the candidates, 77 percent voted for Mondale.[4] When the results were in, one state newspaper headlined, "Alabama saves Mondale hide."[5] Another bannered, "Mondale back in race with Alabama win."[6] While noting that Hart had won on Super Tuesday in Massachusetts, Rhode Island, and Florida, the nationally circulated *USA Today* observed that "Mondale did catch a second breath even if he had to depend on Alabama to do it."[7] Prior to Alabama, Mondale had lost to Hart four consecutive times.

As a result of primary voting and subsequent additions to his delegate roster by the state committee, Mondale had 26 delegates to 12 for Hart, nine for Jackson, and five for Glenn. Glenn dropped out after Alabama and most of his delegates switched to Mondale. The ten superdelegates remained unpledged until the July convention, at which time practically all voted for Mondale. In aggregate voting, of the four major candidates, Mondale received 148,165 votes (36.2 percent of the four-candidate vote), Glenn 89,286 (21.8), Hart 88,465 (21.6), and Jackson 83,764 (20.4). Mondale carried 39 counties, Jackson 16, Glenn seven, and Hart five. Mondale won five congressional districts, Jackson the other two.

THE FALL CAMPAIGN

Most of the factors in the campaign that contributed to Reagan's victory and Mondale's defeat in the other southern states as well as in the nation-at-large were also present in Alabama. With this caveat we can concentrate on how these variables, plus others that may have been unique, affected the race in Alabama.

Alabama Democrats apparently assumed from the outset that there was little prospect of the Mondale-Ferraro ticket carrying Alabama in the November election. Walter Mondale made only two visits to the state during the campaign. He spoke in Huntsville on 9 August, his first trip to the state after his selection as presidential nominee by the Democratic National Convention. On 21 September he spoke to a disappointingly small audience (3,000–5,000, equally divided between blacks and whites) in Birmingham. His basic message was: "When I needed to be nominated, Alabama saved me. Now I need to be elected and Alabama is going to elect me."[8] Following his stop in Birmingham, Mondale went on to Tuscumbia. Then he left the state and did not return again. At the time of this second Alabama visit, Mondale was 26 points behind Reagan in the current survey of voter opinion in the state.

Geraldine Ferraro, despite early protestations that her background as a "tough New York prosecutor" would make her popular in Alabama, came to the state only once. Marty Connors, executive director of the Alabama Republican Party, said that the selection of Ferraro by the San Francisco convention was a signal that Mondale knew how popular Reagan was in the South and was, therefore, choosing to emphasize the Northeast, "where his strength is."[9] Ferraro addressed a banquet of the black causes within the state Democratic Party, the Alabama Democratic Conference, in late August in Montgomery. Ferraro said in her Montgomery address: "We're coming to the South early, we're coming here often and we're coming here to win the election."[10] The press reported that "ADC conventioneers greeted [Ferraro] with polite applause." "They did not," *Birmingham News* reporter Michelle McDonald observed, "seem to be bursting with enthusiasm."[11] Plans for Mondale-Ferraro to campaign more heavily in Alabama were obviously changed when poll data showed there was no hope left of carrying the state. It might be noted that 71 percent of those polled in August in Alabama said that the sex of

Mondale's running mate would not affect their November voting decision.[12]

President Reagan visited Alabama twice in 1984. The first trip came on 4 July when he spoke at the Spirit of America festival in Decatur. In October he spoke to an enthusiastic, mostly student audience of 9,000 on the University of Alabama campus in Tuscaloosa. Preelection surveys showed the President's strongest supporters, in terms of age group, to be persons 18–30. In this bracket Reagan led Mondale 67.3 percent to 29.2 percent in early fall.[13] For both the Democrats and Republicans most campaigning was done by family members and other surrogates.

A number of 1984 analysts found it useful to make a distinction between voter affection for Reagan, on the one hand, and support (or nonsupport) for his policies, on the other. However, this alleged dichotomy has less explanatory value in Alabama. Poll data collected during the fall campaign showed sizable support for both Reagan and his policies. Capstone Poll results published in mid-September demonstrated, for example, that on the issue of a constitutional amendment to permit organized prayer in public schools, 78.3 percent were in favor, while only 15.6 percent were opposed. Further, over half (53.8 percent) backed an amendment to ban abortion except in cases of rape or incest. With regard to economic policy, more than three-fourths of those surveyed (76.1 percent) supported a constitutional amendment to require a balanced budget. On the issue of reducing the deficit, more potential Alabama voters said that they believed Reagan would be better able than Mondale to accomplish this objective. Reagan's reelection would also, the respondents asserted, more likely ensure economic prosperity (44.1 percent to 25.5 percent for Mondale).[14] Most rationally, the Republicans would have seemed to be vulnerable on the issue of budget cuts affecting the disadvantaged, among whom there are many Alabamians both black and white. However, as is generally true, the lowest income groups are the least active politically. Welfare recipients are no more likely to be the controlling element n elections in Alabama than they are in most other states. Among the politically active, the Mondale pledge to raise taxes proved to be no more popular in Alabama than elsewhere, even though generally low income Alabamians presumably would not have been much affected by the proposed tax increases. Alabamians have a strong tendency to vote against new taxes when they have the opportunity.

Mondale was seen by September poll respondents to be more likely than Reagan to protect the civil rights of minorities (43.1 percent to 26.3 percent), to care for society's have-nots (45.7 to 25.5), and to provide equal rights for women (53.4 to 19.8).[15] As far as the more active part of the potential Alabama electorate is concerned, however, they are no more likely to vote on the basis of moral considerations than voters elsewhere. Further, the social gospel is not an integral part of fundamentalist theology.

It was a sign of the gulf separating Mondale-Ferraro from the majority of white Protestant Alabama voters when, during the latter stages of the fall campaign, Mondale attacked the Rev. Jerry Falwell by name. As we have just seen, surveys of Alabama political opinion suggest that Falwell's social agenda receives substantial support from Alabamians. When Ronald Reagan wrapped himself in religious robes at the close of the Republican convention in Dallas, there is little he could have done to endear himself more to white conservative Protestant Alabamians. Church and state have always been united in Alabama. Labor campaign activists found that Reagan had much support among union members because of a more favorable position on social and religious issues. Jim Albright, Alabama Labor Council executive director, said his organization was "trying to convince our people to look at labor issues."[16] Labor distributed close to 200,000 pieces of literature urging Mondale-Ferraro support by union members. Republican campaign workers reportedly distributed 500,000 bumper stickers, 250,000 issue sheets, 200,000 Reagan-Bush yard signs, and 50,000 brochures. Much of the literature stressed the conservative social agenda espoused by Falwell.

Mondale's warning to northern voters that Reagan, if reelected, would attempt to pack the U.S. Supreme Court with social conservatives was not lost on conservative voters. There is still much resentment among white Alabamians toward the social changes that were judicially engineered during the 1960s and 1970s. In summary, the social agenda to which Mondale-Ferraro pointed with alarm was not an object of concern for a majority of Alabamians. To get the emphasis off particular issues, shortly before the 6 November election Democratic campaign leaders placed ads in newspapers calling on Alabamians to return to the fold and support the entire Democratic ticket. Similarly, a brochure called on voters to "pull the lever for Alabama" and back "the party that stood by Alabama and built its past [and which was] the party of its future."

Democratic officeholders up for reelection in 1984 in Alabama attempted (apparently successfully) to distance themselves from the Mondale-Ferraro ticket. Governor Wallace was very evasive in his halfhearted declaration of support for the Democratic slate. When asked in Birmingham in mid-October if he would support Mondale,

Wallace replied, "I don't think so."[17] He said he might write his own name in. State party chair Knight professed surprise. He "had no inkling this was [the Governor's] feeling."[18] Later, Wallace did commit himself to voting for the party's ticket from top to bottom. However, he made no explicit reference to Mondale-Ferraro. In his successful campaign for reelection, Senator Howell Heflin even used in an advertisement a quote from President Reagan praising Heflin's support for the administration's defense build-up program.

The director of the Labor Council said that Mondale's candidacy was hurt by such "disassociation tactics."[19] Joe Reed, chair of the Alabama Democratic Conference, had reminded the white establishment in late August that black votes for Mondale were assured. What was required on the whites' part—specifically, George Wallace, (House Speaker) Tom Drake, (Lieutenant Governor) Bill Baxley, and Howell Heflin—was to deliver white votes.[20] This they would be unable or unwilling seriously to attempt to do, however. Even so, despite the lack of enthusiasm for the Mondale-Ferraro ticket, there were no explicit bolts from the party. There were no "Democrats for Reagan" groups in Alabama. While they gave little doubt that they would have preferred other candidates and a more palatable platform, Alabama Democratic officeholders did give at least nominal support to their national ticket. Under state party rules, it should be added, declining to give such support is reason enough for disqualification to run as a Democrat in future primaries.

Democratic organization apparently left much to be desired. In mid-September the Mondale state campaign staff was reported to be in a state of "disarray."[21] Some political observers credited Public Service Commissioner Jim Folsom, Jr., more than any other, with bringing about Mondale's presidential primary win in March. However, the coordinator role in the fall campaign was assigned to State Senator Gary Aldridge.[22] The less schismatic Alabama Republican Party operated a smoother 1984 campaign. Apparently the wounds of 1980, when there was a serious split between Bush and Reagan supporters, had long since been healed.

A mid-August Capstone Poll showed Reagan with support from 45.7 percent of those surveyed, Mondale with 40 percent.[23] In a poll conducted in September, however, Reagan was supported by 57.7 percent of Alabamians surveyed; Mondale by only 31.8 percent. In the final preelection Capstone Poll Reagan had a 22.5 percentage-point margin over Mondale (54.8 percent to 32.3 percent).[24] Thus as election day 1984 drew nigh, a Reagan victory in Alabama was about as certain as anything can be in politics.

A FUTURE-ORIENTED EXAMINATION
OF THE RESULTS OF THE
PRESIDENTIAL ELECTION IN ALABAMA

President Reagan, of course, swept the entire South, not simply Alabama on 6 November 1984. Out of 1,441,713 votes cast for President in Alabama, Reagan won 872,849; Mondale, 551,899. In percentages this was Reagan, 60.5; Mondale, 38.2. The remaining votes were cast for minor party and independent candidates. Of these, David Bergland, the Libertarian, got the most votes, 9,504, amounting to six-tenths of a percent of the popular vote. Looking at the two-party vote only, Reagan received 61.3 percent; Mondale, 38.7 percent. The popular vote margin of Reagan over Mondale was 320,950. This contrasts sharply with the scant 17,000 vote victory eked out by Reagan over Carter in the 1980 election. Of the 67 counties, Reagan won 54; Mondale 13. The 54 counties in the Reagan column included the most populous counties in the state—Jefferson (Birmingham), Mobile, Madison (Huntsville), and Montgomery. Reagan's popularity in these counties was, in descending order; Madison, 64.5 percent; Mobile, 62.5; Jefferson, 59.4; and Montgomery, 57.8. In all, Reagan received 334,041 votes in these four counties, or close to 40 percent of his statewide total. Mondale received about the same percentage of his cumulative vote in these areas also. In less populous areas, Reagan's percentage frequently was much better—for example, Shelby (south of Birmingham), 77.9 percent; Houston (a rapidly industrializing Wiregrass County), 75.8; Baldwin (east of Mobile), 75.5; Autauga (just north of Montgomery), 71.2; and Chilton (an area of traditional Republican sentiment), 70.5 (see Figure 4–1).

Nine of the 13 Mondale counties have black population majorities—Bullock, Dallas, Greene, Hale, Lowndes, Macon, Perry, Sumter, and Wilcox. Of these jurisdictions, Mondale did best in Macon (site of Tuskegee Institute), where he received 82.7 percent of the vote to only 16.2 percent for Reagan. This was the most lopsided presidential vote among the 67 counties. The only black majority county to support Reagan was Marengo County, also in the Black Belt. Marengo gave Reagan 51.5 percent of its vote; Mondale, 47.1 percent. (This county has a 53 percent black majority population.)

What public opinion polls had reported, the actual election results validated—a racially polarized electorate. In the August Capstone Poll, 59.3 percent of white voters had supported Reagan, only 26.3 percent indicated they would vote for Mondale. In the final poll before the November election, 71.3 percent of white surveyed said they planned to vote for Reagan, while only 21.8 percent intended

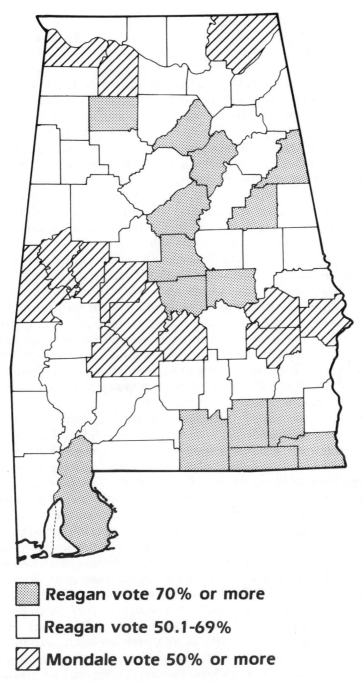

Reagan vote 70% or more

Reagan vote 50.1-69%

Mondale vote 50% or more

FIGURE 4–1   Alabama 1984 Presidential Vote by County

to support Mondale. In the 6 November voting, in a white neighborhood in Birmingham (Roebuck), Reagan received 2,020 votes (89.9 percent of the two-party vote) to only 228 (10.1) for Mondale. Statewide, it is estimated that just 22 percent of white voters (who make up 75 percent of the total electorate) supported Mondale. Regionwide, Texas-based political analyst George Christian saw "a literal white flight from the Democratic Party all across the South."[25] Alabama black state Representative Alvin Holmes argued that "The low-income whites supported Reagan because of his racial policies. . . . They are willing to suffer as long as the blacks suffer." The massive cross-class Reagan support among whites was, he charged, "racism in its finest hour."[26] Mayor Arrington observed that the Democratic Party "just lost in terms of getting support for the top of the ticket from white Democrats. I think they abandoned the party."[27] Governor Wallace, frequently viewed in the past as one of the foremost spokespersons for working-class white concerns in the South and in the nation at large, said following the Mondale defeat that the national Democratic Party was "going to have to rethink some of its positions if it expects to represent the thinking of the average citizen who is tired of big government being involved in running virtually every aspect of our lives." The party should, he contended, come back to the "mainstream of American political life."[28] Mondale's failure to cultivate support more effectively among white voters was viewed as the major shortcoming of his campaign by Lieutenant Governor Bill Baxley.[29]

As the figures thus far indicate, even more strongly than whites supported Reagan, blacks in Alabama—outnumbered though they were—voted for Mondale. In the August Capstone Poll, only 1.9 percent of blacks said they planned to vote for Reagan, while 84 percent favored Mondale. In mid-September, 75.6 percent of blacks surveyed said they had made up their minds to vote for Mondale. In the final poll before the election, 81.5 percent of blacks supported Mondale; Reagan was backed by only 7.6 percent. As we have noted, nine of the 13 Alabama counties won by Mondale on 6 November have black population majorities. A further illustration of racial polarization may be taken from the results in Pratt City, a predominantly black area of Birmingham. Here Reagan got only 109 votes (4.9 percent of the two-party vote) to Mondale's 2,127 (95.1 percent). Statewide, it is estimated that Mondale received 90 percent of black ballots case in November. Blacks constitute about 25 percent of the total Alabama electorate. The heavy black turnout put to rest fears that disappointed Jesse Jackson supporters would be unwilling to turn out in massive numbers for Mondale in the general election.

Within the sector of the electorate that may be classified as blue-collar, consisting in sheer numbers mostly of white voters, Reagan did as well in Alabama as in the South and nation at large. An August Capstone Poll found 47.2 percent for Mondale; 37.6 percent for Reagan.[30] By mid-September, however, 53.3 percent of blue-collar workers polled said they supported Reagan.[31] According to state Democratic Party chair Jimmy Knight, success for the Mondale-Ferraro ticket depended on putting together the 1982 coalition of blue-collar whites and blacks that had that had elected Wallace Governor over Folmar. Obviously, such a coalition was not constructed. Indicative of blue-collar support for Reagan and its coolness toward the Democratic candidate is the fact that President Reagan took generally loyalist Democratic Etowah County (Gadsden), one of the areas of highest unemployment in Alabama. In all, Reagan took 11 of the 13 Alabama counties with the highest concentrations of members of organized labor.

The number of eligible voters at the time of the November election in Alabama was placed at 2,433,448 by Secretary of State Don Siegelman. In June the number of registered voters had been tallied at 2,268,505. This meant that 164,943 voters were added to the rolls in the four months preceding the election. Despite the greater publicity given to black drives, in fact, more whites than blacks were added to voter registration lists in the period 1982–84. White registration is reported to have gone up from 1,656,639 to 1,757,870; black registration from 446,658 to 510,645.[32] The white increase was 6 percent; the black percentage gain was greater, 14 percent. It should be noted, however, that the published figure for registered voters is probably erroneous by as much as 20–40 percent due to the dated character of many county voter rolls. The 1980 presidential election attracted 1,341,929 voters. As we have seen, the 1984 contest drew 1,441,713. The 1984 turnout represented a 99,784 voter increase, or 7.4 percent. Using the inflated registration figures, a 59 percent turnout of enrolled voters is calculated. Correcting the figure downward by 30 percent, the figure would be 84.6 percent.

1984 AND ALABAMA'S POLITICAL FUTURE

The votes may simply not be there to construct Democratic presidential victories in Alabama any more. The traditional loyalty of the majority white Alabama electorate to the Democratic Party has been challenged by Republicans many times; and, generally in recent political history, this challenge has been responded to positively. Thus, as far as presidential contests are concerned, Alabama should be regarded as normally Republican. The 1984 election in Alabama does not represent any great fault line. Alabama has not been consistent in its support of Democratic presidential tickets since the 1940s. Republican candidates received Alabama's electoral votes in 1972, 1980, and 1984—that is, in three out of the last four presidential elections. Not since 1944 has Alabama gone Democratic when a southerner was not on the Democratic ticket. In 1948 and 1968 Alabama supported Democratic splinter candidates (Thurmond and Wallace). In 1952 John Sparkman, then Alabama's junior Democratic senator, ran with Adlai Stevenson, and this ticket carried the state. In 1956 Stevenson's partner was Estes Kefauver of Tennessee, and the Democrats were again successful, in Alabama if not in the nation generally. In 1960 John Kennedy, with Lyndon Johnson of Texas as his running mate, got six of Alabama's eleven electoral votes, while a Democratic splinter noncandidate (Harry Byrd of Virginia) got the other five. Alabama's modern affection for the Republican Party dates from 1964 when Goldwater proved to be enormously popular among the state's overwhelmingly white electorate (pre-1965 Voting Rights Act). In the twenty-year period 1964–84, the Republican Party has carried the presidential election in Alabama four times. Democrats won only one election (Carter in 1976), and Wallace (as an American Independent, 1968) won one. So, in 1984 Alabama did not deviate from its recent presidential voting patterns. This election year was simply a continuation of voting habits begun considerably earlier.

As long as the "rainbow coalition" remains prominent in the national Democratic Party, the prospect for Democratic presidential success in Alabama will continue to be dim. It will remain difficult for Alabama Democratic campaign strategists to construct coalitions of mostly white and conservative Protestant voters with blacks to provide a reasonable prospect of party success in November. Logically, the white Alabama middle-class voter should find a more comfortable home in the Republican Party than in the Democratic Party. If the Republican Party continues to nominate conservative candidates in the Ronald Reagan mold, even if they lack his communicative skills, and if it maintains a reasonably close working relationship with the religious right, Republicans will win favor with a mostly white, mostly socially conservative Alabama electorate. A candidate such as Vice President George Bush or former Senator Howard Baker probably would have less appeal among working-class voters than Reagan did in 1984. Further, a more theoretical conservative, such as Representative Jack Kemp, also might have trouble appealing to a basically nonideological Alabama electorate. Voters do not ballot primarily on the basis of fully developed ideologies, but party and candidate images are important. In 1984 the image of the national Democratic ticket was alien to what the typical white Alabama voter was looking for.

There seems to be a general feeling nationally that the Democratic Party will have to adopt somewhat more centrist positions on issues, if it is to be able to oust Republicans from the White House. To the extent that this occurs the party will be more popular with a majority of the Alabama electorate. A centrist candidate who emphasizes, for example, a strong national defense and a responsible fiscal policy, even while maintaining the party's commitment to civil rights, would have a reasonable chance to win Alabama. This would be particularly true if the Republican candidate also were perceived as centrist rather than as strongly conservative. Senator Howell Heflin, reelected in November 1984 with 62.7 percent of the vote to only 36.3 percent for his Republican opponent Albert Lee Smith, said that his party "need[ed] to start paying a lot more attention to middle-class America and to middle-class Alabamians." In Heflin's view, a "more centralist position" and a "more fiscally conservative approach" were necessary for the Democrats to recapture the presidency.[33]

It is doubtful if the Democratic Party will get markedly more conservative, however, despite its massive defeat in 1984. Again, though, it is conceivable that the party could nominate a candidate so attractive that his basically liberal ideology (as different as it might be from the thinking of the white Alabama voter) could be explained away. This would give the Democratic aspirant at least a better chance to win against a conservative Republican who was not a particularly effective campaigner. And, of course, national or international crises would affect voting in Alabama, as in the rest of the nation.

Alabama had only nine electoral votes to award in 1984. It is unlikely that it will ever be the key element in any presidential candidate's strategy. Alabama is, however, a part of the Sun Belt group of states that, together, have 195 of the 270 electoral votes required to elect a president. Donald M. Rothberg of the Associated Press observed following the 6 November vote that, "If the Republicans get a lock on those votes, it may be a long time before a Democrat moves into the White House." Rothberg concluded, however, that Democrats could do well in states such as Alabama if they would adopt somewhat more conservative positions on issues, not so conservative, however, as to alienate working-class voters, blacks, and other minorities both within the Sun Belt and the nation as a whole. Democratic presidential candidates would fare better than Mondale did in 1984 if they stressed their opposition to high taxes and their support for a strong defense capability. White voters in the Sun Belt, Rothberg felt, did not identify with the union, racial, ethnic, and liberal religious elements composing the coalitions with which the Democratic Party persisted in trying to construct presidential victories.[34] It is doubtful if any of the nonsouthern aspirants for the 1984 presidential nomination would have fared appreciably better than Mondale did in Alabama. A southern running mate, perhaps Senator Lloyd Bentsen of Texas, would have made the race somewhat closer in the state, but it probably would not have changed the result, a comfortable Reagan victory.

In Alabama, as elsewhere in the South, as *Christian Science Monitor* writer Robert Press analogized, "the Republicans attracted a majority of Southern voters to their 'restaurant' " on 6 November, "but only for the main dish—the choice of president." "Most went across the street to the Democratic restaurant for the rest of the meal."[35] Despite the strong tendency toward Republican presidential voting, Alabama remains basically Democratic as far as state and local offices are concerned. Republicans also occupy only a minority of the state's congressional positions.

Republicans put up candidates in only three of Alabama's seven congressional districts in 1984. These candidates ran in the Mobile, Montgomery, and Birmingham districts. Republicans were successful in Mobile (narrowly) and Montgomery. The Democratic incumbent won overwhelmingly in Birmingham, while Democratic representatives were unopposed in the other four congressional districts. As noted earlier, incumbent Democratic Senator Howell Heflin easily defeated one-term former Republican Representative Albert Lee Smith. Some efforts were made by the Reagan-Bush campaign to assist the nonincumbent Republican congressional candidacies in Mobile and Birmingham. Less support was given to Smith's Senate bid. Polls never showed Smith as having any realistic chance of beating Heflin.

Thus, following the 1984 elections, Republican representation in the Alabama congressional delegation remained at three out of nine, two Representatives and one Senator. In only two instances since the mid-1960s have incumbent Republicans been replaces by Republicans. In 1980 one of the Goldwater Five (John Buchanan) was defeated by Albert Lee Smith in the Republican primary. Smith went on to win the general election against a relatively weak Democratic candidate. He served only one term before he was beaten by a stronger Democrat, Jefferson County Commissioner Ben Erdreich. As noted, Erdreich won reelection handily in 1984 and the seat is now probably safely Democratic. After the overwhelming defeat of Republican Jabo

Waggoner by Erdreich, it is doubtful if there will be a serious fight for this seat except perhaps in an extremely favorable presidential year. Even former Representative Buchanan, a moderate Republican, could rarely make much of a dent in the solid black support regularly received by his Democratic challengers during his eight terms in office. The Birmingham district, with its inner-city black and suburban white professional consituencies, is made to order for the election of a moderate Democrat, which Erdreich is. In Mobile in 1984 retiring Goldwater-era Republican Representative Jack Edwards was able to designate as his successor recent Republican convert H. L. Callahan. In all other instances in the modern period, Republican members of Congress from Alabama have been succeeded by Democrats. Thus Alabama should not be regarded as having two safe Republican House seats and one safe Senate seat. Republican Senator Jeremiah Denton, narrowing elected in 1980, has been identified as one of the most vulnerable Republican Senators as far as the 1986 mid-term congressional elections are concerned. At that time the Republican Party in Alabama can be expected to contest seriously only for the two House seats it currently occupies, in addition to the Senate seat. Democrats will probably seek seriously all House seats plus the Senate seat in 1986.

President Reagan's coattails also proved to be very short as far as state and local elections in Alabama were concerned in 1984. Gubernatorial and state legislative positions were not at stake. And municipal elections, which are nonpartisan, are held in summers. Elections for country officers were numerous, however, and results showed generally that if Alabama is moving toward the Republican Party at this level, it is only a very incremental kind of change which is occurring. Just as voters have developed the tradition of supporting Republicans in presidential elections, so they retain the custom of voting Democratic in state and local elections. The best-qualified candidates generally are recruited by the Democratic Party. Further, the Democratic Party in Alabama has shown a remarkable pragmatism. Gone are the "white supremacy" days. The party has successfully brought into one fold for state elections blacks, labor, rural whites, and occupational groups such as teachers and plaintiffs' trail lawyers. Republicans remain stigmatized as the country club set. But it is easier to construct coalitions composed of these diverse groups at the state and local level than it is in presidential elections. At the national level, when the Democratic Party must legitimately give deference to the Rev. Jesse Jackson and his sweeping agenda for social, economic, and foreign policy reform, it alienates white Alabama Democratic voters across the board. Differences between blacks and whites once more come sharply into focus. Cooperation may become impossible. However, since the mostly white Democratic candidates in Alabama do not bring divisive issues into their state and local campaigns, it is easier for whites to support fellow-white Democrats while blacks generally can be expected to find almost any white Alabama Democrat more attractive than the candidates put up by the Republican Party. Thus is does not appear, at least in the short run, that the Republican Party will be capable of translating success at the top of the ticket, such as was enjoyed in 1984, with broad-based support for candidates below the presidential level.

The Republican Party in Alabama put forward candidates for only a minority of the positions up at the state (mostly judgeships) and, more importantly, local levels in 1984. However, while pragmatism has contributed to the continuing hardiness of the Alabama Democratic Party and the weakness of the Republican Party, there is probably a limit to how flexible the Democratic Party can be. It may be impossible to continue, in the long run, as the party, even at the state and local levels, of conservative whites as well as blacks, who require a more aggressive set of public policies. The Democratic Party cannot indefinitely appear to be all things to all people, even within the relatively simple Alabama political setting. One student of southern politics has predicted that within two decades the Democratic Party in the South could well become "a minority party of essentially blacks and 20 to 25 percent of the whites."[36] However, survey analyst Claibourne Darden has observed that there is little justification for the masses of southern white voters to switch to the Republican Party since "the local Democrats are very close (in ideology) to the national Republicans."[37]

At present only 14 of Alabama's 67 counties have Republican local officeholders or are represented by Republicans in the Alabama legislature. Out of 35 state senators, four are Republicans; out of 105 representatives, 12 are Republicans. Each of the state's most populous counties now have Republicans either as state legislators or courthouse officials or both. About 420 offices were at stake in the 6 November balloting. Eighty-five Republicans were in the running for these posts. In 36 counties no local Republicans were on the ballot. Eleven Republicans were unopposed by Democrats, mostly in traditionally Republican Winston County. Of the 74 Democrat vs. Republican contests, Democrats won 55. The relatively few Republican successes at the local level came primarily in areas that are urban or are urbanizing. *Birmingham News* writer Tom Gordon explained Republican success in larger population centers on the grounds that they "have a greater mix of people and governments' responsibilities are such that philosophical or partisan differences more easily emerge."[38]

Encouragingly, for Republicans, the party's base vote has been increasing over the past two decades. It is now estimated by party leaders that a minimum of 37 percent of state voters will support any Republican candidate who makes a serious campaign for state or federal office.[39] This is up from an estimated base of 18–20 percent in the 1960s. In the last Governor's race, Wallace defeated Folmar with a vote of 61 percent to Folmer's 39 percent. This was the strongest race a Republican had made for Governor of Alabama in modern times. The vote received by Gordon Tucker, Republican candidate for president of the state Public Service commission, on 6 November 1984 was 37.3 percent. Tucker was not widely known statewide.

Further, the number of Alabamians identifying with the Republican Party has been increasing, particularly in presidential years. In a survey conducted by the *Birmingham Post-Herald* in January 1980, before a presidential primary, 53.6 percent identified themselves either as "strong Democrats" or "leaning toward the Democrats." The next largest category was independents, 30.2 percent. Just 16.2 percent said that they were "strong Republicans" or were "leaning toward the Republicans." In the same year, but later, in an October poll, before the general election, 20.7 percent indicated a Republican affiliation. Four years later, in February 1984, 26 percent identified with the Republican Party; 45.7 percent with the Democratic Party. The Republicans' best showing came shortly before the 1984 presidential election when 34.2 percent identified with the Republican Party; 41.7 percent with the Democratic Party. Thus, whereas in early 1980 Democrats held a 37 percentage-point Democratic edge. Alabama has no party registration system against which these figures can be checked. Further, other newspaper surveys show that, in nonpresidential years, Democratic identifications apparently revive considerably. In a survey made in October 1982, prior to the Wallace-Folmar gubernatorial general election, 54.6 percent of voters surveyed identified themselves as Democrats, 29.4 were Independents, and just 16.1 made a Republican profession of faith.[40]

The role of the religious right is perhaps the most intriguing element as far as future Republican successes in Alabama are concerned. Operation of politicoreligious conservatives was first seen clearly in Alabama in 1980 in the Republican congressional primary battle in Birmingham between Buchanan and Smith, when the Moral Majority worked strongly on Smith's behalf. But conservative religious groups apparently also were influential in the Mobile congressional race in 1984. Jerry Falwell campaigned personally on behalf of the successful Republican candidate, H. L. Callahan. Also the religious right participated in voter registration drives, signing up many new conservative white voters. Of course, the religious right may not remain consistently active in Alabama election campaigns. However, conservative churches with associated schools have grown rapidly in Alabama in recent years. Also, religious radio stations that propagate conservative political as well as religious ideas are coming on the air with increasing frequency. Thus, there is a basis for ongoing conservative religious and political action. Conservative white voters may be mobilized through these religious, educational, and media institutions much as blacks have been activated historically through local black churches. The next real test of the political power of the religious right will come in 1986 in Denton's reelection effort. Denton has firmly consolidated his support among the conservative religious groups who worked strongly for his election in 1980 in his first try for public office.

There is no prospect for massive conversions of Democratic politicians to Republicanism any time soon. Defections very likely will be few in number. If they occur, they will probably be cases, as in 1984, of Democrats turning Republican to try for congressional seats they may have some prospect of winning. Alabama voters have developed great propensities for ticket splitting, which reduce drastically the coattail effect of even such a popular presidential candidate as Ronald Reagan.

Ironically, in recent years it has sometimes been almost as easy to point to prominent Republicans who became Democrats as to the reverse. The most notable example is former Governor Fob James (1979–83), whose earliest recognized political activity was as a Republican in Lee County. The sincerity of James's conversion was frequently questioned by more devout Democrats. At present Republicans identification in most parts of Alabama, and certainly statewide, would not be of sufficient value to induce official switches. It is plain that, generally speaking, it does not yet hurt to be a Democrat when running for office in Alabama. It is usually an asset rather than a liability. The white majority does not hold state and local Democrats responsible for what they perceive as unsatisfactory about the national Democratic Party.

NOTES

1. *Birmingham News*, 11 March 1984, 1–F.
2. Ibid., 3–F.

3. Statistics cited in this paragraph are from a study by Dr. William Kimmelman, reported in ibid., 1 April 1984, 20–A.

4. The figures used in this paragraph and the two preceding paragraphs rely on data from surveys conducted by ABC News.

5. *Tuscaloosa News,* 14 March 1984, 1.

6. Birmingham *Post-Herald,* 14 March 1984, A–1.

7. *USA Today,* 14 March 1984, 1–A.

8. *Birmingham News,* 22 September 1984, 10–A.

9. *Tuscaloosa News,* 12 July 1984, 3.

10. *Birmingham News,* 25 August 1984, 8–A.

11. Ibid., 26 August 1984, 16–A.

12. Capstone Poll reported in ibid., 12 August 1984, 1–A.

13. Ibid., 16 September 1984, 8–A.

14. Ibid., 17 September 1984, 1–A, 2–A.

15. Ibid.

16. Ibid., 7 October 1984, 2–A.

17. Ibid., 16 October 1984, 1–A.

18. Ibid., 12–A.

19. Ibid., 7 November 1984, 3–A.

20. Ibid., 27 August 1984, 4–A.

21. Ibid., 16 September 1984, 8–A.

22. *Tuscaloosa News,* 22 July 1984, 5–A.

23. *Birmingham News,* 12 August 1984, 1–A.

24. Ibid, 4 November 1984, 1–A.

25. *Tuscaloosa News,* 8 November 1984, 32.

26. Ibid.

27. *Birmingham News,* 7 November 1984, 3–A.

28. *Tuscaloosa News,* 8 November 1984, 2.

29. *Birmingham News,* 4 November 1984, 16–A.

30. Ibid., 12 August 1984, 12–A.

31. Ibid., 16 September 1984, 8–A.

32. *Tuscaloosa News,* 4 November 1984, 24–A.

33. *Birmingham News,* 8 November 1984, 11–A.

34. *Tuscaloosa News,* 11 November 1984, 17–A.

35. Reprinted in *Birmingham News,* 25 November 1984, 2–C.

36. Dan Carter, Emory University historian, quoted in ibid.

37. Ibid.

38. Ibid., 11 November 1984, 1–D.

39. Birmingham *Post-Herald,* 13 November 1984, 1–C.

40. Ibid.

5

Georgia

Thomas G. Walker and Eleanor Main

In his 1971 inaugural address, newly elected Governor Jimmy Carter proclaimed that ". . . the time for racial discrimination is over. . . . No poor, rural, weak or black person should ever have to bear the additional burden of being deprived of the opportunity of an education, a job, or simple justice."[1] Carter's speech, which gained national attention as reflecting the phenomenon known as the New South, signaled that Georgia had undergone a process of political change. The state had advanced from the "politics of the rustics"[2] to a mainstream politics of conservatism and moderation, a "politics of consensus."[3] As the state entered the 1984 presidential election period, candidates faced a much different Georgia than presidential hopefuls had confronted prior to the 1970s. Significant changes had occurred in the state's demographics, participating electorate, and ruling political elites.

Throughout the decade of the 1970s, Georgia's population increased. It became slightly more urban, more industrialized, and more black.[4] Although it grew by 20 percent, Georgia's population did not merit a change in the number of its representatives to Congress. Industrial expansion, measured by a 24 percent increase in the number of employees engaged in manufacturing, was spread throughout the state. According to census definitions, the proportion of the state's population living in urban areas remained virtually constant, but metropolitan area population increased at a higher rate

(21 percent) than nonmetropolitan population. The suburbs grew generally faster than the central cities. The city of Atlanta, atypical of the state and in many ways an extreme example, lost 14 percent of its population while the metropolitan area of Georgia's largest city expanded by 23 percent, and by 1980 one-fourth of the state's population and of its voting age citizenry was black.

These demographic changes, as might be expected, were associated with alterations in the state's balance of political power. Urban-rural cleavages and the north-south split were not as important as they had once been. The previously common alliance between affluent whites and the black population was not always present.[5] The importance of the black vote increased dramatically. Traditional voting patterns shifted, but usually resulted in the selection of fiscally conservative, antifederal government, and racially moderate candidates.

At the state and local level, moderate political changes occurred, but one-party Democratic politics continued to prevail. The Republicans made some inroads at the local level in suburban towns and counties, but maintained only about a 12 percent share of state legislative seats. Blacks and women significantly increased their number of public officeholders, yet each group comprised less than ten percent of the state legislature. However, in the 1970s Georgia sent to Washington its first black representative, and the cities of Atlanta and Augusta have elected black mayoral candidates. Although the number of women and minorities in public office did not constitute large numbers, policy makers did become more aware of the political power exercised by these groups. In spite of the fact that the state House of Representatives overwhelmingly defeated the Equal Rights Amendment, the legislature did change the legal status of women in 1983 by repealing the section of the Georgia code that provided that the husband was the head of the family, his wife was subject to him, and the wife's legal civil existence merged with the husband's upon marriage. Martin Luther King, Jr.'s portrait was hung in the capitol; but in 1984 when the state legislature recognized his birthday as a holiday, it was one of several designated legal holidays among which state employees could select a certain number to celebrate.[6] While these changes in state policy are modest in an absolute sense, they are quite significant departures from the politics of the past. If there remains a politics of race in the State of Georgia, it is the recognition by most candidates that either the black vote must be courted or must be neutralized by dividing it.

More substantial changes occurred at the gubernatorial and congressional levels than in local and state legislative politics. The dominating powers of the past, represented by the Talmadge machine and the great influence of leaders such as Senator Richard Russell, no longer exist. The Georgia congressional delegation in 1984 contained no member whose tenure in office dates prior to 1972. This has resulted in a major shift in political power from the days when Georgia consistently returned to Congress one of the most senior state delegations. Georgia Republican strength in Congress decreased. Voters in the Fifth (urban Atlanta) and Fourth (suburban Atlanta) Districts replaced Republican representatives with moderate-to-liberal Democrats. Representative Larry McDonald, a six-term Democrat and president of the John Birch Society who consistently voted with the most conservative Republicans, was killed when a Soviet fighter shot down a Korean Airline jet and was replaced in a special election by moderate Democrat George "Buddy" Darden. Sixth District Representative Newt Gingrich, first elected in 1968 replacing long-term Democrat Jack Flynt, survived as the only Republican representing Georgia in the U.S. House of Representatives.

Jimmy Carter's election as Governor in 1970 began a trend of selecting moderate chief executives. His emphasis on reorganizing state government was the advent of a change in the perceived role of the Governor. The antics, rhetoric, and often segregationist policies of former Governors, such as Lester Maddox, were replaced by the image of the chief executive as the manager of the state.

Carter's successor in office, George Busbee, relished this executive role. Busbee, the quiet majority leader of the Georgia House, was given little chance to win when he and eleven other candidates entered the race in 1974. The 18-year legislative veteran was little known outside the legislature and his home district. He paled before the flambouyant personality of early front-runner Lester Maddox. Maddox placed first in the primary, but faced a runoff election by capturing only one-third of the primary vote. Busbee placed second, edging former Carter Director of Transportation Bert Lance by carrying the key cities of Macon, Augusta, and Savannah. Busbee's runoff primary campaign urged voters to select "a workhorse not a showhorse." The theme appealed to a majority of the electorate and Maddox was unable to extend his influence beyond his traditional source of support among white, blue-collar workers and older voters. Busbee's emphasis on orderly, business-like government that would benefit all Georgians had struck a responsive chord among the electorate that would carry him through two very successful terms in the Governor's mansion. John Lewis, then Executive Director of the Voter Education Project, described the outcome: "A coalition of Georgia voters, black and white, has rejected the gubernatorial candidate who symbolized the segregationist views of the Old South."[8]

Experience and leadership in the state legislature propelled another relative unknown into the governorship in 1982. Joe Frank Harris, a North Georgia legislator and chairman of the House Appropriations Committee, was running a poor sixth in state-wide polls well into the election year. Harris was able to advance in the polls and upend the favorite, U.S. Representative Ronald "Bo" Ginn of south Georgia, by promising no additional taxes and branding Ginn as a "big spender" in Congress. His campaign was able to attract a portion of the black vote, largely because of the endorsements of key black state legislators, while still supporting conservative policy positions. Harris, for example, favored prayer and the teaching of scientific creationism in the public schools. He opposed ratification of the Equal Rights Amendment and the U.S. Supreme Court's abortion decisions. By portraying himself as a responsible, conservative Democrat and his opponent as a liberal linked to the Washington establishment, Harris defeated Ginn in the runoff primary and coasted to an easy general election victory over modest Republican opposition.

The Harris election was confirmation of a major fact of political life in Georgia. The state legislature serves as the primary arena for grooming political leadership. Four of the five previous Governors—Sanders, Carter, Busbee, and Harris—served in the state legislature. Of these, only Carter did not hold a position of leadership in the statehouse. If there is any kind of statewide political machine in Georgia, it appears to reside in the organization and voter turnout that state legislatures are able to deliver in their home communities.

The currently most-respected public official in the state, U.S. Senator Sam Nunn, is also a product of the Georgia legislature. Interestingly, Nunn is the last major candidate to win election after courting the support of George Wallace. When the venerable Richard Russell died in office in 1971, Governor Jimmy Carter appointed Atlanta attorney David Gambrell to serve in the Senate until a special election could be held in 1972.[9] Gambrell was not to remain in the Senate long, however. Nunn successfully challenged the appointed solon by linking him with liberals such as George McGovern and Jimmy Carter. He promised to "get tough in Washington" and claimed Richard Russell's mantle as an expert on defense policy. Nunn put together a brilliant campaign, which ate into Gambrell's support in metropolitan areas and maintained his own support among moderate and conservative voters in south Georgia. By gaining endorsements from an unlikely collection of individuals such as Lester Maddox, Carl Sanders, and Julian Bond, Nunn's coalition "was held together by one ingredient—political animosity or fear of Governor Jimmy

Carter. . . ."[10] Nunn captured the general election with 55 percent of the vote at the same time Georgia citizens were rejecting the Democratic candidate for President, George McGovern. Since his initial senatorial election, Nunn has continued to build a reputation for hard work, dedication, and expertise. He was reelected in 1978 after winning 80 percent of the primary vote and 83 percent of the general election ballots. Georgia's senior Senator had no serious opposition for reelection in 1984.

The final rejection of old-style Georgia politics occurred in 1980 when voters refused to send Herman Talmadge back to the Senate. Talmadge had represented the state in Washington for 24 years after serving two terms as Governor. For decades he appeared unbeatable. By the end of the 1970s, he was chairman of the Senate Agriculture Committee and a senior member of the Finance Committee. His seniority earned him tremendous power and respect in the upper chamber. Furthermore, his service on the Senate Watergate Investigation panel gave him the luster of a man of seriousness, rigor, and ethics. But the reputation began to crumble when he suffered a devastating divorce, complete with unbecoming charges and countercharges. He was also accused of financial improprieties in 1978 that were of sufficient magnitude to prompt a Senate investigation, which led to his denunciation by that body. Admitted alcoholism also severely tarnished his image among Georgia voters.

In spite of these liabilities, Talmadge doggedly attempted to retain his seat. Challenged in the primary by the more-liberal Lieutenant Governor Zell Miller, Talmadge asked voters to forgive his indiscretions and remember his long years of valuable service. The primary campaign was a bitter one, but Talmadge repelled the Miller threat, taking 42 percent of the primary vote and 59 percent of the runoff ballots. However, he was fatally damaged by the intraparty fight. In the general election, Talmadge faced St. Simons' businessman Mack Mattingly. The Republican challenger had never held public office, but served as the party's state chairman from 1975–77. For the most part, Mattingly refused to attack Talmadge personally, knowing that the voters had fully received such information in the Democratic primary. Instead, the Republican candidate projected the image of a presentable, very conservative alternative, who stressed pocketbook issues and promised to remove politics from the "professional politicians." Talmadge retaliated boy labeling the Indiana-born Mattingly as a carpetbagger and candidate of the country club crowd. In the end, Mattingly did what was previously considered unthinkable. The Republican nominee took 51 percent of the general election vote and sent Herman Talmadge into retirement. The veteran Senator had done well with his traditional constituencies in rural areas and garnered support from blacks and working-class whites. However, Georgia's growing numbers of white-collar, professional, city and suburban voters were ready for a change and endorsed Mattingly. For the Republicans, it was the first statewide victory since reconstruction and gave them hope for the future.

In presidential politics, Georgia's recent past has been inseparable from native-son Jimmy Carter. In both 1976 and 1980, Carter piled up massive majorities in the state's presidential preference primary. In the general elections, Carter carried 67 percent of the vote against Gerald Ford in 1976 and 56 percent in 1980 against Ronald Reagan. In the 1980 contest, Georgia was the only state to give Carter an absolute majority of its votes. A good portion of the Carter vote, however, is undeniably linked to the voters' pride in sending a southerner and a fellow Georgian to the White House. Any other national Democratic hopeful would have had substantial difficulties carrying the state.

Although voters have in large measure rejected the politics of the past, with its frequent segregationist overtones, Georgia remains a conservative state. Its one-party dominance is clearly not sufficiently strong for the state to endorse automatically a Democratic ticket that does not have a distinctively conservative flavor.

THE NOMINATING CONTESTS

Georgia's presidential primary was held on 13 March, one of the Super Tuesday elections that had a significant impact on the Democratic Party's nomination contest. This was only the third presidential preference primary in the state and the first one without Jimmy Carter on the ballot. With candidates Hollings, Cranston, and Askew already eliminated and McGovern deciding to concentrate his efforts in Massachusetts, Georgia provided an important test to Mondale, Jackson, Hart, and Glenn.

Walter Mondale badly needed a victory in the South to rally his supporters and to stem the growing strength of the Gary Hart challenge. Hart, of course, wanted to make a strong southern showing to prove that his attractiveness extended beyond the northern states where he had been so successful. Jesse Jackson, faced with the possibility of losing federal campaign funds because of his modest showing in the earlier northern primaries, needed to garner substantial support from the large number of registered blacks in the state. For John Glenn, whose military background and moderate political philosophy were thought to be assets in the South, a weak showing meant probable elimination.

All four candidates campaigned vigorously in Georgia. Mondale had the support of the unions and the Georgia Association of Educators, but the relatively low level of unionization in the state led him to use these groups primarily to get their members to the polls. Instead, Mondale stressed his tenure as Carter's Vice President. He emphasized his ties to the South and particularly to Georgia. In August 1983, Mondale journeyed to Carter's North Georgia mountain retreat and Carter praised Mondale as a "son of the Southland."[11] Lieutenant Governor Zell Miller, Mondale's campaign chairman, underscored the importance of his appeal to the farmers: "He can make their cap bills nod up and down. He can talk soybeans with them. Glenn can't do that. We have put together a lot of people out in the state who are not in your normal labor-liberal-black group."[12] However, in addition to the Carter loyalists, Mondale did seek support in the black community where he won the endorsements of Julian Bond, Coretta Scott King, and Martin Luther King, Sr. Mayor Andrew Young, who had seemed close to endorsing Mondale the previous year, decided to remain neutral and did not publicity ally himself with any candidate. Young claimed his strategy was ". . . to do the same thing I did in the civil rights movement . . . I was the synthesizer and the harmonizer."[13]

Jackson focused almost exclusively on the black communities of Atlanta and Savannah and in certain predominantly black rural communities. His fervor made up for his lack of an organization. The core of his campaign were civil rights activists and black clergymen. The Rev. Ralph Abernathy, long active in the Southern Christian Leadership Conference and once regarded as Martin Luther King, Jr.'s appointed successor, was state campaign chairman. Jackson told blacks that only he had paid enough dues to warrant their support. He charged that 18 years after the passage of the Voting Rights Act the political system still discriminated against blacks through dual registration, second primaries, and gerrymandering. The day after one large campaign rally and appearance by Jackson in Chatham County (Savannah), 1,300 blacks registered to vote.[14]

Hart and Glenn aggressively pursued independents and Republicans, attempting to prove their electability beyond rank-and-file Democrats. The absence of a Republican contest and the state's open primary laws made such a strategy worthwhile. Early in the campaign, Glenn amassed the support of elected officials; more than 50 state legislators and the powerful Speaker of the House, Tom Murphy, endorsed Glenn before the primary. The most popular officeholder in the state, U.S. Senator Sam Nunn, introduced Glenn with much praise at a number of rallies. Glenn attached great importance to his being ". . . the only real moderate left in the South," and he pointed out that he had ". . . not gone courting the liberal wing which for so long had controlled the Democratic Party."[15] In spite of the aid of elected officials, Glenn's campaign never caught on in Georgia and his early advantage in the state never took root. On the other hand, Gary Hart, who was virtually unknown in Georgia in January, took over like kudzu.[16] Hart's campaign created an excitement that Glenn's and Mondale's lacked. Although the campaign originally concentrated in the Atlanta metropolitan area and the university town of Athens, during the last two weeks hundreds of volunteers, many of them college students, criss-crossed Georgia where no other candidate's supporters canvassed the voters.

A primary turnout of 684,541 voters was an increase of more than 70 percent from the 1980 primary, but still only 29 percent of the registered voters.[17] In the popular vote, Mondale scored an important victory, capturing more than 30 percent of the ballots cast. Hart finished a strong second with 27 percent of the vote. Jackson rallied to take 21 percent, sufficient both to retain federal funding of his campaign and to earn delegates to the convention. Glenn's 18 percent, however, was considered a substantial defeat, contributing to the abandonment of his bid for the nomination.

Mondale's winning coalition was constructed from a number of sources. He attracted the votes of Democratic Party loyalists, union members, and poor whites in South Georgia who had traditionally backed George Wallace. Jackson directly benefited from the low turnout of the white vote. Blacks represented 22 percent of Georgia's 2.4 million registered voters, but they accounted for at least 33 percent of the turnout in the Democratic primary. Approximately 45 percent of the black voters turned out, compared with around 25 percent of the white voters. Jackson was estimated to have won 59 percent of the black vote. He did exceptionally well among both rural and urban blacks, taking 15 of the 19 majority black counties in the state and leading the field in Atlanta and Savannah.

Importantly, Mondale ran a strong second to Jackson among black voters, taking about 31 percent of their vote. The split of the black vote threw Mondale and Hart into a tight race. Fortunately for Mondale, Glenn and Hart divided the votes of those independents and Republicans who participated in the Democratic primary. Hart's second place reaffirmed his basic sources of support. He did well in the predominantly white mountain areas of North Georgia, in the affluent and fast growing suburbs surrounding Atlanta, and in the Athens area. Hart's bid was substantially damaged by his failure to keep pace with Mondale in attracting non-Jackson voters in the major cities. Glenn's modest showing was generally uniform throughout the state, demonstrating no particular sources of significant strength.

Seventy delegates were selected as a direct result of the primary.[18] Georgia's system of awarding bonus delegates to the victor in each congressional district was a definite boon to Hart. Since he had won five of the ten congressional districts, his efforts resulted in a total of 28 delegates. Mondale's delegate count was only 24. Although he had finished first statewide, he led in only three districts. Jackson, winning two congressional districts, was awarded an impressive 17 delegates. The threshold rule Jackson had fought so hard clearly benefited him in the First Congressional District, where he was the only candidate to receive more than the 30 percent required and was allotted all four of the delegates from that district, where 60 percent of the blacks and 20 percent of the whites voted. Glenn failed to gain a single congressional district and walked away with only one pledged delegate.

The battle among the campaigns did not end with the primary. When the 250 state party committee members met to pick the party and elected officials who would fill out the delegate slots, all went well until state party Chairman Bert Lance ruled that the delegates could choose the officers for the delegation.[19] A combination of Hart and Jackson forces nominated Mayor Andrew Young to chair the delegation in place of Joe Frank Harris, who as Governor traditionally would head the delegates. Young and Harris were both out of the country on separate trade missions. It was clear from previous votes at the meeting that a united Jackson and Hart vote could easily out-vote the Mondale forces. When the efforts of Mondale delegates to table the motion failed, a Hart supporter nominated a Jackson delegate to be co-vice chairman of the delegation with Lance. The Mondale delegates then walked out and no vote could be taken. The architect of the plan to unite the Hart-Jackson forces was Stoney Cooks, an Atlanta-based black businessman and national deputy campaign manager for Hart. Cooks is also considered to be Young's closet political and business associate. When Young returned from abroad, he claimed that he did not know he was to be pitted against the Governor, but that if the delegates chose him, he would chair the delegation. Cooks argued that the Governor, who had earlier leaned to Glenn but was technically uncommitted, did not have a national reputation and would not be able to be effective as a mediator at the convention. When Lance accused Cooks of trying to "blind-side" him, Cooks was quoted as saying the Lance's effort to unite the delegation, particularly with the Jackson delegates, were only "plantation favors."[20] The Hart-Jackson delegates' plan fell apart when Jackson forces were informed that the national campaign was not generally looking for an alliance with Hart delegates, and more particularly they did not want Andrew Young, who had been critical of the Jackson candidacy, as chair of the delegation. On 6 June 1984 Mayor Young said publicly for the first time that he would support Walter Mondale for the Democratic nomination and would work to "pull together a unified party to turn out 60 percent of the vote."[21] At a quiet meeting on 9 June, the Governor was elected chair of the delegation.

Ironically, Andrew Young, who had delayed his public endorsement for Mondale for so long and who wanted to play the mediator role, was the one who took the brunt of the black delegates' criticism when he opposed the Jackson minority plank to abolish runoff primaries. Some of the state's leading black politicians, including state Senator Julian Bond, had defended the runoff during the past six months, giving examples of how it allowed moderates to win elections in Georgia. State Representative Hosea Williams, a Jackson delegate, had come out in support of the runoff, explaining that he needed to get into a runoff to win his Fifth Congressional District race against incumbent liberal Wyche Fowler and three other blacks.

Georgia passed the first time on the roll call of the states at the national convention in San Francisco. When the vote came around again, Georgia cast 40 votes for Mondale, 24 for Hart, and 20 for Jackson. Hart had lost delegates since the primary, Jackson had gained three, and Mondale received all the rest. Governor Harris, Senator Nunn and Representative Jenkins voted for Mondale, rationalizing that he was strong on defense and moderate enough for Georgia.[22]

THE CAMPAIGN

The nomination of Bert Lance as chairman of the national Democratic Party, the events that followed, and his subsequent appointment and resignation as general chairman of the Mondale-Ferraro campaign had a thoroughly debilitating, if not totally destructive, effect on the campaign in Georgia. The mismanagement of the Lance nomination became a symbol of all that was wrong with Mondale, his candidacy, his staff, and his campaign.

Bert Lance's current strength and appeal among the Georgia public is not known. In his one campaign for elective office, an attempt to succeed friend Jimmy Carter as Governor, Lance garnered only 15 percent of the 1974 Democratic primary vote. His opponents pictured him as a slick banker with only four years' experience in government as State Highway Commissioner, who was trying to buy the election by spending over one million dollars on the campaign. Generally, during his troubles in Washington, he was sympathetically portrayed as being persecuted by the Washington establishment. After his acquittal in 1980, Lance returned to Calhoun, Georgia, took over the bank there, and was known to have financial business with Arab investors. Viewed as an astute politician, Lance began working toward his political rehabilitation.

In 1982 Lance supported Joe Frank Harris, also from North Georgia, for the governorship. Harris rewarded Lance by naming him head of the Georgia Democratic Party. Lance used the preconvention season to enhance his national reputation; he became an unofficial spokesperson of the southern wing of the party. Although he was a frequent guest on network news shows, he was not questioned about his past business practices. Lance had every reason to believe the events of seven years ago and the trial in 1980 were in the past. Officially neutral during the primaries, Lance used his influence behind the scenes to secure support for Mondale and played the role of mediator and conciliator. He was the only state chair who supported Jesse Jackson's request for lowering the threshold percentage in the delegate selection process. He consistently advocated turning the party more to the center and urged Mondale to adopt a "southern strategy" in choosing his Vice Presidential nominee. The position of chair of the national Democratic Party would have been a complete vindication for him and for Jimmy Carter, who allegedly had suggested the appointment to Mondale. Mondale like Lance, credited him with primary wins in Alabama and Georgia, and also regarded Lance as a well-respected representative of southern Democrats.

The appointment of Lance would send an important message to southerners: the choice of Geraldine Ferraro as the Vice Presidential candidate did not signify that Mondale was discounting the South. Lance's designation indicated that the national Democratic Party would have a leader who not only symbolized the center, but who would actively and energetically work to move the party there by courting the support of conservatives like Joe Frank Harris and George Wallace for the ticket. Instead, the rebellion against Lance's nomination, the lack of support of Mondale's top aides, and the perceived abandonment by Mondale wrested from Lance his ultimate rehabilitation. Responsibility for this debacle was laid directly on Mondale. Mondale was viewed as selling out to the liberal wing of the party, giving in to the antisouthern prejudices of the northeastern "establishment" press, and deserting the man who had worked so hard for his nomination and the healing to the national party. Lansing Lee, executive director of the Georgia Democratic Party, at a news conference, emphasized that the election of state Democrats was the party's only priority: "As for the presidential campaign, that is a national effort. Our position in Georgia is that we will help them if they want our advice and direction. If they don't want our help, then we have a full agenda in Georgia."[23]

Whether or not the state party and state political leaders would have exerted efforts for Mondale-Ferraro if Lance had either not been nominated for national chair or had remained in a national position may be debated. What is clear is that Bert Lance would have campaigned hard for the ticket in Georgia and most likely would have been able to generate some enthusiasm among the state's Democrats. Instead, the leading Democrats did not vigorously campaign for the Mondale-Ferraro ticket because either they were genuinely upset at the treatment of Lance or this whole series of mismanaged events served as a reasonable excuse for them not to be involved.

Disastrous relations with the national campaign staff continued when Mondale was scheduled to appear in Macon at a seminar on military affairs. The event had been added to his swing through the South and was intended to present his position for a strong defense in a state whose citizens and national representatives place a premium on defense preparedness. Every important Democrat in the state was offended when they were belatedly invited to join Mondale. Harris, citing unspecified office appointments, reiterated that his campaign efforts ". . . are going to be pointed toward Georgia Democrats. And whatever the national ticket can gain from that, they're welcome to it."[24] Former President Jimmy Carter and Senator Sam Nunn declined because they each had family plans they could not change; Lieutenant Governor Miller refused because he had a speech scheduled seven hours before the event; Lance gave no excuse when he sent his regrets. The Mondale camp, after announcing that this was to be a unification meeting, had to cancel the appearance.

Almost immediately, Mayor Andrew Young made national headlines when he criticized the Mondale campaign leaders as ". . . smart-ass white boys who think they know it all."[25] Addressing the National Association of Black Journalists in Atlanta, Young spoke of his frustration in trying to get his advice heard. Others in Georgia agreed with his assessment, if not with his choice of words, of the disorganized, directionless campaign. Many elected officials were frustrated by the lack of communication from the Mondale organization.

Mondale, however, refused to concede Georgia. He had a special attachment to the state because of serving as Carter's Vice President and mistakenly thought there was a Carter machine in place that would automatically transfer its support to him. He understood the problems of its farmers, had fought for the rights of blacks, and shared the strong religious values of many of its citizens. C. O. Smith, a businessman from Moultrie, longtime-friend of Jimmy Carter, and active in Democratic politics, became chair of the Georgia campaign. Supporters of Glenn, Jackson, Hart, and Mondale met the candidate at a small gathering in Atlanta in September. Lieutenant Governor Miller, Mayor Andrew Young, former Atlanta Mayor Maynard Jackson, and about 100 other political activists heard Mondale make a strong statement that his vision for America was congruent with those of both white and black southerners. The next day there was a closed-door breakfast meeting that included Nunn, Miller, Young, Jackson, and Hamilton Jordan. Bert Lance personally persuaded a reluctant Governor Harris to join them. The Governor insisted to the press after the meeting that he was there ". . . as governor to welcome him to Georgia. If I wasn't there, people would say I wasn't welcoming him to Georgia."[26] Mondale then went to Agnes Scott College, where he made his first public appearance since the convention with Lance. Lance presented Senator Nunn who, in turn, effusively introduced Mondale. Nunn spoke glowingly about Mondale's plans to set up a trust fund from tax increases to pay off the deficit and about his record on defense. Neither Harris nor Nunn would appear with Mondale again. In his own campaign for reelection, Nunn talked little about Mondale except to give him points for trying to fact up to the deficit question. When asked, he would say that he was supporting the ticket, but that he had ". . . not become a Mondale cheerleader."[27]

The two highlights of the Georgia Mondale-Ferraro campaign were an old-fashioned political barbecue and an Atlanta political rally. The barbecue was held at Talmadge Farms, the long-time home of former Senator Herman Talmadge and the site for many such events in previous years, now owned and operated by his former wife, Betty Talmadge. The ante-bellum house, used in the filming of "Gone With the Wind," was the perfect setting to revive this southern campaign form. It was also a symbol of how the politics of race had changed to the politics of a southern racial coalition for the southern Democrats, when Jesse Jackson had both blacks and whites cheering the Democratic Party, its goal, and nominee. Black- and white-office-holders and campaign workers shared the platform. Former President Jimmy Carter, in his only campaign appearance for his Vice President, delivered an enthusiastic and forceful speech, critical of

Reagan's foreign policies and praised Mondale's experience and knowledge. Walter Mondale responded, standing on a stump, with an eloquent speech, free from the often-criticized high pitched delivery, in an aggressive and robust style. Although the barbecue failed to attract the reluctant Joe Frank Harris, the presence of Lance, Young, and Miller on the platform led to speculation that the campaign was finally getting started. Less than a week later, the campaign appeared to gain momentum when the largest crowd ever, over 20,000, packed Atlanta's Central City Park and its surrounding streets to cheer Geraldine Ferraro as she delivered a sharp attack on the Reagan administration. Once again, Governor Harris failed to lend support by his presence at a rally for the national ticket, remaining in his office at the state capitol just five blocks away from the Ferraro gathering.

In spite of these successful forays into the state by the candidates, the campaign continued to be plagued by a lack of enthusiasm by the prominent Democrats and a general climate of inefficiency, inexperience, and nondirection. Democratic candidates generally kept their distance from the national campaign. At times, the greatest campaign effort seemed to be exerted by blacks and women. Jesse Jackson made a number of appearances in the state. First, he emphasized voter registration, using the preacher's techniques of exhorting the audience to declare themselves by coming down front and then registering. In later appearances, including an election eve rally in downtown Atlanta with Lance and Young, he underscored the need for blacks to vote. However, the Democratic Party provided only $17,500 for the Get Out the Vote campaign among blacks, compared to the $75,000 the Rainbow Coalition used in the state for the primary. Andrew Young consistently was the most likely prominent official to be present at major campaign events. "Women for Mondale-Ferraro" hosted a reception for Rosalynn Carter; and a coalition of women, representing different groups that had worked together for ratification of the Equal Rights Amendment, sponsored a four-day swing through the state the week before the election. Jean Young led the group that was met at different spots by local women and notable visitors such as Mrs. Carter, Joan Mondale, and U.S. Representative Lindy Boggs.

In contrast to the Democrats, the Republican candidates in the state united behind the national ticket. The state Republican Party set into motion "Operation Breakthrough," its long-term plan for turning Georgia into a viable two-party state. This time the effort was directed at increasing the number of Republicans in the state legislature and in local offices. National Republican efforts included voter registration and specific support for the Fourth District Congressional challenger Pat Swindall. Vice President Bush delivered the opening address for the University of Georgia's year-long celebration of its 200th anniversary. The President personally campaigned in suburban Atlanta and in Macon, while Mrs. Reagan made "noncampaign" appearances on behalf of her drug-abuse programs. Compared to the Democratic Party's efforts in the state, the Republicans were a unified, well-organized, and justifiably confident campaign force.

THE VOTE

Georgians streamed to the polls in record numbers on 6 November. The turnout generally surpassed even the most optimistic predictions, with 1.7 million voters breaking the previous standard of 1.59 million in the 1980 presidential election. Sixty-three percent of the state's registered voters participated, causing long lines at many precincts.[28] Officials of the Voter Education project estimated that more than 60 percent of the state's 594,484 black voters went to the polls with some precincts reporting a 75 percent turnout among black voters.[29]

When the votes were counted, it became clear that Georgians had cast their ballots in a manner similar to voters across the nation. Republicans Ronald Reagan and George Bush captured 60 percent of the vote compared to a 40 percent showing for the Mondale-Ferraro Democratic ticket. Republicans swept 135 of the state's 159 countries.[30] As Figure 5–1 indicates, the Democrats won a total of 24 counties generally falling along a line running diagonally across the state. An analysis of the vote distribution reveals that Reagan attracted majorities broadly throughout the electorate, with race and economic status accounting for most of what variation there was in the final tally. Table 5–1 provides the voting breakdown in sample counties having particular demographic characteristics.[31]

Four Georgia counties contain cities with populations in excess of 100,000. Reagan and Mondale split these population centers. Mondale carried Fulton County (Atlanta) with almost 57 percent of the vote. His victory was fueled by large numbers of black voters, who overwhelmingly supported the Democratic ticket. Mondale also captured the Central Georgia population center of Bibb County (Macon). This was a particular embarrassment to the Republicans because the Reagan's state campaign director, George Israel, is mayor of Macon,

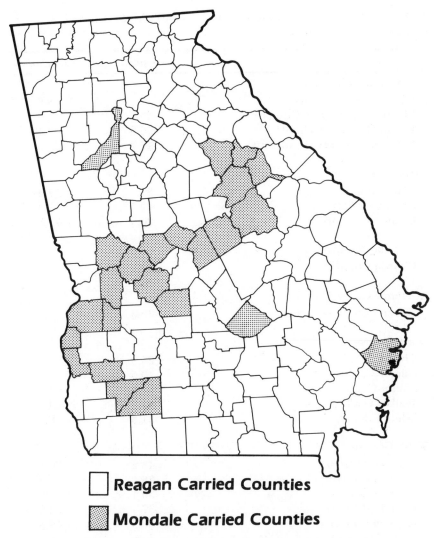

☐ **Reagan Carried Counties**

▨ **Mondale Carried Counties**

FIGURE 5–1   Georgia Counties and Congressional Districts

and both George Bush and the President had made campaign stops in the city. Bibb County was carried by the Democrats largely because of heavy black voter turnout. Republicans won the major population center for Muscogee County (Columbus) in the western part of the state. This county contains Fort Benning and has a distinctly military orientation. The President also captured the seacoast county of Chatham (Savannah) by a 57 to 43 margin. Mondale remained close

TABLE 5–1   1984 Election Results in Counties with Selected
Characteristics (percentage)

	Mondale	*Reagan*
Major Population Centers		
Bibb County (Macon)	51.1	48.9
Chatham County (Savannah)	43.1	56.9
Fulton County (Atlanta)	56.9	43.1
Muscogee County (Columbus)	46.7	53.3
Affluent Suburbs		
Cobb County	22.6	77.4
DeKalb County	42.5	57.5
Gwinnett County	20.5	79.5
Blue-collar Suburbs		
Clayton County	27.2	72.8
Academic Communities		
Clarke County (Athens)	46.8	53.2
North Georgia		
Cherokee County	23.9	76.1
Gilmer County	29.5	70.5
Rabun County	36.6	63.4
Walker County	31.7	68.3
White County	31.5	68.5
South Georgia		
Camden County	43.2	76.2
Coffee County	38.5	61.5
Decatur County	39.1	60.9
Loundes County	37.1	62.9
Mitchell County	50.5	49.5
Greatest Population Growth		
Douglas County	26.5	73.5
Fayette County	18.5	81.5
Gwinnett County	20.5	79.5
Liberty County	46.5	53.5
Rockdale County	24.6	75.4
Greatest Population Losses		
Calhoun County	58.1	41.9
Chattahoochee County	48.3	51.7

TABLE 5–1   *(continued)*

	Mondale	Reagan
Fulton County	56.9	43.1
Stewart County	61.9	38.1
Taliaferro County	63.4	36.6
Black Populations of 60 Percent or More		
Clay County	64.4	35.6
Hancock County	75.3	24.7
Stewart County	61.9	38.1
Talbot County	65.8	34.2
Taliaferro County	63.4	36.6
Terrell County	47.8	52.2
White Populations of 95.5 Percent or More		
Dawson County	32.7	67.3
Fannin County	32.1	67.9
Forsyth County	25.0	75.0
Gilmer County	29.5	70.5
Murray County	31.9	68.1
Towns County	33.5	66.5
Highest Per Capita Personal Incomes		
Clayton County	27.2	72.8
Cobb County	22.6	77.4
DeKalb County	42.5	57.5
Fulton County	56.9	43.1
Glynn County	35.9	64.1
Lowest Per Capita Personal Incomes		
Clay County	64.4	35.6
Crawford County	52.3	47.7
Lee County	30.0	70.0
Quitman County	57.6	42.4
Union County	36.7	63.3
Lowest Percentage of Households Receiving Food Stamps		
Clayton County	27.2	72.8
Cobb County	22.6	77.4
Fayette County	18.5	81.5
Gwinnett County	20.5	79.5
Oconee County	29.7	70.3

TABLE 5–1   *(continued)*

	Mondale	*Reagan*
Highest Percentage of Households Receiving Food Stamps		
Clay County	64.4	35.6
Hancock County	75.3	24.7
Marion County	52.9	47.1
Stewart County	61.9	38.1
Quitman County	57.6	42.4

in Chatham County only because of overwhelming support from Savannah's black community.

The rivalry between North and South Georgia played little role in the 1984 presidential contest. Both areas gave heavy support to Reagan, but in North Georgia, where Republicans have always attracted some support, Mondale's showing was particularly dismal. No county north of Atlanta fell into the Mondale column. In most northern counties, the margin of difference constituted a Reagan landslide with Mondale frequently failing to carry even a third of the votes. In South Georgia, the Democrats fared slightly better. Mondale successfully attracted black voters who constitute large segments of several rural South Georgia counties. Outside of these pockets, however, Reagan dominated.

As in other southern states, race had a major impact on the outcome of Georgia balloting. Exit polls indicated that over 90 percent of the state's black voters supported a Mondale presidency. Charged by the Jesse Jackson nomination campaign and by a well-executed registration drive, black voters were critical in every county in which Mondale did well. Nineteen of Georgia's counties have a majority of black residents. Of these nineteen, Mondale carried all but five. Mondale's voting percentage tended to parallel the proportion of blacks residing in these counties. At the other extreme, 21 counties in the state have populations of which 95 percent or more are white. All 21 were carried by Reagan, with the President obtaining an average of 70 percent of the votes in these counties.

An examination of Mondale's showing clearly indicates that his support was limited to certain areas of the state having a combination of large minority populations and severe economic problems. Unfortunately for the Democrats, these population pockets contained relatively few voters. Outside the Atlanta and Macon areas, Mondale victories came in rural, sparsely populated counties averaging only 8,400 residents. Of the 24 counties that supported the Democratic nominee, 14 had black majorities and the remaining ten had substantial black populations ranging from 31 to 49 percent. The Mondale counties all had severe economic problems or significant concentrations of poverty. The 24 counties that placed themselves in the Democratic column had an average rank of 105 (out of 159 counties) on per capita income, 26 on percentage of households receiving aid to families with dependent children (AFDC), and 29 in percentage of households receiving food stamps. In fact, Mondale counties had an average of 9.2 percent of all households receiving AFDC benefits and 22.35 percent participating in the food stamp program.

On the other hand, President Reagan's most impressive support came from counties characterized by high growth, high personal income, and low rates of welfare and food stamp expenditures. Reagan's vote gathering power, however, was not restricted to these areas. He did well even in several counties having all of the demographic characteristics that would point to a Democratic win. For example, five counties in the state with black majorities ranging from 51 to 61 percent and with exceptionally high welfare payments and low per capita incomes were carried by the President, although in each case the margin was razor-thin.

The 1984 Democratic national ticket offered little to attract the average Georgia voter. Although the black and the poor remained loyal to the party, other voters in this traditionally Democratic state ran to the Republican standard-bearer. The average Georgia voter is conservative, and the Democratic ticket was perceived as too liberal. Walter Mondale's ties to labor, civil rights, and feminist groups imbedded in the minds of the electorate the image of a big spending, Washington liberal—and big-spending, Washington liberals do not win statewide elections in Georgia. The impact of vice presidential candidate Geraldine Ferraro is difficult to assess. Her nomination energized liberals and many politically active women, but her positive contributions were undoubtedly offset by the votes of those not yet ready to accept a woman on the national ticket. More important than gender-related biases in either direction, however, was the fact that Ferraro carried a distinctly liberal image unacceptable to a majority of Georgians. The results of the 1984 presidential election reassert a political reality evident for the past two decades and interrupted only with the candidacy of native son Jimmy Carter: Unless the Democratic Party presents the state with a platform and a ticket more moderate in political philosophy, Republicans will continue to dominate the state's presidential politics.

Outside the race for the White House, Republican forces made significant, although limited, inroads into the Democratic-dominated political power structure. On the congressional scene, Sam Nunn's lock on his U.S. Senate seat appeared almost invincible, as he won his third term carrying 80 percent of the vote. Nunn continues to be one of the most effective politicians in the state, although he is content in concentrating his activities on Senate responsibilities and does not often become involved in internal state politics. Of Georgia's ten seats in the U.S. House, four (the Second, Fifth, Eighth, and Tenth Districts) were not contested in the general election and will remain in the hands of Democratic incumbents. Three were modestly contested by Republican challengers, but incumbents Lindsay Thomas (First District), Richard Ray (Third District), and Ed Jenkins (Ninth District) retained their seats with relative ease. Republican Newt Gingrich easily won reelection in the Sixth District, which extends from the south Atlanta suburbs to the Alabama border. Voters in the Seventh District, which covers the north Atlanta suburbs to the state's northwest corner, returned Democrat Buddy Darden to Washington. It was Darden's first regular election victory after having won a special election to fill the seat left vacant by the death of Larry McDonald. Although Darden won by a ten percentage-point spread, the Republicans had not put up a particularly strong candidate. Darden appears vulnerable to the growing Republican forces in this heavily conservative district.

The congressional race causing the most attention occurred in the Fourth District (the eastern Atlanta suburbs) where ten-year House veteran Democrat Elliott Levitas was defeated by 34-year-old political newcomer Pat Swindall. Swindall, a conservative lawyer and businessman supported by right wing religious groups, ousted Levitas by carrying 53 percent of the vote, following a bitter election campaign. Reapportionment, Reagan coattails, Levitas' complacency, and Swindall's well-financed and organized campaign, all contributed to the end of a decade-long Democratic control of the seat. Swindall joins Gingrich as the state's only Republican representatives in Washington.

The election produced only modest changes in the state legislature.[32] Republicans gained two seats in the state Senate, bringing their total to nine in the 56-member chamber. The minority party also added three seats in the state House, but these victories still leave the GOP outnumbered 154 to 26 in the lower chamber. The General Assembly remains firmly in the hands of the Democrats. Only 18 House incumbents were not returned to the legislature. Of these, six retired, nine lost primary battles, and three were defeated by Republican challengers. On the Senate side, only six incumbents were not returned to service. Three chose not to run for reelection, two lost primary contests, and one Democrat incumbent lost the general election to a Republican challenger. The General Assembly became slightly more diversified in racial and gender characteristics. Blacks increased from four to six in the Senate and maintained their 21 seats in the House. Women retained their two Senate seats, but increased their numbers from 17 to 21 in the House.

Republicans posted some of their most impressive gains at the county level. While these victories were limited to counties surrounding Atlanta, they were of sufficient magnitude to indicate that the GOP is now a major force in local politics. In the affluent northern suburbs of Cobb County, Republicans won a broad spectrum of local races, including the important county commission chairmanship. In fast-growing Gwinnett County to the east of Atlanta, Republicans seized control of the county commission and the county school board. They elected the first woman to chair the county commission, capping a campaign in which the party captured every contested office in a county where no Republican had ever won election in a county-wide race. In Fayette County, north of Atlanta, Republicans captured a three-to-two control of the county commission. In Dekalb County, Republicans made inroads into Democratic domination of local government. And even in the southern Atlanta suburbs of Clayton County, Republicans mounted a broad-scale, effective campaign for local seats that, while unsuccessful, indicated that the party was more than just viable. Although these local victories were limited to the Atlanta metropolitan area, they are of great significance. These suburban counties contain substantial numbers of voters and they have given Republicans a taste of electoral victory that has made the GOP hungry for more.

THE FUTURE

During the past fifteen years, Georgia moved from the politics of race to the politics of racial coalition. For a time it elected moderates; now it is supporting responsible conservatives statewide. White voters are clearly ready to split their tickets, and black voters may be searching for a strategy to maintain their impact on the state Democratic Party.

Georgia has not become a two-party state. Yet Republicans will continue to find support in presidential elections unless the Democratic Party makes a concerted effort to gain their votes by nominating a genuine conservative. Republican Senator Mattingly's reelection bid in 1986 will demonstrate whether or not Democrats who rejected Herman Talmadge's tainted candidacy will vote Republican again for the U.S. Senate. A number of well-known Democrats are likely candidates for this post, including former First Lady Rosalynn Carter, Representative Wyche Fowler, state party chair Bert Lance, former Carter aide Jack Watson, Lieutenant Governor Zell Miller, and former Representative Bo Ginn. Except for Mrs. Carter and Representative Fowler, all of these prospective candidates have lost state-wide primary battles and have been attacked at one time or another for supporting big-spending federal programs. The prospect of requiring $3 to $4 million for a statewide race may discourage some potential challengers from entering the battle against an incumbent who is expected to have financial support from national Republican sources. Mattingly has kept a low legislative profile but is rated high on constituent services. His 1984 endorsement of Senator Nunn is likely to keep Nunn from supporting a Democrat in the general election.

Joe Frank Harris will probably seek reelection in 1986. Although he has been criticized for demonstrating little leadership, he has managed to keep his promise of no new taxes. It remains to be seen how he will implement the suggestions of the Educational Review Commission to improve the state's relatively poor public schools and still keep his promise to maintain present taxation levels. Governor Harris has support from the conservatives, including those of the Christian right. Macon's Republican Mayor George Israel might attempt a race just to gain statewide recognition in preparation for a 1990 race, when there would be no incumbent running.

Republicans may also mount campaigns for specific posts where Democratic incumbents appear vulnerable. Increasing Republican registration in Cobb County in the Seventh Congressional District may encourage popular state Representative Johnny Isakson to run a formidable campaign against Democratic U.S. Representative Buddy Darden. A combination of growing Republican registration in Gwinnett County and traditional mountain Republicanism could give Ninth District Representative Ed Jenkins a reasonable challenge in four to six years. However, until now, the Republican Party has not chosen seasoned professionals to run against incumbent Democrats. Mattingly, Gingrich, and Swindall held no previous elective office before mounting their campaigns. The Republicans do not yet have a farm system in the state legislature or local governments where they can develop candidates to run for higher office.

The religious right has the potential to become a force in Georgia politics. Its presence has been most notably evident in the 1982 Democratic gubernatorial primary and in the 1984 Fourth and Seventh

Congressional District races. Church-going Georgians find it usual to have their ministers speak about political issues and have candidates visit the churches. Many candidates actively seek the endorsement of religious leaders. The religious right's greatest role will undoubtedly be in reinforcing the conservative nature of Georgia's voters and making it difficult for someone perceived liberal on the social issues to be elected to statewide office.

The Democratic Party has managed generally not to be out flanked on the right by the Republican Party and at the same time to maintain its support from blacks. Democratic leaders generally have supported moderate black candidates. Almost lost in the presidential campaign was the fact that Harris-appointed black State Court of Appeals Justice Robert Beneham won 58 percent of the vote in a statewide non-partisan primary in August to retain his position. The campaign was low-key; Benham's picture was not used on campaign posters, except in Atlanta, and the legal establishment and Harris' network campaigned for Benham. But there are not likely to be any gains for blacks in major political positions outside Atlanta. Andrew Young is considered unbeatable in his reelection bid in 1985. Most observers think that the Fifth Congressional District seat will be held by a black when Wyche Fowler steps down. The 1984 primary campaign for the seat became explicitly racial when Hosea Williams and Jesse Jackson claimed that one out of the ten Georgia Representatives should be black. Young and other black leaders felt pressure to support Williams against the white incumbent, who has always been considered supportive of their issues. Fowler won 65 percent of the vote against Williams and three other blacks. However, if a formidable black runs and wins the Democratic primary in this district where 58 percent of the registered voters are black, then any politics of race will be between the Democrats and the Republicans. There is some question whether black leaders in the future will campaign vigorously on the state level for those Democrats who are not going to support their national candidates and issues. Most likely, there will be black leaders who think they must do so in order to make sure they have some input into state politics and appointments. The black leadership in Georgia is not homogeneous, and in the past they have supported different candidates; this will likely continue.

In the intermediate future, it appears likely that Georgia will continue along the political path it has recently followed. The Republican Party will dominate presidential politics and selectively make good showings in races for congressional seats. The minority party will further entrench itself in the local politics of the white, affluent suburbs. However, even the most optimistic members of the Republican

Party predict it will be ten to 20 years before the GOP constitutes a viable opposition party at all levels of government. The Democrats will continue to monopolize state legislative and executive politics and to control the vast majority of county offices. Georgia Democrats will likely adhere to their recent practice of making a sharp distinction between their state organization and the politics of the national party.

NOTES

1. Atlanta *Constitution,* 13 January 1971, B–7.

2. V. O. Key, Jr., *Southern Politics in State and Nation* (New York: Vintage Books, 1949), 106–29.

3. Jack Bass and Walter De Vries, *The Transformation of Southern Politics: Social Change and Political Consequences Since 1945* (New York: New American Library, 1976), 136–57.

4. Census data and information has been compiled from U.S. Bureau of the Census, *Statistical Abstract of the United States: 1972* (Washington, DC: Government Printing Office, 1972); and *Statistical Abstract of the United States: 1982–83* (Washington, DC: Government Printing Office, 1982).

5. See Bass and De Vries, *The Transformation of Southern Politics,* 150–51; and Numan V. Barley, *From Thurmond to Wallace: Political Tendencies in Georgia 1948–1968* (Baltimore: The Johns Hopkins University Press, 1970), esp. 103–9.

6. Martin Luther King, Jr.'s birthday is 15 January. According to law, no state holiday can be celebrated when the Georgia General Assembly is in session. Therefore, holidays such as Jefferson Davis's birthday are observed at a later date by state employees. Governor Harris has proposed that the day after Thanksgiving be the day on which the Martin Luther King, Jr., holiday be observed. Blacks in the state legislature and Coretta Scott King oppose any move from the actual birth date.

7. Numan V. Bartley, "Another New South?" *The Georgia Historical Quarterly* 65 (1981): 119–37.

8. Atlanta *Constitution,* 5 September 1974, A–22.See also Numan V. Bartley, "Moderation in Maddox Country," *Georgia Historical Quarterly* 58 (1974): 340–48 for a discussion of this phenomenon.

9. The primary and general election ballots listed two different races: one was for the unexpired term of the late Senator Richard Russell, beginning 7 November 1972, expiring 3 January 1973; the second was for the full term beginning 3 January 1973, expiring 1978.

10. Milo Pakin, "How Nunn Won a Strange Political Alliance," Atlanta *Constitution,* 31 August 1972, A–1, A–34.

11. Dan Balz, "The Carter Card May Prove to be Mondale's Ace in Georgia," Washington *Post,* 9 March 1984, A–3.

12. Howell Raines, "Southern Primaries Could Spell Trouble for Glenn," *New York Times,* 29 January 1984, I–16.

13. Robin Toner, "Younger Won't Endorse Candidates in Primary," Atlanta *Journal,* 8 March 1984, 9–A.

14. Ronald Smothers, "Bid by Jackson Is Cited in Blacks' Big Turnout," *New York Times,* 15 March 1984, II–14.

15. Howell Raines, "Candidates Battle in Three Southern Primaries," *New York Times,* 7 March 1984, I–18.

16. In a poll of 334 Georgians taken in January 1984, Gary Hart got one respondent (not one percent). Frederick Allen, "South Doesn't Know What to Make of Hart," Atlanta *Journal* and Atlanta *Constitution,* 4 March 1984, A–1, A–16.

17. The Republican presidential preference primary had only candidate, Ronald Reagan, who received all 50,793 votes cast. No delegates were selected on the basis of this primary.

18. The Democratic party's rules included a new method of delegate allocation. A hybrid of proportional representation and winner-take-all by district, the system distributed the majority of the delegates proportionally, but offered one "bonus" delegate to the winner in each of the ten Congressional districts. In January, the voters met in congressional caucuses (the first since 1972) and each candidate's supporters nominated delegate slates. As a result of the presidential preference primary, 48 delegates were selected from these slates. In May the State Committee selected six pledged party and elected official delegates and sixteen at-large pledged delegates allocated according to the state-wide primary vote, except that a candidates falling below a threshold (ranging from 20 to 30 percent depending upon congressional district) did not receive any delegates. Finally, the State Committee chose 14 unpledged delegates, including the four delegates chosen from Georgia by the Democratic House Caucus and Senate Conference of the U.S. Congress. The delegation had to abide by the national party's rules on sex and minority balance.

19. Based on various reports in the Atlanta *Journal* and the Atlanta *Constitution,* 27 May through 31 May 1984.

20. Frederick Allen, "Democrats Try "Eclipse," Atlanta *Constitution,* 31 May 1984, C–1.

21. Atlanta *Journal,* 6 June 1984, A–8.

22. Robin Toner, "State's Delegates Cast Vote, Feel Relieved," Atlanta *Journal,* 19 July 1984, A–8.

23. "Democrats: Lance Affair Regrettable," Atlanta *Journal* and Atlanta *Constitution,* 5 August 1984, A–1, A–18.

24. Frederick Allen, "State Democrats Politely Snub Mondale," Atlanta *Journal,* 16 August 1984, A–1, A–8.

25. Kathryn Hayes, "Young Criticizes Mondale 'Boys,'" Atlanta *Journal* and Atlanta *Constitution,* 18 August 1984, A–1, A–17.

26. Ann Woolner and Robin Toner, "Mondale Takes a Tough, Warm Message South," Atlanta *Journal* and Atlanta *Constitution,* 8 September 1984, A–1, A–15.

27. Ann Woolner, "The Teacher's Mantle Donned by Nunn," Atlanta *Journal,* 2 November 1984, A–26.

28. Atlanta *Journal,* 8 November 1984, B–1.

29. Ibid.

30. Election statistics are based on information provided in the Atlanta *Constitution,* 8 November 1984. Although the figures are complete, the margin of victory in certain counties was very small (six votes in one case). Consequently, any corrected counting errors may affect the final number of counties falling in either party's column.

31. County demographic data used in this analysis were taken from *The 1983 Georgia County Guide* (Tifton, GA: Rural Development Center, University of Georgia, 1983).

32. "GOP, Blacks, Women Gain More Legislative Seats," Atlanta *Constitution*, 8 November 1984, A–16.

6

South Carolina

Laurence W. Moreland, Robert P. Steed,
and Tod A. Baker

INTRODUCTION

Throughout much of this century the presidential politics of South Carolina, in partisan terms, has been a politics of mind-numbing regularity: The years between 1900 and 1944 constituted an era when South Carolina voted not even once for a Republican presidential nominee, and also an era when "not a single county . . . gave a majority vote to any slate of electors other than the national Democratic Party."[1] Only once—in 1944—did the Democratic percentage of the presidential vote drop below 90 percent (87.6 percent)![2] In other contests, too, South Carolinians never deviated from the routine Democratic one-party politics of the state. Between 1900 and 1944 the Republicans failed to win an election entitling them to the Governor's seat or a seat in Congress or even a single seat in either house of the state legislature.

But in the next forty years—from 1944 to 1984—the politics of the state, both presidential and otherwise, reflected dramatic change. Of the ten presidential elections beginning with 1948, national Democratic nominees carried the state only four times (1952, 1956, 1960, and 1976). Indeed, of the six presidential elections after 1960, the Democrats won the state only once, and then only when the ticket was led by a former Governor of a neighboring state (Jimmy Carter). In this forty-year period, the changes at the presidential level were the most striking, yet other political developments also signalled the end of the overwhelming domination of the state's politics by the Democratic Party. As late as 1960, the Republicans failed to contest a single one of the state's six seats in the U.S. House of Representatives, but by 1980 the Republicans held four of them (although the two parties subsequently split the seats evenly in the 1982 elections); even though the Republicans were hardly on the verge of occupying the same position that the Democrats had held from 1900 to 1944, they at least enjoyed an occasional similar satisfaction, as in 1980 when the Democrats failed even to field a candidate against one incumbent Republican representative (Representative Carroll Campbell of Greenville in the Fourth Congressional District). Even in the state legislature, the Republicans began to emerge as a significant, though still small, minority.

To be sure, these changes in the party system in South Carolina came not all at once, but the contrast between the first forty years of this century and the latter forty years has been a sharp one. But then, too, the state itself had changed strikingly in the years after World War II. These demographic changes represented fundamental shifts in employment, urbanization, population, and race. Changes in the national political environment, particularly with regard to race, provided an additional basis, perhaps even a catalyst, for political change in the South Carolina party system.

POLITICAL CONTEXT: FROM THE 1940s TO THE 1980s

Urbanization, Industrialization, and Employment

South Carolina in the late 1940s could be characterized in a fashion that would not greatly differentiate it from its status at the turn of the century. The largest proportion of persons employed outside the home were still employed in agriculture, especially in the lowcountry (the coastal region);[3] consequently, most of the population lived on farms and in rural areas.[4] A wide chasm—socially, politically, and economically—continued to divide the races.[5] In short, in the 1940s the state retained much of its rural character, its agricultural economy, and its racial tradition. By the 1970s and 1980s, however, the trends toward urbanization, industrialization, and the amelioration of racial differences had all subsequently changed the environment in which the party system operated.

In the late 1940s, only four South Carolina counties were characterized by the Bureau of the Census as being in Standard Metropolitan Statistical Areas (SMSA): Greenville County in the northwest piedmont area of the state, Richland (Columbia) and Aiken counties in the midlands, and Charleston County in the lowcountry. By the 1980s, the three urban corridors had substantially expanded, so that of the state's 46 counties, 12 were now characterized as parts of SMSAs (see Figure 6–1). By 1980 the proportion of the population living in urban areas had grown to over half.[6]

This urbanization trend reflected the steadily decreasing reliance of the state on agriculture. In the 1940s agriculture still dominated the economy.[7] By the 1970s, however, only a little more than 3 per-

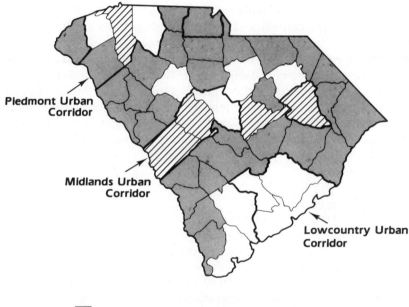

Piedmont Urban
Corridor

Midlands Urban
Corridor

Lowcountry Urban
Corridor

■ 6 or more Democratic election victories,
   4 or fewer Republican victories

☐ even split: 5 Democratic victories,
   5 Republican victories

▨ 6 or more Republican victories,
   4 or fewer Democratic victories

FIGURE 6–1   Democratic and Republican Election Victories in Elections for President, Governor, and Senator in South Carolina, 1970–80

Source: Developed from data from the South Carolina Election Commission for the appropriate years (Columbia, S.C.)

cent white males and about 10 percent of black males could still be characterized as farm workers.[8]

The industrialization of the state occurred first in the piedmont (the northwestern third of the state) with its long-established textile mills and then, to a lesser, in the midlands and coastal areas. By the 1970s the value of textile products produced annually in the state had reached $4 billion.[9] The State Development Board aggressively recruited other industries (represented by Michelin, General Electric, duPont, Westinghouse, Union Carbide, Dow Chemical, Lockheed, Cummins Engine, and others),[10] and nearly $4 billion was invested in the state during each decade of the 1960s and 1970s.[11] The state's economy was also substantially affected by massive defense spending (especially the 11 naval facilities in the Charleston area, including the nation's third largest naval base).

Tourism as well contributed to the changing character of the state's economy. The state's 281-mile coastline (together with the increasingly widespread use of air conditioning) contributed to its emergence as a home to major recreational and retirement communities. More than 12 million people visited South Caroline in 1980.[12] Wealthy resort and retirement developments brought new wealth to the coastal regions: by 1979 Beaufort County—where Hilton Head is located and once one of the poorest counties in the state—had become the wealthiest in terms of per capita income.[13]

In-migration and Population

Shifting patterns in population have also contributed to a changing South Carolina political environment. From 1950 to the present, the state has been a major Sunbelt growth area, characterized by whites moving in and, for much of this period, native blacks moving out. For example, from 1960 to 1970 there was a net in-migration of 44,468 whites and a net out-migration of 176,912 nonwhites—a total net out-migration of 132,444.[14] However, during the decade 1970–80, in-migration accelerated; the state experienced a net in-migration of 272,976 people.[15]

An important consequence of these migration patterns has been that the state's population is becoming less southern. In 1950, for example, only a little over 3 percent of the state's population consisted of nonsoutherners; by 1970 that percentage had almost quadrupled[16] and continued to increase dramatically during the 1970s and early 1980s. While the proportion of the black population has declined in all sections of the state after 1950, the decline was much steeper in the midlands and coastal areas (dropping from almost 50 percent to .37 percent between 1950 and 1980).[17] Nevertheless, 12 of the state's 46 counties retain black majorities, although all are rural, some with quite small populations.

Race

In the period beginning with the passage of the Voting Rights Act in 1965, those blacks who remained in the state became increasingly politically visible as they increased their registration and voting dramatically. In 1960 only 13.7 percent of the black voting age population was registered to vote; by 1976 that percentage had just about reached that of whites (56.5 percent to 58.4 percent).[18]

Of all the changes in the political context in which the party system operates, perhaps the racial change has been the most profound. Forced upon the state's white population through court decisions and acts of Congress, the effective introduction into the electorate of the state's black citizens has provided a basis, paradoxically, both for Democratic decline and continued Democratic vitality in the state's party system.

VOTING AND PRESIDENTIAL ELECTIONS IN SOUTH CAROLINA: 1900–84

The Erosion of Democratic Solidarity, 1944–64

Generally, partisan voting patterns in South Carolina in this century can be roughly characterized as falling into two broad periods: (1) a period of nearly absolute Democratic domination of the state's politics, running from 1900 through 1944; and (2) a transition period, extending from the mid-1940s through the present, characterized by a changed and changing party structure. The state's presidential politics have fluctuated widely during the second period, and the most important trend has been dealignment rather than realignment.

The first period (1900–44) has been briefly described above and is the period about which V. O. Key, Jr., wrote in his influential 1949 analysis. To Key the politics of South Carolina was the "the politics of color."[19] All the characteristics of the one-party South were present in the state: low voter turnout, a high percentage of blacks in the population (but not in the electorate), white demogogues willing (and eager) to make use of the race issue, and an economically unnatural alliance of mill worker and mill owner based on the subjugation of blacks as the political issue of the very highest order.[20]

Between 1948 and 1970, the old structure based on race began to crumble; with the passing of much of the race-based culture, much of the race-based political structure crumbled as well. Although the 1948 presidential election, in one sense, might be taken as the triumph of the politics of color, in retrospect, it can be seen in the long run as one of the early indications that the non-South would not permit the inequality and unfairness of race relations in the South to remain forever undisturbed.

The history of the 1948 presidential election is a familiar one: The southern civil rights revolt against the national Democratic Party got under way as the national Democrats adopted a civil rights stance new for them, causing some southern Democrats to bolt the convention and, in a rump affair in Birmingham, nominate Governor Strom Thurmond of South Carolina for President and Governor Fielding Wright of Mississippi for Vice President.[21] In the general election itself, South Carolina began its break with the national Democratic Party—albeit in a somewhat halting fashion, since Thurmond and Wright were listed on the South Carolina ballot as the Democratic ticket—and cast 72 percent of its vote for what was, nationally, a third party headed by Thurmond. In the ensuring years Governor Thurmond, who was elected to the U.S. Senate in 1954, became the one constant in South Carolina politics, a figure who could count on the loyalty of a large proportion of the electorate, even as other traditional allegiances deteriorated.

In the 1952, 1956, and 1960 presidential elections, South Carolina returned to the Democratic fold, the heat on the national party to a large extent deflected to the U.S. Supreme Court in the mid- to late-1950s by that body's *Brown* v. *Board of Education* decision in 1954. But Democratic majorities were much diminished: Adlai Stevenson won only 51 percent of the vote in 1952 (Independents for Eisenhower won 46 percent) and 45 percent in 1956 (South Carolinians for Independent Electors, pledged to Senator Harry F. Byrd, won almost 30 percent), and John Kennedy squeaked by with a 10,000 vote margin in 1960 (capturing 51 percent of the vote).[22] Moreover, the Republicans were beginning to build a state political organization, bolstered by W. D. Workman's (losing) 1962 U.S. Senate campaign. By the mid-1960s Republican state party chair J. Drake Edens had earned a national reputation for his grass roots organization-building skills.

Republican Ascendancy
in Presidential Politics Since 1964

Beginning in 1964, a number of developments—once again led by Strom Thurmond—gave further evidence of an increasing disengagement by South Carolinians from the national Democratic Party, holding the promise that the Republican Party might become genuinely competitive, at least in presidential elections. On 6 September of that year Senator Thurmond dramatically switched his party allegiance to the Republican Party. Then, with Thurmond's support, South Carolina gave its electoral votes and 59 percent of its popular vote to Republican Barry Goldwater in the 1964 presidential election. By 1968 Thurmond had become something of a kingmaker, playing a major role in helping to keep southern Republican national convention delegates from switching to Ronald Reagan (from Richard Nixon) after Nixon, in a meeting in Atlanta, had given a number of assurances to Thurmond (such as opposition to busing and the nomination of a southerner to the Supreme Court). In a three-way race in November, Nixon won the electoral vote with 38 percent of the popular vote (George Wallace took 32 percent and Hubert Humphrey, the Democratic nominee, got just under 30 percent).[23]

Other developments in South Carolina politics further heralded the disengagement from national Democratic politics. For his support of Barry Goldwater in 1964, U.S. Representative Albert Watson was stripped of his seniority by House Democrats in 1965; he responded by switching parties and by dramatically resigning his seat. Watson then won a 1965 special election as a Republican, the first South Carolina Republican to be elected to the House of Representatives in modern times. In 1966 Senator Thurmond, now a Republican, won reelection to the Senate and Watson was reelected to the House. The year 1966 was important in ways other than the election of two Republicans (albeit newly minted ones) to Congress; in addition, the Republicans nominated a candidate for Governor (which they had not done in modern times). That candidate, a Democrat hostile to school desegregation who had turned Republican, won nearly 42 percent of the vote and carried three of the 46 counties. Some local Republicans did even better as 16 Republicans were elected to the lower house of the General Assembly. With high expectations, Albert Watson four years later (1970) gave up his seat in Congress and carried the banner for the Republicans as their gubernatorial candidate.

Watson's 1970 campaign for Governor was perhaps the last hurrah for overtly racist politics in the state. Even some prominent Republicans, in what was at the activist level an all-white party, were appalled at his attacks on the "black bloc vote," and several condemned Watson's tactics. Watson lost to moderate Democrat John West, with West obtaining about 52 percent of the total vote and virtually all of the black vote.

Watson's loss can be seen as bringing to an end, at least on the overt level of direct appeals to voters, the "politics of color." Even Thurmond, up for reelection in 1972, became concerned over the rising black vote and the continued Democratic loyalty of at least a substantial minority of white voters. In 1971 Thurmond hired a black staffer to man his South Carolina office and began to extend to blacks the same kind of constituent service that had become legendary among whites. Thurmond, always known for this perceptive and sensitive political antenna, was reelected with over 63 percent of the vote.

The 1972 presidential election confirmed the trend toward increased Republican voting in the state. In that year the Democratic nominee (George McGovern) lost every single county in the state; Richard Nixon's percentages in some counties approached 90 percent, resembling the routine Democratic majorities of the pre-1948 era. In the 1976 presidential election, the Democrats earned their only victory of the five elections previous to 1984. However, the election turned on a short-term phenomenon (the nomination of a southern Democrat from a neighboring state running with the image of being outside the national Democratic Party establishment), largely unrelated to the long-term political patterns emerging in the state. By 1980 the short-term factor was less strong, and Carter failed (narrowly, with 49 percent of the popular vote) to carry the state. While Carter carried 35 of the 46 counties, the long-term developments were once again apparent: Although Carter carried a large number of counties, they tended to be the less populous, rural counties with heavy black populations, and he lost eight of the ten most populous counties.[24]

As the above suggests, Republicans have come to dominate the state's presidential politics since 1964. Of the five elections from 1964 through 1980, the Republicans won four, establishing an unmistakable ascendancy in South Carolina presidential politics. The only exception (in 1976) involved the special circumstance of the candidacy of Georgia neighbor Jimmy Carter.

As the politics of color ebbed, it was possible to discern the beginnings of a structure of party competition that characterizes South Carolina politics from the mid-1960s to the present. First, an emerging metropolitan Republicanism became increasingly evident, particularly at the presidential level. White voters, especially in the upper-income areas, were increasingly likely to vote Republican, a trend apparent in all presidential elections since 1956. The pattern varied, however, with the increasing importance of the black vote. Rural, heavily black counties where black registration and voting were low and where the electorate was overwhelmingly white had been more likely to reflect the traditional white southern viewpoint on race and to show increasing Republicanism in the pre-1965 period, particularly in the lowcountry; but by 1968 these same counties now were much more reliably Democratic as the influx of new (black) voters began to be felt.[25] By the 1970s these trends in presidential elections were becoming apparent in other elections as well, although, as noted above, the Democrats still retained the great majority of state and local offices. An examination of all ten statewide elections for President, Governor, and Senator between 1970 and 1980 indicates that the three urban corridors have become the most Republican areas of the state (see Figure 6–1). The rural, heavily black areas of the state have remained more dependably Democratic, but only because of the effective enfranchisement of South Carolina blacks.

A second feature of the contemporary structure of the politics of the state relates to the tendency of many white voters to draw a distinction between national Democrats and South Carolina Democrats. Such a distinction has resulted in the Democratic Party retaining its dominance in winning state and local offices (for example, holding 85 percent of the seats in the state legislature after the 1982 elections), while somewhat paradoxically being relegated to a minority status at the presidential level. A key question of the 1980s, then, is whether voters will continue to see the Democratic Party in this bifurcated fashion, as many Democrats hope, or whether the Republicans will be successful in their efforts to convince the (white) electorate that there is no real difference between the state and national Democratic Parties, that both reflect groups and ideologies out of step with most of the (conservative) South Carolina electorate.

During the 1970s and early 1980s, the Democratic Party, under the leadership of moderate Democrats (John West, Charles Ravenel, Dick Riley, Fritz Hollings, and Joe Riley, among others), has sought to achieve a delicate balance, a balance characterized by moving the Democratic Party from the party of white supremacy to the party of black participation, while retaining the loyalty of at least a substantial proportion of the white electorate. But the Republican Party has responded effectively. It too has attracted a cadre of dependable voters, especially at the presidential level and increasingly at other levels in many areas of the state (particularly in the urban corridors);

these Republican loyalists are nearly all white and are, by almost all measures, quite conservative.[26]

A key question, then, as the 1984 election year approached was whether the 20-year trend away from Democratic domination would be confirmed, modified, or, as many Democrats hoped, reversed.

THE NOMINATING CONTESTS

The Hollings Candidacy

With the beginning of the presidential nominating contests in Iowa and New Hampshire in early 1984, the nominating contests in South Carolina promised to be unexciting and even routine affairs. President Reagan had the enthusiastic support of South Carolina Republicans and, as elsewhere, it was unthinkable that any other Republican would seek to become the party's nominee. For South Carolina Democrats, the situation was not quite so predictable, but the entry of the state's junior Senator, Ernest F. Hollings, into the presidential sweepstakes meant that the state Democratic Party had rallied to his support, not only because of state pride in producing an aspirant for the presidency but also because Hollings had become one of the state's most successful and popular politicians, serving as state legislator, Lieutenant Governor, Governor, and, since 1966, U.S. Senator. There was not much doubt but that he would sweep through the party's 17 March caucuses.

The black vote in South Carolina, however, was not necessarily wholly in Hollings's pocket because South Carolina was "home" to not one but two presidential candidates. While Jesse Jackson had made Chicago the center for his Operation P.U.S.H. (People United To Serve Humanity), he had been born and raised in Greenville, South Carolina, and had often returned to the state to visit his mother. In January 1984, in the first of many visits to the state during the year, Jackson had returned to Greenville for a tearful visit to the housing project where he had grown up.[27] Jackson's symbolic candidacy had caught the imagination of many —especially younger— blacks, and he expected to pick up a respectable vote in the party caucuses, Still, Hollings had obtained early commitments from many black leaders, and he expected to obtain substantial black support.

Hollings had campaigned hard in both Iowa and New Hampshire, visiting each state numerous times, but he had especially concentrated on the New Hampshire primary as an opportunity for a "breakthrough" victory that might catapult him into a position of genuine contention. Three groups of South Carolinians (the "Ernest F. Hollings Home Team") had campaigned for Hollings in New Hampshire, canvassing 75,000 households,[28] and many in the Hollings camp were hopeful that his candidacy would get the boost that would mean national attention and status.

However, Hollings came in seventh in the New Hampshire primary, falling behind even George McGovern and Ronald Reagan (as a write-in) and earning only 3.5 percent of the primary vote. The defeat was devastating, particularly since it made it difficult for the Hollings candidacy to remain alive until the 13 March Super Tuesday primaries, three of which occurred in southern states (Alabama, Georgia, and Florida) where Hollings might be expected to do well. But with a poor showing in New Hampshire after an enormous personal effort on Hollings's part and after describing himself as the only "viable alternative" to Mondale,[29] his continued candidacy seemed unlikely to succeed. Within a few days after the New Hampshire primary Hollings, the candidate most strongly associated with the South, joined Alan Cranston and Reuben Askew and withdrew (on 1 March) from his quest for the presidency.[30]

Post-Hollings Maneuverings

With Hollings's withdrawal only two weeks before the 17 March Democratic precinct caucuses, South Carolina's 48 votes at the Democratic convention were suddenly available to other candidates. This two-week period evidenced essentially two major developments.

First, there was a groundswell of support for Gary Hart's burgeoning and momentarily exciting campaign for the nomination. Neither Hart nor Mondale had scheduled visits to the state during this period, and neither candidate changed his plans to try to capitalize on the changed circumstances; this was not surprising inasmuch as six primaries were to be held on 13 March, and, for Mondale particularly, these primaries were regarded as absolutely crucial to his candidacy. However, Hart's wife, Lee, did visit Charleston briefly the day before the caucuses in an effort to encourage the boomlet for Hart,[31], and full-page newspaper advertisements appeared in the state's major newspapers (while these ads did mention South Carolina, they were not especially designed for the state; they stressed Hart's general campaign themes on new leadership, the nuclear freeze, military strategy, and education). Skeleton campaign organizations were rapidly developed in six of the state's largest cities. Hollings himself joined Hart's camp by endorsing him for the Democratic nomination, and other prominent Democrats soon followed, including Mayor Joseph P. Riley, Jr., of Charleston, several state legislators, and former First District Representative Mendel Davis. Mayor Riley probably spoke for many South Carolinians when he observed that, "Senator Hollings was a candidate of the South," and therefore many "would naturally be influenced by who Senator Hollings thinks will be the best president."[32] Like other South Carolinians, Mayor Riley was not very familiar with Hart or the specifics of his platform: "My interest in Senator Hart isn't so much on the specific issues," he said, but on "a feeling that he's the man for the times. He's got what it takes." In an implicit reference to the view of many whites in the state that Walter Mondale was too liberal, Riley added that Hart possessed a "good, solid pragmatism. He isn't an ideologue, he's an idealist. He has a good solid vision of the future. . . . I think he can win in November."[33] The enthusiasm of many Democrats for Hart appeared to be actually based on a lack of enthusiasm for Mondale, and a candidate, any candidate, other than Mondale looked to have a better chance in November. Many Democrats saw Mondale as fatally linked to "special intersets"—particularly organized labor—in a state where such interests are generally not well-organized.

The second development during this two-week period was an intensive effort by Jesse Jackson. With the withdrawal of Hollings, Jackson's campaign manager in South Carolina (Walker Solomon) called for the Democratic Party's Executive Committee to adopt Jackson as the state's "favorite son," a status previously accorded Hollings who had received the full endorsement of the party. While some white members of the committee were resistant to the favorite son designation, Mondale, Hart, and Glenn supporters on the committee mutually agreed not to oppose it for fear of alienating black leaders, a recognition that a heavy black vote was absolutely essential to Democratic chances in the state.[34] One Jackson supporter, Billie Fleming of Manning, quite succinctly argued that,

> If Jesse Jackson were white, we wouldn't be facing this issue. There was not a single objection when Fritz Hollings was endorsed. For us to procrastinate on Jesse Jackson is an insult to the black people of this state, who have blindly followed the Democratic Party. If it weren't for black voters, some Democratic officeholders in this state wouldn't be there.[35]

A compromise was reached whereby the Executive Committee voted unanimously to "go on record as favoring Jesse Jackson as the South Carolina favorite son" candidate for President.[36] Although this was not the full endorsement that Hollings had obtained, Walker Solomon, chairman of Jackson's South Carolina campaign, said that he accepted it as "the best we could get."[37]

Of the three candidates given much chance of picking up significant support in the state (Mondale, Hart, and Jackson—Glenn was expected to withdraw, and did on 16 March), only Jackson devoted personal time to the state, making campaign stops in Charleston, Florence, and Georgetown just two days before the caucuses.[38] To an enthusiastic crowd of 600 in a black church in Charleston, Jackson sounded his general campaign theme that it was time to move "from the racial battleground to the economic common ground." As for Hart and Mondale, Jackson said the state should reject "Santa Claus politics," which he identified with both Hart and Mondale.[39] Earlier the same day state Senator Julian Bond of Georgia had attempted to rally Charleston blacks to Mondale; a very small crowd had shown up (about 40 persons)[40] in what was a nearly nonexistent Mondale campaign in the state.

As the caucus approached, party country chairpersons in both Spartanburg County (containing the city of Spartanburg and part of the Greenville SMSA) and Richland County (Columbia) observed that Jackson and Hart seemed to be running strongly.[41] Other county chairpersons indicated that the confusion following Hollings' withdrawal had left may Democrats undecided and that many of these would therefore vote for "uncommitted."[42] In fact, many party leaders called for Democrats to elect uncommitted slates rather than vote for particular candidates. The lone candidate to visit the state before the caucuses, Jackson, predicted that he would carry all six of the state's congressional districts.[43]

The Caucus-Convention Results

Under South Carolina's three-tiered system, those who attended the precinct caucuses chose delegates to county conventions; then the county conventions chose delegates to the state party convention, which in turn selected most (41 of 48) of the delegates to the national party convention in San Francisco. (The remaining seven delegates were "superdelegates," elected party officials who officially remained "uncommitted" until the national convention.) Thus, the precinct caucuses were only the beginning of considerable politicking.

At the caucuses themselves, the events of the two previous weeks were reflected in the results: With an estimated 40,000 people participating,[44] over half of the delegates selected to county conventions were uncommitted (53.2 percent), with Jesse Jackson leading (with

25 percent) among those willing to commit to a candidate. Hart came in behind Jackson with about half as many delegates (12.7 percent), and Mondale received only 9.1 percent.[45] Although Jackson led both Hart and Mondale, he fell short of his predictions of carrying the vote; Walker Solomon appeared to be the most disappointed among the three candidates' spokesmen: "I just don't understand why people can't stand up (and) be committed to a candidate. This bothers me."[46] Jackson's failure to obtain the overwhelming support of blacks is well-demonstrated by the all-black caucus in the suburban Columbia precinct of Greenview; there Jackson won 40 percent of the delegates but another 40 percent were uncommitted, including several prominent black leaders holding appointed or elective public office.[47] As elsewhere, older blacks and black leaders tended to be uncommitted or for Mondale; younger blacks tended to support Jackson.

The uncommitted stance of so many delegates reflected perhaps three considerations. First, there was considerable uncertainty as to which candidate might have the best chance at defeating Reagan. As the Horry County (Myrtle Beach) chairman, David Canty, put it, "If Donald Duck could beat Ronald Reagan, they'd vote for Donald DUck."[48] A second consideration was maximizing the state delegation's bargaining position at the national convention. Chesterfield County Chairman J. D. Jones contended that, "If there are enough uncommitted in San Francisco, we can wheel and deal and find somebody to beat Reagan. Ted Kennedy is a dynamic politician. They're holding back to see if something better won't come along or if somebody can't change their minds."[49] And, in addition, at least one county party chairman (Ronnie Cole of Anderson) publicly lamented the lack of a more moderate candidate in the race.[50] A third consideration was the lack of organization that hampered the efforts of those supporting both Hart and Mondale; Mondale's state chairman (Samuel Tenenbaum) noted after the caucuses that Mondale had had no organization in the state.[51]

At the county conventions held on 26 March, the results were similar to those at the precinct caucuses with only a few unpledged delegates moving to commit to a specific candidate.[52] Under party rules, a candidate had to have at least 20 percent of the delegates at the state convention to obtain representation in the state delegation to the Democratic National Convention; for both Hart and Mondale, therefore, it was crucial to pick up support from the uncommitted delegates in order to avoid losing out altogether in South Carolina. In an effort to avoid such a development, Joan Mondale visited the state two days before the state convention, stopping in both Charleston and Columbia to meet with delegates remaining uncommitted.[53]

At the Democratic state party convention held in the state capital on 14 April, all three candidates gained, with Jackson emerging with 17 delegates; Mondale and Hart each obtained six delegates; and 12 delegates remained uncommitted.[54] Even though Jackson emerged with the single largest bloc of delegates, Hart and especially Mondale had made major gains. Going into the state convention, Mondale did not have enough support for even a single delegate, but attracted enough support from previously uncommitted delegates to end up with six national convention delegates. (Hart had picked up five delegates, and Jackson three.)[55] In addition, Governor Richard Riley (one of the superdelegates), while going to the national convention as officially uncommitted, was known to be a good friend of Mondale (as well as of former President Jimmy Carter).

Thus, when the dust had settled on the nominating contests, which for South Carolina had effectively lasted only six weeks, the state's delegation to the Democratic National Convention was highly fragmented. For the Republicans, however, the party was unified, unanimously and enthusiastically supporting Ronald Reagan for renomination and reelection.

The National Conventions

For the Democrats, Mondale appeared to have enough delegates to win the nomination by the time of the July convention; not surprisingly, several of South Carolina's uncommitted delegates jumped on the Mondale bandwagon, and others who had been officially uncommitted but Mondale partisans all along (such as Governor Riley) announced their commitment to Mondale. Of the 22 uncommitted delegates, ten voted for Mondale (for a total of 16 delegate votes); the Governor, the Lieutenant Governor, the state House Majority Leader, and the chair and vice chair of the party, all officially uncommitted in April, voted for Mondale. But, even though the race was all but lost for Gary Hart, he nevertheless picked up an additional eight delegates (for a total of 13); the last-minute move toward Hart of the genuinely uncommitted was generated by the fears of some that Mondale could not win, a view evinced in part by Mondale's blunder in initially selecting Carter confidante Bert Lance as campaign manager. Jesse Jackson gained only two delegates, but still enough to leave him with the delegation's largest vote total (with 19 delegates); indeed, South Carolina was the only state to give Jackson a plurality of its delegates.[56]

South Carolina's Democratic delegates generally were optimistic about Mondale's choice of Geraldine Ferraro as his running mate.

Although conceding that she added "excitement" to the ticket, several wished that a conservative to moderate southerner had been chosen instead; one delegate only wished that Ferraro could have been from Texas (or some other southern state) instead of New York. Party chair William Youngblood acknowledged that "we've got a job ahead of us to" to sell the ticket in the South, adding "But I think we can do it."[57]

For the Republicans, the South Carolina delegation to the national convention in August was unified and unanimous, much like almost every other delegation, in support of the Reagan-Bush uncontested renominations. By convention's end, Roger Milliken, wealthy textile executive and long-time supporter of the South Carolina Republican Party, declared flatly that the Republican Party is "the majority party of the United States."[58]

THE CAMPAIGN

While considerable excitement had been generated among the Democrats by the six weeks of activity during the delegate-selection process in the spring and among black Democrats by the candidacy of Jesse Jackson, the fall campaign itself failed to stimulate much public interest in the state. In mid-September Don Fowler, Democratic national committeeman and former state party chairperson, noted that, "There is a lot of passivity about politics right now. I don't think people have really tuned into the campaign yet."[59] Unfortunately, for Mondale much of the South Carolina electorate never did tune in.

Mondale started in the state from behind and was never able to move from that position. An early poll for Mondale in the spring indicated that over 60 percent of the voters supported Reagan.[60] A Republican poll (by Houston pollster Lance Tarrance) in June found that even a Mondale-Hollings ticket would lose decisively in the state (56 percent for Reagan-Bush, 36 percent for Mondale-Hollings). Lee Atwater, a South Carolinian serving as deputy campaign manager for the national Reagan-Bush committee, interpreted the poll to mean that "Mondale has so much political baggage that Hollings or anyone else can't hold him up in South Carolina."[61] Other polls taken during the campaign reaffirmed the early indications. Two of these, taken in the Third and Sixth Congressional Districts, indicated large Reagan leads.[62] A statewide Republican survey in late September conducted by Detroit pollster Robert Teeter showed Reagan leading Mondale by 58 percent to 35 percent.[63] The Teeter survey showed

Reagan especially strong in urban areas (but still running ahead of Mondale in rural counties, although by reduced margins). But regardless of who took the survey or who commissioned it, the results were remarkable consistent: Reagan regularly attracted the support of nearly 60 percent of the state's electorate.[64]

In the face of a national Mondale strategy that concentrated on the northeast and midwest, the South Carolina Democratic state party chairman gamely insisted, publicly at least, that Mondale had a chance to win the state, that the state had not been "downgraded" in the presidential campaign, and that the bad news polls underrepresented an important part of the electorate—black Democrats.[65] Nevertheless, other Democrats on state and local tickets studiously avoided mentioning Mondale's name in their literature and speeches; as one of the state's best-known political reporters summarized the campaign, South Carolina Democrats were "running away" from Mondale rather than with him,[66] a survival tactic that many had mastered during the McGovern campaign in 1972. When Democratic incumbent Representative Butler Derrick, who was facing a little-known challenger, was asked if he hoped to ride Mondale's coattails, he replied, "Mondale's coattails in my district are about as long as those on my BVDs."[67] All three incumbent Democratic Representatives publicly gave negative assessments of the campaign by early October.[68] The state chair later noted that it was lonely at the top, that "at times I felt I was the Mondale campaign," although Democrats not on the ballot were at least somewhat supportive (Jesse Jackson cooperated fully with the campaign and spoke frequently on behalf of the ticket;[69] Governor Riley and Lieutenant Governor Michael Daniel made appearances for Mondale and the general Democratic ticket, including blitzing the state just before election day).[70]

The state Democratic Party strategy in 1984 was essentially to limit its losses. The Democratic leadership privately did not think that Mondale ever had a chance to carry South Carolina, and the national Mondale campaign chose not to use its resources in the state. Consequently, the state party concentrated its activities (phone banks, for example) primarily in the Fourth Congressional District (Greenville-Spartanburg) in an effort to help the strongest Democratic challenger in his campaign to unseat an incumbent Republican House member. Because the district's basic industry is textiles, an industry severely suffering from foreign competition and therefore not very sympathetic to Reagan administration free trade policies, the Democrats regarded their young, well-financed candidate (Greer attorney Jeff Smith) as having a fair chance of defeating even a three-term incumbent (Carroll Campbell, Reagan's statewide chairman in 1980).[71]

Mondale visited the state once, in a stopover in early August, but did not make any public campaign appearances; he visited Columbia to consult with old friend Governor Richard Riley and to solicit his advice on campaign strategy.[72] Standing on the Governor's lawn at the end of his visit, he told the press that he planned to return to the state "many times," a promise he was unable to fulfill. Mondale's one visit was later sharply criticized by Senator Hollings who contended that "Mondale was all confused when he came to South Carolina. The trip didn't make any sense to me. The Democrats were all huddled like a bunch of chickens in a hail storm at the governor's mansion. He should have gone up to the Piedmont and attacked Reagan on textiles."[73] Former President Jimmy Carter visited Columbia briefly in early September on behalf of his ecumenical Christian ministry project, Habitat for Humanity; he carefully avoided making any comment on the Mondale-Reagan race.[74]

The Reagan-Bush ticket was never in any trouble in South Carolina. Nevertheless, President Reagan, Nancy Reagan, George Bush, and former President Gerald Ford all visited the state during the campaign. Their efforts were to a large extent concentrated in the Fourth Congressional District and were designed to help the state's most closely challenged incumbent Republican representative.

Vice President Bush was the first to visit the state after the national conventions, a campaign stop that, unfortunately for Bush, coincided with the visit of Hurricane Diana. The impact of his Charleston campaigning on 11 September was therefore sharply eclipsed by the hurricane; Bush also made a campaign stop in Columbia later that same day, where he was questioned about a 1980 Reagan campaign promise to reduce textile imports.[75] (Bush had earlier visited the state in June to help kickoff a Republican voter registration drive in Greenville; however, his appearance was thought not to have been of much help to Republican Representative Carroll Campbell inasmuch as Bush at a press conference refused to endorse legislation freezing textile imports).[76] Former President Gerald Ford, in his visit to Greenville in early October on behalf of the Republican ticket, handled the textile issue by ignoring it.[77]

The Reagans, separately, visited the state in October. Nancy Reagan's visit to Columbia on 10 October lasted less than two hours and centered on a visit to a drug education project in an elementary school.[78] President Reagan's visit to Greenville on 15 October was designed to help Representative Campbell. Appearing before a crowd of 8,000 enthusiastic supporters at Greenville Technical College, Reagan essentially ignored the textile issue and focused his speech on Mondale instead; in addition, he contended that the nation needed "elected officials like Congressmen Campbell, Hartnett and Spence."[79]

The 1984 Republican campaign was a unified one as Senator Thurmond permitted his own campaign (for a fifth term to the U.S. Senate) to be integrated with that of the national ticket, something he had never allowed before.[80] Indeed, South Carolina was that rare state where Reagan could run on the coattails of a Republican expected to attract a level of support even higher than the presidential ticket.[81] By early November, nine of the state's 17 newspapers had made editorial endorsements in the presidential election (the other eight did not make endorsements because of corporate or other reasons); all nine endorsed Reagan-Bush.[82]

By election day eve, it was clear that the Democrat's campaign had never really caught fire. A "well known Democratic political consultant" was described by one of the state's leading political reporters as having summarized 1984 as "an incredible dead year here. It's going to go as predicted."[83]

RESULTS AND ANALYSIS

Results

1984 was a year of incumbents in South Carolina as the Reagan-Bush ticket, Strom Thurmond, and all six U.S. Representatives were decisively reelected with margins near or above 60 percent of the vote (see Table 6–1). President Reagan obtained a margin of more than 270,000 votes over Mondale and carried the state with 63.6 percent,

TABLE 6–1   Results of 1984 South Carolina Presidential, Senatorial, and Congressional Elections

Candidates	Percent of Vote	Vote Totals
President		
Reagan-Bush (R)*	63.6	615,815
Mondale-Ferraro (D)	35.6	344,459
Bergland-Lewis (L)	0.4	4,359
Dennis-Brownlee (A)	0.4	3,490
Serrett-Ross (UC)	0.1	682
Totals	100.1	968,805
U.S. Senate		
Strom Thurmond (R)*	66.8	644,815
Melvin Purvis, Jr. (D)	31.8	306,982
Stephen Davis (L)	1.4	13,333
Totals	100.0	965,130

TABLE 6–1   *(continued)*

Candidates	Percent of Vote	Vote Totals
U.S. House of Representatives		
First District		
Thomas F. Hartnett (R)*	61.7	103,288
Ed Pendarvis (D)	38.3	64,022
Totals	100.0	167,310
Second District		
Floyd D. Spence (R)*	62.1	108,085
Ken Mosely (D)	36.7	63,932
Cynthia E. Sullivan (L)	0.1	2,010
Totals	99.9	174,027
Third District		
Butler Derrick (D)*	58.4	88,917
Clarence E. Taylor (R)	40.6	61,739
Robert Madden (L)	1.0	1,510
Totals	100.0	152,166
Fourth District		
Carroll Campbell (R)*	63.9	105,139
Jeff Smith (D)	35.2	57,854
William Ray Pike (L)	0.9	1,431
Totals	100.0	164,424
Fifth District		
John Spratt (D)*	91.4	93,513
Dick Winchester (A)	4.5	4,593
Linda Blevins (L)	4.1	4,185
Totals	100.0	102,291
Sixth District		
Robin Tallon (D)*	59.9	97,329
Lois Eargle (R)	38.8	63,005
Hugh Thompson (L)	1.3	2,050
Totals	100.0	162,384

*Incumbent
R = Republican
D = Democrat
L = Libertarian
A = American
UC = United Citizens

Source: South Carolina State Election Commission, Columbia, South Carolina.

improving almost 13 percent on his 1980 margin over Jimmy Carter (Reagan won in 1980 with 50.7 percent). The number of counties won by the Democratic ticket shrank from 35 of the 46 counties in 1980 to only 12 small, largely rural counties in 1984 (see Figure 6–2).

Analysis: The Presidential Race

The Republicans have now won five of the last six presidential contests in South Carolina. In this era of at least a partial dealignment, it has become clear that at the presidential level the Democratic base now constitutes perhaps only 35 percent or so of the electorate, a base represented by blacks (27 percent of the electorate in 1984) and loyalist Democrats.

The two most important long-term political trends in the state

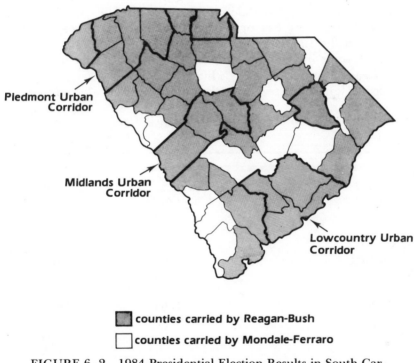

■ counties carried by Reagan-Bush

□ counties carried by Mondale-Ferraro

FIGURE 6–2   1984 Presidential Election Results in South Carolina, By County

Source: Developed from data from the South Carolina Election Commission, Columbia, South Carolina.

relate, first, to race, and, second, to a growing urban-suburban Republicanism. Both trends were confirmed by the 1984 election.

South Carolina blacks overwhelmingly supported the Democratic ticket in 1984. Although after the election there were questionable claims of substantially increased support for the Republican Party among blacks,[84] blacks appear to have given about the same level of support to Reagan as they did in 1980, that is, about 5 percent to 6 percent. A survey of the 22 precincts with black voter registration of 90 percent or higher in the three largest urban counties reveals that the Mondale vote ran at 93 percent (and even higher in precincts with black registration of 95 percent or more).[85] (This finding is consistent with the voting behavior of blacks across the South who supported Mondale by about 94.6 percent.)[86] Not surprisingly, those counties with large black populations were most likely to have supported Mondale (see Table 6–2). Of the state's ten counties with black voter majorities, nine were carried by Mondale. (In the tenth, Bamberg, with 50.7 percent black voter registration, Mondale won 49.9 percent of the vote.) Mondale's other three counties also had high levels of blacks in the electorate (ranging from 41.5 percent to 49.4 percent). In the final analysis, almost two-third's (62.7 percent) of Mondale's votes in the state were cast by blacks; nearly 98 percent of the Reagan vote was cast by whites.[87]

A second long-term trend confirmed by the 1984 election was the

TABLE 6–2   1984 Mondale Counties and Black Voter Registration

County	% Mondale Vote	% Black Registration
Allendale	58.0	59.3
Fairfield	56.7	53.8
McCormick	56.3	51.1
Jasper	54.7	52.3
Williamsburg	53.9	58.1
Clarendon	52.3	51.2
Lee	52.4	55.2
Marlboro	52.1	41.5
Hampton	51.9	51.2
Marion	51.8	49.4
Orangeburg	51.4	53.0
Edgefield	50.0*	47.2

*3-vote Mondale margin over Reagan

Source: Two-party vote percentage calculated from data from the South Carolina State Election Commission, Columbia, South Carolina.

Republicanism that has increasingly characterized urban and suburban areas since the mid-1960s. Reagan carried 34 counties, including all 12 counties in the three urban corridors of the state.
Indeed, of the six counties giving Reagan 70 percent or more, four
were urban or suburban counties (see Table 6–3). In addition, this
urban Republicanism is related to the increasing racial division between the two parties: The five counties with the lowest percentages
of blacks in their populations were among the six strongest Reagan
counties in the state. The two least black counties in the state (Lexington and Pickens), both suburban in character, gave Reagan his
highest percentages (a staggering 81.4 percent and 77.2 percent,
respectively). Finally, an examination of selected white urban-suburban precincts in the three largest counties indicates that both middle-class and working-class white precincts supported Reagan by large
majorities, with margins near or over 80 percent of the vote.[88] A
similar analysis by the Voter Education Project of one hundred precincts estimated that 82.8 percent of the whites in the state voted for
Reagan.[89] White support for Reagan was probably higher in South
Carolina than in any other state in the South or, indeed, any other
state in the nation with the possible exception of Mississippi.

Aside from these two long-term trends, at least three short-term
political forces also favored the Republicans in South Carolina in
1984. Registration and turnout, candidate images, and candidate
strategies all contributed to the Reagan landslide.

TABLE 6–3   1984 Ten Highest Percentage Reagan Counties
and Black Voter Registration

County	% Reagan Vote	% Black Registration
Lexington*	84.4	7.4
Pickens*	77.2	5.5
Greenville*	73.4	14.1
Aiken*	72.3	20.8
Oconee	72.1	7.6
Anderson	70.0	13.2
Berkeley*	69.7	28.1
Horry	69.5	17.3
Dorchester*	68.5	24.4
Cherokee	32.1	18.2

*Counties in one of the three urban corridors

Source: Two-party vote percentage calculated from data from the South Carolina
State Election Commission, Columbia, South Carolina.

Despite intensive drives by both parties to register voters likely to swell the ranks of their supporters, both registration and turnout ultimately favored the Republicans. Jesse Jackson led the effort to register Democrats in the state; he began by changing his own voter registration to South Carolina (he had left the state 20 years earlier) and followed up with rallies and speeches across the state, particularly in an effort to register as many blacks as possible.[90] The Republicans had been seeking to register voters "likely to vote Republican" for at least a year before the election; much of their September registration effort was concentrated in suburban shopping malls.[91] By the time the registration books had closed, however, it appeared that the Republicans had won the registration battle: The percentage of blacks in the electorate was slightly less (at 27.9 percent) than it had been for the 1980 election. The executive director of the Republican Party publicly observed that these figures "bode well for Republican candidates. Sooner or later, the Republican Party has got to get into the black community, but for the purposes of this election, these numbers are encouraging for us."[92]

Turnout, too, was favorable for the Republicans. While the state ranked last in the nation in turnout (at 40.1 percent of the eligible adult population, below 1980's 41.6 percent),[93] black turnout lagged substantially behind that of whites, 56.2 percent to 70.4 percent.[94] Not only had black turnout failed to reach the level that Democrats felt necessary to have a fighting chance in the election (at one point, the party's political director had optimistically hoped for an 89 percent turnout rate among blacks),[95] but black turnout was even lower than in 1980 (about 64 percent). Clearly, South Carolina blacks were not turned into passionate voters by the Democratic ticket.

Candidate images also favored the Republicans, at least among white voters. On the one hand, whites saw Reagan as a strong leader, a point conceded by the Democrats. As the Democratic state chair put it, the Democrats were never able to get the public beyond the perception that Reagan's message was "I am strong and I can lead."[96] A late September Republican survey found that Reagan had an approval rating of 64 percent, higher than any other state political rating except for Senator Thurmond (at 73 percent).[97] On the other hand, Mondale had a negative rating (48 percent negative to 40 percent positive), more negative than his running mate. Mondale's political baggage included his close association with Jimmy Carter ("in the public's mind, Mondale was Carter," as the state Democratic chair succinctly put it). In addition, leaders in both parties believe that Mondale was seen by many South Carolinians as being the prisoner of special interests—big labor, blacks, militant feminists, and gays, among others. Other than blacks, these are groups not at all well-represented in the state, to put it mildly. The support of organized labor probably hurt Mondale from the very beginning, as South Carolina has the least unionized work force in the nation (only 3.6 percent of the private sector work force are members of labor unions).[98]

Candidate strategy also played a role in the Republican victory. Reagan's amazing "50-state" strategy meant that even a small state like South Carolina (eight electoral votes) would get attention. In addition to the various visits of prominent Republicans, including Reagan, state Republicans allocated about $250,000 to the Reagan campaign, including $65,000 from the national Reagan-Bush committee. The Democrats spent far less, unwilling even to reveal the amount during the campaign.[99] On the Democratic side, Mondale's "industrial-core" strategy clearly relegated South Carolina to a diminished status. Moreover, the effort of some southern Democrats—in which South Carolina state Democratic chair Bill Youngblood was instrumental and which was developed at a well-publicized meeting of southern party chairs in Virginia in late August—to use Jesse Jackson to build a biracial populist coalition was not a successful strategy.[100] Indeed, top Republicans believe that Jackson's extensive activity in the state during the campaign only contributed to polarizing the electorate along racial lines. Senator Hollings in a statement just before the election argued that, as a consequence of the Jackson effort, "There will be a strong and bigger white Reagan vote. Instead of 'I am somebody,' it's 'I am some color.' It's not Rainbow. It's Blackbow."[101]

Analysis: The Senatorial Race

The only statewide election on the South Carolina ballot in 1984 other than the presidential contest was the race for the U.S. Senate. The Democrats early on despaired of defeating that legendary figure of contemporary South Carolina politics, Strom Thurmond, and therefore the party virtually defaulted. No Democrat of stature was willing to undertake what would be a difficult and probably hopeless contest, even though Thurmond was 81 in 1984. After election to his fourth term in 1978, Thurmond had said that term would be his last, but with his elevation to the chair of the Senate Judiciary Committee in 1981, Thurmond had changed his mind. In recognition of Thurmond's new prominence and his seeming invincibility at the polls, a number of prominent Democrats, including Charleston Mayor Joseph P. Riley, Jr., and former Governor John C. West, endorsed him for reelection.

The winner of the Democratic nomination was a political new-comer, the virtually unknown Melvin Purvis, Jr. (a Baptist minister from Florence and son of the famed FBI agent who had organized the attempt to capture bank robber John Dillinger in 1934). Purvis was cut adrift by the Democratic establishment, and he spent less than $12,000 on his campaign. Thurmond, on the other hand, spent more than $1.6.[102]

Thurmond's name on the ballot meant that the Republican's all-time top vote-getter would attract many to the Republican column. Thurmond did not disappoint, as he obtained almost 67 percent of the vote in carrying 45 of the state's 46 counties.[103] Although Thurmond carried nine of the state's ten black majority counties, he did not (as usual) attract widespread black support, although we estimate his black support at about double Reagan's (at 8 percent or 9 percent).[104] Despite his age, Thurmond has said he is "not closing the door" to yet another race in 1990, when he would be 87 years old.[105]

The only excitement in the Senate race was speculation, fueled by Jesse Jackson supporters, that Jackson was contemplating a write-in campaign against Thurmond. But on 1 August Jackson took himself out of the running, and, for all practical purposes, the campaign for the Senate was over.[106]

Analysis: The House Races

All six incumbent South Carolina Representatives were easily re-elected, retaining the 3–3 division between Republicans and Democrats. In each of the two districts (the Fourth and the Sixth) in which the challenging party entertained some hope of an upset, the incumbents were decisively reelected (see Table 6–1).

In the First District, incumbent Republican Tommy Hartnett was reelected with 61.7 percent of the vote, defeating former Charleston County Democratic chairman and real estate investor Ed Pendarvis. In a bitter campaign (with Vietnam veteran Pendarvis intimating that Hartnett had dodged the draft), Pendarvis spent only a little over 20 percent of what Hartnett was able to raise and spend.[107]

In the Second District, incumbent Republican Floyd Spence once again faced black Orangeburg physical education professor Ken Mosely. Mosely attracted national interest in his campaign as he was one of the few credible black candidates for Congress in the South.[108] However, despite a more aggressive, better-funded campaign, he could not overcome Spence's heavy support in suburban Lexington County, the state's most Republican county; Spence won an eighth term with 62 percent of the vote.

In the Third District, five-term incumbent Democrat Butler Derrick won 58 percent of the vote against little-known Republican Clarence Taylor in a race that Republicans virtually conceded to Derrick.

In the Fourth District, Democrats hoped to pick a seat held by a popular incumbent Republican, Carroll Campbell. Although the district (just three urban counties) is one of the more heavily Republican areas of the state, Democrats hoped that lawyer Jeff Smith could turn the Reagan administration's stand on textiles into a winning issue.[109] Attractive, from a prominent family, well-financed (largely with his own money), and with excellent political connections (his father, Verne Smith, is a state senator), Smith nevertheless obtained only 35 percent of the vote.

In the Fifth District, John Spratt was elected to a second term without Republican opposition, earning over 90 percent of the vote.

In the Sixth District, the Republicans hoped to pick up freshman Democrat Robin Tallon's seat with former Democrat and radio executive Lois Eargle. However, she was unable to overcome Tallon's base of black support in the state's most heavily black congressional district (about 40 percent of the electorate); Tallon was returned for a second term with nearly 60 percent of the vote.[110]

Conclusion: The Future
of South Carolina Party Politics

In 1984 both long-term and short-term trends ran against South Carolina Democrats at the level of presidential politics. The long-term trends meant that the Mondale-Ferraro candidacies started out from behind; and the short-term trends assured that the ticket would not be able to overcome them. Ronald Reagan was simply an incumbent President exceedingly popular among whites, almost regardless of party identification. Walter Mondale, on the other hand, was seen negatively by much of the electorate and, in addition, failed to create much political excitement, even among his natural constituencies.

That dealignment of South Carolina party politics at the presidential level has occurred is now beyond dispute. Whether white disengagement from the Democratic Party will substantially characterize the state's politics of the late 1980s at other levels remains an open question. The leadership of both parties see the next decade or so as pivotal, a period that may shape South Carolina party politics for decades to come. South Carolina Republicans see their ascendancy as "an evolutionary rather than a revolutionary process," but one that is now on the verge of coming to fruition.[111] Democrats, on the other hand, are working on finding a strategy to stop any further erosion and, they hope, to reverse it.

What is clear is that the politics of the state reflect considerable fluidity. Many whites have "dealigned" to the extent that they have moved away from the Democratic Party, although they have not yet committed themselves to the extent that would bestow majority status on the Republican Party. The mid- to late-1980s may prove decisive in this movement of the white electorate. If the economy is characterized by growth and low rates of inflation, if the public continues to see Republican policies as responsible for such growth, and if the Republican Party can recruit attractive candidates for office, the stage may be set for a long period of Republican ascendancy. Indeed, the Republican leadership sees the 1986 gubernatorial election as a key indicator: If the Republicans capture the governorship with either Representative Tommy Hartnett (who has all but announced for the post) or Representative Carroll Campbell (who may run for the Senate against Fritz Hollings to avoid a brutal primary campaign with Hartnett), majority status for the Republican Party could emerge as early as the 1990s. In this scenario, as Democrats holding local office retired, the Republicans would one by one win many or most of these open seats; in addition, some other Democratic officeholders would probably switch over in an effort to assure their political survival, inasmuch as many might not survive Democratic primaries with increasing proportions of black voters.

Such a success for the Republican Party would probably result in a state party system somewhat reminiscent of V. O. Key's description of South Carolina's politics as "the politics of color." With the inability of the Republicans to penetrate the black community (despite at least some effort), the Republican Party would continue to be overwhelmingly white, and the Democratic Party would become overwhelming black. The party system would come to reflect a dramatic political racial polarization at a time, ironically enough, when racial discrimination at social and economic levels has significantly eroded.

South Carolina Democrats, while gloomy over the failures of the party at the presidential level over the last 20 years, nevertheless point to their continuing strengths: the party still holds all state constitutional offices and commanding but diminished margins in the state legislature (36 to ten in the upper house; 97 to 27 in the lower house); in 1984 the party won about 78 percent of all offices contested in the state. The task for the Democrats will be to hold the party's constituencies in the black community and in the more rural parts of the state and to develop strategies to appeal to South Carolina's working class (which, thus far, has failed to respond to the idea of a biracial populism) and its emergent white middle class. Whether the Democratic Party of this Sunbelt state can persuade whites (as it has blacks) that it—not the Republican Party—is the party of economic upward mobility is a formidable task. In the view of the party's state chairman (who is himself mentioned as an attractive candidate for a variety of elective offices), national Democrats must act more like South Carolina Democrats: "Run fiscally sound ships, be very attuned to economic growth and never forget they are the party of social justice."[112]

Unlike Democrats in other states, South Carolina Democrats—despite their protestations of underlying strength—are clearly worried and have publicly said so. Senator Hollings and Representative Derrick, among others, were concerned about the party's appeal long before the November elections. As Hollings has put it in his usual pithy style, the task is not to reconcile the various interests currently within the party but to "reconcile the Democratic Party with a majority of Americans. There is a majority out there. It's not armbands and alphabet groups. It's individuals and families."[113]

The 1984 presidential election in South Carolina clearly represented a Republican surge, but whether that surge is a prelude to realignment is still too soon to tell. But the signs of Democratic decline and Republican ascendancy are readily apparent. The next decade will likely answer this most fundamental question of contemporary South Carolina politics.

NOTES

1. Donald L. Fowler, *Presidential Voting in South Carolina, 1948–1964* (Columbia: Bureau of Governmental Research and Service, University of South Carolina, 1966), 14. See generally V. O. Key, Jr., *Southern Politics in State and Nation* (New York: Knopf, 1949), 130–55.

2. Chester Bain, "South Carolina: Partisan Prelude," in *The Changing Politics of the South,* ed. William C. Havard (Baton Rouge: Louisiana State University Press, 1972), 606. This and the following paragraph draw on Fowler, *Presidential Voting;* Bain, "South Carolina"; and William V. Moore, "Parties and Electoral Politics in South Carolina," in *Government in the Palmetto State,* ed. Luther F. Carter and David S. Mann (Columbia: Bureau of Government Research and Service, University of South Carolina, 1983), 45–60. See also Laurence W. Moreland, Robert P. Steed, and Tod A. Baker, "Regionalism in South Carolina Politics," in *Government in the Palmetto State,* 5–26.

3. David Duncan Wallace, *South Carolina: A Short History* (Chapel Hill: University of North Carolina Press, 1951), 687–91.

4. Bureau of the Census, *Census of Population: 1950* (Vol. 2, Characteristics of the Population, Part 40: South Carolina) (Washington, DC: Department of Commerce, 1952), 23.

5. Key, *Southern Politics,* 142–50.

6. Bureau of the Census, *Census of Population: 1950,* 15; and *South Carolina Statistical Abstract, 1981* (Columbia: South Carolina Division of Research and Statistical Services, South Carolina Budget and Control Board, 1981), 204.

7. Julian J. Petty, *The Growth and Distribution of Population in South Carolina* (Columbia: State Council for Defense, Industrial Development Committee, issued as Bulletin No. 11 of the South Carolina State Planning Board 1943), 130–35. In the 1940s two-thirds of the state's population still lived in rural areas, half of these on farms. Bureau of the Census, *Census of Population: 1950,* 23.

8. Bureau of the Census, *Census of Population: 1970* (Vol. 1, Characteristics of the Population, Part 42: South Carolina) (Washington, DC: Department of Commerce, 1973), 127.

9. Neal R. Peirce, *The Deep South States of America* (New York: Norton, 1972), 417–18.

10. Jack Bass, *Porgy Comes Home: South Carolina After Three Hundred Years* (Charleston, SC: R. L. Bryan, 1972), 81–84.

11. Peirce, *The Deep South States,* 418; and *South Carolina Statistical Abstract, 1981,* 51.

12. *South Carolina Statistical Abstract, 1981,* 229.

13. Ibid., 149.

14. Edward L. McLean, *Reference Tables: Net Migration, 1960–1970, By Age, Sex and Race for South Carolina Counties* (Clemson, SC: Agricultural Experiment Station, Clemson University, 1976), 2–3, 33–36.

15. *South Carolina Statistical Abstract, 1981,* 202.

16. Jack Bass and Walter DeVries, *The Transformation of Southern Politics* (New York: Basic Books, 1976), 498, 502.

17. *South Carolina Statistical Abstract, 1981,* 202.

18. Bureau of the Census, *Statistical Abstract of the United States, 1980,* 101st ed. (Washington, DC: Department of Commerce, 1980), 514.

19. Key, *Southern Politics,* 130–55.

20. Ibid., 130–31.

21. Ibid., 329–44.

22. Bain, "South Carolina," 607.

23. For further discussion of the events described here and in the following three paragraphs, see generally Bain, "South Carolina," and Moore, "Parties and Electoral Politics."

24. Moreland et al., "Regionalism in South Carolina Politics," 25–26.

25. Bain, "South Carolina."

26. Laurence W. Moreland, Robert P. Steed, and Tod A. Baker, "Ideological and Issue Orientations Among South Carolina Party Activists," paper presented at the 1981 annual meeting of the South Carolina Political Science Association, April 11, 1981, Spartanburg, South Carolina.

27. Columbia *The State*, 29 January 1984, 1–C. *The State*, South Carolina's largest daily and published in the state capital (Columbia), offers by far the best coverage of state political news of any newspaper in the state.

28. Charleston *News and Courier*, 20 February 1984, 15–A.

29. Columbia *The State*, 24 February 1984, 9–A.

30. *New York Times*, 2 March 1984, 1.

31. Charleston *News and Courier*, 16 March 1984, 14–A.

32. Charleston *Evening Post*, 13 March 1984, 2–A; Charleston *News and Courier*, 13 March 1984, 1–B.

33. Ibid.

34. Columbia *The State*, 11 March 1984, 1–A, 9–A.

35. Ibid.

36. Ibid.

37. Ibid.

38. Charleston *News and Courier*, 15 March 1984, 1–A.

39. Ibid., 16 March 1984, 1–A.

40. Ibid.

41. Columbia *The State*, 11 March 1984, 4–B.

42. Ibid.

43. Charleston *News and Courier*, 16 March 1984, 1–A.

44. *Congressional Quarterly*, 24 March 1984, 653.

45. Charleston *News and Courier*, 19 March 1984, 1–B; 26 March 1984, 1–B. These percentages reflect reporting from about 80 percent of the precincts. The Democratic Party never updated the precinct caucus results to include all precincts. See Charleston *News and Courier*, 27 March 1984, 1–B.

46. Columbia *The State*, 18 March 1984, 1–A.

47. Ibid., 18 March 1984, 8–A.

48. Charleston *News and Courier*, 19 March 1984, 1–A.

49. Ibid.

50. Ibid.

51. Columbia *The State*, 18 March 1984, 7–A.

52. Charleston *News and Courier*, 27 March 1984, 1–B.

53. Ibid., 12 April 1984, 10–C.

54. Ibid., 18 April 1984, 12–B.

55. Ibid.

56. *Congressional Quarterly*, 21 July 1984, 1799; Charleston *News and Courier*, 19 July 1984, 3–A; 20 July 1984, 10–A.

57. Columbia *The State*, 13 July 1984, 12–A. After the various disclosures about the Ferraro-Zaccaro finances, the party chair was less hopeful. Interview with William Youngblood, Democratic state party chair, 27 March 1985.

58. Columbia *The State*, 26 August 1984, 2–C.

59. Ibid., 16 September 1984, 12–A.

60. Youngblood interview, 27 March 1985.

61. Columbia *The State*, 2 July 1984, 1–C.

62. A Robert Teeter poll for the National Republican Congressional Committee in September indicated commanding leads for both Fourth District incumbent Republican Representative Carroll Campbell and for Reagan; Reagan's margin over Mondale was 65–32, greater than his margin (57–37) in a similar April survey. Columbia *The State*, 16 September 1984, 1–D. A poll taken for Sixth District Democratic incumbent Representative Robin Tallon in September by Public Opinion Research showed him overwhelming ahead of his Republican challenger; the same survey showed Reagan defeating Mondale by 58 percent to 27 percent. Columbia *The State*, 6 October 1984, 17–A. A poll by President Reagan's pollster, Richard Wirthlin, in early August indicated that the South was Reagan's strongest region and that as of August, Reagan would likely sweep the South. Charleston *Evening Post*, 9 August 1984, 3–A.

63. Columbia *The State*, 4 October 1984, 8–C.

64. These results were consistent across the South; a late-July Darden Research Corp. telephone poll in nine southern states, including South Carolina, found a 60–34 Reagan margin. Darden commented, "The lasting effect of the Democratic Convention in the South is a washout in terms of the presidential race." Similarly, a Louis Harris poll indicated a large Reagan margin (56–43); Harris concluded that the South was Reagan's strongest region and that Mondale was likely wasting his time seeking votes in the South. Columbia *The State*, 5 August 1984, 8–A.
Early in the campaign, the state's congressional delegation was generally not very hopeful about Mondale's chances either in the state or throughout the nation. One of the first South Carolina elected officials to endorse Mondale, U.S. Representative John Spratt, commented, "No one in the House is optimistic about his prospects." Columbia *The State*, 7 September 1984, 19–A.

65. Columbia *The State*, 4 October 1984, 9–C.

66. Ibid., 23 September 1984, 4–B. The reporter was Lee Bandy of the newspaper's Washington bureau; his story was entitled "Democratic Candidates Speak Softly of Mondale."

67. Ibid.

68. Ibid., 7 October 1984, 23–A.

69. Youngblood interview, 27 March 1985.

70. Columbia *The State*, 28 September 1984, 3–D; 3 November 1984, 1–C. In his November appearances Governor Riley insisted that Mondale was the "conservative" choice because Mondale would not pursue "wild and reckless" budget deficits and the nuclear arms race.

71. Youngblood interview, 27 March 1985.

72. Columbia *The State*, 8 August 1984, 1–C; 9 August 1984, 1–A; 10 August 1984, 1–A; Charleston *News and Courier*, 8 August 1984, 1–B; 9 August 1984, 1–A.

73. Columbia *The State*, 7 October 1984, 23–A. Mondale's daughter, Eleanor, visited Columbia on 21 September for a brief visit on behalf of her father. Columbia *The State*, 22 September 1984, 1–B.

74. Ibid., 2 September 1984, 1–D.

75. Charleston *News and Courier*, 12 September 1984, 1–A; Columbia *The State*, 12 September 1984, 1–C.

76. Columbia *The State*, 8 July 1984, 4–B.

77. Ibid., 6 October 1984, 11–A.

78. Ibid., 10 October 1984, 1–A.

79. Columbia *The State*, 16 October 1984, 1–A; Charleston *News and Courier*, 16 October 1984, 5–A.

80. Telephone interview with Republican National Committeeman John Courson, 18 March 1984.

81. See, for example, the Thurmond advertisement in the Columbia *State*, 5 November 1984, 6–A.

82. Columbia *The State*, 4 November 1984, 7–D.

83. The consultant was quoted by Lee Bandy in the Columbia *State*, 4 November 1984, 4–B.

84. A postelection survey of only 300 voters by a Columbia marketing firm, Metromark Market Research, suggested that nearly 20 percent of South Carolina blacks voted for the Republican ticket. Columbia *The State*, 18 November 1984, 4–B. That survey, however, does not at all square with actual voting statistics from heavily black precincts as indicated here.

85. Percentages calculated from data obtained from the South Carolina State Election Commission, Columbia, South Carolina.

86. Voter Education Project, *What Blacks in the South Did on Election Day, 1984* (Atlanta: Voter Education Project, 1984), 6.

87. Voter Education Project, "Blacks Accounted for Over 60% of Mondale's Vote and Under 3% for Reagan's Vote in S. Carolina," press release dated 20 November 1984 (Atlanta, Georgia).

88. Percentages calculated from data obtained from the South Carolina State Election Commission, Columbia, South Carolina.

89. Voter Education Project, *What Blacks in the South Did*, 14.

90. Columbia *The State*, 13 September 1984, 1–D; 8 September 1984, 1–C.

91. Columbia *The State*, 10 September 1984, 2–B; Charleston *Evening Post*, 2 October 1984, 1–A.

92. Columbia *The State*, 30 October 1984, 1–C.

93. U.S. Bureau of the Census estimates, reported in the Columbia *State*, 10 November 1984, 5–C.

94. Voter Education Project, *What Blacks in the South Did*, 14.

95. Columbia *The State*, 21 October 1984, 4–B.

96. Youngblood interview, 27 March 1984.

97. Columbia *The State*, 4 October 1984, 8–C.

98. In 1983 private sector union membership stood at only 51,816, down even from the previous year. Charleston *News and Courier*, 4 September 1984, 6–A.

99. Ibid., 24 September 1984, 5–A.

100. Charleston *News and Courier*, 16 September 1984, 18–A; Columbia *The State*, 21 October 1984, 4–B; *New York Times*, 1 September 1984, 1.

101. Columbia *The State*, 21 October 1984, 4–B. A Gallup survey indicated that, across the South as a whole, 19 percent of the whites said that they were less likely

to vote for Mondale because of Jackson. Reported in Charleston *News and Courier*, 31 August 1984, 2–A.

102. Purvis spent $11,760; Thurmond, $1,638,467. Data provided by the Federal Election Commission (Washington, DC), June 1985. See also Columbia *The State*, 8 July 1984, 4–B; Charleston *Evening Post*, 18 December 1984, 9–A. Less than a month before the election, Purvis had been able to raise and spend less than $8,000. Charleston *News and Courier*, 4 November 1984, 1–E.

103. Calculated from data provided by the South Carolina State Election Commission, Columbia, South Carolina. The one county carried by the Democratic nominee was Fairfield, one of the ten black majority counties.

104. Based on an analysis of data in selected precincts with black registration of 90 percent or higher.

105. Columbia *The State*, 6 November 1984, 1–C.

106. Ibid., 2 August 1984, 1–A.

107. Charleston *News and Courier*, 22 December 1984, 2–C.

108. *Congressional Quarterly*, 13 October 1984, 2589.

109. Columbia *The State*, 7 October 1984, 4–B.

110. *Congressional Quarterly*, 13 October 1984, 2590.

111. Telephone interview with the South Carolina Republican chairman, Dr. George Graham, 5 April 1985.

112. Charleston *News and Courier*, 2 December 1984, 22–A.

113. Columbia *The State*, 15 July 1984, 4–B.

Part III

The Rim South

7

Texas

Dennis S. Ippolito

The 1984 election in Texas was a Republican Party victory of unprecedented and unexpected scope. President Reagan, as expected, carried the state, although the dimensions of his victory were perhaps surprising. Reagan built his 64 percent–36 percent margin by winning handily in every region of the state, in all of its large cities, and indeed in all but a handful of its 254 counties. More importantly, the Reagan victory in Texas was accompanied by major Republican advances in congressional, state legislative, and even local contests. It was this unexpected Republican strength down the ticket that distinguished the 1984 Texas election results from, for example, the 1972 landslide in Texas or the 1984 outcome in most other states.

Whether the 1984 election represents a widespread realignment of partisan voting patterns in Texas is, of course, problematical. It would appear, however, that President Reagan's personal popularity alone cannot explain the profound and possibly lasting changes in party preference and voting that have occurred in Texas. It is clear that population changes over the past two decades have created a very different electorate. Migration into Texas has simultaneously strengthened the Republican Party and the liberal wing of the Democratic Party. Within the state, moreover, the balance of political power has shifted from rural areas to urban-suburban centers. Long-term electoral trends reveal a broadening Republican base, along with sharpening liberal-conservative tensions in the Democratic Party. The 1984 election possibly adds to this a greatly decreased insulation between national and state politics.

Alterations in the Texas political landscape may also be suggestive in terms of regional politics. After an overwhelming Democratic victory in statewide races in 1982, there was a good deal of confidence among Democrats about 1984. National Democratic leaders hoped to pick up the U.S. Senate seat held by John Tower. Mondale forces looked to Texas as, first, a crucial check against the Hart challenge and, subsequently, as a possible breakthrough in the South. Texas, in other words, was viewed as among the more promising Democratic environments in the South. What occurred instead was an erosion of previously strong barriers between presidential and nonpresidential voting in Texas, an erosion that was paralleled, if at all, only in North Carolina. Why and how this took place may provide some indications about the future of party competition in not only Texas but in the rest of the South.

RECENT POLITICAL HISTORY

Over the past three decades, electoral politics in Texas has changed dramatically. One-party Democratic control at all political levels has been replaced by shifting patterns of interparty competition for major offices. In presidential elections, Texas has produced marginal Democratic victories (with the exception of the Johnson-Goldwater race), as compared to very strong Republican majorities. Gubernatorial and U.S. Senate races have featured some highly competitive interparty contests, as well as some Democratic landslides. Texas Republicans have held a respectable, if distinctly minority, share of U.S. House and state legislative seats for much of the past decade but are still unable to mount serious challenges in many congressional and state legislative districts. And outside metropolitan areas, Republican strength in local election has been virtually nonexistent.

The evolution of Texas politics is taking place against a rapidly changing demographic backdrop. From 1940–80, Texas' population increased from less than 6.5 million to nearly 15 million.[1] Between 1970 and 1980, population growth in Texas was more than two-and-one-half times the national average.[2] Texas now ranks third in population size behind California and New York and is expected to pass the latter by the end of the 1980s.

Demographic Changes

Rapid population growth in Texas has coincided with substantial urbanization. The 26 standard metropolitan statistical areas (SMSAs) in the state account for more than 80 percent of the population, with more than 40 percent being clustered in the Dallas–Fort Worth and Houston-Galveston areas alone.[3] There is, in addition, an unusual degree of racial and ethnic diversity. Roughly one-third of the total population is black (12 percent) or Hispanic (21 percent).[4] These two groups also represent 28.8 percent of the voting age population, although their lower registration levels reduce this to about 22 percent.[5] This still represents a major increase over the early 1970s, and minority voters have become an especially important component of the Democratic Party's primary electorate.[6]

While Texas once lagged behind national averages on major socioeconomic indicators, these differences have largely disappeared. Median years of education, for example, are almost identical for adult Texans and the adult population nationwide.[7] In 1982 per capita income in Texas ($11,419) was higher than the national average ($11,106) and also the highest among the 13 southern states.[8] The unemployment rate during 1984 was considerably lower in Texas than nationally and also lower than in most southern states.[9] There are, of course, still rather marked disparities within Texas between the "Anglo" and minority populations on these and related indices, but considerable progress has been achieved in erasing the economic and educational disparities between Texas and the rest of the nation.

Political Changes

If Texas has become less "southern" and more "national" in its demographic composition, its political patterns are not so easily characterized. Texas is no longer a one-party state, but serious competition between the parties has typically been limited to certain offices and certain areas. The most striking break with the past has occurred in presidential voting, and here Texas-national comparisons are instructive.

Presidential elections

For the first half of this century, the Democratic Party dominated presidential voting in Texas. From 1900–48, Republican presidential candidates in Texas averaged just over 20 percent of the total vote, nearly 30 percentage points below their average share of the national vote. Excluding the 1928 election, which produced short-term aberrations in much of the South, the Republican Party was not even minimally competitive in Texas. With the breakthrough elections of 1952 and 1956, however, presidential voting in Texas has tracked the national two-party vote very closely (see Table 7–1). The differential of the earlier period has not only disappeared, but a Republican advantage has begun to emerge.

The dimensions of the reversal in Texas are impressive. Using the total vote for President, the average Republican percentage for the period 1952–84 is just over 50 percent, both nationally and in Texas. The Republican presidential candidate has carried Texas in five of the nine elections, while winning six elections nationwide. The only case in which Texas has not mirrored the national result was in 1968, when Hubert Humphrey received a plurality of votes in Texas, while Richard Nixon gained a bare plurality nationally. Even in this instance, however, the difference between the Republican share of the total vote in Texas and across the nation was quite small—3.5 percentage points. The largest differential in party voting during any single election was only 5.5 percent (in 1972), and in that instance the Republican share in Texas was higher than the national result. In 1980 the Republican presidential vote in Texas was again above

TABLE 7–1   Presidential Voting, Nationwide and Texas, 1952–84

	Republican Percentage of Total Vote		Differential Texas-National
	National	Texas	
1952	55.1	53.1	−2.0
1956	57.4	55.3	−2.1
1960	49.5	48.5	−1.0
1964	38.5	36.5	−2.0
1968[a]	43.4	39.9	−3.5
1972	60.7	66.2	+5.5
1976	48.4	48.0	−0.4
1980[b]	50.7	55.3	+4.6
1984[c]	59.1	63.6	+4.5

[a]George Wallace received 19.0 percent of the vote in Texas, compared to 13.5 percent nationwide.

[b]John Anderson received 2.5 percent of the vote in Texas, compared to 6.6 percent nationwide.

[c]Based on complete, but unofficial returns.

the national vote share (55.3 percent versus 50.7 percent) and was eclipsed, among southern states, only by Florida. In 1984 the Republican margin in Texas was again almost 5 percentage points greater than nationwide. This time, Texas and South Carolina had the second-highest Republican presidential vote shares in the South, with Florida just barely ahead.

In three of the last four presidential elections, then, Texas has produced overwhelming Republican victories. With the national results only slightly less one-sided, this is not particularly striking. It does reflect, moreover, a broader realignment of presidential voting in the South. In Texas and through much of the South, the question is how deeply into state and local elections this presidential realignment will proceed. The evidence has been mixed in Texas, at least up until 1984 when the pace of realignment accelerated rather markedly.

Statewide elections

Below the presidential level, interparty competition has been highly variable. The Republican Party usually manages to do reasonably well in major statewide races, but it has not achieved parity, and its disadvantages become more pronounced with less prominent offices. In gubernatorial races, for example, Republican candidates have received more than 45 percent of the vote in four of the last five elections.[10] In 1978 the Republicans won the governor's race with just over 50 percent of the vote, but the Democratic Party regained control four years later by a solid margin. (By way of comparison, the Republican gubernatorial vote from 1946–66 averaged less than 20 percent.)

U.S. Senate races have also moved into a more competitive range. After decades of futile candidacies, the Republican Party in 1960 managed to capture 40 percent of the vote. The following year, John Tower, who had been the Republican candidate in 1960, won a special election for Lyndon Johnson's vacated seat and subsequently was reelected three times. Democratic control of Texas' other Senate seat has been uninterrupted, although the Republican vote share has averaged almost 45 percent over the last four elections. While incumbency has been an asset to both parties in every general election over the past two decades, it has apparently been more effective on the Democratic side. John Tower's margin was impressive in 1966 (56.4–43.6 percent) but declined in 1972 and almost disappeared in 1978. Lloyd Bentsen, who ousted Ralph Yarborough in the 1970 Democratic primary, received 53.5 percent of the vote in the general election, increased his margin in 1976, and widened it to almost 3–2 in 1982.

Bentsen's performance in 1982 created some optimism among Democrats about the prospects for capturing Tower's seat in 1984. These prospects were presumably enhanced when Tower announced that he would not seek reelection. Instead, the 1984 U.S. Senate race was the worst defeat ever suffered by a Democratic senatorial candidate in Texas. Phil Gramm, the Republican nominee, captured almost 60 percent of the vote, running only several percentage points behind President Reagan throughout most of the state.

In 1982, Democrats also swept—as usual—the other statewide races, such as Lieutenant Governor and Attorney General. For the nine contested statewide offices, the Republican vote averaged just under 40 percent. While not impressive by any conventional standard of interparty competition, this was a pronounced improvement over Republican performances of one or two decades earlier.

The 1982 election races also illustrated a Republican dilemma. By fielding challengers against entrenched Democratic incumbents in the U.S. Senate and Lieutenant Governor races, for example, the Republican generated vigorous reelection campaigns by Lloyd Bentsen and William P. Hobby, both of whom captured approximately 60 percent of the popular vote. That vote, moreover, represented an increase of more than 800,000 voters over the 1978 election. The Republican gubernatorial candidate, William Clements, added almost 300,000 votes to his winning 1978 total, but the additional turnout swamped this improvement. Clements ran ahead of any other Republican candidate in 1982 but still lost by a 54–46 percent margin, with the turnout increase playing a major role in his defeat.

Legislative elections

Below the statewide level, Democratic dominance has been reduced but hardly erased. The first Republican victory in a U.S. House race during this century occurred in 1954, while exclusive Democratic control of the state legislature was broken in 1950. Since that time, there has been a very gradual, modest improvement in Republican representation.

The Texas delegation to the U.S. House, for example, has grown from 23 seats during the 1960s to 27 seats currently. Perhaps as many as half of these seats are distinctly one-party Democratic, while two others (West Houston and North Dallas) are among the strongest Republican congressional districts in the nation. The range of competition for the remainder varies. The 1982 election produced an overall 22–5 Democratic advantage, while changed to 21–6 the following year with Representative Phil Gramm's resignation from the Democratic Party and subsequent reelection as a Republican. And additional Republican gains in 1984 make the ratio 17 Democrats and 10 Republicans for the 99th Congress.

During the 1970s, the number of House Republicans from Texas ranged from a low of two (in 1976) to a peak of four (in 1972 and 1978). The fluctuations for the 1980s will likely be at a much higher range. The combination of traditional Democratic strength, and a redistricting plan favoring the Democratic Party,[11] was thought to preclude any substantial change in the composition of the House delegation, but the 1984 congressional results have obviously altered the competitive balance.

Republican gains in state legislative races have also come very gradually. During the 1970s, Republicans moved up to about 20 percent of the state House and Senate seats. After the 1982 election, the composition of the Texas House of Representatives stood at 114 Democrats and 36 Republicans, while the Democratic edge in the Senate stood at 26–5. The 1984 Texas House elections, however, followed the pattern for congressional elections. A surprising number of seemingly entrenched incumbents were defeated, and the party ratio moved to 97–53. Moreover, House Democratic leaders have predicted that an additional six to ten House members will switch to the Republican Party before the 1986 election.[12] Members of the Texas Senate serve four-year terms, with one-half of the seats up for reelection every two years. In 1984 Republicans contested only four of the 15 Senate seats and made a net gain of one seat.

There are still a number of House and Senate districts where Republicans are simply not competitive, as well as a considerably smaller number that are strongly Republican. Even with the recent Republican gains, Democratic control of the state legislature is hardly in jeopardy. But these state legislative advances are an extremely important development for the Texas Republican Party. If Republicans can hold on to and perhaps even expand these gains, as well as those in the U.S. House, the party will have moved to a competitive stage that seemed unlikely as recently as a few years ago.

Two-Party Politics

The political landscape in Texas has altered a good deal over the past four decades. Realignment at the presidential level is the most visible expression of this alteration. The subsequent impact of this realignment on congressional, state, and local elections has been gradual but nevertheless significant. Indeed, the impact might have been greater had the Democratic Party not been able to insulate state elections from presidential politics. When four-year terms were instituted for the Governor and other state officials in 1971, the Democratic leadership in the state legislature delayed the new cycle until the off-year elections in 1974. In addition, Democratic control of the state legislature has been used for partisan advantage in the redistrictings following the 1970 and 1980 censuses.

The lag in realignment below the Presidency, however, is perhaps best explained by the lingering presence of conservative Democrats in many parts of the state. This has often tended to mute interparty differences and thereby to make it much more difficult for Republican challengers. In 1982, for example, the Republican Party was simply unable to persuade traditionally conservative Democratic voters that their major nominees—Lloyd Bentsen for U.S. Senator, Mark White for Governor, and William P. Hobby for Lieutenant Governor—were "liberals." Two years later, however, the liberal label was effectively applied to the top of the Democratic ticket—not only to Walter Mondale but also to U.S. Senate nominee Lloyd Doggett— and the resulting polarization of Democratic voters produced Republican gains all the way down the ticket.

The central point, then, is that demographic and political changes have made the Republican Party a political force. A more affluent population provides it with a secure socioeconomic foundation. At the same time, the growing influence of minorities within the Democratic Party has exacerbated the conflict between liberal and conservative Democrats. The ideological splits within the Texas Democratic Party—and between conservative Texas Democrats and the national Democratic Party—have provided Republican candidates with abundant opportunities to appeal to dissatisfied Democrats. The Texas Republican Party has begun to develop an effective and sophisticated organization and also has access to substantial amounts of campaign finance, which makes it easier to recruit good candidates and mount serious campaigns. The combination of Democratic factionalism, socioeconomic change, and attractive Republican presidential candidates that has changed Texas politics over the past three decades shows no sign of disappearing.

THE 1984 NOMINATING CONTESTS

The spring primaries in Texas revealed a strong consensus among Republicans, while reinforcing the ideological and geographical splits on the Democratic side. The Republican presidential primary was a mere formality, while the Republican U.S. Senate primary produced a clearcut winner. For the Democratic Party, Walter Mondale eventually gained some two-thirds of the 200-member Texas delegation to the Democratic National Convention, but his victory came amidst confusion and controversy over delegate selection procedures. The Democratic U.S. Senate primary produced a virtual tie among three candidates. The required runoff between the top two candidates was equally close. The primary and runoff between these candidates were decided by only 2,500 votes out of the 2.5 million cast in both contests, and the split between liberal and conservative Democrats could not have been sharper. In a state where, as usual, Democratic primary turnout dwarfed Republican turnout, postprimary polls soon showed a definite Republican advantage in both the presidential and senatorial contests.

The Republican Primaries

President Reagan had only narrowly defeated George Bush in the 1980 Republican presidential primary. In 1984, he eliminated all of the renomination suspense in Texas (and everywhere else) simply by announcing his candidacy for reelection. He was thus the first incumbent President since Richard Nixon to avoid a serious interparty challenge for renomination, and delegate selection in Texas, as elsewhere, was routine. By 5 May, when the Republican primary was held, the Reagan-Bush organization in Texas had already launched a major registration effort for the November election, along with fundraising activities to assist other Republican nominees.

The Republicans did have a four-man race to succeed John Tower as the party's U.S. Senate nominee. U.S. Representative Phil Gramm was the early favorite, and he dispelled whatever doubts existed about his 1983 party switch by winning nearly three-fourths of the 340,000 Republican primary votes. He easily outdistanced another Republican House incumbent, Ron Paul, and came out of the primary with a strongly united state party behind him.

With little excitement Republicans were able to generate was restricted to three congressional districts—two Republican and one Democratic—in which incumbents had decided to run for the U.S. Senate. In two of these, a runoff was required to choose a nominee. In the third, which had been Phil Gramm's district, a recount resulted in a reversal of the unofficial results and provided a 10-vote margin (out of 13,000 votes cast) for Joe L. Barton.

The Democratic Nominating Contests

The decision by the Texas Democratic Party to replace its presidential primary with precinct conventions (followed by senatorial district conventions and a state convention) received very little attention initially. Indeed, state Democratic leaders were convinced that the presidential nomination would be decided before the contest reached Texas and, by late March, had no plans for tabulating the precinct results. At that point, Democratic state chairman Bob Slagle was still predicting that "psychologically" the Democratic nomination would be decided by the time that Texas Democrats convened.[13]

Slagle's prediction was incorrect, and this focused attention on the precinct convention format and rules. The critical points were several. There was no presidential preference on the primary ballot, nonbinding or otherwise. Instead, Democratic voters "qualified" to attend the evening precinct meetings held on 5 May by voting in the Democratic primary earlier in the day. They then returned to their precincts after the polls closed to select delegates based on presidential preference. These delegates, who were not bound, would then attend conventions at the state senate district level. Delegates chosen at the district meetings would then attend the state convention, where the final delegates would be picked.

With no organized reporting system in place by 5 May, the state party had to rely on county chairmen to obtain returns from precinct chairmen and to relay these, in turn, to state headquarters in Austin. With 6,000 precinct conventions across the state, this was no small task, particularly since the state party was unable to provide clear guidelines as to how the conventions were to operate.

As in caucus states, however, the precinct format gave Walter Mondale a boost. Mondale's support among the state's party leadership was quite solid, as was his status with organized labor and other interest groups closely tied to the Democratic Party in Texas. He came out of the precinct conventions with an almost two-to-one lead over Gary Hart and Jesse Jackson. Indeed, Hart managed to gather only a few more delegates than Jackson. Coming on the heels of a decisive Hart defeat in Tennessee on 1 May, Texas was a major, if not fatal, setback to the Hart candidacy.

The presidential results naturally garnered the greatest national attention, but the U.S. Senate primary produced a surprising and quite extraordinary result. When the primary campaign commenced, Robert Krueger, a former member of the U.S. House and ambassador to Mexico under President Carter, was the strong favorite. In 1978, Krueger had lost to John Tower by 12,227 votes out of nearly 2.3 million. His centrist reputation appeared to give him a considerably broader appeal than either conservative U.S. Representative Kent Hance or liberal state Senator Lloyd Doggett. Instead, Krueger was caught in a conservative-liberal crossfire, and he wound up finishing third, some 1,500 votes behind front-runner Hance, with over 1.4 million votes cast. Hance then lost the 2 June runoff to Doggett by 1,435 votes out of the nearly one million cast.

The Doggett-Hance contest foreshadowed some of the problems that Democrats would face in the fall. Hance did well in West Texas and East Texas, bastions of rural Democratic conservatism. Doggett brought together, however, an impressive array of constituent groups—organized labor, teachers, blacks, Hispanics, and homosexuals—that enabled him to carry every major metropolitan area in the state. The runoff campaign was bitter, and the ideological differences between the candidates crystal clear. With Doggett's nomination, Texas had one of the sharpest ideological choices among the nation's fall Senate races. Gramm was a staunch Reagan supporter during his tenure in the House, and he cast both his primary and general election campaigns as Reagan referenda. Doggett, who had served 11 years in the Texas State Senate, was an unyielding Reagan foe, whose reputation as a consumer advocate and business critic made him highly visible and highly controversial.

THE GENERAL ELECTION CAMPAIGNS

There were a number of noteworthy occurrences during the fall campaigns. Dallas was the site of the Republican National Convention, and both Ronald Reagan and especially George Bush followed up their renominations with campaign swings through Texas. Since the Reagan-Bush ticket was a prohibitive favorite throughout the campaign, these appearances were aimed at cementing support and at providing assistance for other Republican candidates. In addition, a special effort was made to improve Republican prospects in counties with large Hispanic populations. Midway through the campaign, Reagan visited Brownsville, deep in the Rio Grande Valley, and made a strong appeal for the Hispanic vote.

Both Walter Mondale and Geraldine Ferraro also campaigned in Texas, with Ferraro in particular being able to draw large and enthusiastic crowds. Their efforts were supplemented by Jesse Jackson, who came in to encourage voter registration efforts in black communities. Despite these efforts, the Democratic presidential effort in Texas operated under a severe handicap. Virtually every poll conducted during the campaign showed the Democratic ticket running well behind Reagan-Bush. As the prospects for reversing this became less and less promising, attention focused on the extent to which other Democratic candidates might escape Mondale's fate.

There were, then, some shared emphases by the competing presidential tickets. Given the size and importance of Texas, the candidates made repeated personal appearances. Both campaign organizations launched major voter registration efforts, with the Democrats concentrating on blacks, Hispanics, and labor, and the Republicans focusing particular attention on college-age youth.

An important distinction between the presidential campaigns, however, was their approach to other party candidates. In effect, the Reagan-Bush organization and the Texas Republican Party tried to use the President's coattails (and resources) to the greatest possible extent. The Mondale-Ferraro organization did not have the capability for matching these resources, nor was it able to offer coattails to most Democratic candidates. Indeed, the question that many Democratic candidates faced was how to avoid or at least minimize the weight of the Mondale-Ferraro ticket.

And here it is important to emphasize several factors that made the 1984 general election campaign truly interesting. First, the Republican Party in Texas chose a party-label strategy. This meant eschewing the "vote for the man, not the party" appeal that Republican candidates had frequently used in Texas. It also meant actively encouraging voters to vote a straight Republican ticket.

The tactical components of this strategy included the use of slate cards in a number of counties, "institutional advertising" that sought to transfer Reagan's popularity to other Republican candidates, and explicit attachments by many of these candidates to the Reagan-Bush ticket. More important, the state party poured money and technical assistance into congressional and state legislative races. Winnable districts were targeted, and organizations were created to provide local linkages between the national and state campaigns.

The Texas Republican Party's "Hispanic Plan," for example, was developed in conjunction with the Republican National Committee's Hispanic Coordinator, Bob Beilon. The basic plan, which was produced in July, emphasized the building of Hispanic Republican organizations at the county level. Counties (and zones within counties) were targeted for Hispanic leadership recruitment, for substantial political advertising efforts, and for vote-delivery programs in support of not just the Reagan-Bush and Gramm campaigns, but also state legislative and even local candidates.

Second, the Republican Party capitalized upon the U.S. Senate race as the vehicle for polarizing Democratic voters. The Gramm-Doggett race was a nasty, bitter, highly negative, and very expensive campaign. For Gramm, this meant emphasizing "family values" at the onset of the campaign. Among the first Gramm attacks, for example, was the charge that Doggett had accepted financial assistance from a homosexual group. (Later advertisements claimed that Doggett supported affirmative action for homosexuals.) A second point of attack for Gramm was tying Doggett as closely as possible to Walter Mondale, to Mondale's tax program, to the national Democratic Party, and especially to prominent liberals in the national party.

The force of Gramm's attack was aided considerably by the Doggett candidacy and by some ill-advised actions by the state Democratic Party. The exceptionally negative tone of Doggett's primary and run-off campaigns made it very difficult for either Krueger or Hance to provide more than token support for his general election campaign. One of Doggett's television commercials, for example, had attacked Hance's sponsorship of income tax cuts with the concluding voice-over that "Kent Hance isn't a congressman, he's a butler." Doggett had previously indulged his penchant for unusual styles of criticism by holding up a plastic jellyfish to describe Krueger's brand of courage. Whether Hance or Krueger could have done much to bolster Doggett's candidacy among conservative and moderate whites is uncertain. The fact is that neither made any great effort to do so, and, after the Democratic primary, few observers expected that they would.

Doggett combined, in sum, liberal ideology and personal abrasiveness. Gramm, who differed only in ideology on this score, at least had the good sense or good fortune to direct most of his personal attacks against Democrats. Moreover, when Doggett tried to soften his image, the results were less than helpful. Both Gramm and Doggett were cited by various advertising "experts" for allegedly misleading or deceptive ads. But Doggett's family campaign commercial—with three generations of the Doggett family gathered round a family dinner, Doggett saying Grace, and an aura that would make a Norman Rockwell picture pale by comparison—was cited by NBC as one of the worst political ads in the entire nation. It was particularly jarring when juxtaposed alongside some of Doggett's more strident attacks on Gramm.

Neither Krueger nor Hance, then, would have facilitated the polarization strategy as well as did Doggett. And the state Democratic Party did not help blunt Gramm's assault, when it voted at its fall convention to incorporate the Democratic National Platform into the Texas Democratic Platform. This meant, among other things, a formal embrace of homosexual rights and other controversial issues that would not otherwise have been part of the party's agenda during the fall campaign.

One of the most important long-term effects of the 1984 campaign, however, may be the organizational improvement in the Texas Republican Party. Fundraising for the campaign was very successful, with $3 million being raised by the state party's finance division. A statewide voter file of over four million households, with voter history information going back to 1980, was developed. Direct mail and telephone programs were expanded. The party's data base division set up word processing and computer system services. And the thrust of these and related efforts was to provide greater cooperation and better services for all Republican campaigns. The experience (and success) gained in the 1984 campaign, then, may prove to be quite important as the Texas Republican Party seeks to capitalize upon its recent gains and, in particular, to create a truly statewide organization.

THE REPUBLICAN PARTY VICTORY

Ronald Reagan's victory margin in Texas was among the highest in the southern states. In addition, the Reagan "landslide" in Texas (or "tidal wave" or "avalanche," as it was variously described) extended from the Presidency to state and local offices. There were major Republican gains in traditionally Democratic areas from East Texas to West Texas. Key local offices in formerly Democratic strongholds, such as Tarrant County (Fort Worth), were captured by Republicans for the first time during this century.

One of the more impressive aspects of the Republican showing was the ousting of Democratic incumbents. The most prominent of these were three U.S. House members—Jack Hightower, Bill Patman, and Tom Vandergriff. They were joined by, among others, 16 members of the Texas House, 13 Democratic judges in Harris County (Houston), and eight Democratic judges in Dallas County.[14] In all, over 100 legislative and local offices changed from Democratic to Republican hands.

There was, then, a Republican Party victory in Texas, but the key to it was the top of the ticket. The combination of President Reagan's enormous popularity in Texas and the accompanying ideological polarization of the U.S. Senate race split the Democratic electorate and linked local races to the conservative statewide trend. Thus, there was not only highly integrated presidential-senatorial voting but quite extensive straight-ticket voting.

The Presidential and U.S. Senate Votes

President Reagan ran exceptionally well across the entire state. In none of the state's eight regions did he fall below 55 percent of the vote (see Table 7–2). And in virtually every region and country, Reagan ran well ahead of the margins by which he had defeated Jimmy Carter in 1980. Reagan carried five of the six most populous Texas counties in 1980; in 1984 Reagan carried them all, increasing his percentage of the vote by an average of more than 7 percentage points.[15]

It was this regional strength that party leaders on both sides considered critical. For Democratic strategists, two regions were of paramount importance: South Texas, with its large Hispanic population, and East Texas, with its rural Democratic vote. The latter is (or was, perhaps) "yellow-dog" Democrat territory, and Democratic state chairman Bob Slagle singles it out as "absolutely critical. . . . We can't afford to lose East Texas and win elections. . . ."[16] In 1980 Reagan and Carter had almost split the 29-county East Texas region, but in 1984 Reagan defeated Mondale by almost a three-to-two margin.

In South Texas, Reagan did nearly as well. Cameron County, with a 77 percent Hispanic population, went to Reagan by a 53–47 margin

TABLE 7–2   Presidential and U.S. Senate General Election Results, 1984, by Region

Region	Republican Percentage of Total Vote		Difference President-Senate
	Reagan-Bush	Gramm	
Panhandle	74.5	69.9	4.6
North Central	67.2	62.3	4.9
East Texas	58.6	53.7	4.9
Upper Gulf	62.6	58.3	4.3
South Texas	55.7	50.9	4.8
Central Texas	62.5	54.6	7.9
West Central	71.6	66.8	4.8
West Texas	65.8	60.7	5.1
State Totals	63.6	58.6	5.0

Source: Complete, but unofficial, election tabulations by the Secretary of State, State of Texas.

in 1984. In Nueces County (Corpus Christi), with an almost 50 percent Hispanic population, Reagan captured 54 percent of the vote. In Bexar County (San Antonio), with a similarly high proportion of Hispanics, the Reagan-Bush ticket received almost 60 percent of the vote.

Just how well President Reagan did among Hispanics has been disputed since the election. According to post-election Texas Poll data, Walter Mondale received 60 percent of the Hispanic vote.[17] This 60–40 split is approximately what Republican Party leaders have claimed, using precinct-level voting analyses. Other studies have indicated considerably wider splits. The Southwest Voter Registration Education Project, for example, reports that Reagan received slightly over 20 percent of the Hispanic vote.[18] The 20 percent level is what Democratic spokesmen claim Reagan achieved in both 1980 and 1984. It is difficult to resolve these disputes, particularly using precinct data, but Reagan clearly improved on his 1980 performance among Hispanics in certain areas. In counties with 80 percent or more Hispanic populations, some showed substantial improvement in Reagan strength, while others were almost unchanged from 1980 to 1984. In Webb County, which is over 90 percent Hispanic, Reagan went from 31 percent in 1980 to 43 percent in 1984. In Hidalgo and Willacy Counties (approximately 80 percent Hispanic), Reagan received approximately 40 percent of the vote in 1980 and raised his total by several percentage points in 1984. In Duval, Zavala, and Starr Counties, Reagan won less than one-fourth of the votes in both 1980 and 1984.

Given Reagan's overall margin, however, there is another side to the debate over the Hispanic vote. Hispanic turnout in 1980 and 1984 was quite similar. If Reagan's Hispanic vote was approximately 20 percent in both instances, as Democrats argue, the degree of defection by whites from the Democratic ticket assumes startling proportions. Indeed, the Texas Poll, which reported a 60–40 Hispanic split, gave the Democrats only about one-fourth of the white, or Anglo, vote.[19] Studies that report Reagan doing less well among Hispanics necessarily show him doing even better among whites.

If all this were confined to the presidential race, the unresolved questions would be interesting but limited. In fact, however, the Republican vote in the Senate race tracked the presidential vote fairly closely. As shown in Table 7–2, most of the regional differentials between presidential and senatorial voting were only about five percentage points, the exception being Central Texas with its eight-point spread. Lloyd Doggett's home county, Travis County, dominates Central Texas, but his support even here was insufficient to carry the region. Thus, Gramm carried every region, as did Reagan, and the only truly close contest was in South Texas.

In Figure 7–1 the geographic sweep of the Republican victory at the top of the ticket becomes even clearer. There were some two dozen of the 254 counties in Texas that went Republican in the presidential race and Democratic in the Senate race. Most of these are quite small, the major exceptions being Travis Country and Galveston County, whose combined populations are about 350,000. There were an approximately equal number of counties that went Democratic in both races, but their populations are typically quite small as well. The very limited crossover voting evident in county-wide results is reinforced by data from the Texas Poll post-election survey, which

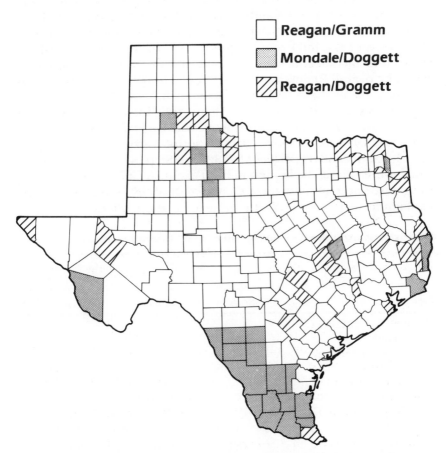

FIGURE 7–1   Presidential and U.S. Senate Results, 1984, by County

shows Doggett receiving the votes of 9 percent of the Reagan voters and Gramm picking up 5 percent of those voting for Mondale.[20]

Congressional Voting

Of the 27 U.S. House districts in Texas, the Republican Party fielded candidates in 18. In these contested races, Republicans won ten seats. Moreover, their share of the 3.6 million votes cast for the U.S. House was over 55 percent (see Table 7–3). Republican incumbents had no serious problems and all were reelected by very substantial margins. The Republican share of the total vote in these districts was almost 80 percent.

There were also 11 Democratic incumbents who ran for reelection. Vote percentages for the eight successful incumbents ranged from 57 percent to 74 percent; Republican candidates captured less than 40 percent of the total vote in these races. In three districts where Democratic incumbents were defeated, the losing margins were narrow. The overall Republican percentage here was just under 52 percent. In none of these races was there much initial optimism among Republicans, in part because the Democratic incumbents had quite conservative voting records in Congress. For example, *Congressional Quarterly*'s 1983 conservative coalition support scores for Hightower, Patman, and Vandergriff were 87, 82, and 85 percent, respectively.[21] These were among the highest in the Texas delegation. Nevertheless, Reagan strength in these quite disparate districts—ranging from the Panhandle to the Fort Worth suburbs to the Gulf Coast—was so

TABLE 7–3   U.S. House Voting, Contested Seats, 1984

		Votes Cast	
Type of Seat	Number of Seats	Total (in millions)	Republican Percentage
Republican incumbent, reelected	4	0.9	79.9
Democratic incumbent, reelected	8	1.4	38.2
Democratic incumbent, defeated	3	0.65	51.8
Open seat, Republican elected	3	0.6	59.6
Totals	18	3.6	55.1

Source: Complete, but unofficial, election tabulations by the Secretary of State, State of Texas.

pronounced that the combination of incumbency and conservatism was insufficient to hold the districts for the Democratic Party.

An unexpected bonus for Republicans was their showing in the three open districts. Republican candidates were expected to be competitive, but their final vote percentages—ranging from 57 percent to 64 percent—were far above even the most optimistic forecasts. Indeed, the Republican share of the total vote in the three open districts was almost on a par with the Democratic share in the re-elected incumbent districts.

State and Local Offices

There were three statewide offices on the ballot in 1984, and, in each instance, the Republican challenger made an unprecedentedly strong showing. The race for Chief Justice of the Texas Supreme Court was decided by a 54–46 margin, while the Court of Criminal Appeals contest was even closer—51–49 percent. The third statewide race, for the Texas Railroad Commission, was won by incumbent Mack Wallace, 50.3–49.7 percent, against perennial candidate John Thomas Henderson, a Democrat turned Republican who received neither funds nor support from the Republican Party. Henderson was the only Republican to receive an endorsement from the liberal *Texas Observer* in 1984. He was also shunned by the Reagan campaign as well as the state party leadership. Despite being outspent $450,000 to $14,000 by Wallace, Henderson almost pulled off what would have been the biggest upset of the year.

In elections for the Texas House, 14 Democratic incumbents were defeated, and Republican candidates also picked up two open seats. With only 42 of the 150 House seats being contested, this was an unusually high success rate. And once again, Republican gains were much greater than had been predicted right up until the election.

There were also numerous Republican victories in county and local races, many of which had never been won by Republicans. In some counties, the Republicans achieved clean sweeps of all offices up for election. The gain of 84 new county offices doubled the previous statewide total for the party.

What made all of this possible was extensive straight-ticket voting, coupled with very high levels of Republican support among new residents and young voters. The Texas Poll post-election survey, for example, reported that 26 percent of those who voted said they had cast a straight Republican ticket, while 21 percent said they voted straight Democratic.[22] Among whites, the Republican edge was 30–14 percent. Among self-described independents, the Republican advantage was 22–11 percent. In some counties, straight-ticket voting was even higher. Dallas County residents, for example, cast half of their ballots for a straight ticket, as did 53 percent of the voters in Harris County.[23] The Tarrance polling organization, which conducted surveys for Reagan and Gramm in Texas, estimated that 35 percent of the 5.3 million votes cast statewide were straight Republican, compared to 12 percent straight Democratic.[24]

In addition, the Republican Party did especially well in the fastest growing areas of the state. President Reagan averaged almost 75 percent of the vote in the seven Texas counties where new residents had increased voter registration rolls by 30 percent or more since 1980.[25] First-time voters in 1984 supported Reagan by a reported margin of 5–1 and Gramm by 5–3.[26] Given Reagan's overwhelming support among young voters, moreover, his margin of victory would have been even larger were it not for the lower turnout level in the 18–29 year old age group.[27]

CONCLUSION—PENDULUMS AND REALIGNMENT

In the wake of their electoral disaster, Texas Democrats have attempted to find solace in the past. Their favorite theory is the pendulum interpretation: Just as Texans in 1982 swung back from their Republican flirtation of 1980, the Texas Democratic Party will rebound from its latest debacle in 1986. Not much, in short needs to be done. Governor Mark White and other party leaders have called for elimination of the caucus system and its replacement by some form of primary, but they have rejected complaints by conservative Democrats that the party reexamine its ties to minorities, organized labor, and other special interest groups. The clearest indication of the Democratic response is that no movement has developed to replace the state party leadership, which is exactly the reverse of the abrupt Republican leadership change after 1982.

Republican analysts, as might be expected, have rather more expansive theories about electoral change in Texas. They see, over the past three decades, a constant progression in Republican strength, which has put Texas on the brink of becoming not a two-party state but a Republican state. For Republicans, party realignment is, at this point, almost irreversible.

If these interpretations are reminiscent of what is being debated on the national level, there is more than coincidence involved. In Texas, as nationally, the Democratic Party has some obvious problems with white voters, young voters, and conservatives. In Texas, as nationally, recent party identification trends point toward substantially increased Republican strength. According to the Gallup organization's fall 1984 surveys, Republican identifiers now account for 35 percent of the electorate, the highest level since 1954.[28] The proportion of Democratic identifiers, 39 percent, is the lowest in over three decades.

In Texas, the shift in party identification has been even more dramatic. As recently as 1980, Democratic identification in Texas was more than double the level of Republican identification.[29] The June 1984 Texas Poll reported an overall Democratic advantage of 37–26 percent.[30] Among new residents (those having lived in the state 10 years or less), however, there was a greater proportion of Republican identifiers (32 percent) than Democratic identifiers (26 percent). Only among lifetime residents was the two-to-one Democratic margin intact.

The post-election polls are very different. They report near parity among Republican, Democratic, and Independent identifiers or even, in some instances, a slight Republican plurality.[31] There are decided Republican advantages, moreover, among whites and young voters. More than half of the whites in the post-election Texas Poll said they identified with the Republican Party, while approximately one-fourth reported being closer to the Democratic Party.[32] The spread among those 18–29 years in the survey was equally wide.

The future of party politics in Texas, then, is likely to reflect in large part the demographic and associated changes that have lifted the Republican Party into a highly competitive position. Its organizational strength and sophistication are impressive. Its candidate recruitment has improved enormously. It has particular appeal in fast-growing, affluent areas of the state.

The future will also be affected, however, by the Democratic Party's response to its current dilemma. At the present time, it shows little inclination for organizational development. It continues to tinker, as does the national party, with convention delegate selection procedures. Its primary electorate is sharply split between conservatives and liberals. Its core electorate for general elections is increasingly narrow. It is, to a considerable extent, a party of minorities, when it comes to contesting elections. Perhaps most importantly, the Democratic Party in Texas has no apparent sense of urgency or realism about its diminishing appeal to conservative and moderate whites.

In Texas, the Democratic Party is really depending on external factors to save it. A major recession, for example, would provide a major boost in 1986. Not having Ronald Reagan on the ticket will no doubt help in 1988. What this suggests, however, is that absent some clear strategy for revitalizing and redirecting the party, Democrats in Texas will be in the dubious position of waiting for Republicans to make major mistakes. This can produce occasional electoral victories. It cannot reverse party realignment.

NOTES

1. According to current estimates, the total population is now well over 15 million. Texas ranked sixth among all states in total population from 1940–60. It moved to fourth in 1970 and to third in 1980.

2. During the 1970s, population growth in Texas was 27.1 percent, compared to a national rate of 11.4 percent.

3. The "metropolitan" population in Texas increased approximately 30 percent from 1970–80, which was about three times the rate of growth nationally.

4. Among southern states, Texas has a relatively low proportion of black residents. The proportion of Hispanics, however, is the highest among southern states and approximately double that of the second-ranking state, Florida.

5. The voting-age population estimates are from *National Journal* 16 (21 April 1984): 764. The registered voter estimate is from James E. Anderson, Richard W. Murray, and Edward L. Farley, *Texas Politics*, 4th ed. (New York: Harper & Row, 1984), 39.

6. See Anderson, Murray, and Farley, *Texas Politics*, 39, 65–75.

7. The gap between Texas and the national standard was largely erased by the mid-1970s.

8. *National Journal* 16 (24 April 1984): 764. Per capita income in Texas rose 39.6 percent from 1970–80. The national increase was 24.8 percent. The "southern states," for purposes of this comparison include Oklahoma and Kentucky, as well as the "Deep South" and "Rim South" states covered in this book.

9. Ibid. In February 1984, for example, the Texas unemployment rate was 5.9 percent, while the national rate was 8.4 percent. Among southern states, only Virginia's was at a lower level.

10. The gubernatorial term was increased from two years to four years through a constitutional amendment adopted in 1972. The first four-year term began in 1974.

11. The first redistricting plan based on the 1980 census was rejected by the U.S. Department of Justice. A second plan, drawn up by a three-judge federal court panel (all Democrats), was rejected by the U.S. Supreme Court but left in place for the 1982 election. The third plan was adopted in 1983, with a Democrat having replaced a Republican as Governor.

12. *Dallas Morning News*, 8 November 1984, 33–A.

13. *Dallas Morning News*, 26 March 1984, 25–A.

14. The outcome in one of the state House races is being disputed. A reversal of the unofficial results would reduce the net Republican gain from 16 seats to 15 seats.

15. The six counties are Bexar, Dallas, El Paso, Harris, Tarrant, and Travis. All but Travis were carried by Reagan in 1980.

16. *Dallas Morning News,* 7 November 1984, 26–A.

17. *Dallas Morning News,* 21 November 1984, 1–A, 6–A.

18. *Dallas Morning News,* 11 November 1984, 36–A.

19. *Dallas Morning News,* 21 November 1984, 1–A, 6–A.

20. Ibid.

21. *Congressional Quarterly Almanac, 1983* (Washington, DC: Congressional Quarterly, Inc., 1984), 41C

22. *Dallas Morning News,* 11 November 1984, 1–A, 6–A.

23. *Dallas Morning News,* 18 November 1984, 8–A.

24. Ibid.

25. *Dallas Times Herald,* 11 November 1984, 12–A.

26. *Dallas Morning News,* 11 November 1984, 1–A, 6–A.

27. Ibid.

28. Washington *Post* National Weekly Edition, 17 December 1984, 38.

29. *Dallas Times Herald,* 11 November 1984, 13–A.

30. *The Texas Poll Report,* June 1984, 1–2.

31. *Dallas Times Herald,* 11 November 1984, 13–A.

32. *Dallas Morning News,* 21 November 1984, 1–A, 6–A.

8

Arkansas

Diane K. Blair

Until very recently, no state was safer for the Democratic presidential nominee than was Arkansas. With the exception of the Civil War and Reconstruction eras, Arkansas voted Democratic in every presidential contest from statehood in 1836 until 1968, when its electoral votes went to George Wallace. Furthermore, it went Democratic by margins that consistently exceeded the national Democratic percentage of the vote. Arkansas was the last of the southern states to cast a non-Democratic vote in the twentieth century, and was also the last of the southern states to finally cast a Republican presidential vote, for Nixon over McGovern in 1972.

Somewhat uncharacteristically, Arkansas' first brush with Republicanism had come in state rather than national elections, with Republican Winthrop Rockefeller's gubernatorial victories in 1966 and 1968. However, these elections proved to be aberrations rather than Republican trendsetters. Rockefeller carefully kept his campaigns separated from those of national Republican candidates, and his winning margins were provided by two electoral groups that were not in the Arkansas Republican ranks before Rockefeller and have never been found there since: blacks and liberal Democrats.[1]

When, after two successive losses, Arkansas Democrats finally began nominating younger, cleaner, more progressive candidates, they returned to power. In fact, for the five gubernatorial elections after Rockefeller's 1968 victory, Republican gubernatorial candidates averaged only 29 percent of the vote. Similarly, with Jimmy Carter rather than George McGovern leading the Democratic ticket, Arkansans trooped joyfully back to the Democratic column in 1976, giving Carter his largest majority (66 percent) of any state but Georgia (66.7 percent).

It is 1980 that stands as the year of the greatest Republican successes to date in Arkansas politics, the only year when Arkansas Republicans were victorious for both the White House and the statehouse. To be sure, neither Ronald Reagan nor Frank White had a very wide winning margin. Reagan's plurality was only .06 percent more than Carter's, and White's 52 percent win over Bill Clinton was an equally slim mandate. Nevertheless, White's election was particularly impressive because it defied the Arkansas tradition, broken only twice previously in the twentieth century, of giving an incumbent governor a nearly automatic (sometimes called courtesy) second two-year term.

The strength of the 1980 Republican tide could also be seen in the U.S. Senate race where Dale Bumpers, elected to the Senate in 1974 with 85 percent of the vote, was reelected with only 59 percent, the second smallest margin in any Democratic Senate candidate in the century. Republican Ed Bethune, who had squeaked into the Second Congressional District seat two years earlier, was the biggest vote-getter of all major candidates, receiving 79 percent over his opponent; and Third District Representative, Republican John Paul Hammerschmidt, had no Democratic opponent at all.

Considering how staunchly Democratic Arkansas has been—the most thoroughly and consistently Democratic state of any in the nation—1980 was indeed a banner year for the GOP. The thrill of victory did not last long, however. In 1982 Bill Clinton won back the governorship from Frank White, in the process rejuvenated a previously moribund Democratic party organization, and of perhaps greatest significance for the 1984 presidential contest, stimulated and solidified the black vote. Arkansas blacks constitute a declining percentage of the state's population (from 28 percent in 1910 to 16.3 percent in 1980), but an increasingly important swing vote in statewide elections. During the Winthrop Rockefeller years, black voters methodically split their tickets with, for example, over 90 percent voting Republican for Rockefeller and Democratic for Humphrey in 1968.[2] The black vote had been rapidly returning to Democratic gubernatorial candidates during the 1970s, but Frank White's 1981 decision to bring former Governor Orval Faubus out of retirement into his administration made the 1982 rematch between White and Clinton something of a holy war for black Arkansans. It is estimated that Clinton got over 95 percent of the black vote; these 90,000 or so black voters were clearly a major factor in Clinton's 78,000 victory margin over White.[3]

Approaching the 1984 presidential election, then, both parties had some basis for optimism, and some grounds for concern. The Democrats could look at 17 out of 20 presidential victories in the twentieth century, an average of 59 percent of the popular vote in these 20 contests, and explain the only deviations by a strong regional sweep for Wallace in 1968 and even stronger national tides for Nixon in 1972 and Reagan in 1980. While Carter's percentage of the popular vote dropped dramatically from 65 percent in 1976 to 47.5 percent in 1980, he still ran much better in Arkansas than he did nationally (41 percent). Indeed, considering the fact that his administration had placed thousands of fiercely unwelcome Cuban refugees in Arkansas in the months preceding the general election, the fact that Carter still carried 50 of Arkansas' 75 counties is a telling tribute to the traditional strength of the Democratic presidential nominee.

Furthermore, in the aftermath of the 1982 elections, Democrats held all statewide elected offices, all but ten of the 135 seats in the state legislature (seven Republicans in the House, three in the Senate), and nearly all local offices as well. One other statistic suggests the residual strength of Democratic tradition: In 1982 560,000 Arkansans voted in the Democratic primary, while only 13,000 voted in the Republican primary.

However, beneath these impressive outlines of Democratic dominance, Republicans could see encouraging indicators of their rising strength. Democratic presidential candidates had won only one of the last four contests, and the average Democratic percentage of the popular presidential vote in Arkansas was unmistakably declining, as the following array demonstrates: ·

Arkansas: Average Democratic Percent of Popular Presidential Vote

1904–16	58.4
1920–32	66.6
1936–48	72.9
1952–64	53.7
1968–80	43.4

While substate elections have remained overwhelmingly Democratic, statewide elections and elections to national office have become increasingly competitive over the past decade. By 1978 two of Arkansas' four U.S. Representatives were Republicans; and in 1982 all four congressional seats were contested in the general election for the first time in the century.

Why had Republicans finally begun to break the Democratic stranglehold in Arkansas? Bruce Campbell has attributed Democratic declines in the South to three major factors: in-migration; generational turnover; and individual conversion.[4] While Campbell's methodology cannot be duplicated here, these factors provide a useful typology for identifying and explaining some of the major forces at work in contemporary Arkansas.

Looking first at in-migration, after decades of population decline, during the last twenty years Arkansas has become an absolute growth state; indeed, between 1970 and 1980, its growth rate (18.9 percent) was one of the fastest in the country, and two-thirds of that growth was due to in-migration. What has made this in-migration so particularly advantageous to Republicans is that it has been concentrated in precisely that northern portion of the state where a sizeable number of mountain Republicans fought for the Union and have maintained their Republican loyalties ever since. Many of these newcomers are associated with the growing industry and expanding economy in northern and western Arkansas; many more are retirees fleeing the snow, crowds, and higher taxes of the Midwest. Certainly not all newcomers are Republicans. Indeed many have some previous Arkansas ties. Nevertheless, as a group, they are measurably less Democratic than are long-time residents.[5]

They are also confirmed, indeed by previous Arkansas standards compulsive, voters. Only in northern Arkansas, particularly Northwest Arkansas, does the voter turnout occasionally exceed 80 percent of those registered to vote. Between 1966 and 1980, while the number of votes cast increased 24 percent in the southern regions of Arkansas, the number of votes increased 74 percent in the northwest. Reagan carried few counties outside Northwest Arkansas in 1980, but he carried this one region with a sufficiently sizeable majority (58 percent) to overcome his narrow losses in the rest of the state.

Campbell's second factor, generational turnover, is more difficult to measure, not only because of the absence of reliable longitudinal survey data in Arkansas, but because many younger citizens have no partisan identification whatsoever. That, however, both confounds and confirms the point. While Republicanism per se has not been running rampant among young Arkansans, they are measurably less likely than their predecessors to be straight-ticket Democrats, and therefore more likely to vote for Republican candidates with attractive personalities or campaign appeals.[6]

Fundamental to the third factor, individual conversion, is the assumption that conservative native southerners would eventually recognize the Republican Party as their more appropriate ideological home. Through the late 1960s—that is, so long as the state Democratic Party was led by such conservative stalwarts as Senator John L. McClellan and Governor Orval Faubus, and the state Republican Party was a progressive Winthrop Rockefeller coalition—these ideological lines were thoroughly blurred. By the 1980s, however, with conservative Frank White and progressive Bill Clinton heading their respective Republican and Democratic tickets, the state parties had finally become fairly accurate ideological mirrors of their national counterparts.

The 1984 elections in Arkansas promised another clearcut referendum between Republican conservatism and Democratic liberalism. President Reagan, of course, would had the Republican ticket as a champion of social and economic conservatism. The National Republican Senatorial Committee targeted Democratic U.S. Senator David Pryor for defeat as "the Senate's No. 1 opponent of President Reagan,"[7] and recruited a strong conservative challenger in Republican Representative Ed Bethune. Governor Clinton, seeking another two-year term, was again promised serious general election opposition. Indeed, the fact that two credible candidates sought the Republican nomination for Governor was another indication of the competitive presence of Arkansas Republicanism. Neither Elwood (Woody) Freeman, an East Arkansas contractor, nor Irwin Davis, a Northwest Arkansas lawyer, had previous elective experience; but both were young, attractive, and articulate, and both promised a more businesslike, business-oriented, conservative administration.

In short, if Democratic declines in Arkansas fundamentally reflect native disaffection from the perceived liberalism of their one "sound" party, 1984 promised at least a good impressionistic test of this "individual conversion" theory. The 1984 election also promised an opportunity for the confirmation, confusion, or refinement of some geographical voting patterns.

Explanations for these patterns have their origins in topographical variations and settlement streams. Because the hilly uplands of northern and western Arkansas were never conducive to large-scale farming, slaves were relatively sparse in these areas. Primarily settled by migration from Tennessee, Kentucky, and Missouri, Union sympathizers were common during the Civil War, loyalties lasted, and Republicanism has long had a foothold. In recent years, substantial inmigration has energized and enlarged the preexisting Republican base, and a still-miniscule black population has little political impact. In contrast, Democrats have remained the heavy favorites in the Mississippi Delta regions of southern and eastern Arkansas. This is where black populations once worked as slaves and later as share-croppers on flat and fertile large plantations, where Confederate and anti-carpetbagger emotions once ran high, and where blacks, now enfranchised, are both numerous and politically influential. It is also evident that these patterns can be completely confounded by a highly unpopular (McGovern) or very popular (Carter in 1976) Democratic nominee. Much, then, depends upon the party's choice of a candi-date.

THE PRESIDENTIAL NOMINATION IN ARKANSAS

Through the 1960s, Arkansas delegates to both parties' national con-ventions were chosen by party elites, usually the state committees. Since then, however, the process has been in a constant state of permutation.[8] Pursuant to a 1975 state law requiring such, both par-ties held their first presidential primaries in 1966. However, after the 1979 legislature amended that law to provide that parties could choose their national delegates by primary, convention, caucus, or any other method permitted by national party rules, the Democrats stuck with a presidential primary in 1980, and the Republicans opted for selection by congressional district committee and the state com-mittee.

Especially with the nomination of Reagan uncontested in 1984, the Republicans saw no reason for changing their system. On 4 February 1984 meetings of party regulars in each of the state's four congres-sional districts selected three national delegates and alternates. On 18 February an additional 17 delegates and alternates were chosen on an at-large basis by the 312-member Republican State Committee. All of this was accomplished with very little controversy and almost no publicity.

However, the Democrats' decision to use a caucus system for del-egate selection, because it was new and because if affected hundreds of thousands of voters grown accustomed to a presidential primary, became so bitterly disputed and controversial that it nearly oversha-dowed the contest by the presidential aspirants per se. The system, patterned after Iowa, began on 17 March in Arkansas' 467 Justice of the Peach (J.P.) districts, where delegates were selected to county conventions on 31 March, which in turn selected delegates to a 5 May state convention where the actual selection of national delegates took place.

The Democrats' decision was based partly on timing (the regular primary could not be held until 29 May, by which time virtually everyone thought the contest would be over) and expense (holding a separate earlier presidential primary would have cost the party about $350,000).[9] However, two additional reasons were operative. First, there was the pressure emanating from the national Democratic Party's Rule 2A, requiring state parties to "take all feasible steps to restrict participation in the delegate selection process to Democratic voters only." Arkansas has no party registration law, attempts to get one enacted by the 1983 legislature were as unsuccessful as past attempts had been; as an alternative, it was felt that the party loyalty oath required of caucus participants would not only effectively exclude the large numbers of non-Democrats who by tradition had always voted in the Democratic primary, but would ease the threat of credentials challenge at the national convention.[10]

Finally, at the time various alternatives were under consideration, it appeared probable that Arkansas' senior U.S. Senator Dale Bumpers would enter the presidential contest, making it even less likely that other presidential prospects would enter Arkansas to compete for 42 delegates against a favorite son.[11] Ironically, by the time Bumpers officially announced that he would not enter the 1984 contest, the Democratic State Committee had officially opted for a caucus selection system in 1984.

The early 17 March date did, as anticipated, draw the personal attention and presence of virtually all the presidential hopefuls and their families. Askew, Cranston, Glenn, Hart, Hollings, Jackson, and Mondale campaigned in Arkansas, in some cases repeatedly. While the press and party activists were excited by this attention, however, the Arkansas voters apparently were not. Despite assiduous party attempts to publicize and explain the "newfangled" caucus system, only 22,202 persons participated on 17 March, less than 5 percent of the 448,174 who had voted in the 1980 Democratic presidential primary. Therefore, while the outcome sheds some interesting light on contemporary Arkansas political patterns, it provided little meaningful comparison with past voting behavior, and only scant clues (other than ominous signals of disinterest) as to possible voter preferences in the fall election.

By 17 March, although Askew, Glenn, and Hollings had also filed, only Hart, Jackson, and Mondale remained viable candidates, and they divided the first and decisive round as follows:

	Popular vote	Percentage popular vote	Counties in which a plurality
Mondale	8,059	36	43
Jackson	7,840	35	14
Hart	5,184	23	18
Uncommitted	1,119	.05	0
Total	22,202	99	75

Figure 8–1 with the strong caveat that it represents a very small and unrepresentative sampling, still provides an interesting illustration of the increasingly geographic nature of Arkansas voting patterns. Hart did best in the Ozark uplands, those areas that have become strongly Republican in national and increasingly so in state-wide contests. Jackson's strongest showing came in the Delta or lowland areas, where Arkansas' black population is concentrated. Mondale carried virtually everything in between, including Arkansas' most populous and urban Pulaski County, where Little Rock is located, and many small, very rural counties.

Further explanations for this breakdown are relatively simple, given

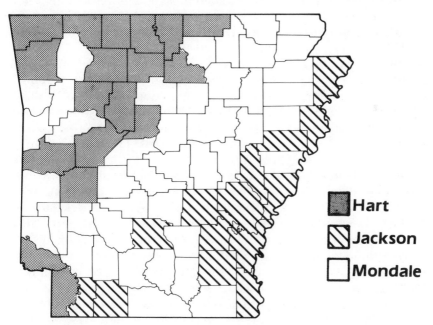

FIGURE 8–1   Counties Carried 1984 Democratic Caucuses

the candidates from whom Democrats had to choose by 17 March—
an important qualification since some of Arkansas' most prestigious
financial and political leaders had earlier committed to Glenn. The
collapse of the Glenn candidacy following his poor showing in the
southern 13 March primaries, however, gave Arkansans a three-way
choice.

Mondale was by far the earliest and best organized with a paid
staff in place by November, 11 full-time workers by 17 March, and
coordinators in every county. This organization was strongly supplemented by the efforts of organized labor and the Arkansas Education Association, the support of many party officials, and the
vociferous endorsement of First District Representative Bill Alexander, Assistant House Majority Whip.

The Mondale effort, then, was ideally suited to a low-turnout caucus system, and his sweep might have been even greater except for
the then-still-surging Hart campaign, effectively capitalized upon by
a small but skilled staff (which came from Iowa and stayed), some
mass media appeals, and a last-minute personal blitz by Hart himself.
Since Hart's major support came from Northwest Arkansas, and 12
of the 18 counties Hart carried had voted for Reagan in 1980, Hart's
support was characterized in the state press as a more "conservative"
vote. However, the youthful and ardently anti-Reagan cast to Hart's
most active supporters sheds considerable doubt upon this characterization.

Jackson's candidacy was enthusiastically supported by black, but
almost only black, Arkansans. (Former Governor Orval Faubus's
expression of support was more a redemptive gesture on Faubus's
part than a serious effort to boost Jackson's delegate strength). Despite some nasty, public, organizational in-fighting, the effort to turn
out black voters was demonstrably successful. Jackson carried the
caucuses in two of the three Arkansas counties with a predominantly
black population; and of the 14 Jackson counties, all but two have
more than twice the statewide 16.3 percent black population. Since
this very visible Jackson turnout did not translate into delegate victories, however, the inevitable results were angry charges, bitter feelings, and the threat of lawsuits and a convention floor fight.[12]

Amid loud denunciations of the entire caucus process from the
statewide press, state legislators, and many county party committees,
the next two tiers in the delegate selection process proceeded with
few hitches and no major shifts from what was anticipated after the
first-round caucus vote. At the state convention on 5 May, Mondale
got 19 of the pledged delegates, Hart nine, and Jackson seven. Of

the seven "unpledged" party officials, four were actually allied with Mondale, one with Jackson, and the other two were genuinely uncommitted.

While Jackson threats (to challenge the discrepancy between his popular strength and delegate totals, and to insist on the abolition of run-off primaries) continued to cast a cloud, and continued references to Dale Bumpers as a Vice-Presidential possibility continued to titillate, what little attention Arkansans had given to the presidential nomination contest shifted to the state's regular primaries on 29 May, in which only 44 percent of the state's registered voters chose to participate.

Predictably, Clinton vanquished three opponents, carrying 70 of the 75 counties and 64 percent of the vote, and Woody Freeman captured the Republican gubernatorial nomination with 67 percent. While the 492,595 Democratic voters presented the usual stark contrast to the 19,562 Republican voters, of potentially greater significance was the fact that the Democratic vote represented a 14 percent decline from the 1982 primary turnout, while the Republican vote represented nearly a 50 percent increase from 1982

THE PRESIDENTIAL CAMPAIGN

The actual presidential campaigns in Arkansas were far more vigorous and visible than have been most presidential campaigns in the past. Although Arkansas has only six electoral votes, both candidates had reason to seek them assiduously. Arkansas, because of its strong Democratic traditions, Reagan's very narrow victory in 1980, and Mondale's close personal ties to some of its Democratic officeholders, was seen as "winnable" by the Mondale camp. To the Reagan camp, these same factors suggested that extraordinary efforts might be necessary to carry Arkansas again.

In terms of organization, both presidential campaigns had hardworking state headquarters run by seasoned professionals aided by numerous volunteers, an elaborate system of regional and district coordinators, and at least some working apparatus in most of the state's 75 counties. Both parties attempted to register their likely supporters and both made strong efforts to get those voters to the polls. Additionally, both organizations spent considerable amounts of time doing advance work as the presidential candidates themselves and large numbers of their surrogates came to personally press their appeals in Arkansas.

Mondale came to Little Rock on 14 August for a "citizens forum" at the Old Statehouse; made a brief appearance in Texarkana (straddling the state line between Arkansas and Texas) on 24 September; and returned to Little Rock on 2 October to speak to the National Rural Electric Cooperatives Convention. Reagan made only one Arkansas appearance; but because of its election eve timing on 3 November, the pomp surrounding his entourage, and especially because he was the first President to visit Arkansas in 36 years, it had much greater dramatic impact.

The vice-presidential candidates also came to Arkansas: Ferraro to a Little Rock rally on 23 October; Bush to dedicate a VA hospital in Little Rock on 5 May, to a bass-fishing contest in Pine Bluff on 14 August, and to a question-and-answer forum in Little Rock on 3 October. Additionally, the candidates sent their families (Maureen Reagan; Joan, Eleanor, William, Ted, and Elaine Mondale; John, Jr., and Donna Zaccaro) and countless spokespersons: Gary Hart, Jesse Jackson, Andrew Young, and Claude Pepper for the Democrats; Gerald Ford (twice), Frank Fahrenkopf, Secretaries Regan, Block, and Hodel, Senators Baker, Hatch, Kasten, Trible, and Stevens, Representatives Kemp, Gingrich, Vander Jagt, Edwards, Sundquist, and McCain, and numerous luminaries ranging from Henry Kissinger to Roosevelt Grier for the Republicans. While most of the Republicans ostensibly appeared in behalf of Representative Ed Bethune's bid for the U.S. Senate and State Representative Judy Petty's bid for the U.S. House seat that Bethune was vacating, they all phrased their appeals in terms of the need in Congress for those who would sustain and advance Reagan's conservative programs.

Strictly in terms of organization, effort, and visibility, then, the presidential campaigns in Arkansas were quite similar. However, in two other respects there were noteworthy differences. First, whereas those representing the national Democratic ticket spoke on a great variety of issues, virtually all the Republicans reiterated the same few themes. Second, whereas Arkansas Democratic candidates increasingly distanced themselves from the national ticket, Republican candidates increasingly moved toward total immersion in Reaganism. The first of these differences seems to have worked to the Republicans' advantage; the second, ultimately, did not.

Regarding thematic emphasis, in Mondale's first Arkansas appearance as the presidential nominee he outlined his national defense program; in his second appearance he dealt with jobs, international trade, presidential leadership, and Lebanon; in his last appearance he lambasted the Republican farm program and suggested his own alternatives. Other Democrats offered criticisms and alternatives regarding civil rights, the elderly, the environment, education, peace, and assorted other issues.

In stark contrast, nearly all Republican speakers dealt in some fashion with the same trinity of themes: We will not raise taxes; we will stand up to our enemies abroad; the Democratic Party has lurched to the left and abandoned its traditional constituency. These three themes were focal nationally as well as in Arkansas, of course; but the singlemindedness with which the third refrain was chorused in Arkansas strongly suggests that much more than a presidential victory was seen to be at stake. The following examples, extracted from literally hundreds of possibilities, were clearly also designed to be the siren song of dealignment, if not realignment.

Consider the following quotes, all from different speakers, at different times and places throughout the campaign. "Mondale has clearly written off the South. Ferraro was chosen to pacify the Socialists in the Democratic Party."[13] Mondale is "way to the left spectrum of American politics. His whole record is to the left with liberal ideas that have failed."[14] "We Democrats are not leaving the party, the party's leaving us."[15] "The Democratic Party has the most liberal platform ever adopted by any national party."[16] "The Democratic Party has become too liberal for most Arkansas voters; the Republicans more closely reflect their conservative values."[17] "John Mc-Clellan would roll over in his grave right now if he saw some of the things that Walter Mondale and Geraldine Ferraro and Ted Kennedy and Tip O'Neill are talking about."[18] "This was the state that gave the U.S. government that great man (McClellan) for so many years. The Democratic Party has gone tremendously to the left. The party has become very left-wing and a lot of us feel that the party left us."[19] "In fact, we were surprised when, in Sunday's debate, he identified only the poor as worse off under Reagan. People probably wondered what had happened to the gays, labor, the liberals, the NEA and all the other types that are now marooned aboard his political ark."[20] "I said then and I say to you now that you should think more about what your grandchildren will think of your vote than what your grandfather would have thought of it."[21] "If the average Southern Democrat went home and told the truth about what he did in Washington, the Democratic Party would be literally repudiated in the South."[22] "What have Democrats been eating or snorting or smoking that caused their majority party to be hijacked by the extreme left wing."[23] And finally, President Reagan himself in Little Rock:

> I know that many of the good people of this state are Democrats, and I respect that tradition. I was a Democrat too for most of

> my adult life, but I changed parties when the leadership of the
> Democratic Party changed course. Its current leaders have made
> that once great party into the plaything of the left . . . They don't
> represent America anymore the way they once did.[24]

Reinforcing this relentless barrage of personal testimonials were
two television advertisements clearly designed for the same dealign-
ment/realignment purposes. In July the Arkansas Republican Party
spent $30,000 for 60 showings of an ad featuring father and son
fishing on the banks of the Arkansas River, with father speaking to
son as follows:

> Y'know, we've got a lot of good family traditions like fishing,
> hard work, and voting Democratic. But the old Arkansas Dem-
> ocratic Party of John McClellan's day is gone. It's been taken over
> by liberals who won't stand up for what's right. But Arkansas still
> has a few good national leaders. Nowadays, they're mostly Re-
> publicans. This year me and Kenny are gonna register and vote
> for some Republicans, 'cause another Arkansas tradition is doing
> what's right.[25]

Immediately preceding the election, a national ad featured a more
upscale father and son duo, with the collegiate-appearing son badg-
ering the father as to why their family always votes Democratic when
the Democrats have offered nothing but taxing and spending. The
son, in effect, asks parental permission to vote Republican, and the
grinning father gives his tacit blessing: "Once you pull that curtain,
son, nobody will ever know."

These appeals to traditional Democrats and their less party-minded
offspring were reinforced by Republican announcements of two
"Democrats for Reagan" lists. The national list included Jackson T.
Stephens of Little Rock, a close friend and avid supporter of Jimmy
Carter, who more recently had headed John Glenn's nomination in
Arkansas. The state list included one retiring Democratic state legislator, one former Democratic state legislator, and a number of
prominent businessmen and farmers once active (though none recently) in state Democratic circles. The Mondale campaign quickly
counterpunched with a list of 46 state legislators who had agreed to
serve on the Arkansas Mondale-Ferraro steering committee. Significantly, however, only one of those on the list faced general election
opposition.

This leads to and highlights the second major difference between
the two presidential campaigns in Arkansas: the cautious distance
delineated by major state Democratic officeholders between themselves and the national ticket; the wholehearted unity between state

Republican office seekers and their national team. The respective stances were first apparent at the two parties' national nominating conventions.

Governor Clinton did attend and speak from the podium in San Francisco. He used the opportunity, however, while paying tribute to Harry Truman, to suggest that Truman would have been disgusted with a party that was still bogged down in old ideas and old politics. The other major officials who attended, again with the exception of Representative Alexander, kept a low public profile; and Senator Pryor, anticipating the stiffest challenge for reelection, stayed away altogether. In contrast, Ed Bethune and Judy Petty used their brief moments on the platform in Dallas, supplemented by a barrage of publicity send back home, to embrace the national ticket and the entire Republican platform.

Although a respectable complement of Democratic officials welcomed and stood with Mondale and Ferraro on the Arkansas visits, those engaged in election contests carefully distinguished their own campaigns from that for the Presidency. Clinton, for example, repeatedly noted on the campaign trail that while he was a Democrat by "both heritage and conviction," he had never hesitated to criticize the party when he felt they had gone astray, and had in fact done so publicly at the national convention in both 1980 and 1984. Pryor repeatedly pointed out that he, like Reagan, supported a constitutional amendment to balance the budget while Bethune had dismissed it as a phony proposal, and Pryor's staff released figures that Pryor and Bethune's percentages of support for Reagan in 1984 (45 percent and 53 percent, respectively) were quite comparable. Tommy Robinson, the colorful and controversial Pulaski County Sheriff who had won the Democratic nomination for the Second Congressional District seat, advertised himself as "an independent voice for Arkansas" with "the courage to fight for right." Additionally, he ran full-page newspaper ads welcoming Reagan to Little Rock and assuring him (and the voters), "When I believe you are right, I will be your strong supporter. When we do not agree, I—like you—will have the courage of my own convictions."[26] The sole exception to this pattern was Representative Bill Alexander who, having won his primary contest by 77 percent, and facing only token write-in opposition in the general election, and also presumably hoping for future advancement in House leadership ranks, became Mondale's most vehement and visible official advocate in Arkansas.

Ed Bethune, Judy Petty, and Woody Freeman, however, continuously released notices of every personal encouragement and endorsement they received from Reagan, invoked his name incessantly on the campaign trail, and invested most of their last major media buys in advertisements featuring Reagan himself asking for their election. Bethune and Petty, in fact, flew to Springfield, Illinois, on 2 November so that they could fly triumphantly to Little Rock with Reagan and be photographed descending with him from the presidential plane.

Considering all the above, it is ironic that although Reagan very substantially improved his own winning margin in Arkansas from 1980 to 1984, his coattails appeared to be considerably shorter than they had been in 1980. However, although all major Republican candidates other than Reagan were defeated, 1984 was not an altogether unsuccessful year for Republicans in Arkansas.

THE OUTCOME AND ITS MEANING

The sheer dimensions of Reagan's 1984 victory in Arkansas are overwhelming, especially in contrast to 1980. In 1980, Reagan won 25 of Arkansas' 75 counties, one congressional district, 48 percent of the popular vote, and a plurality of 5,123. In 1984 Reagan won 65 counties, all four congressional districts, 60.4 percent of the popular vote, and a plurality of nearly 200,000. By any measure, except perhaps McGovern's 1972 loss, Mondale's ten counties and 39.6 percent of the vote constituted a crushing defeat.

Where the Democrats could and did take comfort, however, was in the fact that Pryor was comfortably reelected to the Senate with 57 percent of the vote over Bethune; that the congressional seat vacated by Bethune was recaptured for the Democrats by Tommy Robinson; and that Clinton became the first Governor since Faubus (and only the third in Arkansas history) to win a third two-year term, by 63 percent of the vote. Indeed, in most major races Democrats did even better than these aggregate figures indicate. In numerous counties that Reagan carried, Pryor got more than two-thirds of the vote, and of the eight countries in Bethune's Second District, he carried only his home county of White. Judy Petty raised and spent over a half-million dollars and campaigned indefatigably, all to achieve precisely the same 41 percent of the vote she won when running against a disgraced Wilbur Mills in 1974. On the surface, then Reagan's surge in popularity did little to boost his co-partisans. Before examining this anomaly, however, the geographic and demographic bases to the 1984 election results sharpen the picture of contemporary Arkansas political geography.

Reagan's victory map (Figure 8–2) shows that he managed to extend his base well beyond the traditional areas of Republican strength, leaving to Mondale only a handful of Delta counties where the black vote is sizeable, and two counties (Hot Spring and Clark) where organized labor is traditionally powerful. However, if one looks instead at those counties where Reagan's margin exceeded 5 percent of his state average (Figure 8–3), the strength of Republicanism in northern and western Arkansas is reconfirmed. It was also in these areas that the Republican candidates for Senate (Figure 8–4) and Governor (Figure 8–5) had their only successes.

Also in these counties, which closely coincide with Republican Hammerschmidt's Third Congressional District, Republicans continued their slow but steady increase in state legislative seats, moving from ten to 13 positions: four in the Senate and nine in the House. The fact that Republicans now have a majority in the Third District Caucus in the state Senate, while having less than 10 percent of the legislature generally, highlights the sharp geographic pattern to Arkansas politics, which 1984 strengthened. In this northwestern area, but only in this area, a Republican label has become not only legitimate, but somewhat advantageous.

Two other aspects of Reagan's winning base are worth noting: the stability in Republican presidential voting patterns over the decades, and the significant correlation between Reagan's most favorable counties and the percentage of population growth, both demonstrated in Table 8–1.[27] These two factors, one reflecting stability, the other change, at first appear contradictory; but the explanation underscores the fact that the most dramatic increases in population have been in those northern Ozark counties where native Republicans have been holding their ground for over a century. Whereas the state generally gained 18.9 percent population between 1970 and 1980, Reagan's strongest counties (Figure 8–2) had an average growth rate of 32.9 percent during this same period. Again invoking Campbell's typology, in-migration clearly has been consequential.

In his 1949 treatise on southern politics, V. O. Key described "a strange political schizophrenic, the presidential Republican . . . Locally he is a Democrat, nationally a Republican;" and based upon the fact that the Republican gubernatorial and U.S. Senate votes were generally less than half (48 percent) the size of the Republican presidential vote, Key concluded that presidential Republicans constituted the largest portion of the total Republican presidential vote in Arkansas.[28] Obviously, the presidential vote still exceeds any other kind of Republican vote in Arkansas; but the margins have narrowed

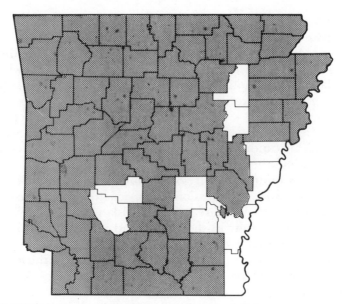

FIGURE 8–2   Counties Won by Reagan, 1984

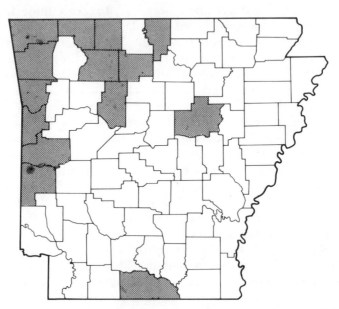

FIGURE 8–3   Counties Where Reagan's Margin Exceeded the Statewide Average by 5% or More

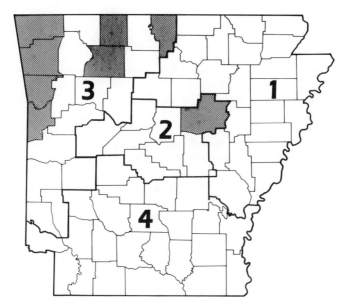

FIGURE 8–4   Counties Won by Bethune (Congressional Districts Indicated)

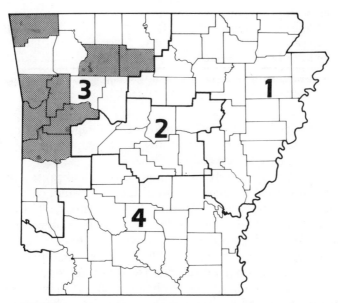

FIGURE 8–5   Counties Won by Freeman (Congressional Districts Indicated)

TABLE 8–1   Simple Correlation Coefficients (Pearson's *r*)
between the 1984 Reagan Vote and Selected Variables

Variables	*1984 Vote for Reagan*
Demographic	
% Population growth 1970–80	.5749
% Black	−.6591
Per capita income	.1807
% Civilian labor force in manufacturing	.1419
% Population with 16+ years education	.1213
% Population born in state	−.5627
% Persons living below poverty level	−.5643
% Population 65+ years of age	.0976
% Urban	−.0650
Electoral	
% Democratic presidential vote, 1928	−.5416[a]
% Democratic presidential vote, 1944	−.5427
% Republican presidential vote, 1948	.5458
% Democratic presidential vote, 1952	−.6063
% Democratic presidential vote, 1956	−.6042
% Republican presidential vote, 1960	.6233
% Republican presidential vote, 1968	.6697
% Democratic presidential vote, 1976	−.6727
% Republican presidential vote, 1980	.8356
% Republican U.S. Senate vote, 1984	.9049
% Republican gubernatorial vote, 1984	.8248
% Republican Lt. Gov. vote, 1984	.7185

[a]Only the Democratic percentage of the vote was compiled for most elections; hence the use of the negative correlation in those years.

(Bethune's popular vote was 69 percent of Reagan's, Freeman's 60 percent), and as Table 8–1 illustrates, all the contemporary Republican votes are closely correlated.

Another pattern strongly confirmed by the 1984 presidential election in Arkansas was the nearly monolithic attachment of black voters to Democratic candidates. Of Mondale's ten counties, all but two have black populations that considerably exceed the statewide average. Indeed, of these ten counties, three have black majorities, and their overall average black population is 36.5 1, more than twice the state 16.3 1 average. Judging by returns from voting precincts that the 1980 census indicated were virtually all black, Mondale received at least 90 percent of all black votes cast. Pryor and Clinton were also beneficiaries of black voters' preferences for Democratic candidates;

in fact, their margins in black communities usually exceeded Mondale's. The lone black candidate on this year's statewide ballot, Republican candidate for Lieutenant Governor Solomon Scaife, got only 26 percent of the statewide vote, and fared no better in black precincts than did the white Republicans on the ticket.

The correlation between Mondale's strength and the size of the black population was such a familiar pattern in 1984 that it needs little elaboration. Where Arkansas does somewhat differ from the national (or at least southern) norm, however, is in the support Mondale received from white voters. In 19 Arkansas counties, blacks constitute less than 1 percent of the population. Despite widespread assertions that Mondale received only 28–30 percent of southern white votes, the Mondale vote in these virtually all-white counties ranged from 23 percent to 47 percent, and averaged 36 percent.[29] Furthermore, if those 11 counties in the Third (and generally Republican) Congressional District are divided from those eight counties in the First Congressional District, Mondale's percentage of presumably white voters was 32.4 percent and 41.5 percent, respectively.

Clearly, Mondale found greater favor with some white voters in Arkansas than elsewhere in the South, and (assuming that estimates elsewhere were accurate) there are several possible explanations: Democratic traditions may still be stronger in Arkansas than elsewhere; the eight northeastern counties where Mondale averaged over 40 percent all lie in the district of Representative Alexander, who is popular in his district and whose wholehearted support for Mondale was widely advertised; these are primarily farming counties, perhaps influenced by the strong effort made by the Arkansas Mondale campaign to criticize Reagan's farm policies. There is also the possibility, somewhat somber in its implications, that it is easier to remain a loyal Democrat in areas where there is little visible evidence of the overwhelming support of blacks for the Democratic ticket.

While survey data strongly suggest the influence of income in voting (a mid-October statewide poll indicated that only 30 percent of those earning less than $10,000 favored Reagan, compared with 62 percent of those earning $10,000–$20,000 and 76 percent of those earning more than $30,000), county-level data do not significantly correlate with income, kinds of employment or education.[30] As Table 8–1 indicates, Reagan's popularity is negatively associated with measures of poverty, but it is difficult to separate the specific impacts of race and poverty since the two factors themselves are associated.

The only other clearly explanatory demographic factor is the percentage of native-born Arkansans, with which Reagan's strength is also negatively associated. This is to some extent the obverse of the population growth factor, and nativism is also closely associated with black and poor populations. What seems most clear from this analysis is that, whatever the topographical and historical origins of the geographic patterns in Arkansas politics, they are clearly based in certain contemporary demographic variables as well.

Considering the extent to which presidential voting patterns in 1984 simply confirmed preexisting trends, it might be fair to conclude that Arkansas, following a strong national trend favoring a very popular incumbent President, in times characterized by relative peace and prosperity, demonstrated once again its ability to ignore party affiliation in a presidential election. However, in virtually all other major races, the traditional Democratic preferences of the voters were still sufficiently strong to withstand the President's appeals. While in its general outlines that is a fairly accurate characterization of 1984 in Arkansas, it is also an incomplete one, obscuring some of the very real progress that emerging Republicanism appears to be making in the state.

First, while it is true that Reagan's popularity had no electoral benefits for the other major Republican contenders, and seemingly even less than in 1980, that may be in part because in 1984 his coattails were anxiously anticipated and cleverly minimized. Clinton, for example, buoyed by a strong Democratic primary victory and encouraging polls throughout 1984, might have permitted himself a much easier pace. However, having been caught napping in the Republican upsurge of 1980, he took absolutely no chances in 1984, waging an expensive and carefully crafted media campaign, and driving his 75 county organizations to fervent local efforts. Similarly, it was clear that Pryor had taken careful note of Bumpers's "embarrassing" loss (through a lackadaisical low-budget campaign) of 41 percent of the vote in 1980 to an unimpressive Republican challenger. Pryor, therefore, raised and spent nearly $1.5 million, repeatedly praised the "ferociously independent" Arkansas voter, hired superb professional consultants, and campaigned tirelessly for a year as though he were an underdog. The coattails might well have been there in 1984, but coattails anticipated are far less damaging than coattails unforeseen.

Second, it should also be noted that Clinton's very vigorous efforts produced exactly the same margin (63 percent) that a minimal campaign had secured in his first election as Governor in 1978; and Pryor had to make an extraordinary effort to achieve 57 percent in 1984, whereas in 1978, after the most bruising Democratic primary in recent history, he had literally cruised through the general election to a 76 percent margin of victory. The clear moral here is that no Democratic candidate for major office in Arkansas, even a popular incumbent, can take the same cavalier attitude toward the general election that was commonplace as recently as six years ago.

Third, if the geographic base of the 1984 presidential election is examined not for Reagan's highest margins, but the Reagan's greatest increases from 1980 to 1984, again there is an ominous message to Democrats. As Figure 8–6 illustrates, Reagan's plurality increased the most, 15 percent or more, in a broad band of counties that runs diagonally across the center of the state from northeast to southwest, but with particular strength in the southern regions.

These 30 counties are considerably less urban than is the state generally (averaging 32.5 percent urban population as compared to 51.6 percent for the entire state) and possess considerably more native Arkansans (averaging 77.4 percent compared to 69.2 percent for the state generally). These counties have also traditionally been among the strongest Democratic supporters, with the insignificant exception of 1972, when the entire state went Republican, but with the possibly significant exception of 1968, when 28 of these 30 counties supported Wallace. It seems safe to speculate that it was in these areas, among

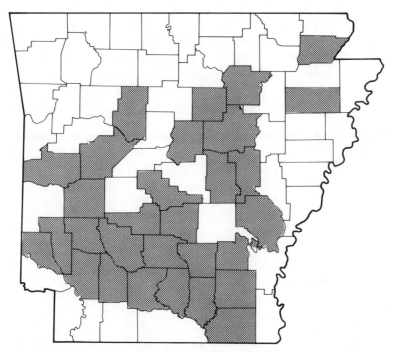

FIGURE 8–6   Counties Where Reagan's Margin Increased by 15% or More, 1980 to 1984

thousands of low- to middle-income rural, white, native Arkansans that the "siren song of dealignment" had its most seductive impact.

No matter how strong the Republican upsurge among the native and transplanted voters of northern and western Arkansas, to move beyond occasional victory to equal competitive strength, Republicans will have to make large inroads into these areas, attracting those who turn-of-the-century Arkansas Governor Jeff Davis once celebrated and mobilized as the "sunburned sons of the soil," and whom Samuel Lubell more recently characterized as "rednecks on the move."[31] Although they are no longer tenants and sharecroppers, many are their descendants; and therefore in terms of economic issues, they are more likely to be attracted by the worker-oriented, kind-hearted Democrats than the business-oriented, hard-hearted Republicans. On social issues, however, such as civil rights and civil liberties, many devoutly embrace a fundamentalist Bible-belt morality; and they are therefore much more likely to be attracted to the puritanical Republican right than to the broad-minded Democratic left.

If they do not yet feel comfortable with the wealthy businessmen, large landowners, and retired Yankees who have led the state Republican Party, they are surely equally uncomfortable with a state Democratic Party in which organized labor, assertive blacks, and liberated women seem to have assumed inordinate influence. The upsurge in Republican presidential popularity in these areas had no apparent negative impact on the candidacies of Clinton and Pryor, but the willingness to desert longstanding Democratic traditions in any race may promise the potential for further Republican gains in the future.

Finally, 1984 opinion survey data, especially when compared with polls taken in the past, offers evidence of some limited realignment, as the following array indicates:[32]

	Democratic (Including Leaners)	Republican (Including Leaners)	Independent
October 1970	59.0%	17.0%	24.0%
31 October 1980	59.0	13.0	28.0
9 November 1980	49.0	16.0	35.0
May 1983	59.9	16.7	23.5
April 1984	59.6	21.7	18.7
September 1984	57.0	26.5	16.5
5 November 1984	53.2	28.0	18.8

In both 1980 and 1984, a popular Republican presidential candidate seems to have reduced, at least temporarily, the number of respondents identifying themselves as Democrats. In fact, disaffection from the Democratic Party was even more pronounced in 1980 than it was in 1984. However, in 1980 disaffected Democrats seemed to move to the halfway house of independency; whereas in 1984, they were more willing to identify themselves as Republicans. This kind of complete switch in party allegiance could have greater permanence than did the more sizeable but only partial switch in the immediate aftermath of Reagan's 1980 victory. Another indication of possible permanence is that the switch to the Republican Party seem to have produced little more change (+6.3 percent) than had other forces operational between 1980 and 1984 (+5.5 percent). Since this data was collected by different pollsters for different purposes, the results must be treated with considerable caution. Nevertheless, it does appear that at least some "individual conversion" is taking place.

Since these polls did not consistently cross-tabulate party identification with age, "generational turnover" is more difficult to measure. In Arkansas, however, as elsewhere in 1984, Reagan's strongest support came the younger generations: He was favored by 63.4 percent of under-30s and by 71.7 percent of 30–44s, compared with 59 percent of 45–59s and only 57.1 percent of over-60s. Also in Arkansas, his strongest support of all came from younger men. In this particular election-eve poll, Reagan was the favorite of 78.1 percent of men under 45 (compared with 56.7 percent of women under 45); his weakest support came from women over 45 (53 percent compared with 63.9 percent of men over 45).[33] While presidential support patterns cannot be equated with party identification, this is fairly strong evidence of at least some generation turnover, tempered by a sizeable gender gap, at work in Arkansas.

Certain electoral conditions will be different, and possibly more favorable to Democrats, in 1988 than they were in 1984. It is already clear that the Democrats will not experiment again with the presidential caucus system; and therefore, to whatever extent its very limited turnout and assorted antagonisms reduced the Democratic vote in the general election, this factor will be eliminated. Furthermore, since Arkansas voters adopted an initiated constitutional amendment in 1984 establishing four-year terms for the Governor and other elected officials, and these elections will be held in the off-years beginning in 1986, whatever energizing effects popular Republican presidential candidates have been having in state races will be eliminated. And certainly, in the aftermath of 1984, there will be loud demands within the national Democratic Party for a 1988 ticket that appeals to rather than offends white southerners.

Even in the eventuality that these pleas are heard, however, Democratic presidential candidates have clearly lost the overwhelming advantage they once enjoyed in Arkansas. While Republicans lost most of their major battles in 1984, they have made considerable progress in strategically positioning themselves for future contests.

NOTES

1. Jim Ranchino, *Faubus to Bumpers: Arkansas Votes 1960–1970* (Arkadelphia, AR: Action Research, Inc.), 73–78.

2. Ibid.

3. John Brummett, "Clinton's Appeal to Blacks Rests on Record, Skill," *Arkansas Gazette*, 6 December 1982, 1–B.

4. Bruce A. Campbell, "Patterns of Change in the Partisan Loyalties of Native Southerners, 1952–72," *Journal of Politics* 39 (1977): 730–61.

5. Diane D. Blair and Robert L. Savage, "Regional Patterns in the Distribution of Political Opinions among Arkansans," paper presented to the Annual Meeting of the Arkansas Political Science Association, February 1983.

6. Ibid.

7. "Pryor Top Foe of President, GOP Panel Says," *Arkansas Gazette*, 31 January 1984, 3–A.

8. In response to post-1968 national Democratic mandates that most delegates be chosen by means open to public participation, the 1972 legislature authorized a presidential primary, then quickly repealed it when the presidential aspirations of then-Representative Wilbur Mills became evident. Thus, in 1972 Democratic delegates to county conventions were popularly selected in the regular spring primary, these in turn selecting delegates to the state convention who then selected the national convention delegates.

9. Only a few of Arkansas counties absorb the cost of paying judges and clerks from public funds. Primaries are largely financed by the party, which in turn is heavily dependent upon filing fees assessed upon the candidates.

10. On two previous occasions when party registration bills were passed, they were vetoed: by Governor Orval Faubus in 1959 and by Governor Winthrop Rockefeller in 1969. In the latter instance, the legislature overrode the veto, only to have the law defeated by voters in a protest referendum.

11. There were also some concerns that, lacking a party registration law, Republicans might join with conservative Democrats to deliberately embarrass Bumpers in his home state.

12. Delegates had been allocated on the basis of previously fixed numbers (population and the Democratic vote for President in 1980 and Governor in 1982) rather than on popular turnout.

13. Bob Leslie, Chairman, Arkansas Republican Party, from radio interview reported in *Arkansas Gazette*, 16 July 1984, 1–A.

14. Vice President George Bush, *Arkansas Gazette,* 9 August 1984, 1–A.

15. Former White House Aide to President Carter David Walters, press conference in Little Rock, *Arkansas Democrat,* 18 August 1984, 6–A.

16. Former Postmaster General Winton Blount, press conference in Little Rock, *Arkansas Democrat,* 18 August 1984, 1–C.

17. Representative Ed Bethune, speaking to the Republican National Convention, *Arkansas Gazette,* 22 August 1984, 3–A.

18. J. J. Vigneault, Executive Director, Arkansas Reagan-Bush Campaign, *Northwest Arkansas Times,* 3 September 1984, 3.

19. Senator Orrin Hatch, speaking in Little Rock, *Springdale News,* 9 September 1984, 6–A.

20. Editorial in *Arkansas Democrat,* 11 October 1984, 12–A.

21. Senator Howard Baker, speaking in Jonesboro, *Arkansas Gazette,* 25 October 1984, 1–B.

22. Representative Newt Gringrich, speaking in Little Rock, *Arkansas Gazette,* 31 October 1984, 9–A.

23. The Rev. Roy McLaughlin, State Chairman, Arkansas Moral Majority, news conference in Little Rock, *Springdale News,* 23 October 1984, 6–A.

24. *Arkansas Democrat,* 4 November 1984, 1–A.

25. Text printed in *Arkansas Gazette,* 20 July 1984, 11–A.

26. *Arkansas Gazette,* 2 November 1984, 12–A.

27. To systematically analyze the bases of the 1984 presidential election in Arkansas, a large number of demographic electoral variables were compiled for all 75 Arkansas counties. These included such demographic measures as the percentages of black, native, and urban population, measures of income, employment, education, age, and poverty, and percentage of population growth; and election percentages for 13 presidential election years, 1928, 1932, 1944–84. Analysis was performed utilizing Pearson's correlation coefficients. Table 8–1 presents the simple correlation coefficients between the 1984 Reagan vote and selected variables. T. R. Carr and Heather Miles gave invaluable assistance with the compiling, coding, and analysis of this data.

28. V. O. Key, Jr., *Southern Politics in State and Nation* (New York: Knopf, 1949), 278—79.

29. For estimates of white southern support of Mondale ranging from 27–30 percent, see *Time,* 19 November 1984, 42; *National Journal,* 10 November 1984, 2132; *Newsweek,* November-December 1984, 7.

30. Data reported here come from "Arkansas Senatorial Polls" conducted throughout 1984, which Senator David Pryor's office most graciously made available.

31. Samuel Lubell, *The Hidden Crisis in American Politics* (New York: Norton, 1971), Chap. 5.

32. All of these polls used a statewide sample of 400 or more. The October 1970 poll was taken by Jim Ranchino & Associates of Arkadelphia. The 1980 polls were taken by Precision Research, Inc., of Little Rock. The May 1983 data is from "A Report of Public Attitudes toward Arkansas Louisiana Gas Company," Precision Research, Inc. The 1984 data is from Arkansas Senatorial Polls, op. cit.

33. Arkansas Senatorial Polls, 5 November 1984.

9

Tennessee

Anne H. Hopkins, William Lyons,
and Steve Metcalf

Every four years, Tennesseans are pulled into the spectacle of presidential politics. The process of nominating and electing a President has been transformed in the last thirty years. Ever increasing expenditures, the use of polls and professional campaign management firms, and major party reform have made presidential elections much more of a nationalized process. Yet the nominating process with its primaries and caucuses, and the general election through the electoral college, are still structurally state-based. And the voters, though participating in a national election, simultaneously participate in state and local elections. Thus presidential elections, though increasingly nationalized, must still play to state forces to be successful.

The purpose of this chapter is to provide a state-level perspective on Tennessee in the politics of the presidential nominating and election process in 1984 and to examine the process and outcome of that election as part of the changing presidential electoral coalition in Tennessee. In order to provide a context within which to understand the outcome of the 1984 presidential election in Tennessee, it is necessary to examine the base of prior electoral behavior in Tennessee both geographically and over time. Additionally, it is important to distinguish among the levels and visibility of the offices contested.

THE PARTISAN CONTEXT IN TENNESSEE

Tennessee is a Border state, which in recent years has been characterized as a competitive two-party or as an example of the increasing Republicanism of the rim South. But this picture of Tennessee electoral politics is overly simplistic and conceals the continuing regional base of electoral behavior and wide variations in partisan support dependent upon the level of visibility of the public office being contested. Tennessee electoral politics has indeed undergone significant changes since the 1950s, but the result has *not* been an evolution to a state with competition across the state or for all offices.

The origin of the current Tennessee party systems lies in the Civil War era. There was significant opposition to secession in the non-slaveholding mountainous areas, and nearly a third of the state voted against secession. Those areas that opposed secession have since formed the core of the Republican voters in Tennessee and are concentrated in East Tennessee and a few West Tennessee counties on the Highland Rim. In contrast, the core of Democratic support has been in Middle and West Tennessee, regions that voted overwhelmingly to join the Confederacy and were slaveholding areas. Writing about Tennessee in 1949, V. O. Key, Jr., noted the "extraordinary durability of voting habits fixed by war and reconstruction."[1] Republicans and Democrats seemed to stay out of each other's turf, and in statewide elections for Governor, the Republicans were "political eunuchs."[2] Turnout was relatively low and the personal organization of Crump in Memphis colored state elections for over two decades (the 1930s and 1940s). As outlined by Key, the geographical base for the two political parties remained essentially unaltered from the 1860s until the 1950s and 1960s.[3] The Democrats controlled all statewide elections for President, U.S. Senator, and Governor, while the Republicans usually elected two members to Congress from East Tennessee and a minority East Tennessee delegation to the state legislature.

It is difficult to identify precisely the point at which significant electoral change began in Tennessee. To permit a broad time perspective in which to assess electoral change in Tennessee, Figure 9–1 plots the percentage Democratic votes for President, U.S. Senator, and Governor from 1932 through 1982.[4] Figure 9–1 indicates that from 1932 through 1944 Democratic candidates won all presidential, senatorial, and gubernatorial elections in Tennessee. After 1944, three points of apparent electoral transition are evident: 1948–52 for presidential elections, 1966 for senatorial elections, and 1970 for gub-

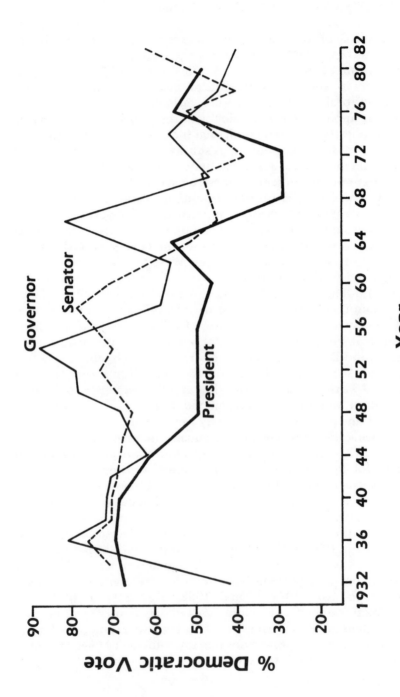

FIGURE 9–1 Percentage Democratic Vote for President, U.S. Senator, and Governor, 1932–82

ernatorial elections. Each of these elections is the point at which
Republican electoral success was first achieved.

The first break in Democratic dominance of presidential elections
occurred in 1948 when the Democratic proportion of the vote dropped
slightly below 50 percent, although Truman won a plurality of the
vote. In 1952 General Dwight Eisenhower carried Tennessee for the
first time for a Republican presidential candidate since 1928. Eisenhower won again in 1956 and Republicans carried the state in 1960,
1968, and 1972 for Nixon and in 1980 for Reagan. Indeed, the only
two presidential elections in which Tennessee voted Democratic since
1952 are the two elections involving fellow southerners—in 1964 for
Johnson and in 1976 for Carter.

The first break from Democratic dominance in races for the U.S.
Senate came much later—in 1966 when Howard Baker defeated
former Governor Frank Clement after a closely contested and divisive
Democratic primary. Four years later, in a banner Republican year
in Tennessee, William Brock was elected Tennessee's second Republican U.S. Senator and Winfield Dunn, a dentist from Memphis, was
elected the first Republican Governor since the 1920. The contrast
between 1966 and 1970 is striking—in the 1966 election when Baker
won first his Senate seat, the Republicans did not even field a candidate for Governor, yet in the next election they were able to emerge
victorious. State political commentators argue that it was critical that
Dunn, from Memphis, was able to pull together the traditional East
Tennessee Republican vote with the emerging Republican presidential vote in suburban areas around Memphis.[5]

Since 1970 Republicans have been competitive in both senatorial
and gubernatorial elections. Baker won reelection to the Senate with
over 60 percent of the vote in 1972 and by a slightly smaller margin
in 1978. Republican Senator Brock was defeated by Democrat James
Sasser in 1976 and Sasser was reelected with over 60 percent of the
vote in 1982. The Democrats recaptured the governorship in 1974,
but following extensive scandals, Republican Lamar Alexander was
elected Governor in 1978 and again in 1982. Thus, since 1970 Republicans and Democrats have vied on a fairly competitive basis (40–
60 percent range) for the major statewide offices.

This recent party competition for the visible offices in Tennessee
seems not to have been translated downward.[6] After some increases
in the 1960, Republicans have not fared well in attempts to expand
their number of seats in the General Assembly. From a low point in
1968–72, the Democrats have expanded the size of their majorities
in both houses of the General Assembly. Similarly, Republican candidates (when fielded) for the Public Service Commission and the

Supreme Court, the only other popularly elected statewide offices in Tennessee, have not been competitive electorally. Indeed, in most legislative races and the less-visible statewide races, the pre-1950s voting alignments seem to be intact.

Republican candidates have become real contenders at least for the visible public offices at stake in Tennessee. Generally, Republicans have gained their electoral success for state offices when Democrats have had divisive primaries or when Democrats have fielded weak candidates.[7] But the Republicans state-level success appears somewhat shallow and contingent on the selection of strong personalities as candidates. Greene has characterized Tennessee politics as personality rather than issue-based and the Democratic party as organizationally weak.[8] Republicans have been more successful at the presidential level. Fund raising has been particularly strong for the Republicans, who have generally not placed much priority on establishing grass-roots (that is, precinct-level) organizations.[9]

This brief discussion of partisan electoral fortunes in Tennessee underlines the limitations that must be attached to the discussion that follows in its focus on presidential politics. Presidential politics in Tennessee is not a mirror of state and local politics and seems to have developed something of a life of its own. The key question relative to electoral politics in Tennessee remains the same, whether presidential or state and local elections provide the focus: Has there been or is there developing an enduring partisan realignment? This question will provide the central point of inquiry relative to analyzing the outcome of the 1984 presidential election in Tennessee.

The regional underpinning of partisanship in Tennessee necessitates an examination of electoral change and the 1984 presidential election at the county level. The desirability of this approach is reinforced by the findings of Hopkins and Lyons that apparent realignments at the state level in Tennessee shield both cross-cutting and cross-canceling realignments at the county level.[10] It will also permit, at least in terms of presidential elections, an examination of the degree to which regionalism endures in Tennessee, a question about which scholars of southern politics disagree.[11]

THE NOMINATING PROCESS

With the renomination of Reagan a foregone conclusion, interest in the nominating process, both nationally and in Tennessee, focused almost entirely on the Democratic Party. Entitled to 76 delegates to the San Francisco convention, Tennessee Democrats selected 44 of these in an open primary on 1 May;[12] an additional 21 pledged delegates that were either party and elected officials (six) or at-large (15) were selected by the Tennessee Democratic Committee and allocated among the candidates on the basis of the primary vote; 11 more delegates were selected by the State Committee but specified as unpledged party and elected officials.[13]

By the May Tennessee primary, the nationwide primary season was about half over. With 40 percent of the delegates still to be chosen, Mondale held an almost two-to-one lead in delegate support over Gary Hart (1,114 to 590), with Jackson trailing in third place (200).[14] For Hart to win the nomination, he would have had to win two-thirds of the remaining delegates; a possible but unlikely occurrence. As Tennessee's primary approached, Mondale had the momentum of recent victories in the Michigan caucus, as well as the Illinois, New York, and Pennsylvania primaries.

Although the three remaining contenders for the nomination committed some time and resources to the Tennessee primary, these were necessarily limited because of the importance of (1) the Pennsylvania primary held one week earlier in which 172 delegates and substantial prestige was at stake particularly for Mondale; (2) the Texas caucus, which followed the Tennessee primary by four days (169 delegates); and (3) the 8 May primaries in which 425 delegates were to be selected (Indiana, Maryland, North Carolina, and Ohio). Nonetheless, as would be expected, the candidates, their surrogates, and Tennessee Democratic party officials all proclaimed the importance of the primary. The primary was of potential importance in the overall race for the nomination, since it provided one of the last chances for Hart to gain an unanticipated win and thereby enhance the possibility of sidetracking Mondale while still enough time was left to win the nomination.

But Tennessee, like the nomination, was not to be Hart's. In early April there was evidence of support for Hart among county chairmen and members of the state executive committee (43 to 42 percent for Hart and Mondale respectively); but among those same leaders, 66 percent believed Mondale would carry their county.[15] These predictions were reinforced by polls of the general population that showed Mondale leading in the state.[16] Since 1972 when Tennessee held its first presidential primary, voter turnout as a percentage of registered voters has been low and has continued to decline (32 percent in 1972; 25 percent in 1976; and 21 percent in 1980). An untypically high turnout would be important if Hart were to make it a close election. A low turnout seemed likely to favor Mondale. His stronger organization boasted linkages to labor (having been endorsed by the state

AFL–CIO and the strong Tennessee Education Association), and support by a number of prominent state Democrats. These included the powerful Speaker of the state House, Ned Ray McWherter, who was an early supporter; Jim Neal, a Nashville attorney and former Watergate prosecutor, who chaired Mondale's Tennessee campaign; Lieutenant Governor John Wilder who switched to Mondale after Glenn withdrew; and the black politically active Ford family in Memphis.

Until close to the primary, the Democratic campaign in Tennessee was oriented toward organization and fund raising. By early February Mondale supporters had established both statewide and state senate district organizations and had raised approximately $100,000. Glenn, who bowed out of the presidential race on 16 March, had organizations in each of the counties and, with the help of incumbent U.S. Senator James Sasser, had raised about $200,000. In contrast, Hart's fund raising and organization at this early date were very limited. Two months later, both Mondale and Jackson had viable organizations. The state AFL–CIO was very active prior to the primary, supplying both direct mail services and phone banks to Mondale. In contrast, Jackson's organization centered on his voter registration efforts, particularly in urban areas. Hart's supporters were much less organized, having started their efforts considerably later than either Mondale or Jackson.

With the exception of Jackson's two-day visit to Memphis in February and a fund-raiser by Glenn, none of the candidates campaigned in the state until a week-and-a-half before the primary. Jesse Jackson was the first to actively campaign in Tennessee. As he criss-crossed the state, he spoke, as he did throughout the campaign, of those who had been left out of the political process. Breaking the tradition of not criticizing the state in which the candidate is campaigning, Jackson attacked the Tennessee legislature for again failing to establish a state holiday to honor Martin Luther King, Jr. Further, after spending the night in a Smyrna subsidized housing project, he criticized the lack of a mandatory school breakfast program (which had just been voted down the previous evening by the state legislature). On Easter Sunday in Nashville, he criticized Tennessee for having "amazing, astonishing, ... disgraceful levels of poverty,"[17] implying the state had not done enough to help the poor.

Gary Hart's efforts in Tennessee had two foci: (1) the rural, agricultural portions of the state's population, which he sought to attract by coupling Reagan's increased defense spending with reductions in spending for farm programs and (2) Walter Mondale, whom Hart sharply criticized as the "special interest" candidate whose delegate committees had accepted contributions from PACs.[18] In a speech at Vanderbilt University in Nashville, Hart argued that the "Democratic Party will not defeat Ronald Reagan if its candidate adopts the ethics of Ed Meese" and called on Mondale to "give the money back, Walter."[19]

These charges gained substantial national attention, and Mondale moved quickly to defuse the PAC issue, ordering his delegate committees dissolved.[20] Other than responses to the Hart charges, Mondale ignored his Democratic opponents and shifted his strategy to attack Reagan. He charged the Reagan administration with weak economic and foreign policies, failed policies on curbing the growth of nuclear weapons, and not understanding the concerns of the average American family.

Turnout for only the fourth presidential primary in Tennessee history declined from its previous low levels, with a mere 16 percent of the registered voters participating in the Republican and Democratic primaries. Just over 400,000 Tennesseans cast ballots, of whom only 80,000 participated in the uncontested Republican primary. Jesse Jackson's registration drive, which is estimated to have produced 50,000 new voters,[21] and a substantial get-out-the-vote drive actuated by his supporters produced a major difference in turnout by race, with approximately 28 percent of blacks voting and less than 15 percent of whites.[22]

Mondale's support in the primary was strong across the state. He carried eight of nine Congressional districts, 85 of 95 counties, won 41 percent of the state Democratic vote, and secured 29 of the 65 pledged delegates. Hart trailed Mondale substantially throughout the state receiving only 29 percent of the statewide vote, and failing to carry any congressional district. Hart ran well in a few high-income areas and carried a suburban Nashville county and three small rural counties; his consistent second place finish secured 21 delegates. The surprise of the primary and also its most interesting aspect was the very strong showing by Jesse Jackson, who ran only 4 percent behind Hart with 25 percent of the statewide vote. Jackson's support was concentrated in the urban areas. Not surprisingly, he carried predominately black Shelby County (Memphis), but the size of his victory there was unanticipated (over 60 percent). Moreover, his plurality victories in Jackson, Nashville, and Chattanooga, cities with substantially smaller black populations, were unexpected. On the other hand, Jackson fared less well in gaining pledged delegates, securing only 15.

The distribution of the candidate vote, coupled with the rules for delegate allocation, gave both Mondale and Hart one extra delegate beyond those which would have been allocated if strict proportionality had been the allocation rule. During the preconvention period, Jackson repeatedly raised the allocation rule as an issue. Jackson's point is best illustrated when the full Tennessee delegation is considered, including the 11 delegates who were required to be unpledged and party or elected officials. In the balloting for the presidential nomination on 18 July, Tennessee's delegation cast 39 votes for Mondale (51 percent compared to 41 percent of the vote), 20 for Hart (26 percent as compared to 29 percent of the vote), and 17 for Jackson (22 percent as compared to 25 percent of the vote). Although one of Hart's pledged delegates defected in the roll call, the primary beneficiary of the unpledged "superdelegates" was Mondale, with Hart and Jackson the losers.

The outcome of the primary in Tennessee seems to have had little effect on the national race to the convention. For Mondale, Tennessee's victory was just another barrier passed; for Hart, it was a lost opportunity in a world of dwindling opportunities; for Jackson, his remarkably strong showing was blunted by its discounting by the national media. The results seem to reflect Mondale and Jackson's superior, though quite different, organizational efforts. Two major observations can be made from the 1984 Tennessee presidential primary. First, the Jackson performance suggests that for the Mondale-Ferraro ticket to have any chance in Tennessee in November, Jackson's supporters are absolutely essential. Further, the very low turnout in the presidential primary coupled with its high costs (local governments paid approximately $1.6 million or $4 a vote) suggests the primary may not survive to the 1988 presidential election.

THE CAMPAIGN:
A VIEW FROM TENNESSEE

Party leaders and delegates to the Democratic National Convention returned to Tennessee with enthusiasm and hope, following a relatively unified convention. Geraldine Ferraro's selection as the party's nominee for Vice President added excitement to the convention, the crucial question was whether the Mondale-Ferraro ticket had any chance of victory in November. Polls taken just after the Democratic convention showed that Tennessee, and the nation in general, liked what they saw in San Francisco. The most optimistic indicator was a Gallup Poll conducted for *Newsweek* that showed Mondale having reversed a preconvention Reagan lead to a two-point advantage (48 to 46 percent).[23] The preferences of Tennessee voters, however, remained relatively unchanged by the convention. In late July a *Nashville Banner* poll indicated a six-point lead for Reagan (47 to 41 percent)[24]—comparable to the results of a late-April Keckley poll that reported Reagan leading Mondale 46 to 41 percent.[25]

While there was excitement and good feeling resulting from the Democratic convention, leaders of the state Democratic Party knew that the Mondale-Ferraro ticket would not be an easy one to sell to Tennessee voters. In the past eight presidential elections, a Democratic presidential candidate had carried the state only twice—in 1964 and 1976—and in both instances, southerners led the ticket. State Democratic leaders were guarded in their assessments: State House Speaker Ned Ray McWherter labeled Mondale an "underdog" and U.S. Senator James Sasser said the campaign was "going to be an uphill battle."[26]

Ferraro's nomination as Vice President was of concern to Democratic Party leaders in Tennessee. Publicly, state Party Chairman Dick Lodge spoke favorably of the Ferraro selection, boasting that he had invited Ferraro to campaign in Tennessee. Speaking to the Tennessee delegation in San Francisco, Lodge claimed that Ferraro's background "is a story that will be familiar to you. It is a story like ours."[27] Senator James Sasser was more pragmatic noting that the "big question is how a woman on the ticket affects voters . . . It depends primarily on Ferraro and the campaign she conducts."[28] The initial effect of the Ferraro selection in Tennessee was clear. While polls indicated that 67 percent of Tennessee voters felt that it made no difference, almost 20 percent said they would be less likely to vote for a ticket that included a woman. On the other hand, 11 percent responded that they would be more likely to vote for Mondale. Thus, despite the existence of a gender advantage for Mondale among women (48 to 39 percent), the selection of Ferraro apparently did not help Mondale's overall support in Tennessee.[29]

While Ferraro's nomination may have affected voter preferences, the Democratic party leaders seem to have been more influenced by the Lance affair. Although the selection of Bert Lance, the Georgia Democratic Party chairman, as national campaign manager might have appeared as a major advantage in the South, this was not the case. Tennessee Democrats were particularly concerned because of an ongoing federal grand jury investigation of Lance's connections to former Knoxville banker Jake Butcher. Butcher was the Democratic Party's unsuccessful gubernatorial nominee in 1978 and a major promoter and financier of the 1982 World's Fair in Knoxville. However, in 1983 Butcher's banking empire crumbled, numerous banks were closed, and he was forced into involuntary bankruptcy. While coverage of the investigation acknowledged that Butcher, not Lance, was the target of the federal investigation, Tennessee Democrats feared the Lance-Butcher connection would be damaging to the Mondale campaign in the state. Had Mondale informed such supporters as Jim Neal, his state campaign chairman, or Speaker McWherter of his intention to appoint Lance, they would have counseled against Lance's appointment.[30]

Despite the apparent liabilities of both the Ferraro nomination and the Lance affair, Tennessee was seen as an important state by Mondale strategists. In fact, it was listed as a state that the Democrats had to carry to win in November.[31] Although optimistic, the goal of Mondale-Ferraro's carrying Tennessee was not *completely* unrealistic. In 1980 Carter lost Tennessee to Reagan by less than 5,000 votes (48.9 to 48.4 percent), and Independent candidate John Anderson received 2.2 percent of the vote. If Mondale could hold the 1980 Democratic vote and pick up most of the Anderson vote, victory by a narrow margin might be possible. Calculating in terms of the primary voting support, the Mondale strategists were counting on Hart and Jackson voters plus significant gains in voter registration among Democrats.

From the early stages of planning the reelection campaign, Reagan-Bush strategists viewed the South as an important component of their victory plan. Although Reagan had carried Tennessee by only 5,000 votes in 1980, the strong performance of Republican presidential candidates in Tennessee since the 1950s and Reagan's general popularity in the South made the Republican strategists' claims of a Southern sweep at least plausible. Republicans were quick to react to the apparent Mondale gains in the polls following the Democratic convention. In late July President Reagan made a campaign swing through the South and declared the national Democratic ticket was "going so far left they had left America."[32] Republicans privately expressed hope that the nomination of a woman as Vice President could be turned to their advantage in the more traditional South. State Republicans were also active in this intraconvention period. Tennessee Republican Chair Susan Richardson-Williams claimed the "Democrats had already written off the South."[33] The state chair was also quick to criticize the Lance selection, arguing that Lance would be of no help in Tennessee.

As the Republicans completed their pep-rally convention, polls and political observers alike were forecasting a sizeable Reagan victory. It is not surprising therefore that the campaign both in Tennessee and nationally failed to capture the public's eye. Both Reagan and Mondale conducted extensive campaigns, which included considerable attention to Tennessee. Mondale and Ferraro came to Tennessee six times. In addition, Jesse Jackson visited Tennessee twice and on one occasion appeared with Ferraro in Memphis to encourage black registration and support for the Democratic ticket. With each visit, Mondale and Ferraro attacked Reagan policies. Mondale appealed to rural Tennesseans with attacks on the Reagan Administration's farm and social security policies. Like the Democrats, Reagan and Bush campaigned actively in Tennessee. Reagan came to Nashville in September to help Grand Old Opry star and popular Tennessean Roy Acuff celebrate his 81st birthday.[34] Also in Nashville, national Reagan-Bush co-chairman Margaret Hance argued that southern Democrats had been "left at the gate" by the national Democratic Party and welcomed moderate and conservative Democrats into the GOP.[35]

The only snag in the growing Reagan support throughout the campaign was a relatively strong performance by Mondale in the first presidential debate, with an accompanying short-term increase in his standing in the polls. Nevertheless, Reagan's lead over Mondale widened between August and November both nationally and in Tennessee. The results of a *Nashville Banner* poll conducted in mid-September showed Reagan with a 26 percent lead over Mondale (58 to 32 percent). Reagan led Mondale in all categories and had recorded impressive gains in all parts of the state. Even among women, where Mondale led by 48 to 39 percent in July, Reagan now had the advantage by a 55 to 34 percent margin.[36] Similar results were reported in the final *Nashville Banner* poll before the election (late October): Reagan maintained a 23-point advantage, leading in all three regions of the state and among all demographic groups except blacks.[37]

The Election Outcome:
The 1984 Election in Historical Perspective

Given virtually continuous polling, the results of the election were hardly surprising. Like most of the nation, Tennesseans overwhelmingly supported the Republican President on 6 November. Reagan carried 73 of Tennessee's 95 counties (see Figure 9–2). Statewide, Reagan garnered 59 percent of the vote, with his strongest showing in traditionally Republican East Tennessee. With the exception of Shelby County, Reagan carried all the state's urban and suburban counties, as well as a number of rural counties in Middle and West Tennessee. Mondale's strength came from heavily black portions of Nashville and Memphis and a scattering of rural, traditionally Democratic counties in Middle and West Tennessee.

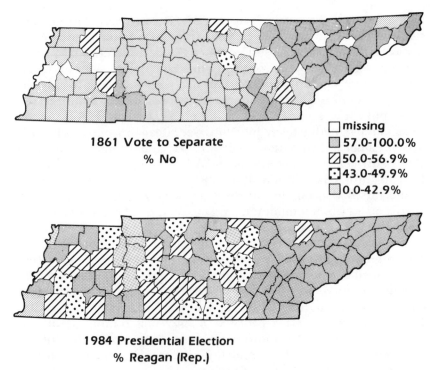

1861 Vote to Separate
% No

☐ missing
▨ 57.0-100.0%
▨ 50.0-56.9%
⊡ 43.0-49.9%
☐ 0.0-42.9%

1984 Presidential Election
% Reagan (Rep.)

FIGURE 9–2   A Comparison of Voting Percentages, 1861 and 1984

A comparison of the two maps in Figure 9–2 suggests the spatial dimension of Republican presidential voting. The 1861 vote to separate from the Union is an often used indicator of the location of the base of partisan voting in Tennessee. Historically, Republicans have been dominant in the mountainous east and on the western portion of the Highland Rim, which opposed slavery; and despite some modifications (for example, Hamilton County–Chattanooga moving to the Democrats), this pattern has persisted to the 1980s. Clearly Reagan's vote in 1984 built on this partisan base. It is obvious, however, that the scope of Reagan's victory extended far beyond that historical Republican base. Republican presidential candidates have been extending their support since the 1950s first to suburban-urban areas, and later and less consistently to rural Middle and West Tennessee. Both suburban-urban and rural support are evident in the Reagan vote in 1984.

Thus, Reagan's victory continued the dominant position of Republican candidates for President in Tennessee that began in the

1950s. At the same time, Tennessee overwhelmingly elected Democrat Albert Gore, Jr., to the U.S. Senate (replacing the retiring Howard Baker) and modestly expanded Democratic control in the General Assembly. This continuation of a bifurcated partisan support dependent upon the particular office contested is as important as the continued support for Republican presidential candidates. However, it is to an analysis of the latter that our analysis is directed.

While regionalism in presidential voting characterizes the 1984 vote, it appears to have declined somewhat, especially since the middle 1960s. The period between 1948 and 1960 were characterized by remarkable regional stability, with aggregate correlations of above .9 among all pairs of elections (see Table 9–1). The shifts that followed, minor as they may appear from an aggregate perspective, are nonetheless important. The major contest initiating this shift was the 1964 election between Goldwater and Johnson. The correlation between percent voting for Goldwater and the "No Vote" in the 1861 secession vote was .72. This represented a rather steep drop-off from the previous years, where the correlations were over ten points higher. Perhaps the loss in predictive power might be better appreciated when we consider that the amount of variance among counties in Tennessee explained by the 1861 vote against leaving the Union was approximately 75 percent for the Presidential elections between 1948 and 1960; only 53 percent of the variance in the 1964 election can be explained by the secession vote.

This difference can be attributed to an alteration of the traditional regional basis of partisanship in Tennessee, one based on the Civil War images of the Republican Party. These images persisted for over a century in this state, and even the emerging presidential Republicanism of the 1950s and early 1960s showed remarkable regional stability. This began to change in 1964. The new Republicans who appeared in that election were more ideologically conservative; many lived in the suburbs of Memphis and Nashville, and identified themselves as southern Democrats. They began voting for a different kind of presidential Republican in the 1964 election and have continued in that practice off and on through the present. The shifts were subtle, as the correlations with other elections are still relatively high. Nonetheless, in reference to the benchmark of the secession vote, the 1964 election stands as a point of departure from tradition.

The county vote in the years that followed has reflected this change in the basis of presidential Republicanism in Tennessee. Although the vote for Richard Nixon in 1968 is largely explained by the secession vote ($r = .85$), we must keep in mind that the candidacy of George Wallace appealed to many of these new conservative presi-

TABLE 9–1 Correlations among Vote to Secede and Republican Vote for President among Tennessee Counties: 1948 to 1984

	No1861	Rep48	Rep52	Rep56	Rep60	Rep64	Rep68	Rep72	Rep76	Rep80	Rep84
No1861	*	.833	.856	.872	.821	.728	.857	.656	.736	.776	.620
Rep48	.833	*	.952	.966	.928	.817	.953	.724	.830	.837	.661
Rep52	.856	.952	*	.955	.954	.860	.943	.780	.878	.874	.718
Rep56	.872	.966	.955	*	.957	.850	.971	.768	.877	.873	.702
Rep60	.821	.928	.954	.957	*	.919	.949	.841	.906	.891	.722
Rep64	.728	.817	.860	.850	.919	*	.855	.877	.943	.899	.723
Rep68	.857	.953	.943	.971	.949	.855	*	.778	.885	.887	.728
Rep72	.656	.724	.780	.768	.841	.877	.778	*	.885	.877	.769
Rep76	.736	.830	.878	.877	.906	.943	.885	.885	*	.937	.825
Rep80	.776	.837	.874	.873	.891	.899	.887	.877	.937	*	.841
Rep84	.620	.661	.718	.702	.722	.723	.728	.769	.825	.841	*
Avg r	.775	.850	.869	.880	.888	.847	.806	.795	.870	.869	.731

n = 95

dential Republicans. The vote in the elections of 1972, 1976, 1980, and 1984 is again much less a function of the pre-1964 regionalism of traditional Republicanism, as the correlations with the secession vote are all in the .6 to .7 range, with the exception of the 1984 contest. Here, a further regional deterioration is evident. Only 38 percent of the variance among counties in the 1984 election of Ronald Reagan is explained by the secession vote of 1861.

Though the basis of regional Republicanism began to shift in 1964, the election in which that shift seems most pronounced was that of 1972. Although there is evidence that the regional patterns of 1972 are not those of 1984 ($r = .769$), the aggregate picture is that regional factors were at work in both these Republican landslides. In 1972, there was a shift in some areas of the state to relatively greater Republican support, but the pattern of support for the victorious Republican nominee was not the same in 1972 as in 1984.

Perhaps the best indicator of the new Republicanism, which began emerging in 1964, is the Ford-Reagan election in the 1976 Republican presidential primary. The correlations between the antisecession vote and each candidate's county proportions and the votes for Republican presidential candidates between 1948 and 1984 appear in Table 9–2. It is obvious that the support for Reagan in the 1976 primary came from the areas of the state not used to supporting presidential Re-

TABLE 9–2   Correlations between Vote to Secede and Republican Vote for President and Ford-Reagan Primary Vote (1976) among Tennessee Counties: 1948 to 1984

		Primary	
	Rep84	Ford76	Reagan76
No61	.619	.574	−.596
Rep48	.661	.656	−.681
Rep52	.718	.585	−.613
Rep56	.702	.671	−.694
Rep60	.721	.591	−.616
Rep64	.722	.477	−.500
Rep68	.728	.675	−.701
Rep72	.768	.318	−.344
Rep76	.825	.499	−.522
Rep80	.841	.472	−.496
Rep84	*	.377	−.398
Ford76P	.377	*	−.996
Rg76P	−.396	−.996	*

n = 95

publicans. The 1976 primary vote indicates a split between the traditional and the new Republicans. Indeed, the 1976 vote for Reagan was negatively correlated with opposition to secession, the vote that had established the pattern of partisan support for over a century. The elections of 1972 and 1984 both show the effects of this newly complicated Republican partisanship. County-by-county results for these two contests are less correlated with both the 1976 primary results and the traditional antisecession vote than are other elections ($r = -.344$ and $-.398$). Thus the landslides of 1972 and 1984 appear to be breaks from the normal pattern of regional partisan support in Tennessee.

One cannot infer from this, however, that the 1984 election was a realigning election even in terms of the nature of presidential Republicanism in Tennessee. Only the passage of time and future presidential elections will provide sufficient evidence for a judgment relative to its realigning or deviating character. And certainly, the 1984 election does *not* indicate a general partisan realignment in Tennessee politics. The accompanying landslide election of the Democrat Albert Gore, Jr., points again to the fact that even for visible offices Tennessee may still be a Democratic state. Additionally, the evidence in terms of party identification, the makeup of the General Assembly, and the composition of the congressional and senatorial delegations is consistent with an assertion of Tennessee being a predominately Democratic state.

In summary, the success of the Republicans in presidential politics in Tennessee has been bolstered somewhat by the "new Republicans" who surfaced in 1964 and fueled the almost successful challenge to incumbent President Ford by challenger Ronald Reagan in 1976. These new Republicans give the party the possibility of gaining a majority, when they find an election that pulls them from what we must surmise are their Democratic roots. The landslides of 1972 and 1984 demonstrate the impact of this shift. What the reduced correlations between each of those elections and the primary votes of 1976 and the antisecession vote indicate is that there is a different geographical basis to the Republican landslides. This is not a necessary function of a landslide; the Republicans could be securing more votes in all areas of the state. Rather, the reduced correlations indicate a difference in the county-by-county vote relative to other counties.

The best inference is that the swing voters who switch their allegiance to the presidential Republicans in certain elections have not undergone partisan rebirth in the Republican Party. For now, it seems as if the presidential election of 1984 was merely a "landslide as usual" for the Republicans in Tennessee. If the Democrats offer a weak candidate, many voters in non-Republican areas will vote for the Republican candidates. Additionally, the evidence indicates that the stability of pre-1964 presidential voting has been substantially reduced in Tennessee. That is, we are finally seeing a tendency to move away from the regional patterns that have lingered so long in Tennessee politics.

These electoral shifts suggest a breakdown of traditional voting patterns that may or not mark the beginning of a new regional pattern. To some degree, present-day demographics point to a continuation of East Tennessee as the area of Republican domination, both at the state and presidential levels. Middle Tennessee will likely continue as somewhat more Democratic than the state as a whole, with large numbers of blacks and a more-developed base of organized labor. The west appears to be the area with the most potential for change. Here there is a base of black support for the Democratic party, but the politics of racial polarization and the innate conservatism of many in the white community point to the possibility for a continuation of, and possibly, an institutionalization of the presidential conservatism so strongly manifest in the 1972 and 1984 elections.

There is some evidence that there has been seepage of presidential conservatism in the areas outside Memphis. The election of Don Sundquist in the Eighth District in 1982 over the challenge of Bob Clement, a well-known traditional Democrat, may be an indicator of new Republicanism at the congressional level. The State of Tennessee might then be moving into an era of more complex regionalism, based less on Civil War geographical cleavages and more on post-1960s racial and socioeconomic politics. At this time, though, it is highly speculative to guess whether any such movement in partisanship within the state might add up to a Republican rather than Democratic domination. The new white Republicanism in West Tennessee balanced against heightened black consciousness and continuing Democratic dominance in contesting the less-visible public offices.

CONCLUSION

The Democrats had their work cut out for them if they expected to achieve a victory for Walter Mondale in the 1984 presidential election in Tennessee. There had been no great outpouring of support for Mondale during the primary process; indeed, he could take little

solace from his victory in the Tennessee primary. His lackluster performance was typical of the situation in many other states, especially
in the South. There was no apparent net effect of the candidacy of
Geraldine Ferraro. From the beginning, all published survey results
pointed to a Reagan landslide victory. And the U.S. Senate race
between Albert Gore, Jr., and Victor Ashe was as much a lopsided
Democratic victory as the presidential contest was for the Republicans. From an analytical perspective, therefore, neither race was ever
perceived to be close enough, or turned out to be close enough, to
allow for meaningful analysis in terms of "Who Won." Rather the
analysis question import became one of "what of within-state realignment in an election with such differing outcomes?"

Aggregate analysis provides some indication that the presidential
Republican base established in the mid-1960s was firmly entrenched,
but no indication of a real move of Tennessee to a Republican state.
One can only infer from the landslide vote for Gore and Reagan that
the effect of nominal partisanship is sufficiently weak so as to allow
for a tremendous amount of ticket splitting. Although the Republican
Party has made inroads, and though these inroads have become somewhat institutionalized, the Democratic edge in identification and their
strength in the state legislature leave them in a continued superior
position prior to most statewide races, if they can field an attractive
candidate. Partisanship alone, however, will no longer suffice for
Tennessee Democrats in an age of personality-based media politics.
The attractiveness of the candidacy of Republican Governor Lamar
Alexander in two successive elections underscores this dilemma for
Tennessee Democrats. In recent years, the politics of the national
Democratic Party has left them with presidential candidates who are
not competitive in Tennessee. However, all things being equal in the
state, an attractive Democrat still enjoys a partisan advantage. While
Republicans seem to be developing a strong base of presidential support within the state, they have not yet translated that advantage into
a strong base for less-visible state races and in the General Assembly.
Republicans must recruit candidates with strong media appeal, and
they must harbor some hope that the Democrats offer unattractive
candidates.

Thus our analysis of the 1984 Presidential election in Tennessee
does not indicate the existence of an enduring partisan realignment.
Instead, although reaffirming both the strength of presidential Republicans and their evolving and more complex nature, the 1984
election continued the pattern of bifurcated partisanship dependent
upon the personalities and the visibility of the offices contested.

NOTES

1. V.O. Key, Jr., *Southern Politics in State and Nation* (New York: Vintage, 1949), 76.

2. Ibid., 61.

3. The two major exceptions to this pattern are the elections of 1928 when Hoover carried Tennessee and 1948 when the Dixiecrat vote significantly lowered the Democratic vote.

4. The year 1932 seems a plausible starting point, given the finding by Greene and Holmes in their study of Tennessee presidential elections that 1932 was the beginning point in the current electoral cycle. Lee S. Greene and Jack E. Holmes, "Tennessee: A Politics of Peaceful Change," in *The Changing Politics of the South*, ed. William C. Havard (Baton Rouge: Louisiana State University Press, 1972), 165–200.

5. This is consistent with Jewell and Olson's arguments about potential obstacles to the development of two-party competition. See Malcolm E. Jewell and David M. Olson, *American State Political Parties and Elections*, 2d ed. (Homewood, IL: Dorsey Press, 1982), especially 31–38.

6. A somewhat contrary argument is made in Leiper Freeman, *Political Change in Tennessee, 1948–1978: Party Politics Trickles Down* (Knoxville: Bureau of Public Administration, University of Tennessee, Knoxville, 1980).

7. Robert H. Swansbrough, "The Tennessee Voter," unpublished mimeo., University of Tennessee, Chattanooga, 1983, 15–16.

8. Lee S. Greene, David H. Grubbs, and Victor C. Hobday, *Government in Tennessee*, 4th ed. (Knoxville: University of Tennessee Press, 1982).

9. For example, see Anne H. Hopkins, "Local Party Organization in Nashville," in *Political Parties at the Local Level*, ed. William Crotty (Knoxville: University of Tennessee Press, forthcoming).

10. Anne H. Hopkins and William Lyons, "Toward a Classification of State Electoral Change: A Note on Tennessee, 1837–1976," *Journal of Politics* 42 (1980): 209–26.

11. Contrast the findings of Greene and Holmes with those of Freeman.

12. Tennessee's election law specifies a closed primary requiring a declaration of party membership on election day prior to the receipt of a primary ballot. In practice, voters simply ask for whichever party ballot they wish.

During the 1983 state legislative session, two attempts were made to alter the primary, first, by changing the date from May to March and, later, by moving to a caucus-based delegate selection system. Failing to alter the primary date, the Democratic-dominated General Assembly passed a bill in May 1983 repealing the presidential primary, but it was vetoed by Republican Governor Lamar Alexander. State observers suggested the attempted move to a caucus was designed to help Mondale and disadvantage Glenn. Although Mondale supporters denied this was their motivation, Alexander used the Democratic squabbling to his advantage by claiming in his veto message that the people of the state deserved direct input into the nominating process.

13. See *Tennessee Delegate Selection Plan for the 1984 Democratic National Convention*. Allocations of delegates among the candidates are based on voter preferences, pro-

vided a given threshold (between 14.3 and 25 percent) is achieved. Forty-four delegates were selected on the basis of the Congressional District vote with variable thresholds; 21 were selected proportionate to the statewide vote, provided a 20 percent threshold was reached.

14. *Time*, 30 April 1984, 15.

15. Conducted by and reported in the respected newsletter, *The Tennessee Journal* 2 April 1984. Two earlier polls of party leaders are also instructive of the evolution of candidate preferences over time. On 25 April 1983 *The Tennessee Journal* reported strong Mondale support (Mondale, 40 percent; Glenn, 22 percent; Hart, 5 percent; Askew, 2 percent; Cranston, 2 percent). By 5 December 1983 support had shifted substantially to Glenn (Glenn, 34 percent; Mondale, 26 percent; Hart, 1 percent; Hollings, 1 percent; Cranston, 1 percent). Hart was the apparent beneficiary of the early withdrawal of Glenn.

16. Polls reported in the Memphis *Commercial Appeal*, 22 April 1984, B–1, and in the Nashville *Tennessean*, 1 May 1984, 1. The latter poll showed Mondale with 39 percent, Hart with 30 percent, Jackson with 12 percent, and 19 percent undecided.

17. *The Tennessean*, 23 April 1984, 1.

18. Early in the campaign both Hart and Mondale had pledged not to accept any PAC funding of their campaigns. The delegate committees, not formally part of Mondale's campaign organization, were designed to facilitate delegate selection, but they later began to funnel money toward Mondale's efforts in several states after his own campaign expenditures were reaching close to the spending ceiling prescribed by federal law.

19. *Knoxville News-Sentinel*, 26 April 1984, 1.

20. Ibid.

21. Ibid., 7 May 1984, F–2.

22. *The Tennessee Journal*, 7 May 1984, 1.

23. *Newsweek*, 30 July 1984, 24. A postconvention Harris poll indicated a two-point Reagan advantage (50 to 48 percent); see *The Tennessean*, 5 August 1984, 8.

24. Nashville *Banner*, 30 July 1984, 1. A Darden poll in late July in nine southern states reported a 60–34 point Reagan margin. See *The Tennessean*, 5 August 1984, 1.

25. *The Tennessee Journal*, 14 May 1984, 1.

26. *The Tennessean*, 22 July 1984, 1; and *The Tennessee Journal*, 23 July 1984, 1.

27. *The Tennessean*, 18 July 1984, 1.

28. Ibid., 22 July 1984, 12–A.

29. Poll conducted by Nashville *Banner*, 30 July 1984, 1, 3.

30. *The Tennessean*, 19 July 1984, 1, 8; and *The Tennessee Journal*, 23 July 1984, 1.

31. *U.S. News and World Report*, 30 July 1984, 18.

32. Rhodes Cook, "Mondale-Ferraro Poll Surge Spurs Reagan Counter Attack," *Congressional Quarterly*, 28 July 1984, 1834.

33. *The Tennessean*, 27 July 1984, 1.

34. Ibid., 14 September 1984, 1.

35. Ibid., 5 August 1984, 1.

36. Nashville *Banner*, 2 October 1984, 1.

37. Ibid., 29 October 1984, 1.

10

Florida

Mark Stern

INTRODUCTION: THE TWO FLORIDAS

In 1949 V. O. Key, Jr., called Florida "the different state."[1] More than two decades later, Manning Dauer echoed this description in his analysis of socioeconomic and political life in the "sunshine state."[2] There remain two Floridas; in the south, a Florida of rapid growth, high urbanization, and interparty competition; in the north, a Florida of little socioeconomic change, with predominant rural interests, and continuing allegiance to one-party, Democratic politics. The frost line, below which a winter freeze is unusual, located about two-thirds of the way up the peninsula, is usually seen as the demarcation line between those two Floridas.[3]

Patterns of support within the state for George Wallace's American Independent Party candidacy for the presidency in 1968 demonstrate this north-south difference. The solidarity of the north Florida vote with the traditional black belt regions of the Deep South, where Wallace's support was most evident, is striking. In fact, Wallace carried at least 32 of the 36 North Florida counties in the 1968 general election, as well as the 1972 and 1976 Democratic presidential primary elections. In the south Florida region, Wallace never carried a majority of the 31 counties in any of these campaigns. North Florida is the "old Florida." South Florida is the "new Florida."

Florida is currently the seventh largest state in the union, and it is projected to be the fourth largest state by 1990.[4] However, most of the change and growth occurs in South Florida. In 1930 almost half of the state population resided in a rural area. By 1950 this figure had dropped to 37.8 percent and further declined to 15.7 percent by 1980. The population currently residing in metropolitan areas is 87.9 percent—a figure higher than all but three other states in the union. In each successive decade since 1940, more than ninety percent of the immigrant population has settled in the southern portion of the state. As a consequence, of the 36 counties above the frost line, 17 are among the 20 least-populous counties in the state. On the other hand, nine of the ten most-populous counties are below the frost line. The two largest counties, Dade and Broward, located in the extreme southeast of the state, account for more than a quarter of the state population (27.36 percent); and the ten largest counties combined hold two-thirds of the total state population.

Of the states defined by Key as part of the South, only Texas has a lower proportion of black residents (13 percent as compared with 13.8 percent). Again, however, North Florida is different from South Florida. All 12 Florida counties with 20 percent or more blacks in their populations are located above the frost line. In addition, although Florida as a whole has a per capita income at almost the national median (98.4 percent of the national figure), 18 of the 20 counties with the lowest per capita income are in the north of the state, while all ten of the highest-income counties are in the southern region. Thus, three of the key socioeconomic attributes associated with the traditional areas of the South are still, to a considerable extent, to be found in North Florida: a rural population, with high proportions of black residents and a relatively low per capita income. South Florida is different: It is highly urbanized, with a low proportion of black residents and a per capita income in excess of the national average.

POLITICAL CHANGE IN RECENT YEARS

Two fundamental changes in Florida politics occurred during the mid-1960s and afterwards, and they are both directly tied to the growth of South Florida. First, a durable Republican political base has emerged below the frost line. Second, the Democratic Party now has two distinct bases of strength: the traditional base in the north; and a new, increasingly important base in the south.[5] A Republican can win the state without carrying the north region. A Democrat cannot win the state without carrying the south region. Overall, as of October 1984 the Democrats had the political advantage, outnumbering Republican voter registrants by a 54 percent to 34 percent margin, with 6 percent of the votes being registered Independent or for "other parties." Also, like the population, voter registration is concentrated below the frost line. Five southern counties alone hold 50 percent of all registered Republicans; 66 percent of the state's Republicans are found in ten counties, and all of them are below the frost line. Eight of the ten counties with the largest proportions of Democrats in the state are located in the south region, and these counties hold 64 percent of all the registered Democrats in the state.

The pattern of elected partisan officeholders, prior to the 1984 general election, also reflects the concentration of Republican strength in the state. Eight of the 40 members (17.5 percent) of the state Senate and 36 of the 120 state House delegates (30 percent) are Republicans, but only one Republican from the north area holds a seat in the state legislature; seven of the 19 Florida members of the U.S. House of Representatives are Republicans, and all come from districts below the frost line. The latest addition to the Republican congressional delegation is Representative Andy Ireland from Central Florida who was elected as a Democrat, but announced a switch in party affiliation in March 1984.

Like their follow partisans in much of the rest of the South, Florida Republicans had a series of "firsts" in the way of electoral victories during the 1960s and 1970s. The first twentieth-century Republican Governor of Florida, Claude Kirk, was elected in 1966 and the first twentieth-century Republican U.S. Senator, Ed Gurney, was elected in 1968. But, unlike some of the other less-traditional southern states, such as Tennessee or Texas, most Republican contenders in statewide elections have been remarkably unsuccessful in Florida. In 1974 the Democrats picked up the Republican Senate seat, but another Republican, Paula Hawkins, was elected to the U.S. Senate from Florida in 1980. Democrat Reubin Askew in 1972 defeated Governor Kirk in his reelection bid. After Askew won reelection, he was succeeded in 1978 by Democrat Robert Graham, who also won reelection. No Republican currently holds a statewide elective office. Thus, Republicans hold a minority of state legislative seats, with almost all of the them in the southern region, and only one Republican holds a position elected on a statewide basis. The significant Democratic Party achievements in the 1970s was the election of Richard (Dick) Stone to the U.S. Senate in 1974. Stone was the first Miami-based Democrat to win a major statewide general election. Significantly, in 1978 the Democratic gubernatorial run-off primary election was a contest between two Miami-based candidates. In prior years, Miami-based Democratic candidates had to fight the stigma of being from the "big" city. Now this has become an asset.

In presidential elections, a rather different picture of Republican strength emerges. The Republicans are the stronger of the two parties in Florida presidential contests. Prior to 1984, the Democrats have only carried the state in two of eight elections beginning with 1952. Lyndon Johnson carried the state in 1964, but only because his net margin of 91,461 votes in Dade County exceeded his loss in the rest of the state by 48,862 votes. He won only nine northern counties and 11 southern counties. By contrast, in 1976 Jimmy Carter carried the state over Gerald Ford by a 166,369 vote margin. Carter was the most successful Democratic presidential nominee since Franklin D. Roosevelt. He carried all but four of the north counties and 17 of the south counties in 1976. As in the rest of the South and in much of the nation, Carter did not do as well in the 1980 bid. Ronald Reagan won almost 59 percent of the popular vote in Florida—his highest popular vote margin in the South. Carter carried only ten north area counties and three south area counties in 1980.

Thus, although he did better in the Florida north region than in the south region, Carter's 1980 election pattern was much like that of most of the Democratic presidential contenders who came before him in the last three decades. While Democrats within the state continue to dominate elections, especially above the frost line, Democratic presidential candidates continue to falter. It is a common, much-cited occurrence in contemporary politics at this stage of southern political history: By and large, southerners still like state Democratic candidates, while the national presidential contenders have lost the support of these voters.[6]

THE 1984 DEMOCRATIC PRIMARY

The 1984 Democratic presidential primary season started off as the Cinderella story of Senator Gary Hart. On 13 March, the week after his stunning upset victory in New Hampshire, Senator Hart staged another major upset victory in Florida. This occurred despite the fact that the Senator had spent only a few days campaigning in Florida and did not field a slate of delegates under his name in a majority of the congressional districts in the state! On the other hand, former Vice President Mondale, in alliance with organized labor and many senior citizens' organizations, had an ongoing active campaign operating statewide. Senator John Glenn had also actively campaigned, especially in the northern areas of the state where there are major military installations and a more "traditional" southern population. The Rev. Jesse Jackson had been in the state, especially activating the black population to register and vote for his candidacy.

Everyone thought they know the likely script-to-be, but two wild cards changed the situation for the Florida primary: Hart's strong showing in New Hampshire and former Florida Governor Askew's poor showing in Iowa. Soon after the Iowa voting results showed former Governor Askew to be a weak candidate, he announced that he would no longer seek the Democratic nomination. In Florida that initially meant confusion took hold among the state party leadership. The major Democratic Party leaders had split over whom to back on the Florida primary ballot, Mondale or Askew. With Askew's withdrawal from an active candidacy, some of the big-name delegates who had been slated for the Governor on the ballot announced their support for Mondale; others announced that they would remain pledged to the former Governor as a "favorite son." The latter group openly stated that they hoped to use this ploy as a means to stay "independent" and keep their votes as delegates free to be used for bargaining at a contested convention. What actually ensued is that after the New Hampshire results were in, many of the "independent," former Askew delegates announced that they supported Senator Hart and that a vote cast beside their names would be a vote pledged to the Colorado Senator's candidacy. As a result, in most of the areas where he started out with no pledged delegate slates, Hart ended up having slates fielded on his behalf. Governor Askew's early exit from primary contesting was indeed a fortuitous event for Senator Hart.

Senator Hart's victory in Florida was broadly based. He carried the largest plurality or majority of the vote in 57 of the 67 counties in the state. As Figure 10–1 shows, Senator Hart carried counties in all section of the state; he won almost 40 percent of the total votes cast. Former Vice President Mondale garnered a third of the votes, and the Rev. Jesse Jackson and Senator John Glenn placed a distant third and fourth, respectively, with 12 percent and 11 percent of the total vote.

Only four counties gave a plurality of their votes to the former Vice President. The two southeastern counties carried by Mondale— Dade and Broward—are dominated, respectively, by the Miami and Hollywood–Fort Lauderdale metropolitan areas. The two northeast counties carried by Mondale are Duval—dominated by Jacksonville— and Nassau—a bedroom country of Jacksonville. The four counties carried by Jackson are all in the Panhandle and have high proportions of blacks in their populations. Jackson's strongest finish, with 39.4 of the vote, was in Gadsden County, which has a majority (58.7 per-

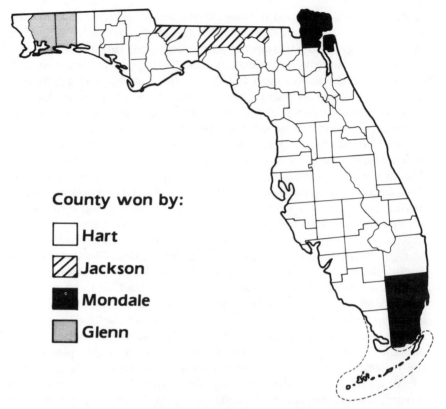

FIGURE 10–1   Plurality of Votes Won by Major Candidates in
the 1984 Democratic Presidential Primary, by County

Source: State of Florida, Department of State, Division of Elections,
"Tabulation of Official Votes Cast: Florida Primary Elections, 13 March
1984".

cent) black population. He also carried a plurality of the votes in
Jefferson County (33.1 percent), Madison County (30.2 percent), and
Hamilton County (26.7 percent). In the latter three counties, the
proportion of blacks in the population is, respectively, 47.8 percent,
42.8 percent, and 38.1 percent. A simple bivariate correlation analysis
shows a +73 relationship between the percent black of the total
voting-age population and the percent vote Jackson obtained in the
ten counties with the highest proportion of blacks in their voting-age
populations.[7] Senator John Glenn carried two northwestern counties
noted for their proximity to the Pensacola military complex.

The Miami Herald,[8] on the basis of a state sample, headlined their
report: "Democrats' Vote Shows Sharp Split." Senator Hart did best,

according to the poll, among the better-educated, younger, more-affluent and "independent"-minded voters. Only among those individuals with some high school education or less, among those with incomes under $10,000 per year, and among those over 60-years-old did the Vice President outperform the Senator in gathering support. Among self-identified "independent"-voting Democrats, Hart garnered 73 percent of the vote. *The Orlando Sentinel*,[9] in an election day survey of Central Florida voters, found that among Hart voters, 10 percent planned to vote for President Reagan if their Democratic preference was not going to be on the general election ballot; 5 percent of Mondale's supporters took a similar position. The Florida Democrats of the 1980s had a pattern of primary vote divisions that was markedly similar to the pattern reported across the nation.

Early in the 1984 primary elections, Hart was the "new" Democrat—an idea overwhelmingly repeated in the national polls and the Florida polls—who swept all before him. This was the story of the 1984 Florida Democratic presidential primary results. Through a stroke of good luck, the early dropout of a favorite-son former Governor, and timing (coming with one week of the New Hampshire upset), the Florida primary became part and parcel of the Cinderella-story spell cast by Senator Hart. Of course, the spell was eventually broken, and after later defeats, the Senator had to give way to the preprimary season favorite. But the Hart sweep in Florida is a sign of the volatility of the Florida electorate in the present era and an indicator of the underlying unpredictability of electoral allegiances. The two candidates initially backed by the major party leaders of the party could not carry the state: former Governor Askew because he dropped out of the race and Vice President Mondale because of the sweep of early primary events. This is the major story of the 1984 Florida presidential primary.

THE NON-CAMPAIGN OF 1984

The weekend prior to the casting of ballots for the 1984 election, Jack Germond and Jules Witcover, in a nationally syndicated newspaper article, summed up the presidential campaign in Florida: "Both candidates have ignored the state. . . . The result is a sort of eerie political silence in a state that otherwise might be considered a prime battleground. And the outcome is likely to be a Reagan victory here by 25 percentage points or more. . . ."[10] President Reagan's actual margin of victory was 30 percentage points in Florida—65 percent to 35 percent! Walter Mondale carried only one county in the state—

Gadsden County: the only Florida county with a majority black population and the same county that gave the Rev. Jesse Jackson his highest vote plurality in the primary election.

The 1984 Florida Democratic presidential campaign effort was minimal, with only one personal appearance by the nominee in the state. The campaign had a token budget of $50,000 to run an office with a seven-person staff and a director who had never previously managed a state campaign. By contrast, the Republican effort involved six professional telephone banks directly under control of the presidential campaign headquarters. Every registered Republican was called. In addition, 13 volunteer Republican telephone banks contacted more than 200,000 Democrats and registered Independents.[11] As the 1984 campaign came to a close, Florida Republicans could not say enough about the virtues of President Reagan or their fidelity to his program—or his coattails. One Democratic candidate for the state House of Representatives lamented about the opposition at a public candidates' forum: "If you all attempt to ride Mr. Reagan's coattails to office, you're going to have to buy him a new coat. You all are about to tear them apart."[12] Yet, despite the Reagan sweep across 66 of the 67 Florida counties, all of the congressional seats remained in the same partisan hands that had held them prior to the 1984 election. The state Senate partisan seat ratio also remained unchanged. In the state House of Representatives, the Republicans were held to a net gain of only six seats, and only one of these seats came from the north section of the state. The 1984 Democratic presidential election campaign never made it to Florida, but the Republican presidential onslaught carried little with it down the ballot line. In essence, the 1984 election appeared to have changed little within the state. But change is occurring, and it is being evidenced in two forms: the shifting patterns of intrastate presidential voting and the shifting patterns of voter registration. It is these long-term developments that we now examine.

SHIFTING ELECTORAL ALLEGIANCES IN FLORIDA

One of the big questions that pervaded the 1984 election campaign across the South was the extent to which the Jackson candidacy would alter the composition of the southern electorate. Some analysts argued that the Jackson candidacy and his subsequent presence in the Democratic campaign would galvanize the black population into active voting support for the Democratic ticket. Others suggested that not only would the blacks be galvanized, but also the white voter population would be galvanized in reaction to the Jackson activity. There was further speculation that Reagan's candidacy, especially in the South where he is a very popular President, would aid in the growth of Republican voter registration. While we cannot extricate all the causes behind the changes in registration figures, the Florida Office of the Secretary of State does publish data not only on major party registration, but also on the number of black and white registrants within each major party. In addition, this data is available for the registration period that closed thirty days prior to the 1984 primary elections, as well as for the period following the primary elections up until thirty days prior to the 1984 general elections.[13]

From 11 February 1984 through 6 October 1984, the Republican voter registration lists grew by 23 percent; the Democratic registration lists grew by 10 percent. At the beginning of the year the Democrats had a 62 percent to 32 percent edge in voter registration; by October the edge had dropped to 59 percent to 34 percent. Overall, as Table 10–1 indicates, ever since 1976 the Republican percentage of the total voters registered has been increasing. A differential in racial registration during the February-to-October 1984 period did occur in two important respects. First, among the Democrats, 231,282

TABLE 10–1   Selected Voter Characteristics, 1976–84 (in percentages)

Characteristics	Year		
	1976	1980	1984
Democratic registrants of total voters registered	67	64	59
Republican registrants of total voters registered	28	30	34
White registrants of total democratic registrants	86	86	83
White registrants of total Republican registrants	99	99	99
Persons registered of total voting age population[1]	67	65	68
Persons voting of total voting age population[1]	51	50	49

[1]Data on the voting age population are from: Frances W. Terhane, ed., *1982 Florida Statistical Abstract* (Gainesville, FL: The University Presses of Florida, 1982), 542–43. The 1984 voting age population is an estimate based on the 1980 census figures and projected median population growth by county as given in the *Abstract,* 44.

whites were added to the voting lists and 70,071 blacks were added to the lists. This represented an increase of 9 percent for whites in the Democratic ranks and 14 percent for the blacks. Second, among the Republicans, blacks increased their numbers from 14,938 to 19,215, a jump of 35 percent on a small base, but white voters increased in the Republican registration lists by 23 percent on a base of 1,530,453. As Table 10–1 shows, the Republican Party remains predominantly a white party. On the other hand, the Democratic percentage of white voters has declined for the first time since the surge of black voters entered the voter registration lists in the 1960s. In fact, blacks constituted about 11 percent of the total voters registered in February 1984 and held that same proportion of the total registration in October 1984, but they have become a slightly large proportion of the Democratic registration base.

Table 10–1 also shows data that deal with overall voter registration as a percentage of the age-eligible voter population and voter turnout. The percentage of the total voting age population that has registered to vote has remained relatively stable since 1976. What has changed in 1984 is that the relative proportion of the total white population registering as Democrats has gone down, while the proportion of the total white population registering as Republicans as gone up. Of course, the Democratic registrants in Florida remain overwhelmingly white and continue to outnumber the Republican registrants, but not by the more than two-to-one margins of ten years ago. Turnout in the 1984 presidential election remained about the same, as a percentage of the total voting age population, as in recent presidential elections. Thus, in Florida, the Jackson candidacy and its activism did not lead to a great increase in the proportion of black voters registered to vote; nor did it lead to an increase in overall voter participation.

How different are the 1984 election results in comparison with other recent presidential elections? Table 10–2 presents the inter-county correlation results for recent Democratic presidential elections. The Mondale election results correlate fairly moderately with the 1968 election results and afterwards. The 1984 results correlate most strongly with the 1972 McGovern election results. McGovern suffered the worst defeat of any Democrat in Florida presidential electoral politics—he lost every county in the state.

From 1948 through 1960 the Florida Democratic intercounty presidential vote had a correlation coefficient of .89 and higher between elections.[15] The Johnson-Goldwater contest upset this pattern of continuity for Florida, as well as the rest of the South.[16] The 1964 to 1972 Democratic election results appear to be consistent within them-

TABLE 10–2 Correlation Coefficient (Pearson's r) of Florida's County Vote between Democratic
Presidential Nominees, 1960–84

Candidate (Year)	Johnson (1964)	Humphrey (1968)	McGovern (1972)	Carter (1976)	Carter (1980)	Mondale (1984)
Kennedy (1960)	.10	−.30*	−.21*	.79*	.66*	.08
Johnson (1964)		.38*	.38**	.14	.07	.36*
Humphrey (1968)			.69*	−.14	−.08	.59*
McGovern (1972)				.04	.17	.78*
Carter (1976)					.90*	.43*
Carter (1980)						.56*

*$p < .01$
**$p < .05$

239

selves, but inconsistent with either the earlier elections or the later Carter elections. Mondale's county vote pattern correlates most strongly with the McGovern vote, but is also significantly related to all of the other Democratic election results from 1964 through 1980. The Mondale vote thus appears to bridge across both the 1964 through 1972 pattern and the Carter pattern.

Another approach that can be used to assess the continuities and discontinuities in recent presidential elections is to examine the socioeconomic bases of support for the candidates of a political party. Selected census characteristics of the population are employed on a county-level basis, with the county vote for each Democratic presidential election from 1960 through 1984. The 1960 census results are correlated with the 1968 through 1972 election results. The 1980 census data is used with the 1976 through 1984 election results.[17]

The traditional Democratic Party vote, in Florida and in much of the South, is based in the rural, slower-growing agricultural areas. The more rural the county and the higher the proportion of the blacks in the county, the more likely the county was to remain staunchly Democratic. Of course, in the aftermath of George Wallace's 1968 through 1976 presidential forays, the 1964 Goldwater campaign, and the Reagan southern appeal, this pattern of Democratic support has eroded, if not disappeared, in many southern states. Within Florida, and the South generally, the base of Republican support had its origins in the larger population centers, which have generally had a wealthier, better-educated populace with a higher proportion of new, nonsouthern residents than is found in the more traditional areas.[18] In Florida the southeast coast Dade-Broward County areas and the southwest coastal Sarasota-Pinellas County areas are typical of the new Republican bases in the state. Table 10–3 shows the correlation coefficient results between the county-by-county vote received by each Democratic presidential nominee from 1960 through 1984 and the socioeconomic variables that have previously been related to the bases of partisan support.

Again it is apparent that the Kennedy base of support is related to the Carter bases of support. The correlation results also indicate that there is a significant inverse relationship between the Kennedy and the Carter votes and county population size, net population change, percentage urban, median age, median education level, and median income level. The Johnson, Humphrey, and McGovern vote patterns tend to be just the opposite of the Kennedy vote pattern. They tended to draw more support from the more urban, higher-status counties. Of course, for Humphrey and McGovern this was in the context of a vastly diminished Democratic vote. The Mondale

TABLE 10–3 Correlation Coefficient (Pearson's r) between Selected Florida County Socioeconomic Variables and County Presidential Vote, 1960–84

Socioeconomic Variable	Candidate (Year)						
	Kennedy (1960)	Johnson (1964)	Humphrey (1968)	McGovern (1972)	Carter (1976)	Carter (1980)	Mondale (1984)
Population size	−.36*	.21**	.51*	.46*	−.20**	−.27**	.16
Net population change	−.53*	.03	.16	−.07	−.34*	−.49*	−.28*
Percentage of population in urban area	−.56*	.18	.46*	.35*	−.68*	−.67*	−.08
Median age of population	−.55*	.05	.17	.08	−.45*	−.49*	−.06
Median education of population	−.64*	.22**	.41*	.25**	−.64*	−.72*	−.22**
Median per capita income of population	−.41*	.13	.33*	.25**	−.74*	−.82*	−.25**
Percentage of population nonwhite	.26*	−.07	.33*	.43*	.38	.56*	.62*

*$p < .01$
** $p < .05$

base, on the other hand, tends to be strongly and positively correlated with only one characteristic: the percentage of the population that is nonwhite. In a diminished fashion, compared to the robust Kennedy and Carter correlations, Mondale also appears to have received support in the slower-growing, lower-socioeconomic status counties. However, because his support was so weak, while it was located in the more-traditional Democratic areas of the state, it was hardly enough to lay claim to a significant return to the traditional Democratic county vote base. In fact, quite the opposite would appear to be the case. The positive and strong Mondale-nonwhite population correlation indicates that it is in the rural areas with a relatively new voting population of nonwhites that Mondale did well in 1984. Yet, in a state with only a small minority of nonwhites, and a relatively small nonwhite participation in what used to be the traditional Democratic Party rural vote, the 1984 Mondale vote is a poor sign future Democratic presidential prospects.

SOME CONCLUSIONS ON THE TWO FLORIDAS

In state elections, the 1984 results reconfirm the existence of two political Floridas. The congressional and state legislative delegations are still predominantly all Democratic from the northern region and mixed Democratic and Republican from the southern region. Nevertheless, at the presidential vote level, a fundamental shift in voting patterns has taken place in recent years, and it bodes poorly for the Democratic presidential prospects in the state. The Democratic presidential party can no longer count on its rural, northern base to carry it to victory with a strong showing in the southern portion of the state. In 1964 Johnson carried Florida solely because of his Dade County vote margin. In 1976 Carter won the state but it took a north-south coalition, a feat that he could not repeat in 1980. By 1984 the Democratic presidential nominee had gained black registrants and clearly had strong black support in the general election, but the Republican Party carried the election and actually out-enrolled the Democratic Party in new registrants.

The 1984 election appears, in retrospect, to be one more confirming sign that the Democratic national presidential party has lost its moorings in a once-solid state of the old Democracy. The Democratic presidential nominees of recent years have no dependable, broad-based support in the state. Their one solid voting bloc, the blacks, are a small minority of the total vote, but an increasingly important part of the Democratic presidential vote. Elections, however, are not won on the basis of small, but stable, minority-based coalitions. Until the Democratic presidential nominees can broaden their southern coalition base, they will be doomed to writing off the South and facing probable electoral defeat nationally. The two political and socioeconomically different Floridas, north and south of the frost line, are realities for only state politicians. National politicians now confront only one political Florida: a state that can now be counted as a reliable part of the national Republican presidential coalition.

NOTES

1. V. O. Key, Jr., *Southern Politics in State and Nation* (New York: Knopf, 1949), 83–87.

2. The census data used in this section is drawn from the following source: Francis W. Terhune, Susan S. Floyd, and Peggy Rosander, eds., *1983 Florida Statistical Abstract*, 17th ed. (Gainesville, FL: The University Presses of Florida, 1983). Election statistics for 1980 and 1982, and voter registration data for 1982 are also reported in the latter compendium in Section 21, "Government and Elections," 534–45. Election data prior to 1980 was collected by the author from individual annual reports issued by the Office of The Secretary of State, State of Florida, Department of State, Division of Elections. Each report contains the official county-based election returns for each election held in a given year.

3. Douglas Price, *The Negro and Southern Politics: A Chapter in Florida History* (Westport, CT: Greenwood Press, 1957), 49.

4. Key, *Southern Politics*, 83.

5. Analyses of recent Florida socioeconomic and political change may be found in Mark Stern, "Florida Elections," in *Florida Politics and Government*, rev. ed., ed. Manning J. Dauer (Gainesville, FL: The University Presses of Florida, 1984); Manning J. Dauer, "Florida: The Different State," in *The Changing Politics of the South*, ed. William C. Havard (Baton Rouge: Louisiana State University Press, 1972); Alexander P. Lamis, *The Two Party South* (New York: Oxford University Press, 1984), 179–92.

6. The literature in this area is vast and growing. A "snapshot" of this process of southern attachment to the "local" Democratic Party and alienation from the "national" Democratic Party may be found in Jack Bass and Walter DeVries, *The Transformation of Southern Politics* (New York: New American Library, 1976).

7. The data for the county population figures is drawn from the *1983 Florida Statistical Abstract*, 24–25. Pearson's *r*, the correlation coefficient used goes from 0.0 when no relationship exists between two variables, to +1.0 when there is a perfect, positive relationship, and −1.0 when there is a perfect, negative, or inverse relationship between the variables. The +.73 figure is considered a fairly strong relationship, that is, Jackson's vote if fairly strongly related to the black percent of voting age population in the county.

8. 14 March 1984, 1–A, 16–A.

9. 14 March 1984, 1–A, 14–A.

10. "Candidates Mostly Ignore Florida," *St. Petersburg Times*, 4 November 1984, A–16.

11. Ibid.

12. "Candidates Spar at Valencia Forum," *The Orlando Sentinel,* 25 October 1984, C–4.

13. Office of The Secretary of State, "Tabulation of Official Votes Cast, Presidential Preferencial Primary, March 13, 1984" (Tallahassee: Department of State); Office of The Secretary of State, "Registered Voters in the State of Florida, February 11, 1984" (Tallahassee: Department of State); and Division of Elections, "Registered Voters in the State of Florida, October 6, 1984" (Tallahassee: Department of State).

14. James L. Sundquist, *Dynamics of the Party System: Alignment and Realignment of Political Parties in the United States,* 2d ed. (Washington, DC: Brookings, 1983).

15. Stern, "Florida Elections," 81–84.

16. Bernard Cosman, *Five States for Goldwater: Continuity and Change in Southern Politics, 1920–1964* (University, AL: University of Alabama Press, 1965).

17. The census material is drawn from the *Florida Statistical Abstract* for the appropriate year. The county election data is taken from the *Reports* of The Secretary of State for each of the elections employed in the analysis.

18. Donald Strong, "Further Reflections on Southern Politics," *Journal of Politics* 33 (1971): 339–56.

11

North Carolina

Jack Fleer

THE TRANSFORMATION OF
NORTH CAROLINA POLITICS

North Carolina voters approached the 1984 elections in a political and socioeconomic context of both change and continuity. Major features of that context include several paradoxes that help define the State of North Carolina. When the elections were held, the transformation of the state and its politics had taken another major step.

North Carolina, according to the 1980 census, is the tenth largest state in the nation. But the six million citizens are widely dispersed in one of the least-urbanized states in the South. The economy of the state has significant manufacturing industries, especially tobacco, textiles, and furniture. But the labor force has one of the nation's lowest manufacturing wages and the fewest members who belong to labor unions. The state has had a progressive image on racial relations, but its black electorate did not expand dramatically between the passage of the Voting Rights Act in 1965 and the 1984 election. Finally voters in North Carolina in recent decades have elected some of the nation's most conservative U.S. Senators and, by state and regional standards, some reasonably progressive Governors. The dynamics and tensions that are generated by these and other conflicting forces influence political decision making in North Carolina.

This examination of North Carolina politics focuses initially on patterns in presidential and state elections between 1972 and 1980. Topics covered include increased competition for major offices, presidential primaries and general elections, relationships between national and state politics, and patterns of voter support for parties and candidates. This background sets a stage for a closer look at state politics in 1984.

POLITICAL COMPETITION FOR
MAJOR PUBLIC OFFICES IN NORTH CAROLINA

Party competition for major statewide and national offices has changed significantly in North Carolina in recent decades. While the state had a meaningful minority party throughout the first half of the twentieth century, the Democratic Party was the predictable majority party in almost every statewide election.[1] However, beginning in 1952, the state's presidential politics became competitive. By 1968 Republican Richard Nixon won the state's electoral votes in a three-way race with 39 percent of the popular vote. Not until 1972 did a Republican presidential candidate win a majority of the state's popular vote. The only previous Republican victory in the state in this century occurred when the Democratic Party leadership was split.[2] Competition between the two major parties in gubernatorial politics began in 1960 and in U.S. senatorial politics in 1966. In each case, however, a Republican did not win these major offices until 1972. Then the state elected its first Republican Governor (James E. Holshouser) and its first Republican U.S. Senator (Jesse Helms) since 1896. With the Republicans winning majorities for three major statewide elections, a new era of party competition began in North Carolina.

Since North Carolina selects its Governor in presidential election years, state politics and presidential politics become more intertwined than in most states. In the nation only 13 states have the combination. Throughout the 1970s and 1980s, struggles within and between the two major parties led by Governor James B. Hunt and U.S. Senator Jesse Helms were reflected in, and had consequences for, the state's presidential choices.

Presidential Nominating Primaries, 1972–80

Presidential nominating politics in North Carolina took a major turn in 1972 with the institutionalization of a presidential primary for determining the preferences of party members among presidential candidates and for allocating votes of national convention delegates in each party. The basic rules of the primary and its implications for convention voting by delegates from the state remained the same throughout the period.

The Democratic Party presidential primary campaigns and results in 1972 and 1976 can be seen as contests between "the Old South" and "the New South." In 1972 former North Carolina Governor Terry Sanford (1961–65), considered a leader of progressive forces in the state and the region, was challenged by Alabama Governor George Wallace, who was riding the wave of southern protest against civil rights advances and growth of national government. Governor Wallace's major victory demonstrated support for his views in the Rim South and in a state with an image for progressiveness in racial relations. Sanford's defeat was a setback for New South politics.[3] The contest was a sideshow for presidential politics in the Democratic Party because the principal candidates passed up the state primary. However the results provided insight for national Democrats on the reception that their ideas would get from North Carolinians.

The 1976 "battle of the Souths" involved change in characters, different results, and more significant consequences for national politics. George Wallace was back, representing the Old South. The New South was represented by Jimmy Carter, former Governor of Georgia and a candidate with more serious designs on the presidency than Governor Sanford. Other candidates were in the race, but the contest was fought between Wallace and Carter. In this instance the New South Carter won.[4] His victory followed fast on the heels of a primary in Florida, where Carter had also defeated George Wallace. Wallace's two losses in his native region put an end to his presidential hopes.[5] North Carolina's statewide support for Jimmy Carter enhanced his drive for the Democratic nomination. Carter's clear majority in North Carolina was unprecedented in a Democratic primary in 1976.

The 1980 Democratic presidential primary was the first in the period to involve an incumbent President, a moderate Southerner. The challenger was Edward (Ted) Kennedy, symbol of the liberal wing of the national Democratic Party. There was no contest. Carter had the support of major Democrats within the state from Governor James B. Hunt, an incumbent seeking renomination, on down. Kennedy's campaign in the state was almost nonexistent. Carter won 70 percent and Kennedy 18 percent of the votes cast with fewer than one-fourth of the eligible electorate participating.[6]

Republican presidential primaries in the state included one contest that was crucial for the party's nomination and two contests in which the outcome was less uncertain and less crucial to the GOP's nominating politics. In 1972, President Richard Nixon, running as an incumbent, won an almost unanimous vote (94.5 percent) from Republican primary participants. His opponent, Representative Paul McCloskey, had withdrawn from the contest with his anti-Vietnam War rhetoric falling on deaf ears within his party.

In 1976 a major contest between incumbent President Gerald R. Ford and former California Governor Ronald Reagan was fought. Reagan won a narrow majority (52 percent) of Republican votes, a victory that surprised Reagan and shocked Ford. The campaign was in part a factional struggle between moderate and conservative wings of the state's Republican Party headed respectively by Governor Holshouser and U.S. Senator Jesse Helms. Reagan campaigned extensively in the state. He ran best in the east and the Piedmont. Senator Helms urged his conservative colleague to challenge President Ford on the "blood issues" that defined factions of the party.[7] The win in North Carolina breathed new life into the Reagan campaign, became a justification for renewed effort, and propelled the contest to a photofinish at the Kansas City national convention.[8]

The 1980 Republican primary was held late in the primary season and was a one-sided contest between Ronald Reagan and George Bush. Reagan had won 12 of 17 primaries and had achieved major victories in other southern states, including George Bush's home state of Texas. Reagan's 67 percent majority in North Carolina continued that pattern and helped him seal the nomination. Once again, the primary can be seen as a contest between the state party's two factions. Once again the faction headed by Senator Helms won.

In five of six primary contests, the voters of the respective parties selected the more conservative candidates defined by the serious options that were available. The 1976 primaries in both parties contributed most significantly to national nominating politics. In four of six contests, North Carolinians selected the eventual party nominees.

General Elections, 1972–80

Presidential elections in North Carolina reflect patterns that have been forming since the 1950s—increasing competitiveness by the Republican candidates and less-certain outcomes in the election results. A comparison of the Democratic vote in North Carolina with the South and the nation is provided in Table 11–1.

TABLE 11-1 Vote for President in State, South, and Nation
Percent Democratic, 1972–80

	North Carolina	South*	United States
1972	29	29	37.5
1976	55	55	51
1980	47	46	41

*Eleven southern states
Source: Data compiled by author.

In 1972 President Nixon won in a contest in which Democrat George S. McGovern lost overwhelmingly in the state, the region, and the nation. McGovern did not campaign much in the region and did not appear in North Carolina during the general election campaign. The liberal stance of McGovern made the state and region inhospitable, if not hostile, to the Democratic standard bearer. Governor Robert Scott of North Carolina stated that "[McGovern's] welfare program and his recommendations for severe defense cuts are not palatable to the people of my state."[9] State Republicans, especially U.S. senatorial candidate Jesse Helms, embraced Richard Nixon with his campaign slogan, "Nixon Needs Helms in Congress." Helms attempted to tie Democratic Senate nominee Nick Galifianakis to the liberal record of McGovern. Galifianakis and gubernatorial nominee Hargrove (Skipper) Bowles tried to separate their campaigns from the presidential contest.

With a southerner heading the Democratic slate in 1976, voters in North Carolina could vote for "someone without an accent" and express their regional loyalties. Carter had campaigned extensively in winning the state's primary. He returned for several major rallies in the fall. Carter was helped by a strong endorsement and effective organization of Jim Hunt who was running for Governor on the Democratic ticket. President Ford did not have support from the Congressional Club, an organization created by Senator Helms and his supporters to lead the conservative wing of the state and national Republican parties.[10] North Carolina gave Carter greater support than he received nationally. A united Democratic Party, not shattered by primary divisiveness, won all major contests in the state.

In 1980 Republican candidate Ronald Reagan won in North Carolina, the South, and the nation despite the presence of a southern incumbent President on the Democratic ticket. However, the southern allegiance and Democratic legacy of the state's voters resulted in Carter's doing better in the state than he did in the nation. Southern politics has taken a dramatic turn when a native of the region running as an incumbent on a Democratic ticket could not muster a majority in the state and regional electorates.[11]

Presidential politics in the state were combined with congressional politics in that the Helms organization and the National Congressional Club supported the election of Reagan and of John East for U.S. Senate. East campaigned effectively via media against the incumbent Robert Morgan, one of the most conservative Democrats in the U.S. Senate. His campaign directors stated that East's success in the state was dependent on Reagan's success. The Congressional Club's "Americans for Reagan" reportedly spent $4.8 million in an independent campaign to elect Reagan. Both Reagan and East, and therefore Helms, won by narrow margins.[12] Thus North Carolina contributed to Reagan's election and to the Republican Party's majority in the U.S. Senate.

In these three presidential elections, North Carolina voters supported the winning candidate for President. However, in 1972 and 1980, Tarheel citizens were more restrained than the national electorate in their support. Voters in the state and the region provided similar percentages for the Democratic candidates. State politics surrounding gubernatorial and U.S. Senate contests were closely related to presidential politics. Through the period, the involvement of Governor Hunt and Senator Helms was substantial. These patterns are major factors in the two principal contests of 1984—the selection of President and of a U.S. Senator for North Carolina. For some observers, the latter contest may well be the "second most important election in the nation."[13]

VOTING BEHAVIOR AND PARTY SUPPORT

Since 1972 the character of North Carolina's registered electorate has remained relatively constant. While the number of registered voters increased from 2.35 million in 1972 to 2.7 million in 1980, the distribution by political party and by race did not change. Democratic registrants exceeded Republicans by three-to-one (72 percent to 24 percent). State registrants were 84 percent white and 16 percent nonwhite, almost entirely black. Approximately two-thirds of voting age whites and one-half of voting age blacks registered.[14] The racial composition of the state's electorate did not change dramatically between the mid-1960s and 1984.[15] Increased competitiveness by Republicans has not altered the party ratios.

The voting behavior of North Carolina's citizens differs from their party registration as indicated by data on party identification and straight or split-ticket voting patterns. Partisan identification in the 1970s was approximately 45 percent Democrat, 17 percent Republican, and 33 percent Independent.[16] Thus the apparent Democratic dominance suggested by registration figures is weakened when psychological affiliation is used. Data on split or straight-ticket voting patterns in the early 1970s provides limited but helpful insight into behavioral tendencies of the state's electorate. DeVries reveals that among North Carolinians "36.8% were behavioral straight Republicans, 34.6% were behavioral straight Democrats, and 28.6% were ticket-splitters." The black's more recent analysis divides the state electorate into 59 percent "expected Democratic voters" and 41 percent "expected Republican voters."[17]

> Examining the three elections according to several major variables—regionalism, race, and urbanization—provides insight into the forces and influences which help determine the results of presidential contests in North Carolina.

From at least the nineteenth century, the Coastal Plains region of North Carolina has been a dependable source of votes for Democratic candidates. The counties in the region have large black populations and rural or small town agrarian interests for the most part. From 1948 through 1964, Democratic presidential candidates received approximately 71 percent of the area's votes.

The Democratic advantage in eastern North Carolina was balanced, though not equalled, by a Republican advantage in the western mountains. This region, characterized by populations that did not share the concerns that led to the Civil War, generally supported Republican presidential candidates but regularly at a lower level—52 percent on the average (1948–64). However, in a state where Democratic candidates won repeatedly and with significant margins, this dependable source of Republican votes provided an important restraint on the Democrats and a base for future growth.[18]

The Piedmont region, most populous and more varied, is at the center of the state and has been the center of competition between major party presidential contestants. The area grew not only in population and diversity, but also in political uncertainty. While Democratic candidates won majorities in most elections (four of five), their margins over Republican opponents were slight.

In the three elections (1972–80), the regional differences were less striking (see Table 11–2). They disappeared in 1972 when McGovern did poorly in all regions. In 1976 and 1980, the Democratic advantage in the Coastal Plains was maintained but at a lower level than previously. The results for the mountains varied. Clearly, the historically strong patterns of regional voting have declined in both importance and persistence.

Since the "civil rights revolution" of the 1960s and the Voting Rights Act of 1965, the number of blacks who are registered to vote has increased and the allegiance of black voters to the Democratic Party, especially in presidential elections, has been clear and consistent.

Data in Table 11–3 show the association between the percentage of blacks in a county population and the amount of electoral support for Democratic presidential candidates. While the 1972 election figures involve less dramatic differences between counties with proportionately large black populations (40 percent plus) and those with small black populations, all three elections provide evidence for the conclusion that as the percentage of population that is black increases the portion of the vote won by Democratic candidates increases. And through the three elections the differences between the counties with least-black populations and the counties with most-black populations have increased, even dramatically, from roughly eight percentage points in 1972 to almost 19 percentage points in 1980.

This finding is a departure from a pattern that existed before the Democratic Party became strongly identified with black interests. The earlier pattern showed white voters in counties with large black but disenfranchised populations providing major support for Democratic candidates.[19] The irony of this change led one study to conclude that "blacks who had been systematically disenfranchised by southern Democrats in the past now provide the most consistent support for Democratic candidates."[20]

At an earlier stage of the development of Republican voting in the

TABLE 11–2   Percent Democratic by State and Region

	1972	1976	1980
State totals	28.9	55.2	47.2
Coastal Plains	28.8	61.2	52.3
Piedmont	29.5	53.0	46.1
Mountains	29.1	53.5	43.8

Source: Data compiled by author.

TABLE 11–3   Percent Democratic Vote by Percent Black Population

Percent Black Population	Percent Democratic Vote		
	1972	*1976*	*1980*
State totals	28.9	55.2	47.2
40% or more	35.5	67.0	62.0
30–39.9%	29.9	58.5	50.8
20–29.9%	28.8	54.2	47.7
19.9% or less	27.4	52.9	43.2

Source: Data compiled by author.

South and the state, metropolitan counties were major areas of growth for the Republican Party. During the 1950s and 1960s, Republican presidential candidates garnered greater support in metropolitan counties than in nonmetropolitan counties.[21] This distinction was less dependable for the GOP in the three most recent presidential elections. The uncertainty of Republican Party support in urban areas is due in part to its failure to secure votes of urban blacks. Furthermore, significant portions of urban, middle-class white voters have maintained identification with the Democratic Party while often voting for Republican candidates.[22] The tension that results is a source of unpredictability for election outcomes.

NOMINATING POLITICS IN 1984

North Carolina's involvement in the 1984 presidential nominating politics focused on its presidential primary held on 8 May. Since Ronald Reagan had no opposition for renomination by the Republican Party, all attention was on the Democratic presidential primary. Simultaneously with the presidential contest, voters in the state Democratic Party could participate in major statewide and local primaries, including a gubernatorial primary in which six of ten candidates were running major campaigns and several congressional campaigns that were strongly contested (especially in the Second District, Fourth District, and Ninth District). The North Carolina primary followed 16 other presidential primaries and many caucuses, involving much sifting of candidates and issues. It was the last primary in a southern state. Also, it was held on the same day as primaries in Indiana and Ohio, which attracted attention from the candidates and media because of their location in the industrial heartland.

The three major candidates remaining in the contest (Jesse Jackson, Gary Hart, and Walter Mondale) each had campaign organizations in the state and each visited the state, especially in the two weeks before the primary. Mondale's organization was headed by former U.S. Senator Robert B. Morgan and included much of the established party leadership throughout the state, such as former Governor Terry Sanford. Gary Hart's team, which was assembled in the period just before the campaign, included many young, upwardly mobile professionals but also several experienced politicos. Jackson's campaign included black leaders from major urban areas, such as LaVonia Allison of Durham who chairs the state's Black Leadership Caucus.

Each candidate visited major urban centers and media markets in the Piedmont crescent, including the Research Triangle (Raleigh-Durham-Chapel Hill), Greensboro–Winston-Salem, and Charlotte. Additionally, Jackson made an extensive tour through the predominantly rural, northeastern Second Congressional District, the population of which is approximately 40 percent black, the highest concentration of minorities in the state. Mondale, stressing his farming background, visited tobacco-producing eastern North Carolina, expressing support for tobacco commodity programs and health-warning labels on cigarette packaging. Hart's visit to the high-tech, academic communities of the Research Triangle emphasized his major appeal. Jackson opposed run-off primaries based on his belief that they discriminated against black candidates. North Carolina had provided several examples of the difficulty of blacks winning run-offs.[23]

Unlike the three previous presidential primaries in North Carolina, the 1984 Democratic primary did not include a southerner among the candidates, although Jackson had been born and educated in the Carolinas. Each candidate was identified with the liberal wing of the national party, a fact that presented difficulties for the party leadership and voters.

Approximately 960,000 Democrats voted. Among registered Democrats this represented 45 percent of the eligible electorate. This substantial increase over the 1980 primary is accounted for in part by the increased registration and mobilization of black voters and the more competitive relationship within the party.

Although Mondale received more votes than his challengers, his large third (36 percent) was not a major victory. Gary Hart received a small third (30 percent), and Jesse Jackson received 25 percent. The remainder went to other candidates and No preference.

While the three candidates' votes were within 11 percentage points, the threshold requirements and bonus votes for the leading candidate enhanced Mondale's delegate count. North Carolina rules presented a good example of the impact of the national rules dispute, which resulted in a call for reform prior to the 1988 convention.[24] The rules, designed to enlarge the delegate strength of the front runner who has a broad base of electoral support, resulted in the following delegate allocation based on the primary vote:

Candidate	Primary Vote	Convention Delegates
Mondale	36.5%	47 (53%)
Hart	30	19 (22%)
Jackson	25	15 (17%)
Uncommitted	5	7 (8%)
Other	4	0 (0%)

Walter Mondale's lead over Hart and Jackson was not great, but he did win pluralities in all congressional districts of the state except the Second District, where Jackson received 41 percent of the vote. Mondale's strongest pluralities were in the western mountain counties (Tenth and Eleventh Districts).

Jackson's greatest support came from eastern North Carolina, especially the northeastern Second District where a large black population and an intense campaign on behalf of a black state representative running for the U.S. House boosted his totals. Additionally Jackson received major support in several urban counties, winning pluralities in Guilford County (Greensboro), Forsyth County (Winston-Salem), and Durham County (Durham). Jackson garnered few votes in the mountainous western third of the state.

Hart's votes were fairly evenly distributed across the state, with greatest support in the west and least support in the east. He did not win a plurality in any congressional district, but he did lead in nine counties, four in the eastern First District.

Racial voting was strong in the North Carolina primary with blacks supporting Jackson and whites split between Hart and Mondale. An exit survey conducted by CBS/*New York Times* reveals the following alignment:

Candidate	Black Voters	White Voters
Hart	1%	41%
Jackson	84	3
Mondale	13	46

This pattern reflected similar voting in other state primaries.

At the Democratic convention in San Francisco, the state's delegates divided their 88 votes as follows: Mondale, 53; Hart, 19; and Jackson, 16. Mondale's strength was enhanced by almost solid support from the officially unpledged superdelegates—state executive, legislative, and party officials. The state's delegation majority contributed significantly to Mondale's winning margin in securing his party's presidential nomination. Since there was no contest in the Republican Party, the state's delegation to the Republican convention in Dallas, Texas, joined in the unanimous endorsement of Ronald Reagan's nomination.

A bruising primary for the Democratic gubernatorial nomination ended with no candidate receiving a majority. The two frontrunners were Attorney General Rufus Edmisten, who received 30 percent of the vote, and former Charlotte mayor, H. Edward Knox, who received 26 percent. A run-off primary was held on 5 June. Edmisten narrowly defeated Knox with 52 percent of the vote. Divisions generated by this intraparty free-for-all would have serious consequences for the fall campaign and elections.

THE GENERAL ELECTION CAMPAIGN IN NORTH CAROLINA

Nationally, the presidential campaign was seen as most important, but in North Carolina the focus was shared by the U.S. Senate contest between incumbent Senator Jesse Helms and his challenger, current Governor James B. Hunt, Jr. Additionally, hard-fought campaigns for governor and for seats in most of the 11 congressional districts contributed to the competitive political environment.

The presidential campaign in North Carolina was waged against a background that included several crucial decisions of Democratic Party nominee Walter Mondale, including the selection of a non-southerner as his running mate, the aborted attempt to name a southerner as the national party chairman, and the decision to tell the truth about raising taxes to reduce the national budget deficit. Additionally, President Reagan's previous success in securing support from the state's voters defined the context within which the campaign was conducted.

Furthermore, Mondale's choice of Geraldine Ferraro lessened the attractiveness of the Democratic ticket in North Carolina, inasmuch as no Democratic presidential victory since 1948 had been achieved in the state without a southerner as one of the two candidates. Additionally, Ferraro's liberal voting record in the U.S. Congress was similar to Mondale's.[26]

Mondale attempted to show his concern for the South by announcing, but then retracting, the choice of former Budget Director Bert Lance of Georgia as the chairman of the national Democratic Party. After meeting a firestorm of criticism, Mondale quickly changed his decision, named Lance as general manager of the campaign, and faced serious questions about his competence in directing the party.[27] Lance subsequently resigned his position. These events signaled a strategy to deemphasize the South in the Mondale campaign.

A third decision that had critical consequences in North Carolina and the region concerned Mondale's announcement that he would raise taxes.[28] This became an albatross for Mondale and many candidates who shared the Democratic ticket with him. Republican candidates from President Reagan on down used this promise to raise taxes to charge that Democratic candidates would "tax and tax, spend and spend" and reverse the "economic recovery" that Republicans claimed they had brought to the country beginning in 1981.

Reagan's previous campaigns in the state had been successful, and throughout the 1984 campaign, the Gallup Poll reported a gigantic lead for the Republican ticket in North Carolina. Between May and late October, the clear margin remained relatively stable (ranging between 21 and 28 percent) and provided a framework that influenced the conduct of the campaign. Democrats knew they had an uphill battle and worried about the prospects for Reagan's coattails in state and local races. Republicans, on the other hand, were pleased to have such support at the top of the ticket and generally latched themselves to the Reagan bandwagon.

Candidates' Visits to North Carolina

Each candidate of the two parties' national tickets visited the state after the nominating conventions. They appeared in major metropolitan areas and key media markets throughout the state.

Walter Mondale, who had visited the state five times in the year before his nomination, included a stop in Asheville on an early trip between the two national conventions. At the Western North Carolina Farmers Market, he focused on Reagan economic policies and their consequences for farm families and the middle class. Mondale continued his standard attack on Reagan's promise to balance the budget and maintain Social Security without a tax increase, and he added a criticism about Reagan's farm policy. He promised to support legislation to protect farm commodities and promote agricultural exports in his administration.[29] The crowd of more than 700 included several state officials, but not the Democratic Party candidates for U.S. Senate and for Governor.

Vice President Bush visited three locations in the state on 10 September, appealing to several groups. At a Raleigh news conference, Bush appeared with Republican U.S. Senate candidate Jesse Helms, a former Democrat, and two former Democratic state legislators who were named leaders of the North Carolina Democrats for Reagan-Bush. Bush appealed to Democrats "who feel the national party in Washington, controlled by the special interests and the most liberal elements of the party, have simply shut them out."[30]

In Archdale near Greensboro, Bush visited a textile plant. He addressed the area's concerns over burgeoning foreign imports of textiles and tobacco and emphasized the administration's preference for free trade.[31]

The major rally of the Bush visit was held at Wake Forest University in Winston-Salem to focus on the Youth for Reagan-Bush. The Vice President's speech contrasted economic and foreign policies in the Carter-Mondale years and in the Reagan-Bush years, praised Reagan for creating a vibrant economy with cuts in government regulations, spending, and tax rates, and praised Reagan's leadership in foreign affairs, saying that America was strong and respected around the world.[32] His themes were standard Bush fare during the campaign.[33] Throughout the visit Republican candidates for local, congressional, and state offices appeared with Bush, who appealed for support of Republican candidates at every electoral level.

On 1 October Geraldine Ferraro visited Greensboro and Raleigh for separate rallies. In each appearance, she emphasized two messages. First, she endorsed Governor Hunt in his bid for the Senate, saying incumbent Senator Jesse Helms espoused "an extremist right-wing ideology" that is out of touch "with the people and traditions of this great state." Second, she claimed that many proposals of the Democratic national ticket—keeping the peace, passing the Equal Rights Amendment, and stopping the arms race—were patriotic acts.[34] All major statewide and some congressional candidates appeared with Ferraro as she brought her historic candidacy to the state, and she was received by enthusiastic crowds. The Democratic Party leadership felt her visit supplied a boost to their sagging fortunes, as reported in the polls. In contrast, state Republican Party Chairman David Flaherty charged that Ferraro is "one of the ten most liberal congressmen in the United States," and he stated, "there are no worries about Ferraro."[35]

The last candidate to visit the state was President Reagan, who made Charlotte, the state's largest city, his first stop after the first debate. Reagan focused on the "economic recovery" and the "national renewal," which he claimed for his administration. He used Charlotte as an example: "Here in Charlotte, construction is up, take home pay is up, sales are up."[36] A crowd, estimated by the Secret Service at around 40,000, greeted the President and the state and local Republicans who appeared on the platform in a patriotic frenzy.

Before the President spoke, Senator Helms announced that a defeated candidate for the Democratic gubernatorial nomination in a bitter spring primary and a former mayor of Charlotte, Eddie Knox, had been named a co-chairman of a national organization of Democrats for Reagan-Bush. This announcement revealed serious divisions within the Democratic Party and would reverberate throughout the fall campaign. It also enhanced the Republican effort to identify former Democrats with the Republican campaign.

While most of Reagan's visit was well-received, one statement was met with stunned silence followed by criticism. Reagan referred to the failure of school busing and assailed Democrats for supporting busing to achieve racial integration in public schools, saying that this process makes innocent children into pawns in an unwanted social experiment. Charlotte had been the site of the first court-ordered busing, and many Charlotte-Mecklenburg civic leaders, expressing community pride in the success of the busing plan and the educational achievements of the integrated schools, later assailed the President for his short-sighted remark.[37] Reagan ultimately apologized for his insensitive remark.

Relationship to Other Races

The wide margin of support in North Carolina favoring the Reagan-Bush team had serious consequences for other contests that were being waged in the region and in North Carolina.[38] While all congressional and statewide campaigns felt the impact of the margin between the two national tickets, examples from the U.S. Senate campaign will make the point.

Senator Helms and Governor Hunt, in their bids for the U.S. Senate seat, discussed their relationships with the presidential candidates often and in contrasting styles. Senator Helms became a cheerleader for the Reagan candidacy, seldom missing opportunities to proclaim his personal attraction for the President and to praise the economic policies of his Republican colleagues. At the same time, he sought and relished chances to tie his opponent to Mondale and his proposals to raise taxes. Governor Hunt expressed support for the Mondale-Ferraro ticket and his opposition to the proposed tax increases. He also focused attention on Helms' criticism of and opposition to Reagan policy proposals in both domestic and foreign arenas, charging that the incumbent Senator was a radical Republican while President Reagan was a reasonable Republican.

In the second of four televised debates between the U.S. senatorial candidates, Helms stated: "Mr. Hunt doesn't want you to know it, but he is a Mondale liberal and ashamed of it and I am a Reagan conservative and proud of it."[39] In the fourth debate in mid-October, Helms proclaimed: ". . . the Reagan Economic Recovery Program must be given the strongest possible support by the Senator you elect in November. . . . Governor Hunt has called President Reagan's program unfair, he's called it a failure, and he says we should apologize for it. The President doesn't need any more critics in Congress. . . . Ronald Reagan is my long-time friend. That friendship is valuable not only to me, it's valuable to North Carolina."[40]

Governor Hunt responded that while he supported the Democratic presidential nominee, he differed with him on some issues. He would vote independently of Mondale in the Senate. Hunt declared: "I think [Mondale] is wrong right now in pushing to raise some taxes. [If I am elected], I will vote against him on that. I will vote for what I think is right."[41] Again in the final debate, Hunt stated: "For 18 months, Senator Helms has tried to tell you that you do not know where I stand. Lately he says I've turned into something he calls a Mondale liberal. But you know better, you've elected me statewide three times. I've served as governor for eight years. . . ."[42]

Throughout the campaign, television commercials with Ronald Reagan speaking from the White House informed the state's citizens of the President's support for Senator Helms. Additionally, Helms spot ads carried the message: "Mondale and Hunt promise to raise taxes. Reagan and Helms oppose tax increases." In campaign appearances Helms spoke mainly of the success of the Reagan presidency, the "economic recovery," and his personal friendship for the President. Reagan could not have hired a better advertising agency.

Similar relationships existed in races for Governor and U.S. House candidates. Hoping for long Reagan coattails, the national Republican Party targeted seven of the state's 11 U.S. House races and poured thousands of dollars into these campaigns. Republican candidates extolled their devotion to and support of Reagan repeatedly in media commercials and personal appearances. The Reagan candidacy received a major boost from these associations, and the state candidates hoped the benefit would be mutual.

Meanwhile, Democrats suffered from what Germond and Witcover labeled the Mondale "leper factor." Although Mondale's superior performance in the first presidential debate encouraged North Carolina Democrats and made Mondale supporters more visible in the state, the positive relationship was temporary. The state's party literature mentioned the national candidates, but gave far more attention to the state candidates promoted as the "Team for Tomorrow." Democratic Party unity rallies, held in each of the state's congressional districts, always included a spokesman for the national ticket, often former U.S. Senator Robert Morgan, who headed the national ticket's campaign in the state.

Voter Registration and Get-Out-the-Vote Efforts

The 1984 campaigns in North Carolina included major efforts to increase the registered electorate and to encourage voter turnout. The 1984 registration drives produced historic highs in absolute number of voters and in percentage of voting-age population to be registered. Approximately 3.3 million voters, 77 percent of the eligible population, were listed on the rolls for the November election.

Beginning in 1981, the state and county boards of elections made a concerted effort to make registration easier and more accessible for citizens. Additionally, black voter groups lead by Jesse Jackson and Andrew Young, and white fundamentalist churches led by Jerry Falwell and Lamarr Mooneyham, contributed to unprecedented increases in new voters.[43] Both parties and candidate groups joined the cause as interest in state races generated new registrants. Twelve years earlier (1972) just over half (56 percent) of the voting-age population was registered.

Modest and meaningful changes occurred in party affiliation and racial composition of the registered electorate from 1980 to 1984. Republican registrants increased from 23 percent to 26 percent, revealing no major partisan shift. Black registrants increased from 16 percent to 19 percent of the electorate. While this change is slight, it represents an increase of approximately 180,000 voters. This was offset by an increase of approximately 400,000 new white voters.

In addition to encouraging voter registration, both political parties and various candidate groups organized what some called the most concentrated get-out-the-vote effort in the state's history. The Democratic Party launched a unified campaign that coordinated local, state, and candidate groups. With adequate financing, computers, phone banks, and thousands of volunteers, the party conducted what state chairman David Price called the most sophisticated voter mobilization drive in the state's history.[44] Democrats sought to use their nearly three-to-one registration advantage to thwart the looming Reagan landslide and its coattail consequences.

But Republicans were convinced equally that they were prepared to get their supporters to the polls. The party and each candidate, especially Jim Martin, organized separate efforts to launch an estimated 35,000 volunteers in neighborhood and friends networks to canvass voters, identify candidate preferences, and remind citizens to vote. Party chairman Flaherty emphasized the need to get Republican-leaning registrants to the polls.[45] Both party chairmen expected the largest turnout in the state's history.

As the polls opened on 6 November 1984, both parties and all major candidates were convinced that voter mobilization would be a key to victory, especially in the closely contested state races. And in the apparently one-sided presidential contest, the Republicans wanted to avoid the possibility of apathy reducing their support. Increased registration drives, intense get-out-the-vote efforts, and last minute campaigning had both parties poised for an historic election day.

GENERAL ELECTION:
RESULTS AND ANALYSES

Introduction

The 1984 general election in North Carolina was historic. For only the second time in the twentieth century, candidates of the Republican Party won three major statewide elections. Furthermore, the depth of the Republican sweep at the lower portions of the ballot was unprecedented, as Republicans won state legislative and county elections in record numbers. The election resulted in the strongest Republican victory since Reconstruction. Voter turnout also set a record as more North Carolinians went to the polls than at any time in history.

Some, if not most, of the tidal wave of Republican success, referred to by one Democratic spokesman as "Hurricane Ronnie," can be attributed to the vast margin of victory garnered by President Ronald Reagan in the state that saved his political career in 1976. But the Republican fortunes are also the product of additional forces at work in North Carolina. A key question being asked is whether the election results are temporary, due to the Reagan "era of good feelings" generated by his "America is back and standing tall" theme? Or have more basic sources of fundamental change in the allegiance of state's voters surfaced that will usher in a new era of highly competitive two-party politics or of Republican dominance after the Democratic Party's dominance in previous state history? Subsequent analyses will examine the results of the election and analyze the principle voting patterns to determine their meanings for future North Carolina politics.

Election Results

The major victory for President Reagan that was predicted in national and state polls throughout the political year was realized with a resounding vote. Reagan won 1,346,481 votes (62 percent) to Mondale's 824,287 (38 percent).[46] While Richard Nixon won a greater percentage (68 percent) of the state's popular vote in 1972 when McGovern headed the Democratic ticket, the impact of Reagan's support reverberated throughout the state and up-and-down the long ballot. Although Tarheels' support for Reagan did not match that of some other southern states (Florida, Texas, and Virginia), the state joined its regional sisters to provide the incumbent President with greater support (63 percent) than any region in the nation.

North Carolina voters elected their second Republican Governor, James G. Martin, in the twentieth century and only the third since Reconstruction. State voters reelected U.S. Senator Jesse Helms over Governor James B. Hunt in an unprecedented battle of the state's political giants, which became the most expensive ($25 million) Senate race on record and likely one of the most bitter and hard-fought. These two contests resulted in Republicans' controlling the top three state offices, as Martin and Helms joined incumbent Republican Senator John East, for the first time in this century.

Additional Republican victories were achieved in U.S. House of Representatives contests, where five Republican candidates were elected in the 11 congressional districts. The victories involved the defeat of three incumbent representatives. In six districts the winning margins did not exceed 2 percentage points. Voters in North Carolina provided the national Republican Party with three of the 14 seats gained in this national election. Two southern states, North Carolina and Texas, accounted for half of the GOP's gain.[47]

Republicans increased their delegates in the two houses of the state's General Assembly, from 24 to 49 representatives (12 of 50 Senate members; 37 of 120 House members). This, too, was a major contingent of Republicans in the century, almost matching the size of the 1972 delegation (50), the previous high. Finally, Republicans increased the number of county boards of commissioners that they controlled from 11 to 20 among the state's 100 counties.

The accumulation of Republican victories resulted in the worst performance of the Democratic Party in the state's history. The Democratic Party was weakened, at least temporarily, in losing a whole generation of experienced leaders and major offices on which to build for the future. When the results are viewed together, North Carolina became one of the two most Republican states in the South. While Republicans may have been disappointed with the length of Reagan's coattails and the leanness of their success nationally,[48] they could look at North Carolina as a "shining city on a hill" where Republican officeholders abound.

Sources of Support

The avalanche of Reagan votes in North Carolina came from all segments of the population, as shown by data in Table 11–4 derived from a Gallup Poll. Reagan received a majority of the votes from all categories of voters except blacks, where his support was quite small. The broadly based coalition does, however, contain evidence of significant divisions. The most serious polarization is found in divisions between whites, 72 percent of whom favored Reagan, and blacks, 79 percent of whom favored Walter Mondale.[49] Another serious division is between younger voters (18–29 year olds) and older voters (50 years and older). The 12 percentage-point difference shows new voters exceeding Reagan's statewide actual vote in giving him 67 percent, and the more mature voters being less inclined to support Reagan than the state at large (55 percent). The development reflects the nationwide phenomenon of youth for Reagan,[50] but the difference between the two age groups is greater in North Carolina than in the nation.[51] Nationally, the two groups gave similar levels of support to Reagan. The third meaningful difference is found between voters with varying levels of education. College graduates and citizens with less than high school educations vary 12 percentage points in their support for Reagan, following long-established patterns of greater support for Republican candidates from persons with higher formal education. Lastly, contrasting support levels exist between men and women but is not as great (10 percentage points) as the purveyors of the "gender gap" and the presence of the first woman on a national ticket might have suggested.[52]

Thus, in North Carolina Reagan did better among whites, younger voters, college graduates and men than he did among blacks, older citizens, less-educated voters, and women. The major component of the lineup is the high support among new voters. This should provide encouragement for the future of the Republican Party if Reagan's

TABLE 11–4 Support among Demographic Voter Groups
President and U.S. Senate (percentage)

	Reagan	Mondale	Helms	Hunt
Statewide	60	37	48	46
Men	65	33	53	42
Women	56	40	43	49
Whites	72	25	58	36
Blacks	15	79	11	83
18–29 year olds	67	32	48	47
30–49 year olds	63	34	48	46
50 and older	55	41	48	45
College graduates	62	36	45	48
Some college	65	33	48	46
High school graduates	63	34	50	45
Less than high school graduates	53	41	48	44
Democrats (self-described)	22	74	15	81
Republicans "	98	1	88	8
Independents "	73	22	54	36

Source: Gallup Poll conducted by telephone survey of 1873 registered voters over the period of 30 October to 2 November 1984. Obtained through the *Winston-Salem Journal,* one of several state news organizations that sponsored the poll in North Carolina.

support can be secured for state Republicans.[53] The almost perfect loyalty of self-described Republicans, the defections of Democratic identifiers, and the lopsided Republican vote of Independents contributed to the Reagan landslide in North Carolina.

Another perspective is provided by consideration of factors that motivated voters to support one presidential candidate over another. Respondents to the ABC Exit Poll were asked to indicate which one characteristic best described why they voted for or did not vote for a particular candidate.[54] The characteristic most frequently mentioned as favorable was "He's a strong leader." Thirty-four percent of the respondents selected this factor, and among them they voted 83 percent for Reagan. The second-most frequently mentioned positive characteristic was "He's fair to all income groups." One out of five voters expressed this view; 86 percent of them supported Walter Mondale. No one characteristic dominated on the question of what motivated lack of support for a candidate. However, 24 percent of the sample selected "weak leader" as a negative characteristic, and 18 percent checked "tied to special interests." In both cases, voters who expressed these views supported Reagan overwhelmingly (91 percent on weak leader; 72 percent on special interests). The leadership dimension was a major consideration nationally in determining votes, and in North Carolina the situation was similar.[55]

Issues also influenced North Carolina voters but were more prominent as negative factors than in motivating favorable votes. Voters were asked to indicate on which one issue they most liked or most disliked a candidate's stand. Thirty-two percent of the respondents disliked a candidate's stand on tax increases; they voted 93 percent for Reagan.[56] The most-frequently mentioned stand that respondents liked was on government spending. The 18 percent of the sample that selected this response divided their votes 81 percent for Reagan and 19 percent for Mondale. These broad responses attest to the significance of economic policies in shaping the outcome of the presidential contest. No one policy stand dominated the favorable category as in the case of the unfavorable category. Walter Mondale's strategy of "telling the truth" to the American people on tax increases and the national budget deficit was a marked disadvantage in North Carolina and the nation. Economic policy interests were in the forefront of voters minds. During the election, in North Carolina and the nation, the Republican Party gained the advantage of being viewed as doing "a better job of keeping the country prosperous."[57]

Throughout the fall and in every Republican campaign, state party leaders hoped that a major vote for Reagan would sweep other party colleagues into office. As stated previously, the strategy of GOP candidates at all levels was to identify strongly with the popular national ticket and hope that the association would reap rewards. State and local Republicans were not disappointed. An example of the benefits of this strategy is found in the widely publicized U.S. Senate election.

Table 11–4 reveals the distribution of votes among the principal demographic groups for Senator Helms and Governor Hunt. Helms received his greatest support from among whites, men, and less-educated voters. Hunt prevailed among blacks, women, and better-educated voters. The unusual finding is that college graduates supported the Democratic candidate more than persons with lower levels of education. This pattern exists in neither the presidential nor the gubernatorial election data for North Carolina. The gender gap and racial polarization were key elements that contributed to the differing bases of support for the two Senate candidates. Also, Helms won 60 percent of the vote of born-again Christians, which comprise approximately one-fourth of the voters in the sample.[58] Finally, Helms received significant support from blue-collar voters in textile manufacturing areas in the rural southern Piedmont.[59] Partisans were strongly loyal, but twice as many Democrats defected to Helms as Republicans to Hunt. Helms had a commanding lead among Independents. With a few noted exceptions, the Reagan and Helms bases of support among major demographic groups were similar, although Helms received many fewer votes than Reagan.

In assessing the outcome of the Senate race, Gary Pearce, co-manager of the Hunt campaign, said that Senator Helms' strategy of associating Governor Hunt with Mondale's tax proposals was critical to the outcome. Senator Helms' press secretary, Claude Allen, stated: "We knew all along that we needed a boost from Reagan." He continued: "Our first ad campaign had Reagan in it. We started with Reagan and Helms, and we're ending with Reagan and Helms."[60] Pearce and David Price, chairman of the state Democratic Party, both felt that the race would have been quite different if Reagan had not built such a huge lead, or if it had occurred in a nonpresidential year. Pearce said Hunt would have been "5–10 points ahead of Helms if the presidential race were closer." He concluded: "This is a tough year to be a Democrat."[61] Thus, the Hunt and Helms camps agreed on one conclusion—the importance of the Reagan landslide and the Reagan economic recovery for North Carolina politics.

The breadth and depth of Reagan's landslide is made clear by Figure 11–1, indicating his voting strength by counties. Fifty-four of

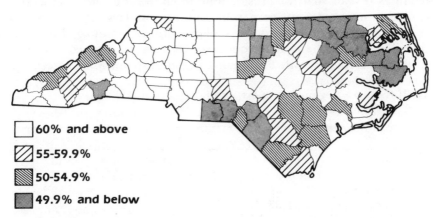

60% and above

55-59.9%

50-54.9%

49.9% and below

FIGURE 11–1   North Carolina Vote for President—Percent Republican

the 100 counties gave Reagan 60 percent or more of the votes cast. In 17 counties, his margin exceeded 70 percent. The Reagan counties are located mainly in the mountainous west and the central Piedmont. But even in the eastern coastal plains, many counties voted overwhelmingly for Reagan. Mondale's strength was primarily in the northeastern counties with large black populations and in a few counties scattered in the Piedmont. The former Vice President won majorities in 15 counties. In only two counties did his support exceed the 60 percent margin.

An earlier analysis of regional voting patterns shows that the traditional patterns declined in significance during recent presidential elections. The 1984 contest resulted in the Democratic candidate receiving slightly greater support in the mountains than in the coastal plains (see Table 11–5). However, both regions were more generous to Mondale than was the Piedmont, where Reagan was far more popular. However, in the contest for U.S. Senate and Governor, the coastal plains remained the major region of Democratic support, exceeding statewide totals. The mountain region remained faithful to Republican candidates for each of the offices.

The 1984 elections sustained the pattern of Democrats receiving greater support in counties with large black populations than in counties with smaller portions of blacks (see Table 11–6). As the percentage of a county's population that is black increases, the portion of its vote won by Democratic candidates increases. The prominence of the black vote in Democratic coalitions is confirmed by this data and other analyses.

Finally, an examination of the vote in the state's six metropolitan counties reveals that for President and U.S. Senate, the Democratic candidates got more support from counties with large urban centers than in nonmetropolitan counties. However, the advantage for Mondale is modest. The nonmetropolitan counties' support comes close to the state totals. Both President Reagan and Jim Martin secured

TABLE 11–5   Regional Support for Major Offices, 1984
(percent Democratic)

	President	*U.S. Senate*	*Governor*
State totals	38	48	46
Coastal plains	42	51	52
Piedmont	37	47	42
Mountains	44	44	44

Source: Data compiled by author.

TABLE 11–6   Percent Democratic Vote by Black Population

Black Population	Percent Democratic Vote
State totals	38
40% or more	50
30–39.9%	45
20–29.9%	39
19.9% or less	32

Source: Data compiled by author.

significant support in the metropolitan counties, which bolstered their statewide majorities.

The widely publicized registration drives and the highly organized voter mobilization efforts did lead to a large number of North Carolinians going to the polls on election day. Approximately 67 percent of the registered electorate voted for Governor and U.S. Senator and nearly 65 percent voted for a presidential candidate. Although the rate of participation did not increase over 1980, the larger registered electorate resulted in the history-making number of participants. The 1980 registration rate was 59 percent, in 1984 the rate was 77 percent. For example, candidates for U.S. Senate in 1980 received the votes of 1,797,665 citizens. In 1984, candidates for the same office attracted 2,239,051 voters. More than 441,000 more votes were cast. Almost 300,000 more votes were cast for President in 1984 than in 1980. The portion of the voting age population that participated increased from 43.4 percent in 1980 to 47.5 percent in 1984. This was the second-highest increase in the nation according to the Committee for the Study of the American Electorate.[62]

SUMMARY AND CONCLUSIONS

Democratic Party dominance in North Carolina politics, which has encountered serious challenges in the past two decades, received further shocks in 1984. The 1984 Republican victories, when added to those of recent years, provide an impressive series of successes for the state's traditional minority party. Republican candidates have won four of the past five presidential elections in the state, four of the last five U.S. Senate elections, and two of the last four gubernatorial elections. Democrats have maintained control of the state's delegation to the U.S. House, statewide executive offices including Lieutenant Governor, Attorney General and seven positions of the council of state, and both houses of the state General Assembly. But even in these positions, the Republicans have increased their support and occasionally increased their victories. It is clear that party and political competition is more intense in North Carolina. Its character and its future must be assessed.

The political developments have occurred in a context of competition involving two opposing sets of leaders.[63] Through the 1970s and into the 1980s, a moderate biracial coalition has supported Democratic candidates, including Governor James B. Hunt and U.S. Senator Robert Morgan. That coalition of blacks, low-income whites, and the more-conservative, white business-industrial establishment is a precarious mix whose diverse components require careful leadership and communications. James Sundquist, referring to similar coalitions throughout the South, describes their leadership as pragmatic, non-ideological, and consensus-oriented. Sundquist states the leaders are "moderate centrists who are skilled in the political straddle, moving just far enough to the center to attract strong black and liberal support but not so far as to drive a large bloc of moderate conservative Democrats into Republican ranks."[64] In a recent campaign debate, Governor Hunt stated their position:

> I am part of a new generation of Democrats in the South. People who believe in three things . . . balanced budget and fiscal responsibility . . . economic growth and providing jobs for people, [and] . . . racial justice and people working together.

Their philosophy is a blend of conservative and progressive themes. Additionally, they have consistently worked with and within the national Democratic Party, while maintaining differences on some policies.

The state Republican Party, with Senator Helms as its leader and principle spokesman, has provided a significantly contrasting message. Helms has preached an economic conservatism of a leaner federal government, reduced taxes, and, with modifications in 1984, balanced budgets. He has espoused social conservatism including strong antiabortion, pro-school prayer, and moral crusade messages. Anticommunism, prodefense, and fervent patriotism are stressed. Finally, a white racial appeal was highlighted by a well-publicized fight against the Martin Luther King, Jr., holiday in 1983. Throughout the period, Helms and state Republicans generally have taken advantage of the party's presidential candidate, with Helms embracing Richard Nixon in 1972 and Ronald Reagan in 1980 and 1984.

Helms has succeeded in challenging the moderate centrist Democrats by describing their candidates as "liberals," by questioning their compatibility with what he describes as a conservative electorate, and by questioning their political integrity and faithfulness to clearly state positions. In 1978, 1980, 1982, and 1984, the Helms organization has used relentless advertising made possible by millions of dollars to cut into Democratic support and to make North Carolina voters suspicious, at the least, of the Democrats' service to the state.

In 1984, Reagan's large victory was aided by his personal characteristics and his leadership image. However, his economic policies, strong defense posture, and social conservatism also appealed to North Carolinians. Republican candidates for U.S. Senate and Governor benefited from Reagan's personal and policy appeal, as Martin and Helms embraced the popular President. Helms' narrow victory was also helped by his advertising campaign, which sowed serious doubts about his opponents' ability to represent the state. Martin capitalized on a splintered Democratic Party. He capped his appeal with a tax reduction package that contained promises for a wide spectrum of economic groups—from business with an inventory tax repeal to low-income voters with repeal of the sales tax on food and nonprescription drugs. Overall, the Republican candidates presented a united and diverse appeal.

Meanwhile, many Democrats were unenthusiastic about their national ticket, divided over their gubernatorial nomination, and insufficiently inspired by Hunt's record and leadership. Importantly, despite these difficulties, Democratic candidates remained competitive except at the presidential level. In 1972 when the majority party faced a similarly bleak future, it rebounded within two years. But what about the future?

Can Republicans build on their 1984 base, or will 1984 be similar to 1972 when Republican successes were significantly reduced in subsequent elections, even though the party was more competitive? Several factors could contribute to Republican prospects for party-building in the immediate future. These include (1) avoiding intra-party squabbling over the party's leadership and direction; (2) the fact that Martin, unlike Holshouser, may succeed himself and thus have eight years at the helm of the state party; (3) Martin's convincing victory within his party and in the general election; and (4) a potentially more-experienced leadership team in a Martin administration. Soon after the election, Martin and Helms announced "Operation Switch" to attract disenchanted Democrats to their party.

The future of political competition in North Carolina varies according to the three levels. In presidential politics, Republicans have

THE 1984 PRESIDENTIAL ELECTION IN THE SOUTH

the edge unless the national Democratic Party changes its image and broadens its appeal. In gubernatorial and senatorial politics, the contest will continue between Democratic moderates and Helms conservatives, with the latter gaining advantage from national coattails and Democratic Party divisions when they occur. Thus these elections will be determined by short-term forces that disrupt the Democratic Party majority. Other statewide executive and legislative offices are likely to remain dominated by Democrats, though competition will grow and pockets of Republican strength will prevail. Democratic Party dominance no longer exists in North Carolina. Future politics in the state will be characterized by competition and change.

NOTES

1. Jack D. Fleer, *North Carolina Politics: An Introduction* (Chapel Hill: University of North Carolina Press, 1968), 125–63; V.O. Key, Jr., *Southern Politics in State and Nation* (New York: Vintage Books, 1949), 205–28.

2. Elmer Puryear, *Democratic Party Dissension in North Carolina, 1928–1936* (Chapel Hill: University of North Carolina Press, 1962).

3. Thad L. Beyle, Merle Black, and Arlan Kemple, "Sanford Versus Wallace: Presidential Primary Politics in North Carolina," in *Politics and Policy in North Carolina*, ed. Thad L. Beyle and Merle Black (New York: MSS Information Corporation, 1975), 115–27.

4. H. Rutherford Turnbull, III, "1976 Democratic Presidential Primary in North Carolina," *Popular Government* 42 (Summer 1976): 16–21.

5. On the demise of Wallace's presidential hopes, see Kandy Stroud, *How Jimmy Won: The Victory from Plains to the White House* (New York: Morrow, 1977), 261–70.

6. *Congressional Quarterly Weekly Report* 38 (10 May 1980): 1239–40.

7. Jules Witcover, *Marathon: The Pursuit of the Presidency 1972–76* (New York: New American Library, 1977), 478–89; W. Lee Johnson, "The New Right in North Carolina," *Journal of the North Carolina Political Science Association* 3 (1983): 9–23.

8. Elizabeth Drew, *American Journal: The Events of 1976* (New York: Random House, 1977), 236–67, and 354–55; Jonathan Moore and Janet Fraser, *Campaign for President: The Managers Look at '76* (Cambridge, MA: Ballinger, 1977) 44, 47.

9. Quoted in *Congressional Quarterly Weekly Report* 41 (22 July 1972): 1818.

10. Johnson, "The New Right in North Carolina."

11. Everett Carll Ladd, *Where Have All the Voters Gone?*, 2d ed. (New York: Norton, 1982), 92–94; also see Everett Carll Ladd, Jr., with Charles D. Hadley, *Transformations of the American Party System*, 2d ed. (New York: Norton, 1978), 279–83.

12. Johnson, "The New Right in North Carolina."

13. *Congressional Quarterly Weekly Report* 42 (25 February 1984): 400–402.

14. North Carolina State Board of Elections, Registration Statistics, appropriate years; *Statistical Abstract of the United States* (Washington, DC: U.S. Bureau of the Census, 1981), 495.

15. Fleer, *North Carolina Politics*, 25–26. See also Michael Crowell, "The Voting Rights Act in North Carolina—1984," *Popular Government* 50 (Summer 1984): 1–9.

16. Schley R. Lyons and William J. McCoy, *Party Politics in North Carolina* (Charlotte: The Political Science Department, University of North Carolina at Charlotte, 1977), 21–23.

17. Walter DeVries, "Ticket-Splitting in North Carolina: The 1972 Elections," in *Politics and Policy in North Carolina*, ed. Thad L. Beyle and Merle Black (New York: MSS Information Corporation, 1975), 104–14; Earl Black and Merle Black, *The Politics of the American South*, Chap. 15, "The Future of Southern State Politics," (Unpublished, 1984), 36. See also Charles D. Hadley and Susan E. Howell, "The Southern Split Ticket Voter 1952–76: Republican Conversion or Democratic Decline?," in *Party Politics in the South*, ed. Robert P. Steed, Laurence W. Moreland, and Tod A. Baker (New York: Praeger, 1980), 127–51.

18. Key, *Southern Politics*, 215–23, 280–85.

19. Donald R. Matthews and James W. Prothro, *Negroes and the New Southern Politics*, (New York: Harcourt, Brace & World, 1966), 115–20.

20. Schley R. Lyons and William J. McCoy, "Government and Politics," in *North Carolina Atlas: Portrait of a Changing State*, ed. James W. Clay, Douglas M. Orr, Jr., and Alfred W. Stuart (Chapel Hill: The University of North Carolina Press, 1975), 89.

21. Fleer, *North Carolina Politics*, 133–35; Donald Strong, *Urban Republicanism in the South* (University, AL: University of Alabama Press, 1960).

22. See Preston W. Edsall and J. Oliver Williams, "North Carolina: Bipartisan Paradox," in *The Changing Politics of the South*, ed. William C. Havard (Baton Rouge: Louisiana State University Press, 1972), 396–402; Charles L. Prysby, "Electoral Behavior in the U.S. South: Recent and Emerging Trends," in *Party Politics in the South*, ed. Robert P. Steed, Laurence W. Moreland, and Tod A. Baker (New York: Praeger, 1980), 110–13.

23. Winston-Salem *The Sentinel*, 20 April 1984, 9; *Winston-Salem Journal*, 22 April 1984, C-3; *Winston-Salem Journal*, 6 May 1984, 1; *The New York Times*, 7 May 1984, 11. See Howard W. Stanley *Race and the Runoff*, Discussion Paper No. 8403, (Rochester, NY: University of Rochester Public Policy Analysis Program, November 1984).

24. "Democratic Nominating Rules: Back to Drawing Board for 1988," *Congressional Quarterly Weekly Report* 42 (30 June 1984): 1568–69.

25. Reported in Thomas E. Cavanagh and Lorn S. Foster, *Jesse Jackson's Campaign: The Primaries and Caucuses*, Election '84, Report #2, (Washington, DC: Joint Center for Political Studies, 1984), 24.

26. "Ferraro Record: A Loyal, Liberal Democrat," *Congressional Quarterly Weekly Report* 42 (14 July 1984): 1680–83; "Women Candidates See Boon, But Southerners Are Worried," *Congressional Quarterly Weekly Report* 42 (14 July 1984): 1685–86.

27. "Lance vs. Manatt: Mondale's First Misstep," *Congressional Quarterly Weekly Report* 42 (21 July 1984): 1731.

28. "Speech: Mondale Accepts Presidential Nomination," *Congressional Quarterly Weekly Report* 42 (21 July 1984): 1793.

29. Terry Martin, "Mondale Says Reagan Hurts Farm Families," *Winston-Salem Journal*, 9 August 1984, 1, and 2.

30. Raleigh *The News and Observer*, 11 September 1984, 1, and 6–A.

31. *Greensboro News & Record,* 11 September 1984, A–1, and A–14.

32. Ted Bilich, "Bush delivers campaign message to campus rally," *Old Gold and Black* (Wake Forest University), 14 September 1984, 1.

33. "The Speech: Peace Through Strength is the Answer," *New York Times,* 5 October 1984, 12.

34. R.B. Brenner and Art Eisenstadt, "Ferraro Visits N.C., Questions Helms' Patriotism," *Winston-Salem Journal,* 2 October 1984, 1, 11; Jim Schlosser, "Ferraro batters Reagan, Helms," *Greensboro News & Record,* 2 October 1984.

35. Raleigh *The News and Observer,* 2 October 1984, 5.

36. Ken Eudy, "President Says City Exemplifies Successes of His Administration," *The Charlotte Observer,* 9 October 1984, 1, 4–A.

37. Frye Gaillard, "President's Busing Remarks Anger Schools Superintendent," *The Charlotte Observer,* 9 October 1984, 4–A; "You Were Wrong, Mr. President," *The Charlotte Observer,* 9 October 1984, 18–A.

38. On impact in the region, see William E. Schmidt, "Southern Republicans Hitch Hopes to a Strong Performance By Reagan," *New York Times,* 14 October 1984, 13.

39. Transcript of debate, Raleigh *The News and Observer,* 11 September 1984, 3–C.

40. Transcript of debate, ibid., 24 September 1984, 1.

41. Ibid., 24 September 1984, 1.

42. Transcript of debate, ibid., 15 October 1984, 4–C, 5–C.

43. Haynes Johnson and Thomas B. Edsall, "North Carolina's 3 R's: Race, Religion, and Registration," *The Washington Post National Weekly Edition,* 15 October 1984, 12–13; North Carolina State Board of Elections, *Registration Statistics,* 8 October 1984.

44. Personal interview, 19 October 1984; Rob Christensen, "North Carolina's most intensive get-out-the-vote effort in the works," Raleigh *The News and Observer,* 4 November 1984, 31–A.

45. Ibid.; personal interview, 19 October 1984.

46. North Carolina election data from North Carolina State Board of Elections, Election Statistics, 27 November 1984.

47. Rob Gurwitt, "GOP Disappointed with Gains in the House," *Congressional Quarterly Weekly Report* 42 (10 November 1984): 2897–2900.

48. "Michel Faults Reagan for Not Boosting GOP Congressional Candidates," *Winston-Salem Journal,* 8 November 1984, 5: Martin Tolchin, "2-Seat Gain Buoys Senate Democrats," *New York Times,* 8 November 1984, 15.

49. Gallup Poll showed 6 percent of blacks undecided; ABC Exit Poll showed Mondale receiving 89 percent of black votes.

50. "Polls on campuses show students back Reagan," Raleigh *The News and Observer,* 29 October 1984, C–1, C–14.

51. Gallup Poll, 7 November 1984.

52. See Diane Granat, "Ferraro: Transforming the Political Landscape," *Congressional Quarterly Weekly Report* 42 (21 July 1984): 1721–23; Nadine Cohodas, "Divided Republican Women Seek to Counter Gender Gap," *Congressional Quarterly Weekly Report* 42 (25 August 1984): 2087–88.

53. Adam Clymer, "Long Range Hope for Republicans is Found in Poll," *New York Times,* 12 November 1984, 1, 16.

54. Based on survey of 1,161 North Carolina voters, ABC News Poll, 6 November 1984.

55. "Key Factors in the '84 Vote," *New York Times,* 12 November 1984, 16.

56. Data from ABC News Poll, 6 November 1984.

57. Gallup Poll, 23 September 1984.

58. *Greensboro News & Record,* 8 November 1984, B–1, B–4.

59. Ibid..

60. Art Eisenstadt, "We Knew All Along That We Needed a Boost from Reagan, Helms Aide Says," *Winston-Salem Journal,* 5 November 1984, 1, 6; Donald W. Patterson, "Reagan's coattails just long enough for Helms win," *Greensboro News & Record,* 8 November 1984, B–1, B–416.

61. Eisenstadt, *Winston-Salem Journal,* 5 November 1984, 1, 6.

62. "Election Turnout Shows Slight Rise," *New York Times,* 8 November 1984, 16.

63. See Alexander P. Lamis, *The Two Party South* (New York: Oxford University Press, 1984), especially Chap. 10, "North Carolina: Clash of Polar Forces—Hunt vs. Helms," and Chap. 15, "Southern Politics in the 1980s."

64. James L. Sundquist, *Dynamics of the Party System,* rev. ed. (Washington, DC: The Brookings Institution, 1983), 374.

65. Transcript of debate, Raleigh *The News and Observer,* 24 September 1984, 1.

12

Virginia

Larry Sabato

Virginia's least-surprising election year since the heyday of the Byrd Organization bequeathed a roster of predictable results. President Reagan and Senator John Warner were treated to an electoral encore by the voters, and all incumbent U.S. House members who sought another term were returned to office (leaving the delegation split with six Republicans and four Democrats). However, the Republican landslides in the presidential and senatorial races were so massive that Democratic representatives in two districts narrowly escaped ouster, though in both cases their winning margins in 1984 exceeded their paper-thin, first-term victories in 1982. Overall, the GOP added another banner year to its nearly unbroken string of statewide successes in recent years.

VIRGINIA'S RECENT POLITICAL HISTORY

Virginia has a nearly consistent record of support for Republican presidential candidates in the post–World War II era, but a more complex picture of the state's political leanings emerges when contests for state offices are considered. Only Harry Truman in 1948 and Lyndon B. Johnson in 1964, among recent Democratic presidential nominees, have proven able to carry the Old Dominion. Even the South's 1976 favorite son, Jimmy Carter, narrowly lost Virginia—the only southern state he failed to add to his electoral column (Table 12–1). Ronald Reagan defeated Carter far more handily in 1980 than Gerald Ford had done four years earlier, securing 53 percent of the vote to Carter's 40.3 percent.

Prior to 1952 Virginia had defected from the Democratic Party in presidential contests only once in post-Prohibition times, when the 1928 Democratic nominee Al Smith—an anti-Prohibition Catholic—proved too much for publicly dry, Protestant Virginia to bear. Franklin Roosevelt returned Virginia to the Democratic column in 1932, where she stayed for two decades. As the national Democratic Party moved leftward, however, friction with the conservative Democratic machine in Virginia became inevitable. The machine's leader, Virginia Governor (1926–20) and U.S. Senator (1933–65) Harry F. Byrd, Sr., developed an antipathy for Roosevelt and, eventually, Truman, whose pro-civil rights tilt was especially offensive to Byrd. By 1952 Byrd had officially adopted a policy of "golden silence" in presidential years—a signal to his machine's troops to vote Republican for President. From 1952 onward, conservative state Democrats regularly split their tickets, backing the GOP presidential standard bearer, while voting solidly Democratic for state and local offices.

The Byrd machine declined after the abolition of the poll tax and the Voting Rights Act of 1965 destroyed the limited electorate that had sustained it, but the habit of ticket splitting remained strong. A

TABLE 12–1 Presidential General Election Results in Virginia, 1948–80

Year	Democratic Candidate	Percent of Vote[a]	Republican Candidate	Percent of Vote[a]
1948	Harry S. Truman*	47.9	Thomas E. Dewey	41.0
1952	Adlai E. Stevenson	43.4	Dwight D. Eisenhower*	56.3
1956	Adlai E. Stevenson	38.4	Dwight D. Eisenhower*	55.4
1960	John F. Kennedy	47.0	Richard M. Nixon*	52.4
1964	Lyndon B. Johnson*	53.5	Barry M. Goldwater	46.2
1968	Hubert H. Humphrey	32.5	Richard M. Nixon*	43.4
1972	George McGovern	30.1	Richard M. Nixon*	67.8
1976	Jimmy Carter	48.0	Gerald R. Ford*	49.3
1980	Jimmy Carter	40.3	Ronald Reagan*	53.0

*Denotes winner in Virginia.

[a]Vote percentages for Democratic and Republican candidates do not add to 100 because of votes received by independents and third-party nominees.

Source: Compiled from returns provided by the State Board of Elections.

heavily Democratic state legislature was regularly returned to office, while from 1968 to 1980 the Republicans won every gubernatorial and presidential election, and captured a majority of the House of Representatives delegation, as well as a Senate seat in 1972. In recent years Virginia's strong two-party competitiveness has been even more evident. In 1981 Democrat Charles S. Robb, President Lyndon Johnson's son-in-law, captured the governorship and led a Democratic sweep of statewide offices. Just a year later, though, the Republicans added the Senate seat of retiring Independent U.S. Senator Harry F. Byrd, Jr., to their column, as Paul S. Trible joined incumbent Senator John Warner (R) in Washington. Simultaneously, though, Democrats recaptured three U.S. House seats from the Republicans, reducing the GOP edge in the state's delegation from nine-to-one to six-to-four.

THE 1984 PRESIDENTIAL NOMINATING CONTESTS

Republicans in Virginia had no nominating contests at all; President Reagan and first-term U.S. Senator John W. Warner were renominated without opposition at the GOP state convention in late May. Democrats were hardly so unified. In the senatorial contest, liberal Delegate Edythe C. Harrison of Norfolk managed to win her party's nod by acclamation at the 18–19 May state convention, but only after Governor Charles Robb and other party leaders unsuccessfully attempted to recruit more than a dozen other individuals to make the race against the heavily favored Warner. By winning the nomination, Harrison became the first woman ever nominated by the Democratic Party for statewide office. (Republicans had nominated a woman, Hazel K. Barger, for Lieutenant Governor in 1961. Barger lost the general election to Democrat Mills E. Godwin.)

The Democratic presidential contest absorbed the state's political interest throughout the spring. Governor Charles Robb and other key Democratic officeholders had endorsed Senator John Glenn of Ohio in 1983, but after Glenn's withdrawal as an active presidential contender in early 1984, Robb urged his supporters to back an uncommitted delegation. However, most state Democrats did not follow Robb's advice in the party caucuses, held 24 and 26 March. As Table 12–2 indicates, Jesse Jackson received a plurality of all the votes cast in the caucuses (32.8 percent). Jackson built his unexpected victory on the strength of huge margins in the Tidewater area First, Second, and Fourth Congressional Districts, where Jackson personally campaigned twice just before the caucuses were held. (Jackson was the only Democratic candidate to visit Virginia.) Even some overwhelm-

TABLE 12–2   Results of the 1984 Democratic Party Caucuses
in Virginia

Candidate	Total Number of Voters Statewide (%)		Number of State Convention Delegates (%)		Eventual Number of National Convention Delegates (%)	
Walter Mondale	6,971	(29.1)	1,050	(30.4)	29	(37.2)
Jesse Jackson	7,858	(32.8)	920	(26.7)	22	(28.2)
Gary Hart	4,168	(17.4)	507	(14.7)	14	(17.9)
Uncommitted	4,959	(20.7)	972	(28.2)	13	(16.7)
Totals	23,956	(100.0)	3,449	(100.0)	78	(100.0)

Source: Provided by state and national Democratic parties.

ingly white Tidewater localities, such as Virginia Beach, emerged from the caucuses with a Jackson plurality. Enthusiasm in the black community, combined with miniscule turnouts of registered voters, accounted for these surprising results. Overall, just under 24,000 voters participated in the caucuses statewide—about 1 percent of the state's registered voters. Still, the turnout was more than double the 1980 caucus participation total of approximately 10,000.

Walter Mondale, who had been expected to win the caucuses outright, finished behind Jackson with 29.1 percent of the votes cast. Robb's uncommitted candidates secured 20.7 percent of the vote, and Gary Hart, despite being the only candidate able to buy a noticeable amount of media advertising, finished last, with just 17.4 percent.

As in many other states, Jackson was unable to translate his vote plurality into a delegate lead. Because his votes were heavily concentrated in relative few localities where his supporters turned out massively, Jackson could win all of the delegates in these areas—but this surfeit of votes could not win Jackson any more than the number of delegate slots previously allocated to his strongholds on the basis of their past backing of Democratic candidates. Thus, Walter Mondale was able to win a 30.4 percent plurality of state convention delegates despite Jackson's raw vote lead. Jackson, at 26.7 percent of the state convention delegates, also finished behind the uncommitted slate's 28.2 percent, for much the same reason.

By the time of the Democratic convention, though, Jackson's percentage of the state delegation (28.2 percent) was a bit nearer his original vote proportion, thanks to some support from a shrinking uncommitted group. Mondale had gained much more, however, and eventually captured 37.2 percent of Virginia's national delegate votes.

Hart concluded the contest at about where he started in the original state caucuses, at 17.9 percent of the Virginia delegation.

RESULTS OF THE GENERAL ELECTION

Given Virginia's predictably Republican voting habits in presidential years, it is not surprising that neither presidential candidate, nor either of the vice-presidential nominees, set foot in the Old Dominion during the 1984 general election campaign. Precious campaign resources on both sides were understandably diverted to more marginal states, and Virginia enjoyed a quiet autumn, punctuated only by more competitive contests for U.S. House seats in six of the state's ten congressional districts. The skeletal Mondale staff in Virginia actually devoted more effort to aiding Democratic House candidates, and the only visible stumping on behalf of the party's presidential nominee was done by liberal former Lieutenant Governor Henry E. Howell, Jr., on his own initiative. And despite protestations to the contrary, the leading politicians of both parties spent more time and energy on the already full-scale maneuvering for Virginia's 1985 gubernatorial election.

The expected occurred on election day, and Ronald Reagan trounced Walter Mondale, securing 62.3 percent of the vote to the Democrat's 37.1 percent (Table 12–3). As in 1980 Reagan's state

TABLE 12–3   Election Results in Virginia, 1984 General Election for President and U.S. Senator

Candidate (Party)	Total Number of Votes	Percent
President		
Walter Mondale (D)	796,250	37.1
Ronald Reagan (R)	1,337,078	62.3
Lyndon La Rouche (I)	13,307	0.6
Totals	2,146,635	100.0
U.S. Senator		
Edythe C. Harrison (D)	601,142	29.9
John W. Warner	1,406,194	70.0
Write-ins	151	0.0
Totals	2,007,487	99.9[a]

Source: Official election results provided by the State Board of Elections.
[a]Rounding error.

showing was a bit better than his national average, and in Virginia it was the worst presidential defeat for the Democrats since Richard Nixon buried George McGovern in 1972 by a margin of 67.8 percent to 30.1 percent. Democratic Senate nominee Edythe Harrison lost to Republican John Warner by an even larger margin, 70 percent to 29.9 percent. Warner received the largest percentage in a two-party contested Senate election since Harry F. Byrd, Sr., won his first full Senate term in 1934 with 76 percent, and Harrison's proportion was the lost for a Democratic Senate candidate in this century, a proportion below even George Rawlings's 31.2 percent in a 1970 three-candidate general election won by the incumbent, Independent Harry F. Byrd, Jr. Harrison won only two small counties (Buchanan and Charles City) and no cities, and Mondale did scarcely better, with victories in just ten of 95 counties and seven of 41 cities (Figures 12–1 and 12–2). Reagan and Warner swept all ten congressional districts, as Table 12–4 shows. Even the reliably Democratic Southside Fourth District turned in substantial Republican majorities, and the margins reached enormous proportions in the Republican Seventh District in the Piedmont region, where Reagan secured 68.5 percent and Warner 76.8 percent of the vote (Figures 12–3 and 12–4, Table 12–5).

Similarly, the Republicans rolled up huge majorities in suburban and rural localities (Table 12–6). Even in the normally heavily Democratic central cities, Reagan nearly obtained a majority, and Warner won 57.6 percent of the vote. In the Republican-leaning suburbs, the GOP candidates grabbed an unusually large share of the vote (66.8 percent for Reagan and 72.9 percent for Warner), as Table 12–7

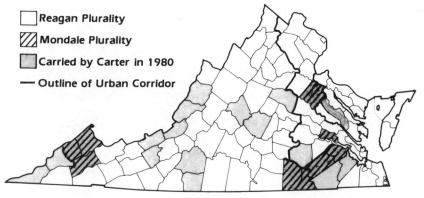

FIGURE 12–1   General Election for President in Virginia, 1984, By Counties

Source: Compiled from official election results provided by the State Board of Elections.

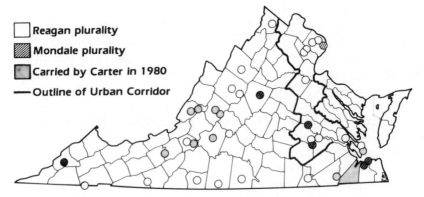

FIGURE 12–2   General Election for President in Virginia, 1984, By Cities

Source: Compiled from official election results provided by the State Board of Elections.

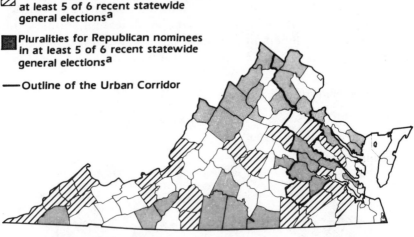

FIGURE 12–3   Virginia's Most Democratic and Republican Counties, as of 1984[a]

[a]Elections used as the basis for this figure are: 1980 and 1984 presidential contests; 1981 elections for Governor, Lieutenant Governor, and Attorney General; and 1982 election for U.S. Senator.

Source: Compiled from official election results provided by the State Board of Elections.

TABLE 12–4 1984 General Election Results for President and U.S. Senator, by Congressional District (percentage of votes cast)

District	Total Votes Cast	Percent of Registered Voting	President			Senator	
			Mondale (D)	Reagan (R)	La Rouche (I)	Harrison (D)	Warner (R)
1	216,882	82.2	37.1	62.2	.7	30.5	69.5
2	177,240	79.0	36.7	62.9	.3	33.5	66.4
3	242,814	80.3	34.7	64.9	.4	26.7	73.3
4	213,728	81.6	43.3	55.9	.9	34.9	65.1
5	205,992	82.5	33.5	65.5	1.1	25.6	74.4
6	206,376	83.5	33.5	65.9	.6	25.4	74.6
7	210,464	82.5	31.0	68.5	.5	23.2	76.8
8	235,116	81.4	38.4	61.1	.5	30.8	69.2
9	205,787	80.7	41.0	58.1	.9	34.9	65.1
10	266,116	81.3	40.7	58.9	.4	33.8	66.2

Source: Compiled from official election results provided by the State Board of Elections.

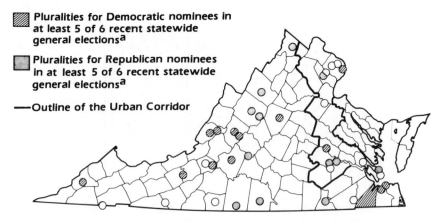

Pluralities for Democratic nominees in at least 5 of 6 recent statewide general elections[a]

Pluralities for Republican nominees in at least 5 of 6 recent statewide general elections[a]

—Outline of the Urban Corridor

FIGURE 12–4   Virginia's Most Democratic and Republican Cities, as of 1984[a]

[a]Elections used as the basis for this figure are: 1980 and 1984 presidential contests; 1981 elections for Governor, Lieutenant Governor, and Attorney General; and 1982 election for U.S. Senator.

Source: Compiled from official election results provided by the State Board of Elections.

TABLE 12–5   Congressional District Voting Patterns in Eleven Statewide Elections, 1972–84

Congressional District (Listed from most Republican to least Republican)	Number of Times District Voted Republican	Number of Times Republican Candidate Secured More Than 55 percent
Seventh (Piedmont)	11	8
Third (Richmond)	10	9
Fifth (Southside)	10	7
Sixth (Roanoke)	10	5
Eighth (Northern Virginia)	8	5
Tenth (Northern Virginia)	7	4
First (Hampton-Norfolk)	7	4
Ninth (Southwest)	6	3
Second (Norfolk-Va. Beach)	4	3
Fourth (Tidewater)	3	3

Note: Eleven elections included in this table are those for U.S. President (1972, 1976, 1980, 1984); U.S. Senator (1972, 1978, 1982, 1984); and Governor (1973, 1977, 1981). The race for U.S. Senator in 1976 is excluded since there was no official Republican candidate.

Source: Compiled from official election results provided by the State Board of Elections.

TABLE 12–6 Urban Vote in the 1984 Virginia General Election for President and U.S. Senator (percentage of votes cast)

Urban Measure	Percent of Total Vote	President			Senator	
		Mondale (D)	Reagan (R)	La Rouche (I)	Harrison (D)	Warner (R)
Urban Corridor[a]	59.4	37.7	61.8	0.5	31.0	69.0
Standard Metropolitan Statistical Areas[b]	66.1	37.5	62.0	0.5	31.0	69.0
Central Cities	16.8	51.5	47.9	0.6	42.4	57.6
Suburbs	49.3	32.8	66.8	0.4	27.1	72.9
Rural Areas[c]	33.9	36.2	62.9	0.9	27.9	72.1

[a]Includes cities of Alexandria, Chesapeake, Colonial Heights, Fairfax, Falls Church, Fredericksburg, Hampton, Hopewell, Manassas, Manassas Park, Newport News, Norfolk, Petersburg, Posquoson, Portsmouth, Richmond, Virginia Beach, and Williamsburg; and the counties of Arlington, Caroline, Charles City, Chesterfield, Clarke, Dinwiddie, Fairfax, Fauquier, Hanover, Henrico, James City, Loudoun, New Kent, Prince George, Prince William, Spotsylvania, Stafford, and York.

[b]The nine Standard Metropolitan Statistical Areas (SMSAs) for Virginia, as established by the U.S. Census Bureau, are Charlottesville, Danville, Lynchburg, Washington, D.C., Newport News-Hampton, Norfolk-Portsmouth, Petersburg-Colonial Heights, Richmond, and Roanoke. "Central cities" and "suburbs" are included in the SMSA figures. The Charlottesville and Danville SMSAs were first designated after the 1980 Census.

[c]All Virginia localities not included in either an SMSA or the Urban Corridor.

Source: Compiled from official election results provided by the State Board of Elections.

TABLE 12-7 Major Statewide Elections in Virginia by Demographic and Black Voting Patterns, 1969–84

Election and Winning Candidate	Percent for Winner			Black Vote
	Central Cities	Suburbs		

General Elections	Central Cities	Suburbs	Black Vote
1969 Governor, Linwood Holton (R)	50.9	56.5	37.2
1970 U.S. Senator, Harry Byrd, Jr. (I)[a]	52.2	55.9	3.0
1971 Lieutenant Governor, Henry Howell (I)[a]	50.6	39.8	91.7
1972 President, Richard Nixon (R)	60.3	70.1	8.8
1972 U.S. Senator, William Scott (R)	42.5	52.7	6.7
1973 Governor, Mills Godwin (R)	43.2	54.6	5.7
1976 President, Gerald Ford (R)	43.6	53.9	5.0
1976 U.S. Senator, Harry Byrd, Jr. (I)	51.4	55.9	4.4
1977 Governor, John Dalton (R)	47.9	59.9	5.0
1977 Lieutenant Governor, Chuck Robb (D)	61.2	51.1	94.9
1977 Attorney General, Marshall Coleman (R)	47.7	56.6	32.7
1978 U.S. Senator, John Warner (R)	45.4	53.7	7.1
1980 President, Ronald Reagan (R)	41.3	58.4	3.4
1981 Governor, Chuck Robb (D)	64.5	49.5	96.4
1981 Lieutenant Governor, Dick Davis (D)	67.2	52.3	95.5
1981 Attorney General, Gerald Baliles (D)	62.7	45.4	95.9
1982 U.S. Senator, Paul Trible (R)	39.6	55.1	5.7
1984 President, Ronald Reagan (R)	47.9	66.8	8.2
1984 U.S. Senator, John Warner (R)	57.6	72.9	21.2

Democratic Primary Elections

1969	Governor, William Battle (first primary)	31.8	40.6	11.8
1969	Governor, William Battle (runoff)	40.7	51.2	4.8
1977	Governor, Henry Howell	59.6	50.6	86.1
1977	Lieutenant Governor, Chuck Robb[a]	35.0	39.1	26.6
1977	Attorney General, Edward E. Lane[a]	37.8	32.0	15.8

[a]Election involved three or more major contenders.

Notes: Party affiliations of winning general election candidates are abbreviated as follows: D = Democrat; R = Republican; I = Independent. Figures for the 1970 Democratic primary for U.S. Senator are not included in this table. Voter turnout in that election was miniscule.

Central cities and suburbs used in this table are designated components of Virginia's Standard Metropolitan Statistical Areas (SMSAs), as established by the U.S. Bureau of the Census: Lynchburg, Washington, D.C., Newport News-Hampton, Norfolk-Portsmouth, Petersburg-Colonial Heights, Richmond, and Roanoke. After 1980 the newly designated Charlottesville and Danville SMSAs are also included. Estimates of the black vote are based on results in the selected predominantly black precincts used in this and previous editions of *Virginia Votes*.

Source: Calculated by the author from data supplied by the State Board of Elections.

shows. Overall, only Richard Nixon of all Republican nominees in the last decade and a half secured a greater proportion in the central cities than did Warner, and Warner bested Nixon in the suburbs, pulling the biggest proportion of the suburban vote of any Republican candidate in this century. The GOP's grip on the suburbs was more important than ever before in 1984, as suburban localities contributed nearly half (49.3 percent) of the total statewide vote, their largest proportion ever (Table 12–8). The central city vote, by contrast, continued its uneven but gradual decline; central cities were the source of just 16.8 percent of the statewide vote total.

Cracks also appeared in the normally monolithic black voters' support of Democratic candidates. Ronald Reagan was held to 8.2 percent in the selected predominantly black precincts of Table 12–9— only a little better than average for a GOP nominee though an improvement over Reagan's 3.4 percent in 1980. But John Warner posted an average percentage of 21.2, about triple the 7.1 percent he gained in his initial 1978 Senate bid. Only Linwood Holton (at

TABLE 12–8   Metropolitan Proportions of Statewide Vote, 1969–84
(percent of total statewide vote)

	Election	*Central Cities*	*Suburbs*
General Elections			
1969	Governor	21.5	35.0
1970	U.S. Senator	22.6	35.4
1971	Lieutenant Governor	18.6	28.4
1972	President	21.7	41.2
1973	Governor	22.0	37.6
1976	President	20.1	41.5
1977	Governor	20.6	39.0
1978	U.S. Senator	19.8	39.1
1980	President	17.0	44.3
1981	Governor	17.8	46.5
1982	U.S. Senator	18.0	46.9
1984	President	16.8	49.3
Democratic Primary Elections			
1969	Governor (first primary)	28.1	26.3
1969	Governor (runoff)	27.3	28.8
1977	Governor	26.9	37.8

Source and *Notes:* See Table 7.

TABLE 12–9 Voting in Selected Predominantly Black Precincts in Virginia Cities, 1984 General Election for President and U.S. Senator (percentage of votes cast)

City	Number of Precincts	Total Votes Cast	Percent of Registered Voting	President			Senator	
				Mondale	Reagan	La Rouche	Harrison	Warner
Charlottesville[a]	1	1,026	69.4	81.1	18.6	0.3	63.0	37.0
Virginia Beach[b]	1	1,178	74.8	66.2	33.6	0.2	62.9	37.1
Hampton[c]	2	3,532	76.9	79.0	19.0	2.0	74.8	25.2
Newport News[d]	8	8,122	74.1	91.8	7.3	0.9	82.7	17.3
Norfolk[e]	10	15,282	72.5	94.9	4.9	0.2	89.4	10.6
Portsmouth[f]	2	3,543	81.8	94.5	4.9	0.6	82.9	17.1
Richmond[g]	15	16,702	70.4	91.2	7.9	0.9	68.6	31.4
Emporia[h]	1	387	38.8	90.5	7.7	1.9	68.6	31.4
Petersburg[i]	4	3,764	74.9	91.6	0.8	79.4	20.6	
Totals	44	53,536	72.6	91.1	8.2	0.7	78.8	21.2

[a]Firehouse precinct.
[b]Seatack precinct.
[c]Phenix and Pembroke precincts.
[d]Dunbar, Lee, Marshall, Chestnut, Jefferson, Huntington, Washington, and Newsome Park precincts.
[e]Precincts 1, 2, 4, 5, 6, 7, 8, 9, 17, and 42.
[f]Precincts 26 and 27.
[g]Precincts 301, 303, 304, 306, 602, 603, 604, 605, 701, 702, 703, 704, 705, 707, and 801.
[h]Ward II.
[i]5th Ward-1st precinct, 5th Ward-2nd precinct, 6th Ward-1st precinct, and 6th Ward-2nd precinct.
Source: Official election results provided by the State Board of Elections.

37.2 percent in his 1969 gubernatorial triumph) and Marshall Cole-
man (at 32.7 percent in his successful 1977 race for Attorney General)
have exceeded Warner's proportion of the black vote among Republican candidates in modern times. Despite these black defections
to the Republicans, about a third of all the votes received by Mondale
and Harrison statewide were cast by blacks.[1]

Not only was the black vote more bipartisan than usual, but black
turnout in 1984 (72.6 percent of those registered) fell well below the
state average of 81.5 percent (Table 12–10). Black turnout actually
decreased proportionally from its 75.4 percent mark in 1980 and its
76.4 percent standard of 1976. White turnout was up substantially
in 1980, to almost 84 percent of registered white voters—fully 11
percent higher than black turnout.

The increased white voter participation helped to fuel Virginia's
best turnout ever (Table 12–11). While Virginia's participation rate
of 51.9 percent of the voting age population (age 18 and over) still
fell a bit below the national average of 52.9 percent, the gap was the
smallest in this century, as the state's voter turnout moved upwards
much more substantially than the minimal national gain of .3 percent.
Virginia's 3 percentage point gain in potential votes cast in 1984
(compared to the previous presidential election) was the second best
among the 50 states, after North Carolina's 4.1 percent increase.[2]
Since the percentage of registered Virginia individuals actually voting
in 1984 (81.5 percent) was approximately the same as in 1980 (81.4
percent), the state's increased participation was a direct result of the

TABLE 12–10   Turnout in Selected Black Precincts vs.
Statewide Turnout, 1976–84 (percentage of registered voters)

Year	Election	Overall Turnout	Selected Black Precincts
1976	President	80.8	76.4
1977	Governor	61.9	62.8
1978	U.S. Senator	60.3	56.4
1980	President	81.4	75.4
1981	Governor	64.9	67.5
1982	U.S. Senator	65.1	68.9
1984	President	81.5	72.6

Notes: Overall turnout includes black turnout; therefore, the differential between
black and white turnout in each year is obviously greater than the figures in this
column can indicate.

Black turnout is measured by use of the predominately black precincts cited to
analyze the black vote in this volume. See notes to Table 9.

Sources: Previous editions of *Virginia Votes*.

TABLE 12–11   Participation in Presidential Elections in
Virginia, 1948–84

Year	*Total Potential Voting Population*	*Total Votes Cast*	*Percentage of Potential Votes Cast*	*National Average (est.)*	*Increase in Turnout from Preceding Election*
1948	2,015,000	419,000	20.8	51.5	6.0
1952	2,083,000	620,000	29.8	62.0	47.8
1956	2,198,000	698,000	31.8	60.1	12.6
1960	2,349,000	771,000	33.3	63.8	10.5
1964	2,539,000	1,042,267	41.2	61.3	35.1
1968	2,717,000	1,361,491	50.7	60.2	30.6
1972	3,197,000	1,457,019	45.6	55.1	7.0
1976	3,528,000	1,716,182	48.6	53.3	17.8
1980	3,817,000	1,866,032	48.9	52.6	8.7
1984	4,203,000	2,180,515	51.9	52.9	16.8

Note: Total potential voting population from 1948–68 includes all persons twenty-one years of age and older, while the figures for 1972–84 include those aged eighteen and above.

Source: The State Board of Elections provided figures for "total votes cast," and either the Tayloe Murphy Institute or the U.S. Census Bureau provided figures for the "potential voting population."

vigorous efforts at new voter registration undertaken by the State Board of Elections, local registrars, and many political and religious groups.

DEMOGRAPHIC ANALYSIS

While the margins were swollen, the pattern of Reagan's and Warner's support among voters resembles those of other recent successful GOP nominees. As Table 12–12 indicates, Reagan and Warner secured near-unanimous support among Republican identifiers, and about four-fifths of the self-described Independents as well. Warner was about twice as successful as Reagan in attracting Democratic crossover votes, with a quarter of all Democrats casting their ballots for Warner and 12 percent for Reagan. Overwhelming backing for the GOP candidates was evident among conservatives, as expected, but moderates also sided decisively with the Republicans in 1984. Amazingly, Warner garnered nearly half (46 percent) of those who described themselves as liberals, and even Reagan won well over a third (37 percent) of the liberal vote.

TABLE 12–12   Demographic Breakdowns of 1984 Vote for
President and Senate

Groupings	*Percent for*			
	Mondale (D)	*Reagan (R)*	*Harrison (D)*	*Warner (R)*
Party				
Republican	3	97	4	96
Democratic	88	12	75	25
Independent	22	78	17	83
Ideology				
Liberal	63	37	54	46
Moderate	40	60	31	69
Conservative	15	85	14	86
Sex				
Men	31	69	26	74
Women	40	60	33	67
Race				
White	25	75	21	79
Black	90	10	76	24
Age				
18–24	32	68	28	72
25–49	35	65	30	70
50–64	36	64	30	70
65 or over	37		28	72
Occupation				
Professional/managerial	35	65	29	72
White collar	27	73	24	76
Blue collar	41	59	36	64
Labor Unions				
Union Member	50	50	43	57
Nonunion	32	68	27	73
Religion[a]				
Protestant	30	70	25	75
Catholic	34	66	29	71
Education				
Less than high school				
graduate	42	58	34	66
High school graduate	32	68	30	70

TABLE 12–12   *(continued)*

| | Percent for | | | |
Groupings	Mondale (D)	Reagan (R)	Harrison (D)	Warner (R)
Some college and college graduate	32	68	25	75
More than college graduate	45	55	39	61
Annual Income				
Less than $20,000	46	54	40	60
$20,001–$30,000	32	68	25	75
$30,001–$40,000	33	67	28	72
More than $40,000	32	68	28	72

[a]Members of "other" religions were too few to include in the calculations shown here.

Source: These figures are taken from the NBC News Election Day Exit Poll of Virginia. A total of 2,550 Virginia voters were interviewed as they left their polling places on election day. The margin of error for the breakdowns shown in this table is about ± 3 percent.

There was a sizeable gender gap in Virginia in 1984, but both sides of the chasm were in the Republican camp. Reagan's support among men was about 9 percent greater than among women, but 60 percent of the women also backed him. Warner's gender gap was a slightly smaller 7 percent, and fully two-thirds of the women voting in 1984 chose the male Senate candidate over the first female candidate for the U.S. Senate in Virginia's history.

As we saw earlier, blacks favored the Democratic candidates, but the mirror image of this result deserves attention, too: Whites voted heavily Republican. Reagan received three-quarters of the white vote (and about 80 percent of the white male vote). And whites actually voted more en masse for Warner than blacks did for Harrison; Warner won 79 percent of the white vote (and about 83 percent of the white males who cast a ballot). Not for almost two decades has a Democratic nominee for Senator, Governor, or President received a majority of the white vote in Virginia.[3]

Reagan's support among age groups was the reverse of the usual pattern: The younger the voter, the more likely he or she was to vote Republican. (Warner's backing was spread evenly across the age spectrum, though.) All occupational categories favored the GOP; blue collars somewhat less so than others.

Labor union members, presumably Mondale's strength, actually split their ballots evenly between the Democratic and Republican presidential candidates, with Warner securing 57 percent of their votes. The Republicans also carried all religious, educational, and income groups, though they were weaker among Catholics, those with less than a high school education as well as those with more than an undergraduate college degree, and those who made less than $20,000 annually.

ELECTIONS FOR THE HOUSE OF REPRESENTATIVES

There was no change in the party line-up of Virginia's congressional delegation in 1984, with incumbents in nine districts being reelected and a Republican, D. French Slaughter, replacing retiring GOP Representative J. Kenneth Robinson in the Piedmont Seventh District. This placid result obscures the competitive battles that were waged in six of the ten congressional districts, however.

In the Roanoke Sixth and the southwest Ninth Districts, freshmen Democrats James R. Olin and Rick Boucher were relatively hard-pressed to survive the Reagan and Warner landslides in their districts. But the incumbents were beneficiaries of widespread ticket splitting, and Olin defeated former state Senator Ray Garland with 53.5 percent of the vote, while Boucher bested Delegate C. Jefferson Stafford with 52 percent. As close as these results were, Olin and Boucher actually increased their winning percentages from their 1982 showings of 49.7 percent and 50.4 percent, respectively. As Table 12–13 shows, both Democrats outspent their GOP foes, and that, combined with incumbency, moderate voting records, and good constituency service over the prior two years was sufficient to secure second terms for them.

None of the other congressional contests were nearly as close (Table 12–14). In the eastern First District, freshman incumbent Republican Herbert Bateman easily won a rematch with Democrat John Mc-Glennon, securing 59.1 percent in 1984 compared with 53.9 percent in his initial 1982 victory over McGlennon. In the Seventh District—the state's most Republican—a heated and hard-fought campaign melted into a Slaughter landslide, as he defeated Democrat Lewis Costello by 56.5 percent to 40.2 percent (with conservative Independent Robert E. Frazier, Jr., receiving 3.3 percent). The moderate-conservative Costello had been enthusiastically backed by Governor Robb and his associates, but the daunting Warner and Reagan margins in the Seventh made Costello's task impossible (though Costello did manage to run far ahead of both of his Democratic ticket-mates).

The two northern Virginia districts, the Eighth and Tenth, pro-

TABLE 12–13   Election Results and Campaign Expenditures,
.1984 General Election for U.S. Representatives in Virginia

District	Candidates	Total Campaign Expenditures ($)	Total Number of Votes	Percent
1	John McGlennon (D)	263,552	79,577	39.8
	†Herbert H. Bateman (R)*	488,829	118,085	59.1
	Eli Green (I)	NA	2,154	1.1
	Write-ins	—	6	—
	Totals		199,822	100.0
2	†G. William Whitehurst (R)*	64,147	136,632	99.8
	Write-ins	—	256	0.2
	Totals		136,888	100.0
3	†Thomas J. Bliley, Jr. (R)*	236,529	169,987	85.6
	Roger L. Coffey (I)	NA	28,556	14.4
	Write-ins	—	24	—
	Totals		198,567	100.0
4	†Norman Sisisky (D)*	104,131	120,093	99.9
	Write-ins	—	69	0.1
	Totals		120,162	100.0
5	†W. C. (Dan) Daniel (D)*	65,739	117,738	100.0
	Write-ins	—	40	—
	Totals		117,778	100.0
6	†James R. "Jim" Olin (D)*	442,953	105,207	53.5
	Ray L. Garland (R)	256,045	91,344	46.5
	Write-ins	—	9	—
	Totals		196,560	100.0
7	Lewis M. Costello (D)	269,756	77,624	40.2
	†D. French Slaughter, Jr. (R)	490,746	109,110	56.5
	Robert E. Frazier, Sr. (I)	14,001	6,397	3.3
	Write-ins	—	25	—
	Totals		193,156	100.0
8	Richard L. Saslaw (D)	286,348	97,250	43.4
	†Stanford E. Parris (R)*	842,249	125,015	55.8
	Donald W. Carpenter (I)	NA	1,814	0.8
	Write-ins	—	12	—
	Totals		224,091	100.0

TABLE 12–13   *(continued)*

District	Candidates	Total Campaign Expenditures ($)	Total Number of Votes	Percent
9	†Frederick C. "Rick" Boucher (D)*	467,458	102,446	52.0
	C. Jefferson Stafford (R)	456,967	94,510	48.0
	Write-ins	—	0	—
	Totals		196,956	100.0
10	John P. Flannery II (D)	409,695	95,074	37.5
	†Frank R. Wolf (R)*	623,774	158,528	62.5
	Write-ins	—	23	—
	Totals		253,625	100.0
	Grand Total	5,782,919		

Notes: N/A = not available
† denotes winner
* denotes incumbent

Source: Official election results provided by the State Board of Elections; campaign finance data provided by the Federal Election Commission. (The Federal Election Commission only requires the filing of campaign finance data by candidates who spend more than $5,000. The presumption is that the candidates for whom no report was filed spent less than the threshold sum.)

duced twin victories for the incumbent Republican representatives. Eighth District Representative Stan Parris obtained his first full-fledged majority ever[4] in defeating Democratic state Senator Richard L. Saslaw with 55.8 percent of the vote. In the Tenth District incumbent Frank R. Wolf won an unusually large (for northern Virginia) 62.5 percent in turning back the challenge of Democrat John P. Flannery II, whose wife and campaign manager, ABC newswoman Bettina Gregory, had attracted a fair amount of media attention for her husband-candidate. Only Flannery and Saslaw among all the congressional contestants throughout Virginia had been nominated in contested primaries.

Three other representatives—Republican G. William Whitehurst of the Second District, Democrat Norman Sisisky of the Fourth District, and Democrat W. C. "Dan" Daniel of the Fifth District—were unopposed, and Third District Republican Thomas J. Bliley, Jr., drew on a minor Independent candidate. Bliley greatly outspent his un-

TABLE 12–14 Comparison of General Elections for U.S. Representative in Virginia, 1972–84

District	Incumbent as of 1984 (Party)	Year of First Election	Percent of Total Vote						
			1972	1974	1976	1978	1980	1982	1984
1	Herbert H. Bateman (R)	1982	—	—	—	—	—	53.9	59.1
2	G. William Whitehurst (R)	1968	73.4	60.0	65.7	99.9*	89.8*	99.9*	99.8*
3	Thomas J. Bliley, Jr. (R)	1980	—	—	—	—	51.6	59.2	85.6*
4	Norman Sisisky (D)	1982	—	—	—	—	—	54.4	99.9*
5	W. C. (Dan) Daniel (D)	1968	99.9*	99.4*	99.9*	99.9*	99.9*	99.9*	100.0*
6	James R. "Jim" Olin (D)	1982	—	—	—	—	—	49.7	53.5
7	J. Kenneth Robinson (R)	1970	66.2	52.6	81.6*	64.3	99.7*	59.9	[56.5]
8	Stanford E. Parris (R)	1972a	44.4	42.4	—	—	48.8	49.7	55.8
9	Frederick C. "Rick" Boucher (D)	1982	—	—	—	—	—	50.4	52.0
10	Frank Wolf (R)	1980	—	—	—	—	51.1	52.7	62.5

aParris was first elected in 1972 but was defeated for reelection in 1974. He won the seat back in 1980.

Notes: In all instances where percent figure is followed by an asterisk (*), the incumbent ran unopposed or was opposed only by an independent or minor party candidate. In the 1984 races, J. Kenneth Robinson (7th district) retired. The bracketed figure shows the proportion of the vote secured by his successor, D. French Slaughter.

Source: Compiled from official election results provided by the State Board of Elections.

derfinanced challenger, and in fact all of the congressional winners drew upon a larger warchest than their unsuccessful foes.

Overall, Republicans secured a comfortable majority (55.1 percent) of the congressional vote in party-contested districts in Virginia (Table 12–15). The GOP House candidates have amassed more voters than their Democratic foes in party-contested district consistently since 1966. Further, the 1984 totals show the Republicans rebounding from their relatively slim 52.4 percent to 46.3 percent edge over the Democrats in the recession midterm year of 1982, when Democrats picked up three House seats. Unfortunately for the GOP, the Republican resurgence in 1984 was fairly evenly distributed, and the proportionate increase in votes did not translate into seat gains.

CONCLUDING COMMENTS

The 1984 elections in Virginia were among the least competitive in the state's post-Byrd Organization history. The Senate race was as lopsided as an election probably can become in the era of two-party competition. Harrison was outspent by Warner $2.4 million to $500,000; she was a liberal in a conservative state in a conservative year; her sex was an asset in some ways (attracting free media attention because of its novelty, for example), but more than one-third of those polled on election day by NBC News[5] admitted to a belief that "Virginia was not ready for a woman senator"; and she was little-know, without any real electoral base, having been defeated in 1982 for reelection to the state House of Delegates from Norfolk.

Warner had his own substantial advantages. In addition to his moderate-conservatism, his incumbency, and a lavish campaign warchest—the most ample ever in Virginia—Warner enjoyed wide popularity and favorable evaluations of his job performance; as a veteran, a former Secretary of the Navy, and the next-in-line to become chairman of the Senate Armed Services Committee,[6] Warner was in a far better position than Harrison to appeal to military-minded Virginia; and, of course, Warner benefited from the same Republican "era of good feelings" (generated by a robust economy and other conditions) that catapulted Reagan to a landslide reelection.

Mondale's crushing defeat stretched the Republican string of presidential victories in Virginia to five in a row (and eight of the last nine). Except in extraordinary circumstances,[7] Virginia can be safely counted in the GOP column of presidential election days. It was almost inconceivable from the outset of the 1984 campaign that Ronald Reagan could lose Virginia, or that a ticket as liberal as Mondale-

TABLE 12–15   Vote by Parties in Virginia General Elections for U.S. Representative, 1966–84

| Party | Percent of Vote | | | | | | | | | | Average |
	1966	1968	1970	1972	1974	1976	1978	1980	1982	1984	1966–84
All House elections											
Democratic	57.3	48.4	51.4	49.4	54.8	45.5	42.0	31.3	47.2	43.3	47.1
Republican	39.3	43.5	45.8	46.4	39.1	45.8	56.3	64.7	51.7	54.6	48.8
Others	3.4	8.1	2.8	4.2	6.1	8.7	1.7	4.0	1.1	2.1	4.1
Total	100.0	100.0	100.0	100.0	100.0	100.0	100.0	100.0	100.0	100.0	100.0
Party-contested House elections only											
Democratic	43.9	47.4	47.2	40.7	44.8	47.0	41.0	40.5	46.3	44.1	44.3
Republican	56.1	49.7	49.7	54.3	48.8	50.0	58.5	55.7	52.4	55.1	53.0
Others	0.0	2.9	3.1	5.0	6.4	3.0	0.5	3.8	1.3	0.8	2.7
Total	100.0	100.0	100.0	100.0	100.0	100.0	100.0	100.0	100.0	100.0	100.0
Number of Democratic House seats	6	5	4	3	5	4	4	1	4	4	4
Number of Republican House seats	4	5	6	7	5	6	6	9	6	6	6

Total: N = 10
Source: Compiled from official election results provided by the State Board of Elections.

299

Ferraro could carry the state. These assumptions were clearly borne out in November, to the delight of Republicans and the chagrin of Democrats in the Old Dominion. For both groups, it was merely another chorus in an increasingly familiar electoral tune heard in Virginia since 1952.

NOTES

1. Exit polls and the data in Tables 12–9 and 12–10 suggest that no more than 13 percent of the 1984 electorate (or about 283,500 voters) were black. Of that number 96.2 percent (or 272,700 approximately) cast a ballot for President, while 83.7 percent (or 237,300) voted in the Senate contest. Mondale received 91.2 percent of the black votes (0r 248,700) and Harrison garnered 198,600; therefore, black voters comprised about 31 percent of Mondale's statewide vote total, and 33 percent of Harrison's.

2. The District of Columbia also had a larger increase in voter participation than Virginia, posting a 5.8 percent gain.

3. William B. Spong, Jr., was the last to do so, in his successful general election contest for the U.S. Senate in 1966. But Spong had received a minority of the white vote in the 1966 Democratic Senate primary, when he upset incumbent A. Willis Robertson, and Spong was defeated for reelection in 1972, when he received less than 40 percent of the white vote.

4. Parris had been elected with less than 50 percent of the vote (due to multi-candidate fields) in 1972, 1980, and 1982. He was defeated for reelection in 1974 and did not run in 1976 and 1978.

5. See Table 12–12, source for details about the NBC News exit poll.

6. With the retirement of Senator John Tower (R-Texas) in 1984, an ailing Senator Barry Goldwater (R-Arizona) became the Armed Services Committee chairman. Upon Goldwater's planned retirement in 1986, and assuming continued GOP control of the Senate in 1987, a questionable assumption at this writing, Warner would take command of the committee.

7. For example, the nomination of a conservative southern Democrat or the inclusion of a popular state Democratic figure, such as Governor Charles Robb, on the ticket *might* be enough to tip Virginia to the Democrats, assuming that the basic circumstances of the election year (state of the economy, international relations, and the like) also favor the Democrats.

Part IV

Conclusion

13

The 1984 Presidential Election in the South: Race and Realignment

Harold W. Stanley

Walter Mondale intended to make the South a major battleground on which to decide the 1984 presidential election, but the South ultimately proved to be a solid base of support for President Reagan. Reagan led Mondale in the rest of the nation by 16 percentage points, in the South by 25. A regional view of the 1984 campaign in the South provides helpful perspectives on the results as well as on two related topics—whether the politics of race has returned in force to the region and whether partisan realignment is occurring in the South.

THE SOUTH: DEMOCRATIC HOPES, REPUBLICAN GAINS

Reagan won ten of the eleven southern states in 1980. Democrats planned to reverse such Republican victories and restore the South to the Democratic column in 1984. Narrow Reagan wins in 1980, the arithmetic of the electoral college, less hospitable alternatives elsewhere, and the Democratic tradition of the South made the region a relatively attractive target for the Democrats. During the Democratic convention, Mondale's men expressed high hopes for the South. In the words of Bob Beckel, a key Mondale aide: "When you look at the electoral map, you cannot win without making electoral inroads in the South. We expect to make inroads in the South. . . . We've targeted a lot of resources on the South."[1] Richard Moe, a longtime Mondale associate, said, "No Democrat in this century has been elected without winning Texas. I don't think we're going to break that rule."[2] (They didn't.) Moe acknowledged that "it's uphill in the South" but suggested that the prospect of a heavy black turnout made every state but Virginia and Florida a potential target.[3]

Initial Democratic optimism about southern electoral votes was not merely wishful thinking. The 1980 elections had set back Democrats in the South. Since 1980, Democratic resurgence typified the region. After the 1980 elections, Democrats held only six of the eleven southern governorships. By 1984, they held ten, leaving only the governorship in Tennessee to the Republicans. In the 1980 elections, southern Democrats lost six seats in the U.S. House. Two years later they regained six House seats from the Republicans and won one of the three newly created districts.

Even at the presidential level, Democrats had grounds for optimism.[4] Blacks strongly disapproved of Reagan's presidency, providing a sizable support core that could be expanded and on which Democrats could build in the South. Even Reagan's large 1980 lead in Texas could be jeopardized by Democratic registration and turnout gains like those that helped turn Republicans out of office in 1982. In 1980 Reagan had carried Alabama, Arkansas, Mississippi, North Carolina, South Carolina, and Tennessee by fewer than 40,000 votes each. Voter registration gains by southern blacks after 1980 were expected to overcome such narrow leads for 1984.[5] This prediction was premised on two conditions events proved wrong: Mondale could secure southern white support comparable to Carter's in 1980 and white mobilization would not offset the black voter registration gains.

Mondale's problems elsewhere stood out in bold relief in the South. Extended consideration of the extent to which Mondale acquired southern white support and the problems he had seeking it precede consideration of the extensive registration drives among southerners of both races. Then two large themes—racial polarization and partisan realignment—receive sustained and separate discussion.

Southern Whites

In courting the southern white vote, Mondale had disadvantages. Mondale not only lacked Carter's regional roots, he also lacked Carter's more moderate political stance. Then, too, Ronald Reagan, a popular incumbent, seeking reelection during a time of economic recovery, was a far more formidable political figure in 1984 than earlier, although in 1980 he had proven formidable enough. Consequently, Mondale in 1984 gained only 27 to 29 percent of the southern white vote, not Carter's 1980 level of 37 percent.[6] Given the lack of white support for Mondale, even a vastly expanded, more solid black vote would not have provided the margin of victory in any southern state.

The track record of liberal, nonsouthern Democratic candidates in the South in 1968 and 1972, not Carter's 1980 showing, provided a better basis for predicting Mondale's appeal in the region. Even though Democratic support by white southerners dipped in 1984, it was no lower than the levels for Humphrey and McGovern. Both of these campaigns, like Mondale's, had a liberal look and no southern running mate. Humphrey had the Wallace candidacy to contend with, but Humphrey-Muskie in 1968 and McGovern-Shriver in 1972 gained only 26 and 20 percent of the southern white vote. Mondale-Ferraro met a similar fate. Given the declining Democratic loyalties and the increasing conservatism of southern whites even within the last decade,[7] it is surprising that Mondale's support among southern whites was not lower still.

The liberal image, the lack of southern origins, and the popularity of Reagan made it difficult for Mondale to gain the support of southern whites. Mondale had other problems as well—the nomination of Ferraro for Vice President, the promise to increase taxes, the inept attempt to install Lance in some politically prominent position, and the lack of firm, visible support from southern Democratic leaders. Although some believe Mondale's solid black support is a principal reason southern whites favored Reagan, later discussions of the roots of Reagan's popularity and the role of racial backlash leads to doubts that racist motivations matter that much.

Ironically, the South probably saved Mondale's quest for the nomination. Even though Mondale trailed Gary Hart in primaries or caucuses in six states on the same day, Mondale's nomination drive was revived by first-place finishes on 13 March, Super Tuesday, in the Alabama and Georgia primaries. Had he failed to finish first in those two states after losing New Hampshire, Maine, Vermont, and Wyoming to Hart, the viability of Mondale's candidacy might have resembled that of John Glenn's, who dropped out of the race after Super Tuesday. (Had Glenn dropped out before Super Tuesday, Hart might have placed first in Georgia, making talk of Mondale's "comeback" unlikely.)[8] In the South Mondale did receive critical shares of the black vote in some cases, but the bulk of his support came from whites. Overall, Mondale placed first in four southern primaries, and lost two—Florida to Hart and Louisiana to Jackson. Mondale bested the opposition in three southern caucuses and lost two—trailing the uncommitted vote in Mississippi and the uncommitted as well as the Jackson vote in South Carolina. At the convention, Mondale was supported by a majority of the delegates in seven southern states and a plurality of delegates from the other southern states except South Carolina (where Jackson's delegate total edged out Mondale's).

Although Mondale enjoyed considerable southern support for the nomination, the relative nonparticipation of southern whites during the primaries and caucuses provided ample warning of the limited appeal of the Democratic candidates to southern whites.[9] Glenn's candidacy had initially generated interest but by the time of the first southern primaries, Glenn's campaign was at death's door. Many southern leaders who had lined up behind Glenn retired to the sidelines once Glenn withdrew. The relatively high turnouts in southern primaries and caucuses resulted from vastly greater black participation rates despite white falloff. Louisiana was an extreme case but even in the rest of the South, southern whites had very low rates of participation in the Democratic nomination process.[10] The racial composition of primary and caucus electorates reflects the higher black participation rates. For example, on Super Tuesday, blacks made up 23 percent of the registered voters in Alabama and 21 percent in Georgia. Blacks cast a far larger share of the Democratic presidential primary votes in both states, network exit poll estimates ranging from 31 to 40 percent in Alabama, 28 to 41 percent in Georgia.[11] Essentially, southern white voters sat out the Democratic nomination process while Jackson's candidacy enthused and mobilized blacks.

A Southern Vice President?

A conventional Democratic gesture by Mondale toward the South would have been to pick a southern running mate. But no particular southerner as Vice President would have made it more likely that Mondale would carry the South.[12] Even with Senator Bentsen as his running mate, Mondale's winning Texas was not assured. Mondale himself would have to win the hearts and minds of enough southern whites, and hold the high loyalty of southern blacks, to carry enough southern states to make a national electoral vote victory thinkable. As one Democratic consultant explained Mondale's choice of Ferraro: "It is important for Mondale to choose Ferraro because he has to do something dramatic—he had to change the whole tone and image of his campaign. Every indication was that conventional politics would not work for him."[13]

Ferraro's nomination provided an element of excitement Mondale's campaign had been missing. Seen by many as a bold stroke, picking Ferraro gave Mondale's campaign a needed lift at a helpful time, even if that lift did not prove lasting. At the time, some Democrats feared the selection of Ferraro made an uphill fight in the South all the more difficult. One journalist put it memorably: "To Southerners, Ferraro sounds like an Italian sports car, not a vice-president, and they prefer stock car racing anyhow."[14] A 69-year-old Tennessee Democratic National Convention delegate spoke for many when he said: "I'm a good southern Democrat, and if she is on the ticket and Mondale is the nominee I will support her. But I'm not ready for a lady in that high place, and my people aren't ready." Others worried about the appearance that Mondale, already committed to labor, had given in to another special interest group—here, the National Organization of Women.[15] After the election, Reagan's pollster, Richard Wirthlin, characterized his poll findings on Ferraro: we found "a lot of Americans applauded selecting a woman as the running mate. But we also found that because she was a woman from New York and a liberal, the decision strengthened us in the southern states."[16] In the blunter assessment of Edward Rollins, Reagan's political director, "She made the South ours."[17]

Taxes

The pick of Ferraro was seen by many as a beneficially bold stroke. Mondale's next bold strokes—the appointment of Bert Lance to high party office and the promise to raise taxes to narrow the deficit—definitely set the campaign back. The candor about taxes initially rattled Reagan, as he and Bush had problems coordinating clear statements that Reagan would not raise taxes. Reagan solved this one by granting an exclusive interview to his press secretary on the subject. Ultimately, Mondale's promised tax hike cost him dearly in the nation and in the South, since it gave new life to the notion that Democrats were out to "tax and tax and spend and spend." As Al Lapierre, executive director of the Alabama State Democratic Party, explained during the campaign, southerners "see the old Mondale, and the tax issue sealed it. They don't trust him not to go out and spend it."[18] Reagan's pollster agreed: "what was most helpful to us . . . was Mondale's declaration that he would increase taxes. He made a two-part statement: He would increase taxes to reduce the deficit, but people didn't hear the second part of his commitment. The only thing that came through was 'Walter Mondale will increase taxes.' "[19]

The Lance Affair

Mondale, because he did not select a southerner as Vice President, decided to send the South a message by appointing Bert Lance, Georgia state Democratic Party chairman, to head the Democratic National Committee. The Lance affair, reviewed in the Georgia chapter, merits further consideration from a regional viewpoint.

The timing and the manner of the Lance choice were terrible. The DNC chairman, Charles Manatt, was replaced as the Democratic National Convention was opening in his home state of California in the city of Mayor Feinstein, whom Mondale had just considered but passed over for the vice-presidential nomination. No one was consulted outside the Mondale inner team. As North Carolina's Democratic chairman David Price put it, "We have been happy with Chuck Manatt and had no inkling that this was coming."[20]

Of course, Lance brought baggage. Wonders about Lance's financial footwork resurfaced. Lance's financial practices had not led to a conviction—the jury deadlocked 10–2 for conviction on two counts and the government chose not to retry the case[21]—but this proved too fine a point for many to appreciate. Lance learned that as Faulkner said of the South itself, the past was not even past yet. Many thought Mondale was throwing away the ability to hit Reagan hard on "the sleaze factor" (a criticism soon completely undermined by questions about Ferraro's finances) and in the process dusting off bad memories from the Carter administration best left to gather more dust. The uproar Lance's appointment created over the next three weeks was met by apparent indecision, presenting Mondale "as a man who either couldn't make up his mind or was easily swayed by pressure and adversity."[22] The whole affair took the shine off a highly touted Mondale organization, cutting into the favorable publicity and momentum generated by Ferraro's nomination and the Democratic convention.

Why did Mondale pick Lance? As one Mondale adviser recalled, "When we headed South (for Super Tuesday after the loss of New Hampshire and several New England states) we couldn't find our so-called friends down there with the FBI. But Bert was there (for Super Tuesday). He stood by us, day after day, and slugged it out for us."[23] Lance offered Mondale essential future help as well. Lance had established a working relationship with Jesse Jackson during the primary and caucus season and Jackson's active support could help ensure high black turnout rates for Mondale in November.

Also, Lance probably could have helped Mondale reach moderate and conservative white southerners by mobilizing some southern

Democratic political leaders to support Mondale visibly. (Lance had mobilized the southern state party chairmen to work as a regional force within the Democratic Party and headed the group to campaign on behalf of Democrat Harold Washington in 1983 in Chicago's racially charged mayoral election.[24] In the 1984 campaign, Mondale's lack of active support from mainstream southern democratic leaders made it difficult for him to exploit Reagan's vulnerabilities in the South—for instance, "textile layoffs and imports, high interest rates and a struggling agricultural economy."[25] Mondale's South Carolina chairman pointed to the need and its consequences: "If you take a Dick Rile [South Carolina Governor] and put him out on the stump and get him enthusiastic, it could make all the difference in the world. For a textile worker to vote for Ronald Reagan is like a chicken voting for Colonel Sanders. But people with credibility in the state have got to tell people that."[26] Governor Riley's visible support for the Democratic presidential candidate came in the last two weeks of the campaign when he made televised appeals to vote a straight Democratic ticket but did not specifically name Mondale in his appeal. Without the controversy surrounding his past, Lance may have helped Mondale in various ways, but at best he would have narrowed Reagan's lead in the South. The missed opportunity cut into Mondale's appeal but questions about Mondale's choice of Lance and Mondale's handling of the controversy cut deeply, too.

Lance left the Mondale campaign supposedly on his own initiative, although the lack of visible support from Mondale helped him out the door. On balance, the southern party chairmen were not anxious to keep Lance. According to one high-ranking party official: "All they (the Mondale aides) heard from southern leaders, who were supposed to benefit from this, was 'keep him out of my state.' "[27] A top Mondale aide summed up the Lance affair best: "We screwed up."[28]

Most southern party leaders, in public at least, put a brave face on the mess Mondale made with Lance. Some commented that the whole episode was a media and Republican issue that would not last and would not affect the loyalty of Democratic voters. True, but these events left their mark on political activists. Some southern party leaders had been excited by the appointment (former Representative Bowen of Mississippi had initially called the Lance appointment "a mighty nice consolation prize" for the vice presidency),[29] some were relieved, if not delighted, once Lance resigned; others were furious. Georgia Lieutenant Governor Zell Miller, chairman for Mondale's primary campaign in Georgia, said publicly what some only thought or said in private: "I'm going to vote for Walter Mondale. I'll help him in my limited way. But my enthusiasm gas tank is on empty. In fact, I'm sniffing and I can't even smell the fumes. . . . Some of the folks in that [Mondale] organization know as much about southern politics as I do about the Farmer-Labor Party in Minnesota."[30] Because of the Lance affair, Walter Mondale could not campaign in Georgia for weeks without running the risk of being snubbed by state party officials.[31]

The Lance affair raised doubts pertinent to the South (and elsewhere) about Mondale's campaign to come. Clearly, the South was important if Mondale was to win, but Mondale's best idea about helping himself down South produced more problems than promise about a strong campaign to come.

Campaigning in the South

The Lance affair produced problems enough, but the results of the early campaign stress on the South were distressing indeed. The South was targeted, resources committed, and an ambitious personal courtship got underway. During August, before the Republican convention, Mondale and Ferraro made several campaign stops in the South, appearing in Mississippi, Texas, North Carolina, Alabama, and Tennessee. Mondale also planned but then cancelled a trip to Georgia. (Reagan and Bush scheduled campaign trips to Texas immediately after the Democratic convention, allegedly to seize the opening Mondale had left by passing over two Texans—Senator Bentsen and Mayor Cisneros—and not picking a southern running mate.)

Despite spending time in the South early to woo the voters and make the region competitive, results pleasing and favorable to the Democrats were not forthcoming. Public polls reported a 27 percentage point Reagan lead in the South during the last week of July and the middle of August.[32] Reagan's pollster claimed a more modest but still impressive 14-point margin (Reagan 52, Mondale 38 in 12 southern states), finding that in mid-August Reagan was stronger in the South than at the end of the Democratic National Convention.[33]

The South did not respond favorably to Mondale and Ferraro. This mirrored the situation in the rest of the nation but the South had been singled out for special attention and was seen as critical to success. In part, the flaps over Lance's position and Ferraro's finances eclipsed other more favorable focuses. Mayor Andrew Young's remark about the caliber and color of the Mondale advisers ("smart-assed white boys and they think they know it all. But I can't afford to let them lose this election.")[34] indicated that, among other things, even in the middle of August, the Mondale camp had some way to go to get the campaign running smoothly. On 7 September Mondale finally visited Georgia for a Democratic unity meeting. The most significant message given the Georgia Democrats, according to Hamilton Jordan, was the assurance that Mondale had not yet written off the state.[35] Most Mondale or Ferraro campaign appearances in the South were dogged by reporting that the visit was designed to counter rumors that the Democrats had written off the state.

Democrat campaign swings in the South failed to narrow Reagan's large lead. Indeed, national pollsters such as Lou Harris and Gordon Black had publicly suggested Mondale should not waste time on the South. Lou Harris noted that his post-Democratic convention poll showed a close race nationally but a decisive Reagan advantage in the South: "I could argue maybe they (Mondale and Ferraro) ought to write off parts of the South and forget it."[36] Time spent campaigning in the South was time some thought should have been spent on shoring up the Democratic base in the East.

Voter Registration Drives

Amidst numerous problems, one bright spot for the Democrats was the initial gains in black registration. By May 1984 southern blacks had made enormous strides in voter registration, actually outstripping white registration gains absolutely. Between November 1980 and May 1984, almost 700,000 additional blacks registered in the South, whereas white registration fell by 227,000. But by November 1984 the figures had changed to 1,342,000 additional blacks and 3,078,000 additional whites.[37] The political payoff of the black registration gains was offset by the registration of southern whites apt to support Reagan.

> "One of the lessons we learned," said Rex Harris, [Jesse] Jackson's campaign manager in [North Carolina], "is the quickest way to register white conservatives is to hold a black registration drive. . . . The black preachers wrote the book on this," gloated Gary Jarmin, field director of a nationwide voter registration drive in . . . predominately white churches. "God bless them for it." Concedes Harris: "We may have created a monster."[38]

The Republican Party and evangelical pastors were among those who worked to push up white registration to reduce or reverse the political consequences of the black registration gains. " 'It scares the bejeebers out of me,' the Texas Republican chairman, George Strake, said [in June] of the masses of southern blacks who registered to vote for Mr. Jackson in his campaign for the Democratic nomination."[39] North

Carolina's Republican chairman, David T. Flaherty, sent out 45,000 fund-raising letters in August, warning, "Your vote may be canceled because radical Jesse Jackson has already registered enough liberal Democrat voters in North Carolina to cancel your vote for President Reagan and our other Republican candidates." Flaherty promised top priority to "a massive voter registration drive designed to offset the tremendous increase in black voter registration in North Carolina."[40]

The timing of the registration gains—a black surge followed by a larger white surge—suggests the white gains were in large part a reaction to the black mobilization. But this is a stronger conclusion than the facts support. Some of the white registration increase was racially motivated, but the critical question is how much. No precise answer can be provide here, but a fuller consideration of the context suggests the registration gains by whites cannot be interpreted as solely white racial countermobilization. Other motivations mattered significantly.[41]

Considering who mounted the registration drives and why (interesting points in themselves) does not determine why individuals registered, how they voted, or why they voted as they did.[42] Much of the white increase stems from roots more mundane than racism. The southern voting-age population contains more than four whites for every black, so one expects far greater absolute registration gains among whites. Presidential elections elicit peak voter interest even in the South, naturally more people register in a presidential election year. Moreover, since a change of address can require reregistration, a significant level of registration activity can be anticipated even without major registration drives.[43]

The different timing of the black and white registration surges can be explained in part by the different peaks of political interest. Little Republican politicking occurred in the South during the first half of 1984. Reagan was unopposed for the presidential nomination and Republican contests for state and local offices were few and elicited little participation. The Reagan campaign did not register voters during early 1984 but identified likely Reagan supporters among the unregistered for later registration by other Republican campaigns. On the Democratic side, Jesse Jackson's presidential bid attracted new black voters and reinforced efforts already underway to register blacks. Southern whites, as noted, were not enthusiastic about the Democratic presidential choices as the nomination process unfolded. These considerations combined to create in the South during the first half of 1984 a context of growing political awareness among blacks and relative inattention on the part of whites. Consequently, black registration gains since 1980 far outstripped white registration gains, even in an absolute sense, in early 1984, after which white registration gains surpassed the black.

Democrats had hoped that the black registration increase between 1980 and 1984 would overcome Reagan's 1980 margin of victory in several southern states. In eight of the 11 southern states this happened; in at least four of these the black registration increase exceeded Reagan's margin plus the white registration gain since 1980 (see Table 13–1).

In voter registration, blacks accomplished what Democrats sought, and black turnout exceeded 1980 levels.[44] This is all-the-more surprising since get-out-the-vote drives in the black community were weaker than they would have been with a closer presidential contest. Indeed, some Democratic funds were diverted from the South in the closing days of the campaign, since southern states seemed out of Mondale's reach.[45]

At the presidential level, the white vote was so lopsided for Reagan that even greater black voting gains could not have changed the outcome. Below the presidential level, the black vote provided critical support for several Democrats: U.S. Senator Howell Heflin (Ala), Steve Neal (N.C.–5), Bill Hefner (N.C.–8), Ben Erdreich (Ala.–6), Wayne Dowdy (Miss.–4), and Robin Tallon (S.C.–6).[46] This is a short, but not exhaustive list, of Democrats who won because of the black support they gained. Other Democrats had a more comfortable margin of victory and perhaps a weaker challenger because of the level of black support anticipated and secured, so the importance of the black vote to the election of southern Democrats is greater than the list suggests. At the state and local level, Democrats' putting together biracial coalitions to win the election in the South is not so forbidding a task as might be inferred from the 1984 presidential results. U.S. Senator Howell Heflin won 46 percent of the white vote plus over 80 percent of the black vote and retained his seat (Table 13–2). Twenty-two years ago those numbers would have meant defeat. In 1984 they meant he won with 62 percent of the vote overall. Democratic U.S. Senate candidate Jim Hunt in North Carolina gained 34 percent of the white vote and 86 percent of the black vote but lost only narrowly, despite the presidential landslide for the Republicans, after his opponent Senator Jesse Helms outspent him by several million dollars.

Strong registration gains and high Democratic loyalty marked southern blacks in 1984. The more sizable white registration gains

TABLE 13–1 Registration Increases by Race, 1980 to 1984, and Reagan's Winning Margins, 1980 and 1984

State	Reagan's 1980 Lead over Carter	Registration Increase, 1980 to 1984		Reagan's 1984 Lead over Mondale
		Whites	Blacks	
Alabama	17,462	128,000	166,000**	320,950
Arkansas	5,123	41,000	41,000*	198,128
Florida	627,476	652,000	102,000	1,281,534
Georgia	−236,787	302,000	144,000**	362,094
Louisiana	84,400	151,000	96,000*	385,713
Mississippi	11,808	59,000	129,000**	230,185
N. Carolina	39,383	308,000	179,000*	522,194
S. Carolina	11,456	89,000	69,000*	271,080
Tennessee	4,710	17,000	62,000**	278,498
Texas	629,558	1,070,000	250,000	1,484,152
Virginia	237,435	261,000	104,000	540,828

*indicates black registration gain exceeds Reagan's 1980 margin

**indicates black registration gain exceeds Reagan's 1980 margin plus the white registration gain

Sources: 1980 election returns from Congressional Quarterly Weekly, 25 April 1981, 721–25; 1984 election returns from The New York Times, 22 December 1984, 10; voter registration figures from The Voter Education Project, rounded to the nearest thousand.

TABLE 13–2   Presidential and Senatorial Voting by Race, 1984 (by percentage)

State	Black		White		
	D	*R*	*D*	*R*	
Voting for President					
National	89	7	35	64	
South	89	9	28	72	
Alabama	93	6	17	82	
Florida	84	13	29	71	
Mississippi	89	9	14	85	
North Carolina	85	12	24	76	
Tennessee	95	5	31	69	
Texas	86	12	22	77	
Virginia	90	10	25	74	
Voting for U.S. Senator					Senate Winner
Alabama	81	6	46	48	Heflin (D)
Mississippi	81	10	17	81	Cochran (R)
North Carolina	86	13	34	64	Helms (R)
Texas	88	9	29	68	Gramm (R)
Virginia	76	24	21	79	Warner (R)

Note: The South includes Kentucky and Oklahoma, as well as the states of the former Confederacy.

Source: CBS News–*New York Times* Exit Surveys as reported in a Joint Center for Political Studies press release, 14 November 1984, and *Focus,* November-December, 1984, 5. Florida and Tennessee figures are from the ABC News Exit Poll press release. Virginia figures are from the NBC News Election Day Exit Poll as reported in the Sabato chapter.

cannot be viewed chiefly as the result of racial backlash. Neither can the limited white support for Democrats, a topic to which we now turn.

RACIAL POLARIZATION

Does the racial polarization in partisan support—the over 70 percent Republican vote of southern whites and the nearly 90 percent Democratic vote of southern blacks—principally indicate southern politics revolves around race, with whites opposing causes and candidates backed by blacks? Similar racial voting patterns, only slightly less pronounced, prevailed in the rest of the nation, but racial concerns have long been thought to have a peculiarly southern focus.

Several commentators thought the southern results arose from resurgent racism. The Alabama and Mississippi chapters presented examples of such commentary, so one should suffice here. On election night on CBS, Bill Moyers explained the firm backing of Reagan by white southerners this way: "You know, the overwhelming reason, I think is race. It's not white drift so much as it is white flight. . . . when they say in the South that the national Democratic Party is too liberal what they really mean is that Jesse Jackson is too powerful in the Democratic Party." Moyers ticked off several signals Reagan and the Republicans had sent white southerners:

> They've retreated from affirmative action. They have supported tax exemptions for schools that practice racial desegregation. They're opposed to busing. The President went down to Charlotte [N.C.] and made a speech . . . saying busing had failed when in fact busing had succeeded in Charlotte. The newspaper the next day had to call his hand on that but by then the message had gone out on local television that the president was against busing. George Bush was in Mobile, Alabama . . . and made to an all-white group a speech saying the party of Mondale and Ferraro and Tip O'Neill is not the Democratic Party that the people of Alabama remember. Well, the party that the people of Alabama remember is the party of the old George Wallace and Bull Connor and the days when the white segregationists were in control of the South.

Noting "it has become politically palatable again for white southerners to feel the way they did for a long time," Moyers concluded, "old ways die hard."[47] In Moyers's view, the growing black presence in the Democratic Party ("when the blacks move in, the whites move out") and Reagan's invitations to return to the old ways caused white southerners to become the staunchest Reagan supporters.

To place such emphasis on the racial issue underestimates the depth and breadth of Reagan's appeal to white southerners, an appeal with far stronger roots than hints of a return to a segregationist past, the reactions to the blacks's dislike for Reagan, or Jesse Jackson's involvement in Democratic politics. Few southern whites have an interest in politics limited to countering black political influence. To start and stop analysis on the assumption that race is all that matters distorts rather than delivers an understanding of southern politics. A review of nonracial reasons for the racially polarized election results as well as aspects of southern racial politics helps drive home the point that race was but one factor, probably not even the most important, in the 1984 outcome.

Evidence of the affection of southern whites for Reagan and their disaffection with national Democratic candidates, particularly liberal ones, has not been lacking. More than a continuation of pro-Republican trends traceable to the Eisenhower years was at work here. Reagan loomed large as a very popular political figure. A reviving economy, a strong defense, resurgent patriotism, and shrewd public relations helped. Reagan's emphasis on conservative religious issues had particular appeal to southern whites. No single cause, such as racial issues, pulled the southern white into Reagan's corner.[48] Republican campaigners stressed three themes profitably: no tax increase under Reagan, Reagan will stand up to our enemies abroad, and the Democratic Party's veer to the left leaves it no longer worthy of its traditional support (see the Arkansas chapter for excellent examples and a broader discussion). As noted in the Alabama chapter, both Reagan's personality and policies receive high marks from southern whites. Reagan enjoyed very high approval ratings from southern whites, but southern blacks were at the opposite extreme. In early 1984 southern whites approved the way Reagan handled his job as president by 78–22 percent, the way Reagan handled the economy by 73–27, and the way Reagan handled our relations with foreign countries by 62–38. The corresponding figures for southern blacks were 29–71, 29–71, and 13–87. (Each of the approval figures for southern whites ranged 12 to 14 percentage points above those for nonsouthern whites.)[49]

Reagan's strong popularity among southern whites contrasted sharply with Mondale's weaker appeal. Only 18 percent of southern whites thought Mondale provided strong leadership a great deal of the time; 59 percent thought so for Reagan. One-third of southern whites thought Reagan really cared about people like them; only 19 percent thought the same of Mondale.[50]

One's evaluation of the economy's performance is a strong determinant of voting for or against the incumbent president.[51] Southern whites and blacks had distinctly different views on the state of the economy under Reagan. CBS New/*New York Times* Election Day Surveys found 51 percent of southern black voters thought the U.S. economy was worse today than four years ago. Of southern white voters, 67 percent thought the U.S. economy was better. The 59 percent of the southern voters, both white and black, who thought the economy better voted for Reagan by a nine-to-one margin; the 18 percent who thought it worse voted for Mondale by a nine-to-one margin. Such divergent, vote-shaping economic evaluations are but one potent reason the racially polarized results need not have stemmed from racist motivations.

Reagan's one overt attempt to raise the race issue in the South came when he spoke against busing in Charlotte, North Carolina. As discussed in the North Carolina chapter, the rhetoric backfired locally. Charlotte provided the national test case for busing in 1971. Following the unanimous Supreme Court decision in favor of busing, members of the community had worked vigorously to make the school system and court-ordered busing succeed. Even Republicans in Charlotte were embarrassed by Reagan's statements on busing.[52]

If the race issue were the principal reason white voters deserted the Democratic Party, the courting of black voters by southern Republican candidates would be rare. In fact, southern Republicans increasingly seek black votes. As noted by Walker and Main in the Georgia chapter, "If there remains a politics of race in the state of Georgia, it is the recognition by most candidates that either the black vote must be courted or must be neutralized by dividing it." In 1984 Senators Thad Cochran of Mississippi and John Warner of Virginia made major efforts to gain black support. Jim Martin, the successful gubernatorial candidate in North Carolina, did the same. Even Senator Helms of North Carolina made campaign appearances before predominantly black audiences in 1984.[53] Senator Thurmond of South Carolina has cultivated black votes since the early 1970s.[54] Such moves can be explained by electoral self-interest. In South Carolina blacks make up 28 percent of the registered voters. If blacks also make up 28 percent of the voters and back one candidate solidly, that candidate can win if he gains only 31 percent of the white vote. By courting black votes, Republicans can provide insurance against such a solidly opposed black vote, as well as offset votes lost elsewhere. Since serious searching for black support would hinder efforts to raise the race issue among whites, Republicans, by their campaign tactics, indicate the race issue is not the preferred principal means of moving more southern whites away from Democratic voting habits.

Several scholars contend racial attitudes during the 1960s and 1970s drove formerly Democratic whites to the Republicans. Scholars suggesting a sizable role to racial backlash have relied on testable but untested assertions (E.M Schreiber) or a small portion of the available evidence (James Sundquist and Kevin Phillips).[55] Survey findings frustrate those researchers claiming racial backlash as the cause of Democratic decline. Paul Beck, as well as Raymond Wolfinger and Robert Arseneau, provide thorough analyses of the available survey data, finding white racial attitudes had little to do with the Democratic decline.[56] During the 1980s and 1970s, native white southerners showed increasing conservatism on social welfare issues such as government-guaranteed jobs and standards of living, government health insurance and medical care, and federal aid to education, leaving the native white electorate at odds with much of the Great Society. Racial issues were not the single force separating southern whites from the national Democratic Party. As Bruce Campbell notes, this broad ideological misfit, rather than simply a preoccupation with race, holds more promise as the reason the southern white population became less Democratic.[57] Since the 1960s had far more salient and turbulent racial politics, if the greater stimulus then failed to move southerners away from the Democrats, one should question the role of race in the less racially charged context of 1984.

Southern whites have long been staunch Reagan supporters (Figure 13–1), they did not suddenly look more favorably upon the Republicans once Jesse Jackson rose to prominence within the Democratic Party.[58] The marginal change Jackson's involvement made for some southern whites may well have been outweighed by more pressing evaluations of Reagan and his record in contrast to Mondale. A Gallup Poll in August 1984 "found no sharply hostile reaction to the Jackson campaign among southern whites. Jackson's endorsement made 19 percent of southern whites less likely to vote for Mondale, and 8 percent more likely. Many of the whites responding negatively to Jackson would probably have voted against Mondale for other reasons having little to do with race."[59] An earlier, roughly comparable question offers a revealing contrast. In 1956 and 1960, between one-third and a majority of southern whites claimed a Negro group's endorsement of a candidate would make them less likely to vote for the candidate. Only one southern white out of 750 respondents (0.1 percent) replied that this would make them more likely to vote for the candidate.[60]

Some southern whites do vote out of racist motivations. Since 1960 Democrats have not been able to rely on this group in presidential politics. These racially roused southern whites deserted the Democrats to support Goldwater in 1964, Wallace (or perhaps Nixon) in 1968, Nixon in 1972, perhaps returned to the Democratic fold to back a fellow southerner in 1976 (although Carter did not get a majority of the white vote even in the South), and probably did not stick with Carter when offered the choice between Reagan and President Carter in 1980. To hold that in 1984 the issue of race has driven off more southern whites from the national Democratic Party neglects the way the Democrats have not been able to count on whites reachable on the race issue since 1960.

If one equates the typical southern white's less liberal political opin-

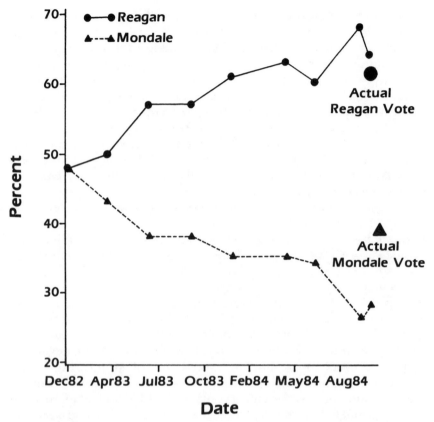

FIGURE 13–1   Reagan-Mondale Trial Heats in the South, 1983–84

Question: "If the presidential election were held today, for whom would you vote?"

Source: Darden Poll of the South (registered voters in Alabama, Florida, Georgia, Louisiana, Mississippi, North Carolina, South Carolina, Tennessee and Virginia), as reported in *The National Journal,* 7 July 1984, 1326; *The Atlanta Journal,* 4 August 1984 (76:F–6), and 2 November 1984 (134:D–4, D–5); and *The Philadelphia Inquirer,* 29 October 1984 (132: C–13).

ions with racism, "racism" can then be considered quite powerfully present by definition. Yet once one recognizes the reality that southern whites can have nonracial reasons for holding conservative opinions, the role of racism is not determined by assumption or definition but becomes a matter for investigation. To ask rhetorically, "Conservative on what issues? Race?" is no excuse for failure to consider the fuller context in which racial motivations may have played a part but were not the only motives. In summary, the lingering importance of race does not provide an adequate explanation of Reagan's popularity among whites, or the racially polarized vote.

Racial concerns were not the principal reason southern whites found favor with Reagan, but racial divisions within southern Democratic parties seem likely to intensify for the foreseeable future. Black political leaders in the South have grown increasingly disturbed that blacks, the most loyal support group for the Democrats, have a smaller share of Democratic nominees and officeholders than the black proportion of the voting-age population or registered voters. Such disenchantment led to various proposals, including the threat of an independent black Senate candidacy in Mississippi, a tactic certain to doom Democratic election chances. The independent candidacy was abandoned partly because it would have been too late in starting and might have hindered a black Democratic congressional candidate's chances. But the disappointments giving rise to its consideration remain.[61] Such increasingly strong black demands on the southern Democratic parties—Mississippi seems the extreme case—come as southern whites are very willing to abandon the Democratic presidential nominee for a palatable Republican candidate and have shown some willingness to do so for the lesser offices. Black leaders have several grievances, the runoff and the reluctance of whites to vote for blacks being prominent among them.

Jackson's presidential campaign focused attention on the run-off requirement for the Democratic nomination in several southern states, a rule he claimed disadvantaged blacks politically.[62] Since blacks seldom make up a majority of a district's voters, and whites are reluctant to vote for blacks, the insistence on a majority vote for the nomination imposes a high hurdle for blacks. Southern Democratic leaders insist that abolition of the runoff would divide the Democrats and promote Republican prospects. Jackson first said the runoff's abolition was essential to secure his support for the Democratic nominee, then later accepted a commitment to study the effects of the runoff.

The reluctance of whites to vote for black Democratic candidates is a major frustration for blacks. The 1984 results revealed that the problem endures. Although blacks provide a solid core of support for white Democratic candidates, black Democratic candidates have had severe problems securing white votes. The exceptions are few. In the Democratic primary in North Carolina's 62 percent white Second Congressional District, the white incumbent turned back a strong black challenger who needed 34.5 percent of the white vote to win but received just under 32 percent.[63] Even so, this percentage of the white vote was one of the higher figures for black candidates in the 1984 elections. Some blacks were elected in predominantly white districts, the election of State Court of Appeals Judge Robert Benham, "the first black person elected to statewide office in Georgia," being the most notable case.[64]

Reagan's popularity and the Republican gains did not result primarily from white racial backlash. But racial tensions within the Democratic Party could grow as a result of the current disenchantment of black political leaders with the Democratic Party.

PARTY REALIGNMENT?

Given the overwhelming Republican wins in the South in three of the last four presidential elections, one might conclude that partisan realignment has occurred, perhaps even that the South has shifted from one-party Democratic status to one-party Republican status. Of course, such regional Republican strength reflected the outcome in the rest of the nation, but the end of the South's isolation from national political currents is noteworthy in itself.

Previous Republican gains in partisan identification have been slow or reversed, but early 1984 data reveal that Republicans have increased their proportion of identifiers in the South (Figure 13–2). Compared with 1980, counting partisan "leaners" as Independents, Republican identifiers have increased from 21 to 27 percent of the southern voting-age population, Independents are up from 31 to 36, and Democrats have declined from 47 to 37 percent. Republican identifiers have increased especially among the young, decreasing the share of both young Democrats and Independents.[65] Southern whites under 30 interviewed in the first half of 1984 claimed the following partisanship: 35 percent Republican, 38 percent Independent, and only 25 percent Democratic. Comparable figures for 1980 were 22, 45, and 31.

In the South, Republicans are in a much improved position. The growth in Republican identifiers and Independents (who now match the proportion of Democratic identifiers) creates a more favorable electoral context. Moreover, as the Louisiana and Texas chapters emphasized, some southern states' Republicans now have better organizations in place to capitalize farther on auspicious electoral openings. Possibly Reagan's popular policies now have legs of their own, capable of enduring for Republican benefit even when Reagan is no longer the one to espouse them. The 1984 elections gave Republicans results worth relishing. Such rosy prospects are a boon for recruiting capable candidates, encouraging politicians to switch to the Repub-

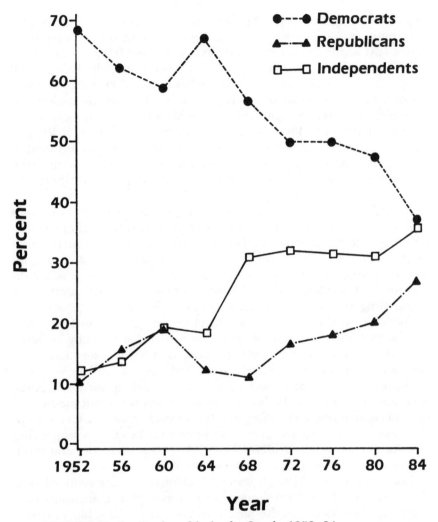

FIGURE 13–2   Partisanship in the South, 1952–84

Note: Partisans are weak or strong identifiers. Partisan leaners are combined with independents.

Source: American National Election Studies data, calculations by the author, for the eleven states of the former Confederacy.

licans, and undertaking the development work needed for further Republican growth.

Whether the pro-Republican aspects of the 1984 results will prove lasting is another matter. For years southern Republicans have been perched on the edge of a breakthrough. After the 1980 elections,

Republicans seemed likely to gain even greater victories in the South, but Democrats rebounded, taking back many of these Republican gains. Just as the Democratic resurgence in 1982 followed the Democratic setback of 1980, the same could happen in 1986. Reagan will not be on the ballot. If his popularity has lessened and the economy soured, the Republican prospects in the South and the nation will look bleaker. After Reagan the leadership of the Republican Party is an open question. The same is true now for the Democrats. Reagan has shown the difference an individual can make. As Lamis noted in closing the Mississippi chapter, what the future holds for the pro-Republican trends evident in the 1984 results depends in significant part on the future actions of political elites.

In presidential politics, the South seems now to be the Republican's to lose rather than the Democrat's to win. To carry southern states, a Democratic presidential candidate must be capable of securing high black turnout and solid black support yet moderate enough to gain the critical margin of white votes. Given the sure presence of a conservative (or moderate) Republican opponent, the Democrat's task of courting the moderates while keeping firm black support is no simple feat. At the state and local level Democrats do this frequently and successfully. The adoption of such winning ways by national Democratic candidates is made less likely by what it takes to gain the Democratic nomination. Carter managed the feat in the South in 1976, but his moderation was a handicap in seeking the Democratic nomination. To carry the South, his moderation was supplemented by his regional roots, enabling him to win each southern state except Virginia. In 1980 he lost every southern state but Georgia, proving that for Democratic presidential candidates, southern ties and moderation may be essential but are not sufficient.

The continuing, although lessened, Democratic dominance below the presidential level cautions against a sweeping conclusion proclaiming realignment in the South. In the early 1960s, blacks firmly realigned with the Democrats. Although whites have grown much less Democratic, the slack has been taken up by Independents rather than Republicans, so despite the recent Republican gains, dealignment may be a better characterization of current white voter attitudes toward the parties. Of course, the growth among Independents advantages Republicans in the short run as the Democratic hold on white voter loyalties declines.

The degree of Democratic one-party dominance in most areas of the South does not extend to supporting liberal presidential candidates. Southern Democrats do not offer the state and local electorates liberal-conservative choices akin to the Mondale-Reagan election.

When they do nominate a more liberal candidate, such as Doggett in the Texas Senate race, the results reaffirm the wisdom of not offering such a choice more often. Consequently, southern Democrats are not as electorally endangered a species as the Mondale-Reagan results suggest, although southern Democrats suffer from a national party appreciably to the left of a majority of the southern voters.

In 1984 the apparent spillover effects from the presidential to the subpresidential levels were greater than the Democrats would have liked and less than the Republicans had hoped. In senatorial races, Democrats gained a seat in Tennessee; at the congressional level, Democrats lost eight seats but regained one; at the gubernatorial level, they lost North Carolina. In Texas and North Carolina, as discussed in those chapters, Republicans made unprecedented inroads at the state and local level. The Reagan tide did not lift all Republican candidates—some seemed to be in what Jesse Jackson would call those boats stuck on the bottom—but Reagan's coattails may have provided the critical victory margin for U.S. Senator Jesse Helms and in a few of the eight House seats the Republicans won. Southern Democratic candidates are experienced in the techniques of distancing themselves from the national ticket and work hard to minimize unfavorable coattails. And, as the Arkansas chapter documented, coattails anticipated can be coattails curtailed.

Figures 13–3 and 13–4 display the gains of the Republicans in the South since 1952, providing historical perspectives on the most recent Republican victories. Clearly, Republican strength is top-heavy, the presidency and U.S. Senate showing the greatest Republican successes. Republicans have made inroads into the southern delegations in the U.S. House of Representatives, although the Republican wins in 1984 only bring Republicans back to the level of 1980. At the gubernatorial level, Republican weakness resembles that of the late 1960s. At the state legislative level, the trend is up but the rate of increase is very slow. Fitting a trend line to the data for Republican state legislative seats—a calculation one cannot take too seriously— indicates that at the present rate of growth, Republicans will have a majority of the state legislative seats for the lower chambers in the South in 2045 and in the upper chambers in 2066. More seriously, Republicans are far from majority control of any southern legislative chamber. Republicans now hold about one-third of the lower chamber seats in Florida, North Carolina, Tennessee, Texas, and Virginia. Only in Tennessee do Republicans hold almost one-third of the upper chamber seats.

The simple but mistaken suggestion that Republicans could win

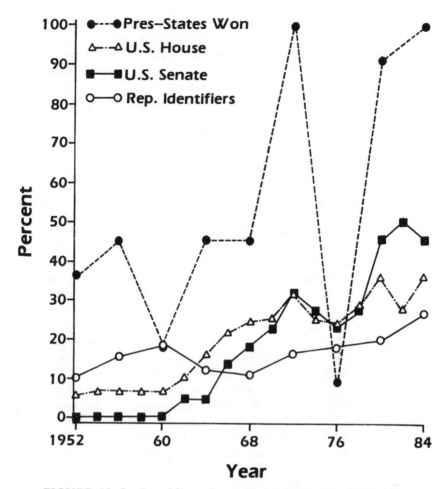

FIGURE 13–3   Republican Strength in the South, 1952–84:
Partisanship, the Presidency, and Congress

Sources: Republican partisan identification calculated by the author
from American National Election Studies data. Partisan division of congressmen and electoral votes taken from James Q. Wilson, *American Government: Institutions and Policies* (Lexington: Heath, 1980), 152; and
Congressional Quarterly Weekly, 8 November 1980, 3297, 3315, 3325–26;
6 November 1982, 2785–86, 2793; and 10 November 1984, 2893, 2907–
10.

more if they contested more at the state and local level reveals the
difficulties Republicans face in increasing their share of elective offices. Many Democratic incumbents win uncontested elections for
federal, state, and local offices in the South because running Republicans against popular Democratic incumbents makes those incum-

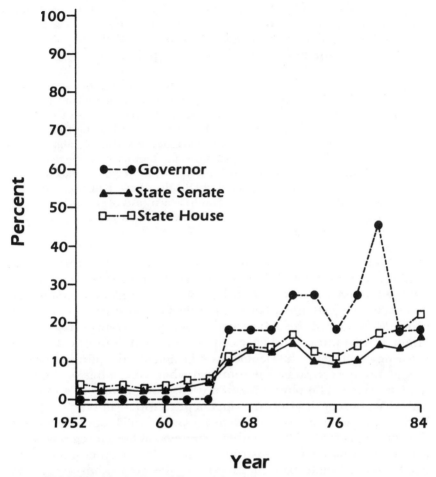

FIGURE 13–4   Republican Strength in the South, 1952–84: Governors and State Legislators

Sources: Partisan division of state legislative seats taken from Jack Bass and Walter DeVries, *The Transformation of Southern Politics: Social Change and Political Consequence since 1945* (New York: Basic Books, 1976), 34–37; U.S. Bureau of the Census, *Statistical Abstract of the United States: 1984* (104th ed.), Washington, 1983, 260; and *USA TODAY,* 9 November 1984. Partisan division of governors taken from James Q. Wilson, *American Government: Institutions and Policies* (Lexington: Heath, 1980), 152; and *Congressional Quarterly Weekly,* 8 November 1980, 3328; 6 November 1982, 2807; and 10 November 1984, 2913.

bents mobilize their supporters, thus aiding other Democratic candidates. Texas Republicans had a good year in 1984, but they had candidates in only 67 elections to the 150-member state House and in only four of the 15 state Senate elections.[66] As noted in the Texas chapter, Texas Republicans learned in 1982 the political disadvantages of taking on popular Democratic incumbents.

Alan Ehrenhalt, writing in early 1984, described the problem the South presents for Democratic presidential politics:

> Republicans are the majority party for one crucial reason—they win the South. . . . Jimmy Carter's showing as an incumbent in 1980—a southerner carrying nothing in the region except his home state—is the clearest possible evidence of what the Democrats are up against. Republicans have not talked much about a southern strategy lately, but that is because they have not needed to. It is the Democrats who need a southern strategy, and except for the nomination of Carter in 1976, they have had none to offer. Unable to compete in the South, which casts over a quarter of the electoral vote, they have been beaten from the start, whether they knew it or not.[67]

Here "southern strategy" means no more than special efforts to win southern electoral votes. The South may require special attention, but the limited appeal of recent Democratic presidential candidates nationally suggests the Democrats have far more than a regional problem. Some calls for a Democratic "southern strategy" reflect the origins of that phrase and have connotations that, if practices, would prove destructive for the Democrats.[68] Originally, the phrase covered special attempts to court the southern white vote, while writing off the black vote. The phrase is often used to stigmatize an opponent with charges that disaffect the opponent's support in other regions. Racial issues were not the sole determinant in 1964, but Goldwater's showing suggested such a southern strategy, although regionally attractive, was nationally disastrous. National Democratic candidates need a larger white base of support in the South, but seeking to secure an adequate white base by spurning the black seems needlessly hazardous. Mondale's problems with the southern white vote were far more extensive than the growing role of blacks within the party. Mondale would not have gained appreciably more white votes by disaffecting black voters. To reduce motivations for the southern white vote to racial backlash ignores the very real problems presidential Democrats have had in securing southern support (not to mention national support). A more promising southern strategy for the presidential level would duplicate the biracial coalitions successful state and local Democrats put together. Since blacks provide from a quarter to over half of the Democratic support in the southern States, Democrats might more effectively build upon rather than abandon that base of support.

CONCLUSION

For the 1984 election, black voter registration gains in the South were substantial. The larger white registration surge, marginally aided by racial backlash, cannot be stereotyped as principally stemming from such a cause. Black voter turnout lagged behind the high expectations fueled by the registration increase, but since Reagan carried more than 70 percent of the southern white vote, even higher black turnout would not significantly altered the outcome.

Given Reagan's popularity nationally and within the South, a Mondale victory would have been difficult to achieve. Picking a non-southern, liberal, and female running mate; elevating, then dropping Bert Lance; and promising to raise taxes—such moves by Mondale made a difficult campaign even more so in the South. Moreover, most southern Democratic elected officials and leaders refrained from taking an active, visible role on behalf of Mondale. Democrats in general election contests worked to distance themselves from the party's presidential candidate.

To read Reagan's strong support among southern whites as a confirmation of the importance of race to southerners underestimates the firmness, depth, and breadth of Reagan's appeal in the South. Economic recovery, a strong defense, reviving patriotism, religious emphasis, strong leadership—such themes struck a responsive chord among white southerners. Such themes had a reality of their own and were not merely rationalized reflections of a voting choice resulting from preoccupation with race.

White southerners have been shedding the habit of voting Democratic, but in recent decades that habit did not stretch to include strong support for liberal candidates. So it was in 1984. At the presidential level, Republicans benefit from the likely prospect of a more liberal than moderate Democratic candidate whose limited white southern support will not make up the margin of victory, even if blacks remain solidly Democratic. Such an addition of most southern states to the Republican base in the West would make Republican victories all but certain. Below the presidential level, Republicans have brighter prospects than before, but less promising than for the presidency. Southern Democrats typically win elective office, not by presenting themselves as "Mondale liberals" but by offering a more moderate political stance, successfully securing enough black and white votes to beat back the Republicans. The ability of southern Democrats to build such biracial coalitions has hindered Republican prospects at the state and local level. Republicans, lacking a support base in the black community, must typically muster 60 percent or more of the white vote against Democratic candidates who are much closer to the Republican's positions than was Mondale to Reagan's. Consequently, Republican strength at the lower levels such as state legislatures, although greater than before, is far below the strength with which Republicans contest for the higher-level offices. For Republicans to win 60 percent or more of the white vote requires the abatement of economic class differences that often demand political expression. As Thomas Cavanagh put it, "While Democrats cannot win if they cede 70 percent or more of the white vote, neither can the Republicans hope to maintain this percentage for any length of time. Such an outcome would require transcendence of the very real class differences among southern whites, differences that are sharpening over time as the region's urban areas continue to modernize and develop."[69]

The linking of white racial backlash to the Republican rise and the Democratic decline in the South downplays the general conservatism of southern whites and ignores the steps Republicans are taking to appeal to black voters. Whether Democrats can retain solid black support hinges on the success of the Republican courtship, the ability of the Democrats to resolve the tensions within biracial coalitions, and whether blacks remain content with the pace of progress toward desired political ends within the Democratic Party. The reluctance of whites to back black Democratic candidates and the use of the runoff are but two of the more visible sources of disenchantment between blacks and the Democratic Party. If state and local Democratic candidates can count on strong biracial support, the bright Republican prospects at the presidential level will contrast sharply with the darker prospects at the state and local level.

NOTES

1. Baltimore, *The Sun,* 21 July 1984 (67:A–11). All subsequent references of the form (67:A–11) refer to the location within *Newsbank* (Microform), Political Development, 1984, fiche.

2. *Philadelphia Inquirer,* 22 July 1984 (77:E–14).

3. Baltimore, *The Sun,* 22 July 1984 (77:F–2, F–3).

4. One expects upbeat, optimistic predictions from Democratic National Convention delegates about the Democrat's chances of winning back home. Even so, when asked, "How would you describe Mondale's chances of carrying your state against Ronald Reagan?" a majority of the delegates polled from Florida, Louisiana, and Virginia thought Reagan had the stronger chances. A majority of the delegates from Georgia, North Carolina, Tennessee, and Texas rated the state a tossup or Mondale's chances stronger. Results for the other southern states were not reported. Polling

occurred between 14 June and 9 July (*New York Times*, 16 July 1984, A–15). Individual state polls of registered voters conducted in May and June showed a Reagan lead of 10 to 33 points in each of these states (*National Journal Convention Daily*, 15 July 1984, 1, 10, 21).

5. Don Campbell, "What Happened to Mondale's Great Southern Strategy?", *The Rochester Democrat and Chronicle*, 14 October 1984, 12a.

6. Calculations by the author using National Election studies data for 1968, 1972, and 1980 in the eleven southern states. While voting data for 1984 are from the CBS News/*New York Times* Election Day Exit Polls, the ABC News Election Day Exit Polls, and the NBC Election Day Exit Polls. ABC and CBS poll results are taken from network press releases, the NBC results are reported in *Time*, 19 November 1984, 42.

7. For the trend toward conservatism within the white South, see Everett Carll Ladd, Jr., with Charles D. Hadley, *Transformations of the American Party System: Political Coalitions from the New Deal to the 1970s*, 2d. ed. (New York: Norton, 1978), 139–40, 166–77.

8. *Congressional Quarterly Weekly*, 17 March 1984, 625.

9. Mondale did receive sizable black support in the southern primaries and caucuses. The three television networks's exit poll estimates of Mondale's share of the black vote ranged from 34 to 47 percent in Alabama and from 27 to 30 percent in Georgia. ABC claimed Mondale gained 25 percent of the black vote in Florida; CBS found Mondale received 22 percent of the black vote in Tennessee, 16 percent in Texas, and 13 percent in North Carolina.

10. Southern Regional Council, "An Analysis of Voting Patterns in Alabama and Georgia: The Presidential Primary Election of March 13, 1984 (Targeted Precinct Analysis)."

11. Estimates are taken from network press releases for the ABC Exit Polls and CBS News/*New York Times* Exit Polls. NBC Exit Polls and black percentages of registered voters are from *Time*, 26 March 1984, 19. In the other southern states, CBS News/*New York Times* Exit Poll estimates of the percentage of primary of caucus voters who were black and Voter Education Project figures for the percentage of registered voters who were black (in parentheses) are: North Carolina 27 (19), Tennessee 26 (13), and Texas 33 (9). Florida was an exception to the disproportionate black turnout in the rest of the South. An ABC News Exit poll estimated Florida blacks made up 11 percent of the Super Tuesday voters, the same share blacks make up of the registered voters.

12. Analyzing presidential voting from 1948 to 1972, Steven J. Rosenstone found "The only electoral advantage a party gains from a regionally balanced ticket is the extra 2.5 percent that the running mate pulls in his home state." (*Forecasting Presidential Elections* [New Haven: Yale University Press, 1983], 88).

13. David Garth, quoted in *Newsday*, 13 July 1984 (65:G–12).

14. *San Francisco Chronicle*, 14 July 1984 (62:E–3, E–4, E–5).

15. Noting that Mondale had accelerated the southern trend to the Republicans because of his alliance with the AFL–CIO, Democratic political analyst Horace Busby said, "It's a concealed issue in this whole thing for Southerners. Southern whites are pulling out of the party because of it." *Newsweek*, 29 October 1984, 40). A Gallup Poll in August found that when asked to specify groups having "too much influence" over national policy, twice as many southern whites cited labor leaders as cited blacks

(59 to 30 percent). Reported by Thomas Cavanagh, in "Election Roundup," *Focus*, November-December 1984, 4.

16. Richard Wirthlin, 13 December 1984 interview with the editors of *Public Opinion*, quoted in Everett Carll Ladd, "The Election of 1984," *The Ladd Report #1* (New York: Norton, 1985), 36.

17. *Time*, 19 November 1982, 42.

18. *Philadelphia Inquirer*, 29 October 1984 (132:C–13).

19. Richard Wirthlin, quoted in Ladd, "The Election of 1984," 36.

20. Raleigh, North Carolina, *News and Observer*, 16 July 1984 (69:C–13, C–14).

21. Dale Russakoff, "After the Fall: The Brief, Unhappy Return of Bert Lance," *The Washington Post National Weekly Edition*, 13 August 1984, 12.

22. Jules Witcover, "How Manatt Decision was Made, Unmade," *National Journal Convention Special*, 21 July 1984, 6.

23. *San Jose Mercury*, 17 July 1984 (70:A–11). Such praise of Lance by the Mondale campaign irked many who thought others had done more to achieve the Mondale wins on Super Tuesday in Alabama and Georgia. "Knowledgeable political activists in both states say with resentment that Lance 'didn't win one vote in Alabama' for Mondale, and was less influential in Georgia than were Georgia Association of Educators chief Jim Williams, state AFL–CIO director Herb Mabry and Lieutenant Governor Zell Miller." (Russakoff, "After the Fall," 12).

24. Russakoff, "After the Fall," 12.

25. Jim Walser, "Mondale Effort in Key Region Grounded in Discord, Disarray," *Charlotte Observer*, 2 September 1984 (91:F–11).

26. Sam Tenenbaum, Ibid.

27. *Miami Herald*, 4 August 1984 (77:G–9).

28. *San Jose Mercury*, 17 July 1984 (70:A–11).

29. Jackson, Mississippi, *Clarion-Ledger*, 15 July 1984 (64:B–2, B–3).

30. *Atlanta Journal*, 3 August 1984 (77:G–8).

31. Mondale sought to arrange a Democratic unity meeting in Georgia on 13 August, personally calling Georgia party and political officials to set up the meeting. Mondale cancelled the meeting when commitments to attend were not forthcoming *Atlantic Journal*, 23 August 1984 (86:D–3, D–4). *Newsweek* (27 August 1984) reported the only local official who would welcome Mondale to Macon was Mayor George Israel—Ronald Reagan's campaign chairman in Georgia.

32. Several polls documented the wide Reagan lead during this period. Two examples are the Darden Poll for the earlier period and the Gordon Black Poll for the middle of August. Darden: *Atlanta Journal*, 4 August 1984 (76:F–6). Black: *Rochester Democrat and Chronicle*, 19 August 1984 (76:G–9, G–10).

33. *Louisville Courier-Journal*, 21 August 1984 (76:F–8, F–9).

34. *Charlotte Observer*, 18 August 1984, (86:D2, 77:A–13).

35. *Washington Post*, 9 September 1984, A–7.

36. Harris quoted in Jackson, Mississippi, *Clarion Ledger*, 2 August 1984 (77:D–1). Gordon Black supported Harris's view—see *The Rochester Democrat and Chronicle*, 19 August 1984 (76:G–1, G9–10). In late September Harris said, "I don't know what possesses him to make him keep going back to the South. It's like a moth going to

the flame. . . . the South is totally lost for Mondale": *Philadelphia Inquirer,* 23 September 1984 (88:E–10). In October Harris noted, "The president's base in this election is the South, not the West": *The Dallas Morning News,* 3 October 1984 (126:A–7).

37. These registration figures by race reflect Voter Education Project estimates and compilations of official figures. The figures through May are taken from *American Political Report,* 18 May 1984, and *Focus,* June 1984, 9. The figures through November were supplied by the Voter Education Project.

38. Tom Fiedler, "Whites Top Blacks in Voter Registration," *The Miami Herald,* 5 October 1984 (125:C–3).

39. *New York Times,* "Black Registration Alarms G.O.P. Leaders," 7 June 1984, B–12.

40. The Republican gubernatorial candidate James G. Martin's campaign repudiated the letter and continued recruiting black support. Raleigh, North Carolina, *News and Observer,* 14 August 1984 (82:B–11).

41. My analysis of increased southern voting between 1952 and 1980 found that racial attitudes, once other political attitudes and pertinent demographic characteristics were taken into account, did not account for the surge in white electoral participation during the Civil Rights era ("The Political Impact of Electoral Mobilization: The South and Universal Suffrage, 1952–1980," Diss. Yale University 1981, 160–63.

42. Democrats and allies took a general approach, assuming most unregistered individuals, once registered and voting, would be Democratic supporters. Given Reagan's level of general popularity, such an approach among unregistered whites may have worked against the Democrats. Republicans mounted a major, focused drive to identify, register, and turn out likely Reagan supporters. Many of the newly registered Reagan supporters may become and remain Republican supporters, but this depends in part upon future choices and circumstances. A preelection retrospective on the various registration drives is Ann Cooper, "Voter Turnout May be Higher on November 6, But for the Parties, It May Be a Wash," *The National Journal,* 3 November 1984, 2068–73.

43. Nationwide, in the 12 months prior to November 1980, 12.7 percent of the citizens of voting age had moved. (Some 27.3 percent had moved in the three years prior to November 1980—U.S. Bureau of the Census, Current Population Reports, Series P–20, No. 370, *Voting and Registration in the Election of November 1980* [Washington, DC: 1982], 68). Figures for the South in 1984 are not yet available but if these figures pertain, more than 4 million white southerners would have had the need to register again during 1984 for the simple reason of change of address. The laxer the registration recordkeeping (and some areas of the South still lag by the standards of modern recordkeeping), the more likely it is such changes of address add another registered voter to the rolls without removing that same voter at the previous address. CBS News/*New York Times* Election Day Exit polls in the South show 9 percent of the voters had registered in 1984 for the first time, while 10 percent registered in 1984 but not for the first time.

44. The preliminary release of the Bureau of the Census survey data on registration and voting in November 1984 reports 54.1 percent of the blacks in the eleven states of the former Confederacy claimed to have voted, up from 48.4 percent in 1980. Some 66.4 percent of southern blacks reported being registered, up from 59.8 percent for 1980. Of southern blacks who claimed to be registered, 83.0 percent reported voting in 1984, 81.0 percent in 1980. Corresponding percentages for southern whites

are as follows: turnout: 56.7 (1984) and 57.3 (1980); registration: 67.1 (1984) and 65.7 (1980); and turnout of those registered: 85.4 (1984) and 86.3 (1980) (Bureau of the Census Current Population Reports, Series P–20, No. 397, *Voting and Registration in the Election of November 1984 Advance Report,* [Washington, DC: Government Printing Office, 1985]).

45. *The Washington Post,* 4 November 1984, A–7.

46. Cavanagh, "Election Roundup," 4.

47. CBS Election Night Coverage, 6 November 1984. Moyers did note other possible reasons for Reagan's popularity (strengthening the military, renewed patriotism, Reagan's personality, and his rhetoric) but singled out race as by far the most important.

48. If the 1984 election had pitted Ronald Reagan against a Democratic candidate who matched Reagan in other respects but had Mondale's positions on racial issues, the likely outcome would have been a Democratic victory in the South. Of course, outside the South such a Democratic candidate could have encountered considerable problems in carrying Democratic constituencies.

49. 1984 American National Election Studies data, calculations by the author, for the 11 states of the former Confederacy. On these questions the sample size for southern whites is 342 to 361, for southern blacks 46 to 48.

50. Ibid.

51. Morris P. Fiorina, "Economic Retrospective Voting in American National Elections: A Micro-Analysis," *American Journal of Political Science* (May 1978): 426–43. See George C. Edwards III, *The Public Presidency: The Pursuit of Popular Support* (New York: St. Martin's Press, 1983), 263–64, for a useful summary of recent literature bearing on this point.

52. *Charlotte Observer,* 9 October 1984 (113:G–11).

53. Helms's campaign may provide the clearest example of using a racially sensitive issue to gain white support. Jesse Helms overcame Jim Hunt's large, early lead in the opinion polls after he gained national publicity for opposing the Martin Luther King, Jr., federal holiday in the Senate in the fall of 1983. Helms's support among North Carolina whites rose. Thereafter the lead in the opinion polls flipflopped but the race remained tight. Margaret Edds and Mason Peters, "A Political Uprooting Apparent in Northeastern North Carolina," *Norfolk Virginian-Pilot,* 7 October 1984, (123:C–11, C–12, C–C13). See also Richard Whittle, "Helms-Hunt Contest Pits 'Bull against Bull,'" *Dallas Morning News,* 19 October 1984 (118:G–5).

54. For an excellent review of Thurmond's efforts to court blacks, see the article by James M. Perry in *The Wall Street Journal,* 2 October 1978, 1, 4.

55. James L. Sundquist, *Dynamics of the Party System: Alignment and Realignment of Political Parties in the United States,* 2d ed. (Washington, DC: Brookings Institute, 1983), 403–4; E.M. Schreiber, " 'Where the Ducks Are': Southern Strategy versus Fourth Party," *Public Opinion Quarterly* (Summer 1971): 157–67; Kevin P. Phillips, *The Emerging Republican Majority* (New Rochelle, NY: Arlington, 1969), 205–12.

56. Paul Allen Beck, "Partisan Dealignment in the Postwar South," *American Political Science Review* (2): 492–94; Raymond Wolfinger and Robert B. Arseneau, "Partisan Change in the South, 1952–1976," in *Political Parties: Development and Decay,* ed. Louis Maisel and Joseph Cooper (Beverly Hills: Sage, 1978), 200–2.

57. Bruce A. Campbell, "Patterns of Change in the Partisan Loyalties of Native Southerners: 1952–1972," *Journal of Politics* 39 (August 1977): 748–54.

58. A different reading was provided by Mayor Andrew Young who noted in August what some Democratic strategists feared—Jackson scares off some whites: "I know Jesse, I like Jesse and I think I understand Jesse. But Jesse scares the hell out of white folks. It's counterproductive to cuss white folks out. We have got to educate them and win them over." *Atlanta Journal,* 18 August 1984 (86:D–2).

59. Cavanagh, "Election Roundup," *Focus,* November-December 1984, 5.

60. Author's calculations from American National Election Studies data, 1956 and 1960.

61. Jackson, Mississippi, *Clarion Ledger,* 8 September 1984 (101:F–13).

62. Jesse Jackson makes his case in "Moving to the Common Ground," *Washington Post,* 25 March 1984, C–7; "Runoffs and Voting Rights," *Washington Post,* 16 April 1984, A–13. For a discussion of the racial and political impact of the runoff and the likely consequences of either retaining or abolishing it, see my "Race and the Runoff," Public Policy Discussion Paper No. 8403, University of Rochester, November 1984.

63. Dr. Brian Sherman, Voter Education Project, press release, 27 May 1984.

64. *Atlanta Journal,* 15 August 1984 (73:E–4, E–5).

65. Calculations by the author from 1984 American National Election Study data. The interviews occurred between 11 January and 19 June. The sample size for southern whites under 30 is 248 for 1980 and 111 for 1984.

66. Fred Bonavita, *Houston Post,* 14 and 21 October 1984 (115:B–3, B–7).

67. Alan Ehrenhalt, "The South: Key to Political Realignment," *Congressional Quarterly Weekly,* 3 March 1984, 531.

68. William Safire provides a revealing account of the meaning and origins of "southern strategy" in *Safire's Political Dictionary* (New York: Ballantine Books, 1978), 671–72.

69. Cavanagh, "Election Roundup," 5.

About the Editors and Contributors

Robert P. Steed (Ph.D., University of Virginia) is professor of political science at The Citadel. He is codirector of The Citadel Symposium on Southern Politics and has coedited three books: *Party Politics in the South* (1980, *Contemporary Southern Political Attitudes and Behavior* (1982), and *Religion and Politics in the South* (1983). He has done substantial research and publication in the areas of southern politics, party activists, the presidency, political socialization, and South Carolina politics. He is currently codirecting a multistate study of state convention delegates.

Laurence W. Moreland (M.A., Duke University) is associate professor of political science at The Citadel. A codirector of The Citadel Symposium on Southern Politics, he has coedited three books: *Party Politics in the South* (1980), *Contemporary Southern Political Attitudes and Behavior* (1982), and *Religion and Politics in the South* (1983). In addition to his current research on state party activists based on a multistate study that he is codirecting, he has coauthored a number of publications and professional papers on southern politics, elections, and party leaders.

Tod A. Baker (Ph.D., University of Tennessee) is professor of political science at The Citadel. He is codirector of The Citadel Symposium on Southern Politics and is presently codirecting a survey of state convention delegates in 13 states. He has authored or coauthored a number of professional papers and publications in the areas of urban politics, southern politics, South Carolina politics, and party activists. He has coedited three books: *Party Politics in the South* (1980), *Contemporary Southern Political Attitudes and Behavior* (1982), and *Religion and Politics in the South* (1983).

William C. Havard, Jr., (Ph.D., University of London) is professor of political science at Vanderbilt University. Nationally recognized as a leading authority on southern politics, he has published extensively in a variety of areas and has served in numerous capacities in many professional organizations and societies, including the American Political Science Association and the Southern Political Science Association. His many books and monographs include *The Changing Politics of the South* (1972), which remains a valuable examination of southern political developments during the period from the end of World War II to the early 1970s.

Charles D. Hadley (Ph.D., University of Connecticut) is associate professor of political science at the University of New Orleans. He is coauthor (with Everett Carll Ladd, Jr.) of *Transformations of the American Party System* (1978) and has published in a number of journals, including *Public Opinion Quarterly* and the *Journal of Politics*. His current research interests include black politics in the South and recent developments in Louisiana politics.

Alexander P. Lamis (Ph.D., Vanderbilt University) is associate professor of political science at the University of North Florida and author of *The Two-Party South* (1984), as well as articles and professional papers on southern politics. He taught at the University of Mississippi from 1981 to the spring of 1985; he also holds a J.D. from the University of Maryland Law School.

William H. Stewart (Ph.D., University of Alabama) is associate professor of political science at the University of Alabama. His research on southern (and Alabama) politics has been the basis of numerous books, monographs, book chapters, and journal articles. He has served since 1980 as an election consultant on Alabama politics for ABC News. He has also served as a consultant to a number of Alabama political figures, law firms, and governmental units.

Thomas G. Walker (Ph.D., University of Kentucky) is associate professor of political science at Emory University. He as authored or coauthored four books, including *Political Parties, Interest Groups, and Public Policy* (1980) and *Public Opinion and Responsible Democracy* (1976). He has also written a number of professional papers and journal articles and is presently engaged in a wide range of research on the American legal system.

Eleanor C. Main (Ph.D., University of North Carolina) is associate professor of political science at Emory University. She currently serve as chairperson of Emory's Department of Political Science. She is coeditor of *Health Care Evaluation* (1977) and has coauthored articles in, among others, *Urban Affairs Quarterly* and *Journal of Social Psychology*. She has made paper presentations at a number of professional conferences and has served as advisory editor to the *Social Science Quarterly.*

Dennis S. Ippolito (Ph.D., University of Virginia) is Eugene Mc-Elvaney Professor of Government and Chairman of the Department of Political Science at Southern Methodist University. He is the author or coauthor of seven books and monographs, including *Political Parties, Interest Groups, and Public Policy* (1980) and *Hidden Spending: The Politics of Federal Credit Programs* (1984). He has presented a number of papers at professional meetings and has published widely in a variety of journals, including the *Social Science Quarterly,* the *Journal of Politics,* and the *Western Political Quarterly.* At present he is doing research on political parties and presidential choice.

Diane Kincaid Blair (M.A., University of Arkansas) is assistant professor of political science at the University of Arkansas. She is the author of one book and over a dozen book chapters and journal articles. She has served in a number of appointive positions and has done extensive work (research and writing) for Arkansas Governors Bill Clinton, David Pryor, and Dale Bumpers.

Anne H. Hopkins (Ph.D., Syracuse University) is professor of political science at the University of Tennessee. The author of four books and monographs, including *Tennessee Votes: 1796–1976* (1978), she has written a number of book chapters, journal articles, and professional papers. She has served on the editorial boards of the University of Tennessee Press, the *Journal of Politics,* the *American Politics Quarterly,* and *Administration and Society;* and she codesigned and moderated a series of six television programs on the Tennessee Constitution.

William Lyons (Ph.D., University of Oklahoma) is professor of political science at the University of Tennessee. He has published extensively in many of the leading political science journals, including the *Journal of Politics,* the *Social Science Quarterly, Legislative Studies Quarterly,* the *American Journal of Political Science, Public Administration Review,* and *Political Methodology.*

Steve Metcalf (MPA, University of Tennessee) is a Ph.D. candidate in the University of Tennessee's graduate program.

Mark Stern (Ph.D., University of Rochester) is professor of political science at the University of Central Florida. He has published a number of book chapters and journal articles and has presented a variety of papers at professional conferences. For seven years he served as a political analyst for Florida elections for the ABC Network News Election Service. He is presently engaged in extensive research on the 1965 Voting Rights Act.

Jack Fleer (Ph.D., University of North Carolina) is professor of political science at Wake Forest University. His publications include one book, *North Carolina Politics: An Introduction* (1968). He has engaged in extensive professional and scholarly activity, including serving as an editorial consultant for the Duke University Press and the *Journal of Politics*. He has also served as state supervisor for the NBC News North Carolina Elections Project.

Larry Sabato (D.Phil., Oxford University) is associate professor of government and foreign affairs at the University of Virginia. A Rhodes Scholar, he is recognized as the leading academic authority on Virginia politics. His six books include *The Rise of Political Consultants, The Democratic Party Primary: Tantamount to Election No Longer,* and *Goodbye to Good-Time Charlie: The American Governorship Transformed.* He has also written a variety of election reports and has served as an election analyst for numerous newspaper and electronic media reports.

Harold W. Stanley (Ph.D., Yale University) is assistant professor of political science at the University of Rochester. A Rhodes Scholar, Professor Stanley has done work at Oxford University as well as at Yale. He is the author of one book, *Senate vs. Governor, Alabama 1971,* and a number of professional papers. He is currently involved in research and writing on southern politics.